SOCIALISM AND THE CHALLENGE OF WAR

SOCIALISM AND THE CHALLENGE OF WAR

Ideas and Politics in Britain 1912-18

J. M. WINTER

Centre for the Study of Social History
University of Warwick

Routledge & Kegan Paul
London and Boston

First published in 1974
by Routledge & Kegan Paul Ltd
Broadway House, 68-74 Carter Lane,
London EC4V 5EL and
9 Park Street,
Boston, Mass. 02108, USA
Set in Monotype Imprint
and printed in Great Britain by
Willmer Brothers Limited, Birkenhead
Copyright J.M. Winter 1974

ISBN 0 7100 7839 0
Library of Congress Catalog Card No. 74–75861

Contents

Illustrations

Acknowledgments

Many people have given generously of their time and advice in the preparation of this book. The following people consented to interviews during the course of my research: Mrs M.I. Cole, Sir G.N. Clark, Mr M.B. Reckitt, Mrs Frida Laski, Mr R. Page Arnot, Dr John Bowlby, Mrs Lucy Middleton, the late Sir Richard Rees, and the late Mr Leonard Woolf. Mrs Middleton, Mr Michael Vyvyan, and Lady Allen of Hurtwood granted me permission to consult valuable private papers in their possession.

Permission to cite from unpublished manuscript material has been granted from: the Passfield Trustees, for the Passfield Papers; the General Secretary of the Labour Party, for the party archives at Transport House; the Master and Fellows of Balliol College, for the A.L. Smith Papers; Mrs M.I. Cole, for the Cole Papers and Bedford Collection at Nuffield College, Oxford; the Society of Authors, for the Shaw Papers; the British Library of Political and Economic Science, for the Beveridge Papers, Lansbury Papers, and the City of London ILP Papers; the Trustees of the Beaverbrook Library, for the Lloyd George Papers; and the Fabian Society, for the Fabian Society Papers, at Nuffield College, Oxford. Transcripts of Crown copyright records in the Public Record Office appear by permission of the Controller of H.M. Stationery Office.

Mrs Eirene Wagner of the Labour Party Library gave me invaluable help in the exploration of the party archives at Transport House. Mr C.G. Allen of the British Library of Political and Economic Science has been a constant help, as have been the staffs of the British Museum, the Institute of Historical Research, the Public Record Office, and the Cambridge University Library.

The editors of *Past & Present*, the *Historical Journal*, and the *Journal of Contemporary History* have kindly allowed me to

vii

incorporate in this book material which has been published in their respective journals.

The criticisms and suggestions of Dr H.M. Pelling were of the highest value throughout my research. The late Professor D.M. Joslin first directed my attention to Tawney's ideas and encouraged me at many difficult points. His tragically early death is a heavy loss to me and to many other people who knew him as a kind counsellor and friend. Professor Fritz Stern's influence on my work will be apparent to all who have had the privilege of his friendship and advice. Many other people have taken the time to read and comment on various drafts of this book. Among them are: Professor G.S. Simpson, Professor G.R. Elton, Mr Negley Harte, Professor Jonathan Malino, Mrs Sara Malino, Professor F.J. Fisher, Professor R.K. Webb, Professor J.L. Talmon, Professor Royden Harrison, Professor Ralph Miliband, Mr Joe Lee, Mrs Jose Harris, Dr Ben-Ami Shiloni, Professor Emmanuel Sivan, Mr Harvey Mendelsohn, Mr John Hutcheson, and, not least, my parents. My wife patiently shared the years that went into this book. Only with her encouragement and support was it possible to complete it.

My students in Jerusalem did more than they know to help me clarify my ideas. A scholarship from the London Friends of the Hebrew University of Jerusalem helped me to extend my research, and a grant from the Faculty of Humanities of the same university helped to defray typing costs. Mr Andrew Wheatcroft's help in seeing this book through the press was invaluable.

Jerusalem   October 1972

Abbreviations

BSP	British Socialist Party
CAB.	Cabinet Papers, Public Record Office
CPB	R.H. Tawney's Commonplace Book
COS	Charity Organization Society
FRD	Fabian Research Department
FO	Foreign Office Papers, Public Record Office
GFTU	General Federation of Trade Unions
ILP	Independent Labour Party
ISB	International Socialist Bureau
LG	Lloyd George Papers, Beaverbrook Library
LPEC	Labour Party Executive Committee Minutes
LSE	London School of Economics
MFGB	Miners' Federation of Great Britain
NEC	Labour Party National Executive Committee
NGL	National Guilds League
PCTUC	Parliamentary Committee of the Trades Union Congress
PLP	Parliamentary Labour Party
PRO	Public Record Office
T-V	Tawney-Vyvyan Papers
TUC	Trades Union Congress
WEC	War Emergency: Workers' National Committee
WEWNC	War Emergency: Workers' National Committee Executive Minutes
WEA	Workers' Educational Association
WO	War Office Papers, Public Record Office

Introduction

All political thought is concerned with the origin and the resolution of social conflict. War, as the most violent form of organized human conflict, is bound to cause anyone who thinks seriously about society to re-examine his ideas and to try to make some sense of the contradictions and dilemmas of war.

In addition, protracted armed struggle between industrialized nations as in twentieth-century Europe has brought home the stresses and sacrifices of war to an unprecedentedly large proportion of the population. Continuity of daily life and disengagement from public affairs have been possible for many during wars between industrially backward societies. But in this century few have escaped participation in the waging of war.

An account of the impact of modern war on political ideas, therefore, involves the discussion of two related but independent problems: (1) the way in which war affects the internal development of political thought, as seen in the work of certain outstanding or representative thinkers; (2) the way in which war affects the propagation, dissemination and acceptance of ideas among broad sections of the population, who may be unconcerned, on the whole, with systematic social analysis. Here the efforts of politicians and their followers to adopt and enact an ideological programme must be considered.

This approach is appropriate to the study of British socialist thought in the period of the First World War for a number of reasons. First, socialism at all times develops internally and externally, in the sense stated above, since it is at once a body of doctrine about society, the validity of which is independent of political fortune, as well as a theory of action. Second, war in this century presented problems which have severely tested socialist ideas. Both the structure of social analysis and the tactical and strategic concepts which socialists advanced in the pre-war years were called into question by the experience of war.

A study of the impact of war must begin in the years before its outbreak. Only against the background of pre-war movements can one measure the immediate effects of the conflict. To evaluate the effects of the First World War, one must look to British society on the eve of the conflict.

The three years before August 1914 form a single, turbulent period in the history of the British working class. Beginning in the summer of 1911, there occurred the outbreak of the greatest series of industrial disputes in Britain since 1889–90. First the dockers, then the railwaymen, then the miners struck in turn, and their actions seemed part of a pattern of discontent which contemporaries called 'the labour unrest'.

The causes and consequences of this wave of popular protest were urgent questions which commanded the attention of all who reflected on political and social issues in the pre-war years. Socialists, in particular, felt compelled to take account of the new situation and, at this time, many admitted the need to examine and if necessary to revise their political ideas. An important reappraisal of the theory and tactics of British socialism was therefore begun, only to be interrupted by the advent of the war. This pre-war phase in the development of British socialist thought is one of the main subjects of the first part of this book.

What did it mean to be a socialist in Britain prior to the First World War? There were probably as many answers to this question as there were people to ask it, as even a glance at the voluminous literature of the period will suggest. Today, some would take this diversity to be a sign of a healthy British suspicion of all 'Continental' theorizing or as an example of the time-honoured tradition of toleration in action. Contemporaries, however, were not so sanguine. Many saw, in the failure of socialists to make clear their beliefs and to act on them, a root cause of the apparent purposelessness of organized Labour's parliamentary and industrial policy. To stop the drift at a time when the working class was demonstrating in a more militant fashion its dissatisfaction with social conditions was, therefore, an urgent political necessity.

Numerous men and women joined this pre-war debate over socialist objectives, which filled the columns of the Labour press and inspired a substantial number of articles, pamphlets and books.

Most of these writers agreed as to the need for a new approach in socialist thinking, but their comments are all too frequently marked by a vagueness which made (and make) it difficult to grasp the essence of many socialists' ideas. A prominent example is that of J. Ramsay MacDonald, secretary of the Labour Party from its inception as the Labour Representation Committee in 1900 to 1912, and chairman of its parliamentary contingent until August 1914. MacDonald, who remained a master of obfuscation throughout his eventful political life, wrote about socialism regularly and with consistent imprecision. He likened it, in a typical passage, to 'a city towards which roads run from all points of the compass – a pilgrims' way for the devout, a trade route for the merchant, a bridle path for the philosopher; and so,' he concluded, 'we have many aspects of Socialism'.[1] Did these approaches to socialism all share the same destination? And if so, what were its outlines? MacDonald's answers to these questions were not apparent.

Others, both within and outside the Labour Party, were not far behind in looseness of rhetoric or reasoning. J. Keir Hardie, one of the founding fathers of the Labour Party and probably the most forceful socialist speaker in pre-war Britain, was said by his colleague and close friend, J. Bruce Glasier, to have been 'singularly indifferent to abstract theories of any kind', in part 'because he distrusted logic altogether as a method of thinking, and felt that when you attempted to compress truth into mere word boxes you distorted or falsified it'.[2] Glasier himself, a poet and evangelist in socialist garb, chairman of the Independent Labour Party from 1900–3 and editor of its paper, the *Labour Leader*, from 1905–9, was probably the one man in the Labour movement most committed to the hyperbolical exposition of socialist ideas.[3] Consider for example a passage in his last book, *The Meaning of Socialism*, written at the end of the First World War, but similar to many of his pre-war statements: 'Not one but ten thousand dragons, devouring and fouling the earth there may be, but, Socialism, lo! its light is the advent of peace, the epoch of man released from the brute, the reign of equality.'[4]

After reading MacDonald, Hardie and Glasier, as well as other public figures, the educated layman in early twentieth-century Britain, like the historian today, would not yet be able, with any precision, to determine what Labour leaders meant by 'socialism'. For the only direct and coherent answers prior to the First World War to the question: What is socialism? one must look outside

3

both Parliament and the head offices of the major trade unions, where day-to-day tasks undoubtedly took first priority. Not that the thought of the many men who made up the leadership of the Labour movement was unimportant or uninteresting; on the contrary. They simply were not often inclined to work out the difficult theoretical problems which are inherent in any socialist position.

It is one of the purposes of this study, therefore, to present the efforts of those individuals in Britain who, under the pressure of specific events, did attempt to work out a consistent socialist philosophy. In the first instance, then, this inquiry turns to these two questions: What was the content of the work of the most rigorous and original British socialist thinkers, and what brought these people to advance their particular views?

The first socialists whose work is examined are Sidney and Beatrice Webb. Already in their fifties at the time of the 'labour unrest', the Webbs had behind them a considerable body of historical and polemical writing and more than twenty years' active political work on behalf of the Fabian Society. It might have been expected that they would have already retired to a quiet scholarly life, concerned only with their books and the affairs of the academic institution they helped to found, the London School of Economics. But the Webbs in 1911 were far from the end of their public service. They were also much more open to new ideas and aware of the need to revise their opinions in the light of events than most of their critics would have us believe.

First, they helped launch their new journalistic venture, the *New Statesman*, in 1913, with a series of articles on the question: 'What Is Socialism?' These essays furnish one of the most concise statements of their political ideas. In addition, the Webbs initiated at this time, through the Fabian Society, a research project on the issue of the control and internal management of industry. Part of the reason for their study was that both the work of certain French writers called 'syndicalists'[5] and, more importantly, the renewed trade-union militancy of the period had given added significance to the idea of workers' control. This set of problems engaged the attention of the Webbs and many other socialists in 1913–14.

One of the people who joined the Webbs in their pre-war inquiry was a young Oxford don, G. D. H. Cole. In this period he was also engaged independently in an effort to provide a radical socialist alternative both to syndicalism and to the Webbs' ideas. His first book, *The World of Labour*, was written in response to

4

the 'labour unrest' and published in 1913. It was the first of his many attempts to work out the framework of what was to be called 'guild socialism', an evolutionary theory of workers' control, which other writers associated with the literary journal, the *New Age*, had begun to formulate a few years earlier. Before August 1914, Cole had succeeded in tracing the outlines of a coherent critique of the Webbs' views and in suggesting at least the beginnings of a new approach in socialist strategy.

A third socialist, R. H. Tawney, who was ten years older than Cole, but twenty years younger than the Webbs, also responded to the 'labour unrest' by beginning a comprehensive examination of his political ideas. Tawney was a Christian who came to socialism with very different assumptions than did most of his contemporaries. The Commonplace Book or diary which he kept at Manchester from 1912–14 contains a complete and moving statement of his socialist beliefs, largely based on his moral outlook.[6] His ideas differed on many important points from those of both the Webbs and Cole, and are examined in chapter three of this book.

Taken together, the work of these thinkers was an important contribution to the development of socialist thought. Their writings contain the most complete statement of the theoretical and practical problems which British socialists faced in the years prior to the First World War. Their views outline the choices open to socialists at that time and reflect standpoints held throughout the Labour movement.

Tawney, Cole, and the Webbs shared the assumption that a socialist philosophy worthy of the name had to be supported by a theory of the state, an account of the origins of social inequality under capitalism, and an explanation of how a plan of action could remedy the ills which plagued contemporary society. Much of their writing focused on these problems. But, in a number of ways, there the similarity ends. These thinkers did not develop a unified set of ideas but distinct and at many points competing and contradictory positions. No synthesis emerged from their pre-war analyses, but rather a statement of three alternative visions of socialism. Each thinker's work, therefore, is presented separately, in the first part of the book.

The second part of this study is concerned with the effects of the war itself on these socialist thinkers and on the development and dissemination of their ideas. Once again, the distinction between socialism as a theory of society and as a theory of action is crucial. On the one hand, the world conflict did not generate any important body of analytical work in Britain which is comparable to the pre-war reappraisal of British socialist ideas or to the wartime writing of European socialists, such as Rosa Luxemburg's *Junius Pamphlet* or Lenin's *State and Revolution*. It is clear then, on one level, that the most creative period in British socialist thought in the first two decades of this century was not the war, but rather the two years prior to its outbreak.

The war experience, however, was crucial in another way. The First World War provided tasks which one approach to socialism, that of the Webbs, was admirably suited to meet. Webbian socialism, with its emphasis on institutional, administrative action, emerged from the war as a far more potent force in large part because of the war itself and the nature of the demands it made on the Labour movement. On the other hand, the atmosphere of war was uncongenial to the propagation both of Cole's ideas of class warfare and of Tawney's Christian social philosophy.

This is not to suggest that Labour was about to adopt a quasi-Marxist or Christian ideology as its own, but was prevented from doing so by the war. The point about the war is, rather, that it made certain that when the time came in 1917 for the reconstruction of the Labour Party as a national organization committed to socialist objectives, it would be to Sidney Webb and his ideas that the party leaders would turn. The contrast with the cool, if not hostile, relationship between the Webbs and the leading figures of the pre-war Labour movement could not have been more striking.

Not only did the attitude of the Labour leadership to socialism change during the war; so did the attitude of socialists to the Labour Party. By 1918, the tactical dispute in Britain had been decided for all but a handful of revolutionaries who eventually formed the Communist Party. In the last year of the war, both Tawney and Cole were among the many people who joined the Webbs in active support and counsel of the reconstructed Labour Party. It became then, as it is today, the major institutional focus for socialist political activity.

In other ways, too, the war experiences of these people are instructive. The Webbs helped to run the home front. Tawney was a soldier. Cole opposed the war and operated on the fringes of the pacifist movement. Virtually every socialist in Britain had to choose one of these responses to war.

There was an intellectual consistency to the behaviour of these socialists during the First World War. In fact, their war experiences are comprehensible only in terms of their pre-war assumptions and preoccupations. Because of the differences in their outlooks, a comparison of their actions and reflections necessarily involves separate studies.

The Webbs' institutional orientation has been examined here primarily in terms of Sidney's leadership of the War Emergency: Workers' National Committee and his work with Ramsay Mac-Donald and Arthur Henderson, party secretary since 1912, in the Labour Party executive committee after mid-1917. Special attention has been paid to the reasons why MacDonald and, in particular, Henderson sought out Webb's advice and enabled him to formulate virtually every major aspect of Labour Party policy. This point has required an examination of MacDonald's period as a political exile and Henderson's response to the Russian Revolution, which prepared the ground for their alliance with Sidney Webb.

G. D. H. Cole's inclination to emphasize industrial action and his hesitant pacifism precluded both his joining Webb in political work until very late in the war and his organizing, on the other hand, an outright challenge to the state during the conflict. Consequently, his ideas seem far more disembodied than those of the Webbs. He did work as a technical adviser to the Amalgamated Society of Engineers during the war, but unfortunately, the files of that union were not open to research. Attention has been turned instead to his continuing theoretical work and to his efforts on behalf of the National Guilds League, a body which he helped to form in 1915 for the dissemination of guild socialist ideas.

As has been noted above, Tawney's war, as opposed to Cole's and that of the Webbs, was primarily the war of a volunteer soldier and survivor of trench warfare. His war reflections, as much as his whole moral theory, are subjective, and therefore more time has been spent in an analysis of the personal component of his thought and the course of his war experience.

This book does not pretend to be an exhaustive history of British socialism. There were certainly other men whose writings during the First World War constitute an important contribution to British socialist thought. The Shop Stewards' Movement, for instance, produced socialist writing of force and substance, but it was on the whole less directly concerned with theory than with the pressing problems of the day.[7] On the other hand certain thinkers, such as Bertrand Russell and Harold Laski, did begin to explore socialist ideas along many of the same pluralist lines that Cole was advocating during the war. These writers, however, did not begin theoretical work on socialist problems until after August 1914.[8] It is not possible, therefore, to apply to their writing the same dual analysis of pre-war and war-time developments which governs this study. Their ideas and those of other socialists are discussed, then, in terms of the work of the principal figures of this book.

A word or two should be added about the question of the 'significance' of these thinkers and their work. Some historians think that ideas are worth examining only if they are held by present or future political leaders or their mentors. History, according to this school, is about power and the men who seek and all too frequently abuse it. There is clearly little room here for an account of the thought of four people who, in the pre-war period, at least, exercised no political power and very little direct political influence. For those who see the history of Labour purely in terms of parliamentary struggles or 'high politics', parts of this book may seem somewhat off the beaten track.

But significance is not so easily determined. A whole generation of people, both active and inactive in politics, was introduced to political ideas through their work. Cole at Oxford[9] and Tawney at the London School of Economics[10] taught hundreds of men and women who both studied social problems and acted to solve them. Sidney Webb was a minister in both Labour Governments of 1924 and 1929–31, and until their discovery of the wisdom of Soviet Communism in the 1930s, the Webbs were the acknowledged elder statesmen of British socialism.[11] Surely their work in the Labour movement deserves more than a passing reference. This study has tried to tell at least part of that story.

A further aim of this book has been to try to examine socialist thought in a somewhat more precise way than has been done in the past. It is hoped that it will add to the general appreciation of the variety and content of British socialist ideas.

Above all, the work is intended as one contribution to the study of the complicated historical problem of the relationship between war and social change. The assessment of the social consequences of war, to the victor as well as to the vanquished, has unfortunately become an almost universal task for the politician and the historian in this century. This may explain the familiar sound of the arguments which have been examined in this book. But the resonance may also be the result of the differences between the two world wars. The struggle against Hitler did not present the same problems of commitment and participation which faced socialists in the First World War and which confront many in various parts of the world today. It is in the language of 1914 or 1917, and not that of 1939, in which the current debate of the role of the left in wartime is carried on. The concerns of the generation of the First World War are sadly still with us today.

NOTES

1 J. Ramsay MacDonald, *The Socialist Movement*, 1911, p. xi. Throughout the notes, the place of publication is London unless otherwise stated.
2 J. Bruce Glasier, *James Keir Hardie: A Memorial*, Manchester, 1915, pp. 59, 61.
3 On Glasier, cf. L. Thompson, *The Enthusiasts*, 1971.
4 J. Bruce Glasier, *The Meaning of Socialism*, Manchester, 1919, p. 19. Professor Beer of Harvard does not press Glasier's ideas too much, but suggests that his writing was typical of the 'distinctive ethical tendency' of British socialist thought. S. H. Beer, *Modern British Politics*, 1965, p. 128. For other pre-war socialist writing, the reader is referred to *The Miners' Next Step*, Tonypandy, 1912, written by Noah Ablett and other Welsh militants. This interesting tract dealt with the problem of leadership, but was not a full statement of socialist ideas. More elaborate, but less original, were the writings of the (Marxist) British Socialist Party, which offer little more than slogans first voiced by their energetic leader, H. M. Hyndman, twenty years earlier. Cf. C. Tsuzuki, *H. M. Hyndman and British Socialism*, 1961.
5 Syndicalism was primarily a French doctrine of revolutionary class struggle, which emphasized industrial action and hostility to the state, leading to the overthrow of capitalism through a general strike. Cf. F. F. Ridley, *Revolutionary Syndicalism in France*, Cambridge, 1970 and Élie Halévy, *Histoire du socialism européen*, Paris, 1948, pp. 226–34.
6 J. M. Winter and D. M. Joslin (eds), *R. H. Tawney's Commonplace Book*, Cambridge, 1972.
7 Cf. J. T. Murphy, *Preparing for Power*, 1934; B. Pribicevic, *The Shop Stewards' Movement and Workers' Control 1910–1922*, Oxford, 1959, and J. Hinton, 'The Clyde Workers' Committee and the dilution struggle', in A. Briggs and J. Saville (eds), *Essays in Labour History 1886–1923*, 1971, pp. 152–89.
8 Bertrand Russell did publish the lectures he gave on German socialism

in 1896, but in a later reprint of them, he noted, 'The point of view from which I wrote the book was that of an orthodox Liberal.' B. Russell, *German Social Democracy*, 1965, p. v. His most important war-time essays are: *Political Ideals*, 1917; *Principles of Social Reconstruction*, 1916; and *Roads to Freedom*, 1918. Laski's wartime writings are to be found in *Studies in the Problem of Sovereignty*, New Haven, Conn., 1917 and *Authority in the Modern State*, New Haven, Conn., 1919.

9 Cf. the comments of various writers at the beginning of volume one of A. Briggs and J. Saville (eds) *Essays in Labour History*, 1960.

10 Cf. this appraisal of Tawney's influence by an historian who shares none of his views: 'People won't believe this, but when the historian comes to write – if an historian still comes to write – an intellectual history of the early twentieth century, Tawney will be one of the figures he will really have to concern himself with. Not Toynbee, whose influence is neither here nor there (not in this country at any rate). Not Maitland, who carried very little influence in the public mind, even indirectly. But Tawney, who wrote for a purpose – wrote beautifully, and wrote history which was in great parts – I am looking for a polite word – in great parts mistaken.' G. R. Elton, *The Future of the Past*, Cambridge, 1968, p. 16. For a more sympathetic account which concurs with Elton's view on Tawney's importance, cf. the late Professor W. H. B. Court's autobiographical essay, 'Growing up in an age of anxiety', in his collection of essays, *Scarcity and Choice in History*, 1970.

11 We await Professor R. Harrison's authorized life of the Webbs for a full account of their work and its significance. Until it appears, the best introduction is M. I. Cole (ed.), *The Webbs and Their Work*, 1949.

I

SOCIALIST THOUGHT AND THE LABOUR MOVEMENT 1912-14

1

The Background

After years of work for social reform and the repeal of the Poor Law of 1834, Sidney and Beatrice Webb left Britain in June 1911 for a voyage round the world. They retired temporarily from their work at a critical moment in the history of the British Labour movement. When they returned home the following year, it seemed that the complexion of the political world had changed. In June 1912, Sidney Webb addressed the National Committee for the Prevention of Destitution. 'The country to which I return,' Webb remarked, 'strikes me, in many ways, as intellectually a new England.'[1] What were the events which had taken place in the twelve months that the Webbs were on tour to convince Sidney of this fundamental change?

British parliamentary affairs were at a particularly turbulent stage when the Webbs turned their attention to non-European civilization. The electorate had gone to the polls twice in 1910 and had returned the Liberals to power, but without the same freedom of action which they had enjoyed after their overwhelming victory of 1906.[2] Two hundred and seventy-two Liberal M.P.s faced exactly the same number of Conservatives in the House of Commons in 1911. The government was able to break this stalemate only through the support of the Irish Nationalists, led by John Redmond, and the Labour Party, led by J. Ramsay MacDonald. The leverage of these two minority groups over Liberal policy was strictly limited, though, since neither had anything to gain from the return to office of the party of Arthur Balfour and Bonar Law. An uneasy, informal alliance of anti-Conservative forces in Parliament was formed in 1911, and lasted until the outbreak of war.

The Liberals' pre-war legislative record was an impressive one. It was achieved over the strenuous objections of the Conservatives, whose opposition to change was voiced at times in the most acrimonious terms. The first item on the Liberal agenda, on which the 1910 elections had been fought, was the plan to restrict the veto power of the House of Lords. This obstacle had endangered the ambitious budgets of David Lloyd George, the Chancellor of the Exchequer, and had been used to block any move towards Home Rule for Ireland. On 15 May 1911, the Parliament Act passed its third reading in the Commons. The Lords did not challenge the measure, but chose rather to 'perish in the dark', in Lord Selborne's felicitous phrase.[3]

Eleven days previously, Lloyd George had introduced his monumental National Insurance Bill. His scheme provided the entire working population with insurance against sickness and provided workers in certain vulnerable trades, such as building, shipbuilding, and engineering, with insurance against unemployment. After the controversy over the Lords' veto, the Conservatives chose not to oppose the Insurance Bill in Parliament. Instead they organized popular meetings throughout the country to protest against the measure, and hoped that the hostility which they expected to greet the plan when it came into operation, would undermine the government.

The only principled opposition to the Insurance Bill was stated by six dissident Labour members, who were socialists and objected to the contribution of fourpence per week which most eligible workers would pay for the privilege of insurance.[4] But despite their refusal to back the bill, Ramsay MacDonald held the bulk of the Labour Party together in its support. It passed its third reading in the Commons on 8 December 1911.

One additional piece of legislation was of great interest to the Labour members. On 10 August 1911, the same day on which the Lords approved the Parliament Act, the Commons voted an annual stipend of £400 per year for each member of the House. This provision was especially important to the Labour Party, whose financial basis had been severely shaken by the important Osborne judgment. On 21 December 1909, the Law Lords upheld the objection of a member of the Amalgamated Society of Railway Servants to the statutory levy of that union for the support of the Parliamentary Labour Party (PLP).[5]

The effect on the Labour Party was immediate and drastic. Without redress, the party was likely to go bankrupt.[6] On this point Labour presented a united front. MacDonald claimed that by this decision the courts had allowed Capital to regain the 'privileged position' which it had lost with the coming of the Labour Party.[7] Despite the usual extravagance of his language, MacDonald was speaking for the vast majority of his party and its supporters, who saw the repeal of the Osborne judgment as a primary Labour demand. His party's support for the National Insurance Bill was the price which Ramsay MacDonald willingly paid for the Liberals' action on the payment of members.[8] With the passage of this latter measure, at least part of what the chairman of the PLP in 1910–11, George Barnes, called the 'entrance fee'[9] into the House of Commons was finally met by the state.

What Labour members should do once they got into Parliament, though, was a matter of considerable dispute in these years. The party's objectives at this time were unclear, to put it mildly. Its independence from the prodding of the Liberal Whip was a point which MacDonald frequently took pains to establish, but his leadership in Parliament did little to convince anyone of his case.[10] When pressed to explain his defensive and often hesitant action, as in the case of the Insurance Bill, he fell back on reciting a catalogue of the party's problems. 'Am I "letting the cat out of the bag," ' he asked the Trades Union Congress (TUC) in 1912, 'when I confess that during the last four or five years we have been keeping our political machinery going in the face of the most terrible consequences and tremendous difficulties.'[11] Aside from the Osborne judgment, which was 'bleeding the Labour movement on its political side', MacDonald had to contend as well with what he called the 'extravagant expectations' which many working men had 'indulged in . . . regarding the work that the Labour Party would do immediately. Not a few imagined that its advent removed the flaming sword from the gates of Paradise. These delusions had to go as all dreams go.'[12] Whenever explanations were demanded, MacDonald brought up the chastening facts of the balance of power in the House which, he said, gave him little room for manoeuvre and no alternative but to support the Liberals. He asked his critics 'to remember that, while there is a morass on one side of the road, there is a wild beast waiting to devour us on the other, and in keeping out of the morass, I am not going to put myself into the jaws of the wild beast'.[13] The position was not an easy one. 'If we go that side we are scorned,' he explained, 'and if we go to the other we are laughed at! I am sorry to say that there is not so very much honour in politics now, but there we are.'[14]

What was left for Labour to do? MacDonald insisted:[15]

> You have got to keep straight in the middle of the road of progress, and really straight, not nominally straight. You have to keep your end in view, and your end is in front. You have to keep the doctrines, but your doctrines were not handed down to you in the sixties by a few people who wrote some interesting phrases.

With such advice, is it a surprise that many contemporaries were hard pressed to decide what the Labour Party stood for?

Did the party stand for socialism? The answer must be a negative one before 1914, and the Webbs would have been the first to agree. Even though many of its major spokesmen, Keir Hardie, Fred Jowett, and MacDonald himself were members of the ILP and avowedly socialists, the pre-war party was committed to nothing other than the election of as many M.P.s as possible. It could hardly have done otherwise, though, since its loose structure as a federation of unions and socialist societies gave the decisive voice in the party to trade unionists, many of whom were definitely not socialists. Most people were of the opinion, at least before 1912, that the ideological position of the party was best left undefined, in the interests of the peaceful coexistence of all its members.

The Labour Party did apply successfully for membership in the International Socialist Bureau (ISB) in 1908, which was a commitment of sorts. But the party was ushered into the European socialist movement by the back door, as it were. No less a dialectician than Karl Kautsky, the German socialist leader and authority on Marx, moved the resolution on 12 October 1908 which declared that[16]

> the English Labour Party is to be admitted to the International Socialist Congresses because although it does not avowedly recognise the class struggle, it actually carries it on; and because the organisation of the Labour Party being independent of the bourgeois parties is based upon the class struggle.

These distinctions may have missed many of the party's members, including Arthur Henderson who, on becoming secretary of the party in 1912, automatically became secretary of the British section of the ISB.[17] When it was suggested to him that this post ought to be manned by a socialist, he joined the Fabian Society.[18]

In 1912 the (Marxist) British Socialist Party (BSP), led by H. M. Hyndman, decided to challenge the Labour Party's credentials as a member of the ISB, on the grounds that it was 'not only not an avowedly Socialist Party, but it declines to adopt a Socialist programme and frequently acts and votes in an anti-Socialist sense', an apparent reference to the Insurance Bill voting.[19] Henderson's appointment to the secretaryship of the ISB 'even though he is a non-Socialist' seemed to have been the last straw for them.[20] Henderson himself penned a long reply to these charges, which were rejected by the Brussels office of the ISB.[21] Still, the Labour Party record on socialism was ambiguous enough to prompt Camille Huysmans, the secretary of the ISB, to ask the party secretary to send him 'all the Socialist Bills [proposed] in the House of Commons, since the entrance of Labour members in the House'.[22] Henderson, it seems, did not reply, nor could he have done so easily, since his party was not prepared to fight for such legislation in the pre-war years. It did make a public gesture now and then in favour of 'the nationalisation of railways, mines, and other monopolies',[23] but the measure was never pressed in Parliament, partly for fear of splitting party ranks. When the party executive met on 6 February 1911 to decide which 'Bills [were] to be Balloted for in order named' during that session, a Railway Nationalisation Bill was on the list of seven, but it brought up the rear.[24] The slow build-up of party strength rather than ideological assertions that were bound to fail was, then, the order of the day for the pre-war Labour Party.

Such tactics may have been necessary, given the state of the forty-man Parliamentary group which, as MacDonald repeatedly stated, rarely acted as a unit.[25] But his choice of the quiet, unassertive line of development severely limited its effectiveness as a party of protest. The Labour Party was in no sense the leading force in the working-class movement prior to the First World War. This fact was demonstrated perhaps most forcibly in 1911–12 during the course of the major industrial disputes which were known collectively as the 'labour unrest'. These strikes, which erupted and took their course independently of Labour Party policy or action, were the most important events in labour history in these years.

The first signs of the new spirit of militancy in the pre-war Labour movement could have been seen in the conduct of the Cambrian Combine dispute which began in the Rhondda Valley of South Wales in September 1910. Two months later most of the collieries in Glamorgan had been affected. The strike, fought for a minimum wage, was marked by two features which were to recur with disturbing regularity in the course of the next two years: sporadic rioting and the use of troops to restore order. On 7 November, strikers tried, in the words of the official inquiry into the dispute, 'to compel the officials, stokers, and others at Glamorgan Colliery, Llwynypia to leave work and this led to serious rioting in Llwynypia and Tonypandy on 7–8 November 1910'.[26] A strike which broke out separately in the Aberdare Valley also led to rioting in early November, when a train carrying colliers was attacked by strikers at a point between Aberdare and Cwmaman.[27]

On the evening of 8 November, Winston Churchill, the Home Secretary, decided to dispatch a contingent of Metropolitan police to Glamorgan, and to hold back on troop deployments only if rioting stopped immediately. By midnight, he received word that the streets had not yet been cleared, and so sent several cavalry units into the disturbed areas.[28] General Neville Macready took control of the situation, and acted at times as if he were occupying enemy territory. 'A system of intelligence similar to that used in war time' was 'evolved', and provided a constant flow of information about the plans and movements of the workers' leaders.[29]

The general placed responsibility for the disorders on the preachings of a 'small, but energetic section' of miners dedicated to what he called 'extreme socialism'.[30] But he did not absolve the colliery managers from their share of the blame for the trouble. Too frequently, he noted, they acted with total disregard for the consequences of their measures, and looked to the army to support them in any steps they took.[31] An official of the Home Office who was in Wales, J. F. Moylan, substantiated these charges, and added details which reveal the owners' fears of an impending insurrection. On one occasion a clerk of the Tonypandy Colliery office of the Cambrian Combine called for troops to meet an invasion of '400 armed strikers' who turned out to be 'the Lancashire Fusiliers taking their walk'.[32] 'The same manager,' Moylan continued, 'asked if he could have a line of sentries on the hill tops!'[33]

The two sides of the 'labour unrest' were already in evidence in the Rhondda Valley in 1910 – defiant industrial action on the one hand and resistance based upon the often-exaggerated dread of civil disorder on the other. These lines of conflict and trepidation extended to the nation as a whole during the dock strike of the following summer.

It was in the summer of 1910 that the dockers' leaders, Ben Tillett and Tom Mann, who had become prominent during the great dock strike of 1889, and the far more conservative J. Havelock Wilson, united to demand that an industry-wide conciliation board be established for the docks, as had been done for the railways. In these boards, the workers' leaders hoped to achieve recognition for their union, to exact a minimum wage, and to regulate the conditions of employment in shipping throughout Britain. The Shipbuilders' Federation not only refused to consider these proposals, but would not even negotiate with the new aggressive union leadership, much to the chagrin of the Board of Trade. A strike was unavoidable, and Mann, Tillett, and Wilson built their organization to meet the coming test of strength. The new National Transport Workers' Federation was formed in November 1910.

On 14 June 1911, during the hottest summer in years, an international strike of seamen was called by the new Transport Workers' Federation. Although the continental dockers failed to join the strike, the disruption it caused in Britain and the bitterness it engendered, lend weight to Élie Halévy's description of the conflict as 'nothing short of a revolutionary outbreak'.[34] Within a fortnight, the shipping industry was brought to a complete standstill.

On 30 June 1911, a conference at Hull between the parties to the dispute was arranged by G. R. Askwith, the Chief Industrial Conciliator at the Board of Trade. The meeting ended in failure, since recognition of the men's union was refused by the owners. A crowd of two thousand strikers then marched on the docks to prevent the unloading of a steamer, the *Calypso*. Police were stoned at the entrance to the Albert Docks. Reinforcements were called in, and twenty-three people were seriously injured.[35] The next day a steamship of the White Star Line was set on fire at Liverpool.[36] The disputes at these two ports were settled in a few days, but not before the trouble spread to Glasgow, where police were stoned while guarding the offices of the Clyde Shipping Company,[37] and also to Manchester, where a baton charge dispersed a large and supposedly menacing crowd.[38] Sixteen were hurt in Cardiff on the night of 23 July.[39]

By the end of July, the workers' demand for a conciliation board was dropped, but employers were forced to concede wage demands throughout much of the industry. The unions had won a partial victory, but the fact and fear of violence which accompanied the dock strikes overshadowed the terms of settlement. The bitterness of class war was growing more intense. 'Remember,' Keir Hardie told a meeting at Wigan on 2 July, 'all the time at election time you are "citizens", when you strike you are the mob.'[40]

Two days after the last dockers had returned to work, the industrial situation took a further turn for the worse. Two hundred people were injured during clashes in Liverpool on 13 August 1911. The trouble was sparked off by a minor incident. After a man refused to climb down from the windows of the Lime Street Station Hotel, he was pulled down by police, who then had a riot on their hands. The Riot Act was read, and mounted police charged into the working-class district.[41] Two days later, police tried to transport to gaol in five prison vans the men who had been sentenced for rioting offences. Three thousand men blocked the road. Shots were fired, killing two men and wounding two others.[42]

The day after this fatal incident, the second phase of the 'labour unrest' began. The four railway unions called their men out, first in sympathy with the Liverpool seamen, and then on a national scale with demands of their own.[43] Within two days, the government knew it was facing a total disruption of economic life, and acted quickly to meet the crisis. Eleven thousand infantry and two thousand cavalry were sent to London from Aldershot.[44]

One of the people who witnessed the movement of troops in London during the rail strike was Ramsay MacDonald. On 22 August 1911, he told the House of Commons of his experience four nights before, while walking home to his rooms in Lincoln's Inn after thirty-six hours' negotiation.

'When I got to Southampton Row', MacDonald recalled, 'I was held up whilst about 1,000 mounted men went past, going towards the East End.' Turning to Churchill, he added:

I want to put in the warmest and firmest protest I possibly can against this recurrence to medieval ideas of how law and order are going to be maintained. This is not a medieval State, and it is not Russia. It is not even Germany.

He finished his angry speech with the charge to the Home Secretary to 'think a little bit more before he starts drafting his troops into places where they are very unwelcome and unbidden guests'.[45]

Fortunately, the confrontation which MacDonald feared did not take place. After veiled threats by Asquith had failed to end the strike, Lloyd George won the day by brilliantly appealing to the employers' and workers' patriotism. At the time of the rail strike, the Agadir crisis was still unresolved. Britain and Germany were on the brink of war, the Chancellor insisted, and a general railway stoppage would imperil the national interest, since troop movements depended heavily on rail transportation. Lloyd George's master-stroke was an unqualified success. The strike was settled the same day, and a compromise was worked out through a Royal Commission and the railway conciliation boards.

But again there had been bloodshed. At Llanelly in South Wales on Saturday 19 August, a train driven by blackleg labour was blocked and boarded. The engine-driver was badly hurt, and the fire of the locomotive was extinguished. At this point the Worcestershire Regiment was ordered to clear the tracks, and once again, the Riot Act was read. When the crowds refused to disperse, bayonets were fixed and two men were shot dead, one in his garden adjacent to the tracks. Then the situation got out of hand. The goods shed of the Great Western Railway Company was broken into and set alight. Trucks standing on a siding were also fired. They contained gunpowder which exploded, killing four and wounding a dozen others.[46] Five days of ugly rioting, at times with anti-Semitic overtones, followed in Tredegar, Ebbw Vale and Rhymney.[47] The tenor of the discontent was very ominous indeed.

Keir Hardie knew who was to blame for the deaths in Llanelly. He told the House of Commons:

> It is no business of the troops to pursue a flying crowd, to clear the streets, and perform police work. At Llanelly there was no riot of serious consequence, there was no looting or burning of railway wagons until the soldiers shot two men dead. That was the beginning of the serious trouble at Llanelly.

He was even prepared to make more specific charges. 'The men who have been shot down,' he asserted, 'have been murdered by the Government in the interests of the capitalist system. The intention was to help the railway directors to suppress this rising among the men.'[48]

The new working-class militancy and the violence which accompanied it were profoundly unsettling events, not only in their immediate impact, but also in what they foreshadowed. Employers, government officials and cautious trade union leaders had reason to be worried. G. R. Askwith told the Cabinet just before the summer's events that[49]

it looks as if we were [sic] in the presence of one of those periodic upheavals in the labour world such as occurred in 1833–34, and from time to time since that date, each succeeding occurrence showing a marked advance in organization on the part of the workers and the necessity for a corresponding change in tactics on the part of the employers.

'Almost imperceptibly,' he noted, 'a new force has arisen in trade unionism, and at every hand there is evidence to show that the power of the old leaders has been superseded.' The consolidation of the unions of unskilled labour had given leaders like Mann and Tillett 'enormous power', and consequently, Askwith warned, 'anything might happen in the near future', possibly a general strike.[50] The trouble on the docks and railways was just the beginning, or so it seemed to this well-informed observer, of a very dangerous period of industrial conflict.

The Times contributed its own suggestion in August 1911 about the proper way to deal with the dislocation caused by strikes. It proposed the formation of a 'Public Security Brigade' to break a future transport stoppage. Its appeal had the full flavour of class prejudice behind it. It speculated, 'Men of a moderately athletic tendency would find it easy enough' to carry on essential work, 'and not disagreeable for a short time.'[51]

One of the government's major fears in the summer of 1911 was that the discontent would soon spread to the coal industry. R. A. S. Redmayne, Chief Inspector of Mines, reported to Churchill in July 1911 that 'underground mining labour in many of the mining districts of Great Britain is in a very disturbed state, and I think there is a great probability of the spirit of unrest culminating in a general strike'.[52] He saw four underlying causes of discontent at work. First was the consolidation of the power of the Miners' Federation of Great Britain (MFGB). Second, the men were no longer 'as submissive to their old official leaders as they formerly were', and 'younger and more violent men were urging a more "forward" policy'. Then there was the fact that the miners had not been through a big strike for years and did not, therefore, 'fully

THE AJAX OF INDUSTRY.

Plate 1   'THE MINER: "If I'm expected to support all this, I ought to be assured of a secure footing." '   *Labour Leader*, 6 October 1911

THE MODERN DRAGON.

Plate 2   'Labour: "When will the State destroy this monster?"'
Labour Leader, 20 October 1911

appreciate' the consequences. The final and more subtle source of unrest was, according to Redmayne, the introduction of the three-shift system in northern collieries which 'had disrupted the home-life patterns of miners'.[53]

It came as no surprise, therefore, when the MFGB voted on 18 January 1912 overwhelmingly in favour of strike action.[54] On 18 February, the miners' executive took the decision to terminate work at the end of the month unless their demand was met for a minimum wage per shift of five shillings for men and two shillings for boys.[55] On 28 February, the Prime Minister met the miners' leaders at the Foreign Office, and declared his support for the principle of a minimum wage, but not for the '5 and 2' as the miners' claim was known. He asked the union to accept this 'considerable advance' in labour policy and to withdraw their strike notices.[56] Their refusal brought on the national coal strike of 1912.

More than one million men joined the strike in the first ten days of March. The economic dislocation it caused was severe. The pig-iron industry practically came to a halt, and 60 per cent of the men in all iron and steel works were laid off by 23 March. Five-sixths of the tin-plate mills were forced to close, and 80 per cent of the potters in North Staffordshire were out of work in the wake of the strike. The glass-making industry was also badly crippled.[57]

Clearly the government had to act quickly. After three weeks of tense stalemate, a Bill was rushed through Parliament to settle the strike. At 3 o'clock in the morning of 27 March, and over the objections of the Labour Party, the Miners' (Minimum Wage) Bill passed its third reading by a vote of 213 to 48.[58] It provided the right to the minimum wage for miners. Wage rates would be fixed separately by twenty-three district boards, on which union men would sit. Men could be exempted from the minimum wage by the boards according to the district rules or by proof of the irregularity of their work. No provision was made for the '5 and 2', but, on the other hand, the principle of the minimum wage had been established in law.

Later the same day, the miners' executive agreed to ballot on 'resuming work pending the settlement of the minimum rates of wages' by district boards. On 4–6 April the vote was taken. It showed a narrow majority for continuing the strike. But the executive decided that, since a two-thirds majority was required to

B

call a national strike, so a similar majority was needed to continue one. They therefore advised their men to return to work, and officially ended the strike.[59]

In May 1912, a hundred thousand dockers struck again, this time against the practice of the Port of London Authority of using non-union labour. The strike ended in total failure by the end of July, with Lord Devonport, the authority's chairman, unyielding and unrepentant.[60] Overall, 40,890,000 work days were lost in industrial disputes which began in 1912. The total was greater than the sum of work days lost over the previous eight years.[61] By the time the Webbs had returned to England in June 1912, the 'labour unrest' had become by far the most important element in working-class politics.

For all British socialists, the questions at hand in 1912 were apparent. What caused the 'labour unrest'? Where did this new wave of discontent lead? How would they respond to the challenges of labour militancy? In addition, they had to examine their conception of the Labour Party's role in the Labour movement in the light of the insignificant part it had played in the events of the previous year.

On the other hand, MacDonald tried to make the most of the party's record. He told the TUC in 1912:[62]

The events of the last two years have shown us the wisdom of creating a Labour Party. You cannot come out on strike, whether you like it or not, without the Board of Trade, or the Prime Minister, or the Cabinet, or the Chancellor of the Exchequer interfering. You cannot lay down tools or declare war on a class of aggressive capitalists; you cannot paralyse industry except we have pressure [sic] brought to bear from your side [in Parliament] . . . What are you going to do? Can you afford to meet year by year in the Congress just to pass resolutions and send them up to Whitehall? No. You have got to get the men standing in the House of Commons and making speeches in the House of Commons like those which have been delivered so eloquently during the sittings of this Congress. (Cheers)

But what did his oratorical effort in Parliament actually achieve during the previous year? The only point on which the party was firmly committed to fight was the '5 and 2', and that battle was lost.

Closer to the mark was the opinion of Sidney Buxton, President of the Board of Trade, when he informed the Cabinet, shortly after the end of the miners' strike, of[63]

> the almost complete collapse of the Labour Party in the House as an effective influence in labour disputes. They were not consulted with regard to, and had no share in the Seamen's or Transport Workers' movement last summer. During the railway strike, they attempted to act as a go-between for the men and the Government. But they had very little influence over the actions of the men, or on the result. During the Miners' Strike . . . the Labour Party exercised no influence at all.

Furthermore: 'Their elimination is a distinct loss to industrial peace; and they may be forced to seek to regain their influence by taking up a more aggressive attitude on labour questions.'[64] In any event, a reappraisal of Labour Party policy was in order.

It is important to bear in mind the fact that, both within and outside the pre-war Labour Party, there was no consensus about its proper function or even about its future as a political force. The 'labour unrest' brought this problem to the fore and forced many people to reconsider their commitments. Those who thought out the issues most carefully knew that if they wanted to follow, if not to guide, the movements of the day, they had to do more than merely repeat past slogans and programmes. It was their business as socialists, then, to work out anew the political ideas which they hoped would give form and purpose to the growing protests of the labouring population. This ferment in pre-war British socialist thought may best be studied in terms of the original and incisive work done at this time by four people: the Webbs, R. H. Tawney, and G. D. H. Cole.

NOTES

1 Sidney Webb, 'The moral of the labour unrest', *Crusade*, 3, 7, July 1912, p. 116.

2 Cf. N. Blewett's authoritative work, *The Peers, the Parties, and the People: the General Elections of 1910*, 1972.

3 As cited in G. Dangerfield, *The Strange Death of Liberal England*, 1936, p. 63.

4 The six dissenters were George Lansbury, Keir Hardie, Philip Snowden, and Fred Jowett of the ILP; Will Thorne of the Social

Democratic Federation; and James O'Grady of the National Amalgamated Furnishing Trades Association. Cf. their statement 'Why we opposed Insurance Bill', *Labour Leader*, 15 December 1911.

5 H. M. Pelling, *A History of British Trade Unionism*, 1962, pp. 130–2.
6 Levies were collected in 1910 from 217 affiliated societies of the TUC to defray the costs of the appeal, which totalled £2,838. More importantly, twenty-five injunctions had been granted against affiliated societies by the end of that year. Cf. *TUC Annual Report 1911*, pp. 129–32; and *TUC Parliamentary Committee Seventh Quarterly Report*, December 1910, p. 28.
7 J. Ramsay MacDonald, *The Socialist Movement*, 1911, p. 75.
8 Beaverbrook Library, Lloyd George Papers, C/6/5/5. Master of Elibank to Lloyd George, 5 October 1911.
9 *Hansard's Parliamentary Debates*, 5th ser., 20, 18 November 1910. Hereafter referred to as 'Hansard'.
10 A more sympathetic treatment of MacDonald's record may be found in R. McGibbin, 'James Ramsay MacDonald and the problem of the independence of the Labour Party,' *Journal of Modern History*, 42, 2, June 1970, pp. 216–35.
11 *TUC Annual Report 1912*, p. 213.
12 *Ibid.*, and J. Ramsay MacDonald, 'The trade union unrest', *English Review*, 6, November 1910, pp. 128–39.
13 *TUC Annual Report 1912*, p. 213.
14 *Ibid.*, p. 214.
15 *Ibid.*
16 Labour Party Library, Labour Party Papers, LP/INT/1/488.
17 Labour Party Papers, Minutes of the executive of the British section of the ISB, 4 May 1911.
18 H. M. Pelling, *A Short History of the Labour Party*, 1961, p. 32.
19 Labour Party Papers, LP/INT/1/488, and ISB minutes, 26 July 1912.
20 *Ibid.*
21 *Ibid.* and LP/INT/11/1/394, MacDonald to C. Huysmans, 16 October 1912.
22 LP/INT/11/1/ 480, Huysmans to Arthur Henderson, 17 June 1913.
23 As cited in Henderson's reply to the BSP charges, LP/INT/11/1/488, p. 2. A bill for the nationalization of the mines was presented in the Commons on 9 July 1913, but did not receive a discussion. Cf. R. P. Arnot, *Miners: Years of Struggle*, 1953, p. 153, and E. E. Barry, *Nationalisation in British Politics*, 1965, pp. 180–91.
24 Labour Party Papers, Labour Party Executive Minutes, 6 February 1911. Hereafter referred to as 'LPEC'. The Bills were, in order of priority, the Trade Union Amendment Bill, the Unemployed Workmen Bill, the Education (Administrative Provisions) Bill, the Electoral Reform Bill, the Eight Hours Day Bill, the Bill to Provide against Eviction of Workmen during Trade Disputes, and the Railway Nationalisation Bill.
25 LPEC, 5 December 1912.
26 *Colliery Strike Disturbances in South Wales. Correspondence and Report*, 1911 Cd 5568, 64, p. 2.

27 *Ibid.*, p. 4.
28 *Ibid.*, p. 7.
29 *Ibid.*, p. 50.
30 *Ibid.*, p. 49.
31 *Ibid.*
32 *Ibid.*, p. 31. K. G. J. C. Knowles, in his *Strikes*, Oxford, 1952, discusses the same points relating to the Cambrian Combine dispute.
33 *Ibid.* For a more sympathetic view of Churchill's role, cf. R. S. Churchill, *Winston S. Churchill Young Statesman 1901–1914*, 1967, pp. 373–9.
34 É. Halévy, *The History of the English People in the Nineteenth Century. Epilogue*, 1936, 2, pp. 441–86. Cf. also 'Beginning of seamen's strike', *The Times*, 15 July 1911; Ben Tillett, *History of the London Transport Workers' Strike 1911*, 1912; E. H. Phelps Brown, *The Growth of British Industrial Relations*, 1960; and, G. R. Askwith, *Industrial Problems and Disputes*, 1920.
35 'The seamen's strike', *The Times*, 30 June 1911.
36 'The seamen's strike', *The Times*, 1 July 1911.
37 'The seamen's strike', *The Times*, 4 July 1911.
38 'The shipping strike', *The Times*, 5 July 1911.
39 'The seamen's strike at Cardiff', *The Times*, 24 July 1911.
40 'Mr Keir Hardie and the police', *The Times*, 3 July 1911.
41 'Street fighting in Liverpool', *The Times*, 14 August 1911.
42 'Fresh rioting in Liverpool', *The Times*, 16 August 1911.
43 'Spread of the labour war', *The Times*, 16 August 1911.
44 'Railway strike ordered', *The Times*, 18 August 1911.
45 Hansard, 5th ser., 1911, 29, 22 August 1911.
46 'Fatal riots at Llanelly', *The Times*, 21 August 1911.
47 'Anti-Jewish riots in Monmouthshire', *The Times*, 22 August 1911. 'The Anti-Jewish riots in Wales', *The Times*, 24 August 1911.
48 Hansard, 5th ser., 29, 22 August 1911.
49 Public Record Office (PRO), CAB.37/107 (1911), no. 70. G. R. Askwith, 'The Present Unrest in the Labour World', 25 June 1911.
50 *Ibid.*
51 'General Strikes and General Strike breakers', *The Times*, 26 August 1911.
52 PRO, CAB.37/107 (1911), no. 78.
53 *Ibid.*, pp. 1–2.
54 British Library of Political and Economic Science, MFGB executive minutes, 18–19 January 1912.
55 MFGB executive minutes, 18 February 1912.
56 MFGB executive minutes, 28 February 1912.
57 'The coal trade dispute', *Board of Trade Labour Gazette*, 20, 4 April 1912, pp. 127–8.
58 Hansard, 5th ser., 36, 26 March 1912.
59 MFGB executive minutes, 4–6 April 1912. The vote was 201,013 for resumption and 244,011 against.
60 'Labour fights for dockers', *Labour Leader*, 4 July 1912; and, 'The Dock Strike Ending', *Labour Leader*, 1 August 1912.

61 Pelling, *History of British Trade Unionism*, pp. 261–2.
62 *Trades Union Congress Annual Report 1912*, p. 213.
63 PRO, CAB.37/110 (1912), no. 62. S. Buxton, 'Industrial unrest', pp. 4–5.
64 *Ibid.*

2

The Webbs' Approach to Socialism

THE CHANGED WORLD OF LABOUR

While they were in India, the Webbs learned of the 'labour unrest' from one of the many dedicated young men who were drawn by them to socialism and the Fabian Society – Clifford Sharp.[1] He had worked with the Webbs on their Poor Law Crusade, and realized that the combined effect of the Insurance Act and the industrial discontent was to divert attention fatally from that Fabian campaign. The Webbs' plans for reform, embodied in the Minority Report of the Poor Law Commission of 1905–9, which Beatrice largely wrote, were brushed aside, as it were, by 'Lloyd George's Ambulance Wagon'.[2] But though the passage of the Insurance scheme had abruptly ended one major phase of the Webbs' work, the 'labour unrest' inaugurated another.

Sharp wrote to Beatrice in March 1912 that, in the Webbs' absence, the 'whole politico-economic situation' had changed.[3] He told them of the strikes and their consequences. The 'upheaval,' he declared, 'must leave a permanent and a deep mark on our industrial and political history. The "State within the State" has suddenly come to its full power.'[4]

> [Labour] will surely never forget that it has had 'the strongest Government of modern times' practically on its knees suing for peace. And that must give a tremendous impetus to industrial versus political methods. Within a week the Miners' Federation has converted Parliament and the nation to accept a legislative measure for which they would have had to fight 10 years if they had relied solely on political action through the Labour Party.

'Things will never be the same,' he claimed, 'this affair marks the beginning of a new phase in the class war – possibly a very dangerous phase.'[5] Sharp told Beatrice that they had their work cut out for them on their return.[6]

> Socialist thought, (as well as outside public opinion) is in a condition of flux, – and during the next few years it must harden in one direction or another. What direction, will, I think, depend largely on personalities. It may be that the political Socialist movement will be swallowed up in a movement, much more vague philosophically, but much more concrete practically, on the lines of industrial unionism. On the other hand it may be that in ten years time Socialism will be the dominant force in the country. Everything seems to me to depend on the success of Socialists in directing the course of progress during the immediate future, in accordance not necessarily with their own doctrines, but with the real semiconscious expectations of the working class.

The Webbs could not have missed the obvious invitation in Sharp's final remarks: 'Everybody is as it were waiting for a lead – and as things stand political Socialism is not offering one. If it does not strike fairly soon I think it will not have another chance.'[7] After their return to England, the Webbs tried to provide that lead.

It was with his characteristically unshakeable optimism that Sidney Webb noted the emergence of a 'new England'[8] on his return in 1912. He immediately concluded, as had Clifford Sharp, that there were new and virtually unlimited possibilities, on account of the 'labour unrest', for the advance of socialist ideas. It must have been the case, Webb insisted in his 1912 presidential address to the National Committee for the Prevention of Destitution, that during his absence from England:[9]

> The common ideas about the organisation and control of industry have changed. There has evidently been in the past twelve months, a tremendous education of public opinion. What the workmen are demanding is something more than a mere rise in wages.

They wanted more than schemes like the Insurance Act, which dealt only with the effects of economic helplessness and ignored its roots. Their action, he believed, had turned public debate back to consider whether the source of discontent was not the very organization of industrial life. This question was beginning to dawn on many observers. 'Even the House of Commons,' Webb remarked, 'which is about the last place for facts or ideas to penetrate, seems at one moment', the passage of the Minimum Wage Act, 'to have realized as in a flash the depths of its own ignorance, and the impotence to which it had actually come.'[10]

In addition, Webb believed that the political implications of the immense economic power of the working class had been established as never before. Indeed, the 'labour unrest' was the occasion for 'the sudden revelation of the Governing Classes being no longer Governing Classes at all'.[11] The strikes had demonstrated, he argued, that a formidable body of radical opinion existed outside Parliament with which politicians of all persuasions had to deal. Henceforth, Webb said, the Cabinet 'need be in no fear of being in advance of public opinion. There is nothing that would be deemed too revolutionary. The individualist Mrs Grundy is dead.'[12]

Socialists too had to act on the new developments in political opinion. Webb realized that the industrial democracy which he had first described in 1897[13] had changed, and in the light of those changes, he and Beatrice proceeded to re-examine their political tactics and philosophy. Sidney Webb included himself in the category of those whose attitudes had been shaken from below, as it were, by the 'labour unrest'. 'In short,' he remarked, 'though we in England have by no means become wise, we are perhaps all of us, through our humiliation, in a healthier state of mind.'[14]

Beatrice Webb shared her husband's appraisal of the changed state of the Labour movement in 1912.[15] While still abroad, she responded to Sharp's news of the 'labour unrest', admitting that 'All these exciting events must to some extent alter the character of our work – give it perhaps a new direction.'[16] Beatrice further developed her ideas about the new situation in an interview with the *Christian Commonwealth*. Paraphrasing Sidney:[17]

> Mrs Webb explained that the England to which they had returned differed very strikingly from that which they had left in June 1911. 'It is, in many respects,' she said, *'an awakened England* which confronts us today. A new spirit and temper are being manifested by the industrial classes, and an entirely new group of questions has emerged.

The Webbs had previously concentrated their attention on the consumer and the relief of poverty. By 1912 they realized that they had to shift their attention to the producer and the relations of production. Beatrice admitted that[18]

> In the new demand of labour for a partnership in the management and control of industry as well as a fairer share of its profits we deal with an issue which is on an altogether different plane from that which has hitherto presented itself. It cuts across the issue with which we have been concerned in the crusade against the Poor-law. The evils against which we waged war along the lines of the Minority Report of the Poor-law Commission, which the National Committee [for the Prevention of Destitution] was formed to prosecute, might occur, if not prevented, in any form of society; but the new demand for industrial self-government brings into prominence a quite different group of considerations which are concerned with the structure of the industrial organisation rather than with the groups of questions involved in the effort to break up the Poor-law.

These new questions preoccupied the Webbs until the outbreak of the First World War. Their examination of workers' control of industry and the overall restatement of their political theory grew out of their recognition, in Beatrice's words, that the 'labour unrest' had 'raised, in an acute form the question of the possible alternatives to the existing system of private ownership' and management of the means of production.[19] At that critical moment the Webbs felt called upon to provide an intellectual lead to British socialism. Moral outrage alone was no longer enough. Too often it obscured, by the force or brilliance of its rhetoric, the confusion about what the socialist reconstruction of society really meant. The Webbs were deeply aware, in the pre-war period, of:[20]

> The existing chaos and disorder among Socialists, whenever we are asked for constructive proposals, together with our apparent inability to state, with any degree of unanimity or precision, what we are asking for with regard to the future organisation of industry and commerce.

They saw as well that the increased power of the Labour movement, so forcefully demonstrated by the strikes, brought with it added responsibilities for socialists. 'The Socialist Party,' Beatrice observed in 1913, 'has aroused great expectations as to the construction of a New Social Order. Unless we can meet these expectations by carefully drafted and tested specifications, we shall be adjudged by the rising generation of thinkers and workers, intellectually bankrupt.'[21] The Webbs' re-evaluation of the ideas and tactics of British socialism was an attempt to remedy this situation.

THE WEBBS' SOCIALIST IDEAS

The state

The Webbs' examination of their socialist ideas began with a statement of their views on the state. Their principal definition of the state as an association of consumers sharply separates their socialist thought from the Marxist tradition. They also departed at the outset from those, like the guild socialists and syndicalists, who distrusted the state and therefore directed their efforts towards the development of workers' organizations as the true road to socialism. The Webbs, in contrast, asserted that industrial life was marked by a conflict of interest between producers and consumers, which should not be confused with or obscured by the class struggle. Their ideas were incompatible with a straightforward Marxist analysis of industrial society.

The Webbs' political thought is based on two central assumptions: first, that the consumption of necessary goods and services is the fundamental common interest of all men; and second, that government inevitably represented within given geographical boundaries 'the interest of the citizen as a consumer'.[22] The Webbs' socialist state was therefore one whose initial purpose was the satisfaction of consumer needs. They did admit, however, that an industrial and political order 'based exclusively on the interests of consumers can secure merely the material comfort of the race'.[23] The role of the citizen as producer had to be recognized as well, through the trade unions. But the Webbs placed political power firmly in the hands of the consumers, through the institutional apparatus of the state.

The Webbs would neither describe nor define the state as the agency which exercised police power, or (in Max Weber's contemporary axiom) that institution which had 'the *monopoly of the legitimate use of physical force* within a given territory'.[24] Rather, the Webbs' state was, ideally, that set of institutions which dealt exclusively with the administration of public services and engaged in 'housekeeping on a national scale'.[25] They did not regard this as a utopian view. They noted optimistically that the state before August 1914 was well on the way to the complete reversal of its traditional and violent role. The pre-war state, they observed, had become a large-scale employer engaged in a number of service industries, and the adoption and development of these new functions had fundamentally 'changed its character'. In fact:[26]

> The government has passed from being an autocratic monarch, whether a person, a class, or an official hierarchy, to whom we owe loyalty and obedience, and has become a busy house-keeper, whose object is to serve the citizens, and to whom we owe only such adherence to common rules and such mutual consideration as will permit the civic household to be comfortable.

By the extension of welfare services throughout the world, over the previous century, government had begun to adopt the spirit of co-operation. The Co-operative Societies rather than the trade unions, the Webbs observed, provided the example of contemporary institutions which operated on this admirable principle. Here was the model of the future socialist state. Indeed, the fact that government was coming more and more to resemble a Co-operative Society had 'made Social Democracy possible'.[27]

Associations of producers, on the other hand, were based on very different principles. In fact by 1914 industrial democracy and social democracy were no longer intimately related in the Webbs' political thought. Their pre-war views reflect a far more hostile view to trade unionism than did their previous writing. In 1897, they had commented that:

> These thousands of working-class democracies, spontaneously growing up at different times and places, untrammelled by the traditions or interests of other classes, perpetually recasting their constitutions to meet new and varying conditions, present an unrivalled field of observation as to the manner in which the working man copes with the problem of combining administrative efficiency with popular control.

Then they regarded trade unionism as a reflection of 'the irresistible tendency to popular government, in spite of all its difficulties and dangers' which gave the Webbs 'a sense of the vastness and complexity of democracy itself'.[28] Sixteen years later, the Webbs' view had changed.

All associations of working men as producers, including the trade unions, the Webbs noted after the 'labour unrest', 'always tend to develop, sooner or later, into what Adam Smith called "conspiracies against the public" '. And as soon as such groups come to power, they become[29]

> in fact, an oligarchy. This was the tendency that ruined the craft gild; this is the tendency shown to-day by every professional association exercising governmental powers; *this is the tendency manifested by every trade union whenever its position permits.*

All producers' associations were based, in the Webbs's view, on objectionable principles – exclusiveness, selfishness, and coercion. Therefore, they concluded, 'to base any government organisation on Associations of Producers is to negative Democracy'.[30]

Associations of consumers, on the other hand, do not suffer from the same parochialism of outlook or policy. These groups[31]

> even if enjoying governmental power, have no interest in, and therefore, no tendency to, any restriction of membership, and no vested interest to protect against the whole body of citizens. Whatever may be their other defects, they constitute an automatic Democracy.

The Webbs' acceptance of the state as a vehicle for social change and their optimism about the gradual growth of its function and structure was a result of this identification of socialism with Co-operation. By 1913, they were prepared to assert that[32]

> The State has become, in fact, a sort of extended Co-operative Society, performing for the great public of consumers the services they require, and supplying these, not necessarily compulsorily, or even universally, but often only by definite individual request.

The Webbs greeted this supposed development with unqualified approval. 'To the working-class Socialist,' they observed:[33]

> it seems that the modern function of the State – its character as a Co-operative Society, of which we all automatically have the privilege of membership – is destined altogether to outweigh, and finally to submerge, the function of the State as a

coercive authority. The old State, with its semi-civilized population, concerned itself solely with the maintenance of order. The new State, able more and more to take order for granted, devotes its energies to securing progress.

Coercion and service are competing alternatives in the Webbs' pre-war political thought. The capitalist state was based on the former principle; the socialist state would operate on the latter. Under socialism, the state would emerge from its barbaric infancy to take up its mature role as the beneficent and pacific guardian of the national interest. Their future socialist state was, therefore, one in which 'conformity to common rules designated only to secure the common comfort' would replace 'the authoritarian conception of dominion (*Verwaltung, autorité régalienne*) with its correlative of loyalty to a monarch, and obedience to coercive laws'.[34]

The Webbs were nevertheless aware of the dangers inherent in the concentration of power in the state. They knew that their state shared the disadvantages of all large-scale organizations, that is, the problems of bureaucracy, which they considered unavoidable and tolerable evils.[35] On the other hand, the Webbs insisted, 'It is a curious misconception which associates Socialism with a gigantic, centralised, bureaucratic, coercive and all-pervading government, administered from the State capital.'[36] As an antidote to oppressive centralism, they formally supported the maintenance of strong subsidiary pressure groups and local associations. Still, political sovereignty was indivisible in their view, so that local government groups, trade unions, and Co-operative Societies, for example, would all serve only as advisers to the state, to help assure the multiplicity of popular controls over government.[37]

The growth of lesser authorities and various subsidiary groups was essential to the successful operation of the Webbs' socialist state. Such developments were slow and undramatic, and added further limits to the speed at which political changes were likely to occur. While it was their belief that 'the progress of Socialism resembles the approach of the hyperbole to its asymptote', they still held that 'we cannot increase our Collectivism faster than the nation is able to build the necessary social tissue'.[38] Political convulsions or violently disruptive actions, such as revolution, were, therefore, ruled out by the Webbs from the start. The evolution of their socialist state was to be on the whole as peaceful as the future society it would serve.

The organization of industry

The Webbs believed that the non-violent transformation of modern society would be accomplished only through the re-structuring of government and the extension of state control over industry. In their view, the communal ownership of the means of production would change the nature both of the state and of industrial organization. Government and the economy then would be in a symbiotic relationship. By engaging primarily in industrial functions, as opposed to foreign affairs or the maintenance of internal order, the state would become, the Webbs argued, essentially benevolent and democratic, that is, in line with the real interests of the people. At the same time, a state-controlled economy would be able finally to abolish primary poverty, so that at least a minimum of civilized life could be shared by all. The resulting prosperity would allow the state then to proceed to its higher goal: to preserve and improve the physical, intellectual and spiritual resources of the nation.[39]

Their research in the pre-war period on the control of industry led the Webbs to reaffirm their view that state and municipal enterprise offered the only effective and practicable alternative to capitalism. The advantages of state control were numerous. They assumed that corporate selfishness would be limited in governmental dealings by the ethics of a professional managerial class. Only under state control could there be co-ordination and unity of administration. The just regulation of the market was also possible under a system of collective ownership. Consumption could be restricted by raising prices, and conversely, subsidies could be used to lower the prices of items of desirable consumption, such as education and medical services.[40] In addition, without exorbitant prices and monopolistic private control there was likely to be, the Webbs believed, greater equality of remuneration. And above all, they foresaw under state socialism an 'almost certain increment in values attendant on increases of population and national prosperity'.[41] The Webbs' major assumption here is that contact with their new state would cultivate that sense of community and mutual service which they believed to be essential to any socialist experiment.

The Webbs admitted that the neglect of the producers' viewpoint in favour of the consumers' was a glaring omission in the political organization of the contemporary state. There was a real need, they noted in 1914, for the incorporation of the 'personality' of the producing class in the formation of public policy. The lack of any adjustment on the part of the state to meet producers' demands was, the Webbs thought, the cause of the contemporary discontent with governmental action and the basis of the widespread fears about the effects of nationalization.[42]

They were prepared to admit that some of the criticisms of state control were legitimate. Indeed, they knew they were unable to offer conclusive answers to those who asked if state ownership would really change the relations of production. In particular, they admitted that manual workers were much worse off than administrative workers in government employment. Manual workers had insecure tenure, severely limited rights to unionize, and they did not participate in any stage of management. There seemed to be little improvement over capitalist methods of remuneration and workshop discipline. Still, they held that most men who worked for the state had greater continuity of employment, a fixed standard of life, and, in all probability, disinterested managers. It appears that the obvious class bias in the selection of the Civil Service did not occur to the Webbs at this time. They seem to have felt that under socialism, not only the nature of the state, but also the character of the men who ran it, would be uplifted.[43]

Nationalization was, therefore, a necessary, although not a sufficient, step in the process of improving the condition of industrial life. State socialism undoubtedly had its drawbacks, but they were convinced nevertheless that none of the other alternatives to capitalism suggested by contemporaries were likely to provide a more equitable system for the organization of industry. They rejected profit-sharing and other co-partnership schemes, since they totally ignored the question of the status of the worker in industry.[44] Co-operation, too, the Webbs admitted, afforded operatives in their working lives no alternative to the capitalist system.[45] Syndicalism, on the other hand, took the problem of the producer's status within industry and society as the key to the socialist reconstruction of society.

But the syndicalists' proposals[46] shared the problems implicit in all schemes for workers' control of industry. Indeed all producers' associations, the Webbs argued, were completely inadequate units around which to reorganize industry. Such associations had failed consistently throughout Europe in the past since (1) they were unable to maintain adequate workshop discipline, (2) they did not have the requisite knowledge of the market, and (3) they did not have sufficient flexibility to be able to change processes to meet new demands and to provide new products.[47] No one could deny, the Webbs asserted, the 'inability' of producers' associations 'to cope with industry, conducted on a large scale, and in small-scale industries their failure to make headway against, or even to keep pace with the capitalist system'.[48]

The Webbs' criticism of syndicalism is very revealing. Their treatment of this radical doctrine shows clearly their ambivalence toward trade-union and working-class militancy as a whole. Indicative of this view is a comment of Sidney Webb to E. R. Pease, secretary of the Fabian Society. Webb wrote after the 1911 unrest, 'I am sorry that the strikes cannot help making for Tom Mann and the General Strike, but it was time Trade Unionism woke up again and asserted itself.'[49]

The Webbs admitted that Syndicalism was 'a very natural, and we must concede, very pardonable reaction from the intolerable social condition of today, and from the quite inexcusable neglect of Cabinets and Parliaments to deal with these evils'.[50] They pointed out that syndicalists were 'trying to express what is a real and deep-seated feeling in millions of manual working wage-earners, which cannot and ought not to be ignored'.[51] But though syndicalism was a necessary irritant, in their view it was fraught with very dangerous tendencies. Thus:[52]

> whilst we think that the Syndicalist agitation supplies a useful corrective, and brings into prominence working-class feelings that we are too prone to ignore, we regard the Syndicalist proposals, not only as ethically objectionable, but also as fundamentally impracticable.

The Webbs found it morally repugnant that the syndicalists preached 'to the workers a deliberate disregard of the duties of citizenship, the persistent abstention from voting, and the abandonment of all interest in Parliament and Local Authority, for the sake of advancing their own interests'.[53] This parochialism and selfishness was, the Webbs insisted, 'hardly the road to higher things'. They also condemned the tactics of 'ca'canny' and other restrictive practices which, they believed, reflected 'a serious deterioration of moral character in those who consent to take part in it'.[54]

Syndicalists and those others who made the class war into the prime fact of modern life, were, the Webbs believed, not merely wrong. They also contributed to an atmosphere which was, 'to say the least of it, not conducive to that growth of fellowship upon which alone a decent social order can be built'.[55] And the syndicalists, unlike the Marxists, also intended to perpetuate the division of society after their revolution, which was surely not the way to a just and peaceful society.[56]

Syndicalism, they asserted, would not even remedy the problem of the centralized state. It would either reproduce such an authority, or set up dual sovereignty which was bound to lead to civil strife. Furthermore, since syndicalism robbed the workers of trade unions as defensive organizations by transforming them into instruments of political power, the Webbs argued that a new crop of unions would have to be raised to fulfil their present important functions.[57] Finally, the tactics of the general strike could not, in their opinion, be relied on to effect 'huge constitutional changes'.[58] The Webbs concluded therefore, that[59]

the very foundation of the Syndicalist community is wrongly chosen . . . we must reconstruct society on a basis not of interests, but of community of service, and of that 'neighbourly' feeling of which local life is made up, and of that willingness to subordinate oneself to the welfare of the whole without which national existence is impossible.

They rested their argument once again on the belief that state socialism would lead to this new communitarian spirit in industrial as well as in political life.

Prospects: the dangers of militarism

The Webbs did not expect to see the advent of socialism in their lifetime or indeed in the foreseeable future. The cautiousness and conservatism of their estimate of the movement towards socialism is striking. In 1913 they asked rhetorically:[60]

What is the probability of this movement extending to such a degree as to give its tone to the nation? What are the chances of seeing say, within the next hundred years, one or more of the great States of the world organised, to any considerable extent, on the Socialist principles that we have described?

In answering this question themselves, the Webbs did not assume that the development of the socialist society was inevitable. They were certain that society would evolve, but they added significantly, *'in what direction we know not'*.[61] If the Western world did not move towards equality and freedom and away from unfettered capitalism, then, the Webbs prophesied, there was little more to look forward to than continued discontent and revolts which would multiply as long as men were aware of injustice. But revolt was bound to end dismally in repression, the Webbs believed, unless the nation as a whole developed the capacity for 'scientifically directed common action'. Without such a shift in public policy, the Webbs foresaw the time when 'any effective economic and political power of the working class might be destroyed'.[62] The formulation and dissemination of socialist ideas were attempts to avoid this catastrophe, but would they, in themselves, be enough? the Webbs asked rhetorically.

On the one hand, they felt confident that history was on their side. Behind every institutional change, the Webbs posited:[63]

> there drives on silently the persistent pressure of a people traditionally free; aware of its power; clearing its eyes from the illusions of the past; becoming steadily more alive to its common interests, and, if we mistake not, resolved to make Democracy a reality in industry as well as in politics.

But on the other hand, two problems led them to seriously qualify their optimism. The first was militarism. They argued, one year before the outbreak of the First World War:[64]

> The political ambitions of the different Great Powers, sharpened by their industrial and commercial rivalry, will – unless there is a change of heart – inevitably lead to constantly increasing armaments and to periodical wars of a destructiveness which the world has never yet witnessed.

They did not offer any specific remedy to this problem, which was neglected, on the whole, in their pre-war thought.

The second factor which supported a pessimistic view of the future of British socialism, and Western European civilization as well, was, the Webbs believed, the decline in the birth-rate of the 'higher races' among all but the lowest strata. This point merits further consideration, since it exposes one of the serious limitations of their political thought – their racialism.

Race and the non-white world

A fuller understanding of the Webbs' pre-war political ideas may be gained through an analysis of their views on race and the non-white world. In their comments during and after their round the world tour in 1911–12, we can see the extent to which they accepted and helped to propagate a number of crude assumptions about racial and national character which were widely shared in late-Victorian society. Today we take for granted that socialism implies a belief in human equality and the right of all peoples to self-determination. Webbian socialism did not rest on this premise.

By contemporary standards the Webbs' racialism was unexceptional. They adhered to the common belief that ethnic groups had distinct moral and intellectual characteristics which were biologically and culturally transmitted from generation to generation. These differences were not immutable, in their view, but they largely determined the present capacity of peoples to undertake the tasks of social organization.

It is easy to see how the Webbs built on this notion a fairly typical justification of Empire as a benevolent necessity.[65] Their paternalism was the common response of Victorian intellectuals of all political persuasions to cultures and societies of which they had little knowledge and less understanding.[66] As did many of their contemporaries, the Webbs saw in Asia and Africa what was, with the one notable exception of Japan, a world of politically immature people, not yet sufficiently advanced to be able to master the arts of social administration. The rudimentary skills of modern political life, therefore, had to be taught to the black and yellow races by the example of white imperial authority. In this way, and given enough time, racial backwardness, they felt, could ultimately be overcome.

But just because the white presence in Asia and Africa was a positive force, it did not follow for the Webbs that a substantial number of non-whites, or even of 'inferior' Caucasians, such as Slavs or Jews in Western Europe was similarly conducive to progress. On the contrary, they expressed fears that the Europeans' capacity for social improvement would be diminished severely if race-mixing on a large scale were to take place. And this threat to the 'racial vitality' of the advanced white nations was made even more serious, they believed, by the decline in European fertility rates, a phenomenon which had aroused considerable comment prior to the First World War.[67] Only if the white race remained intact and if Western Europe held its own demographically, the Webbs asserted, could socialists' hopes be realized. To this end they urged that miscegenation had to be kept to a minimum and that the tendency of Europeans, especially the more educated and highly-skilled, to limit the size of their families, had to be reversed.

The Webbs' comments on the non-white world are worth examining in detail for our purposes, since they so clearly reveal much more about their own preconceptions and prejudices than about the subjects they were supposedly investigating.[68] One salient example of the inegalitarian side of the Webbs' socialist thought is the opinion of Chinese racial character which they expressed during their tour of the Far East in 1911.

Their visit to China came at a particularly turbulent time, amidst the turmoil and uncertainty of the last days of the Manchu dynasty. What was the Webbs' explanation for the panic and disorder they observed? The source of the chaos was to be found, they claimed, in the moral defects of the Chinese as a race, which rendered them incapable of orderly government and social improvement.[69] For one thing, the open practice of homosexuality was proof for the Webbs of the degeneracy of the Chinese. After having visited numerous 'boys' homes' for male prostitutes, Beatrice noted in her diary that 'It is this rottenness of physical and moral character that makes one despair of China – their constitution seems devastated by drugs and abnormal sexual indulgence. They are essentially an unclean race.'[70]

Beatrice's reaction to the Chinese at times bordered on physical disgust. She confided to her sister Kate Courtney that she had been appalled in her walks through the streets of Peking by the 'horrid expression' on the face of the Chinese, 'undisciplined and yet servile, with a curious feminine and rather feline sweetness'.[71] She mentioned again how she felt that the Chinese 'all look as if they were devastated by personal self-indulgence and vice of one kind or another'. 'It is not pleasant,' she concluded bluntly, 'to be among a people one dislikes so much.'[72]

After a visit to Canton, Beatrice was equally distressed. 'Certainly judging by the look of their home life,' she wrote after a tour of one residential area, 'the Chinese are a horrid race.' And she added: 'If there is any spectacle more repulsive than a Chinese home,' well-staffed by concubines, 'it is a Chinese Temple, with its hideous idols, its fortune tellers, and Quack Medicine Vendors, its dirt and elaborate golden decorations.'[73] Of the Great Wall of China, she had no better opinion. 'It is a monument of extravagant stupidity', merely a reflection of the Chinese 'belief that mere size and bulk and material strength will avail to maintain a nation; without regard to the infinitely more important forces of intellect and will and character.'[74] It was hardly a surprise to her, then, that such a depraved people, given up to pleasures of which she did not approve, lacked as a race the idealism and self-control to build a decent life for itself.

Sidney tried to give this view of the Chinese a more scientific form. Writing from Peking, he suggested that the Chinese race provided 'a striking example of arrested development'. Here he thought that:[75]

> A biological analogy may help to make the position clear. The highly developed insect has gone very far, but it is along a line in which further progress seems impossible. The lowly vertebrate may be less developed, but has greater potentialities.

One could hardly blame the Chinese for their political ineptitude and the resultant instability, which were simply the outcome of the stunted growth of that race. Pressing further his biological metaphor, Sidney argued:[76]

> The whole Chinese nation reminds us, in fact, of a race of ants or bees of gregarious habits, but incapable of the organization of the ant-hill or the hive. They show us, indeed, what homo sapiens can be if he does not evolve in the social organism.

The Webbs' reaction to the other indigenous inhabitants of the Asian mainland was similarly marked by this crude social Darwinism. Koreans, Burmese, Indians all suffered in varying degrees, the Webbs believed, from the same inability to generate and operate by themselves the organs of social administration.[77] In their view, none was so hopelessly retarded as were the Chinese, but there was still, they believed, a yawning and as yet unbridgeable gap between Asian and European political achievements.

But as the South Africans do today, the Webbs were prepared to admit that in one specific case – that of Japan – the rule of white political, intellectual and moral superiority did not apply. Here again, their remarks bring into focus more general aspects of their ideas. More central to their thought than their racialism was the principle that social maturity was synonymous with administrative ability. And on this count, the Japanese were most impressive. In Japan they discovered in abundance all the positive qualities of social and political organization which in China and the rest of Asia were so conspicuous by their absence. Consequently, they accorded to the Japanese a special status, which set them distinctly apart from the rest of the non-white world.

Years before their visit to the Far East, the Webbs had developed a profound admiration for the Japanese as the only coloured nation that could be compared favourably with any European state. Indeed, in the first decade of the twentieth century, Japan was acclaimed by a chorus of voices in Britain, including those of the Webbs, as the paragon of national efficiency.[78] In large part, this phenomenon was the direct result of her stunning military victory over Russia in 1904-5, which British socialists greeted warmly. First there was the defeat of the Czar to be applauded. But more importantly for the Webbs, there was the example of what a strong centralized government could accomplish in industry as well as on the field of battle, if guided by national idealism similar to that of the Japanese.

Beatrice Webb shared the sense of astonishment many less philosophical Europeans felt at the emergence of this non-white power. 'They have suddenly raised the standard of national efficiency,' she observed in late 1904, 'exactly in those departments of life where we Western nations imagined ourselves supremely superior to the Eastern races.'[79] In the previous months she claimed to have seen:[80]

> in myself and in others a growing national shamefacedness at the superiority of the Japanese over our noble selves in capacity, courage, self-control, in benevolence as well as in all that makes up good manners! They shame our Christianity, they shame our administrative capacity, they shame our inventiveness, they shame our leadership. . . . They seem both more scientific and more religious than ourselves – [and have] a nobler purpose and more ably-contrived processes wherewith to carry out this purpose.

Their success was bound to tell in Europe, she added, 'in favour of organization, collective regulation, scientific education, physical and mental training – but not on the whole in favour of democracy'.[81] This last drawback did not deter Beatrice from claiming that Japan's development helped to prove and in the future would continue to 'bear out the Collectivist as against the individualist theory of the Political State'.[82] And 'for many a long day,' she observed, 'the reformer will be able to quote on his side the innovating collectivism of the Japanese; the idealist, the self-abnegation of all classes of the community in a common cause.'[83]

In fact, the British public, she thought, was already beginning to draw the necessary conclusions. After the Anglo-Japanese Treaty was renewed in 1905 for a further ten years, Beatrice optimistically noted that the upsurge in pro-Japanese feeling in England was 'accompanied by an increase of faith in collective regulation and collective action as against the old ultra competitive creed'. 'How the old-fashioned radical hates the Jap!' she wryly noted.[84] There was every reason, therefore, for socialists to take heart from Japan's rise to world prominence, since she was proving 'the superlative advantage of scientific methods in the international struggle for existence'.[85]

The Webbs' expectations were fulfilled when they finally visited Japan in late 1911. During their eight weeks' stay they had a good opportunity to see for themselves the results of that 'capacity for scientific method and for disciplined effort' which, they believed, distinguished the Japanese from other Asians.[86] They were immediately impressed both by the intellectual calibre of the government officials they met and by their dedication to the ideal of national service.[87] They were struck, too, by the fact that Japanese culture was not the prerogative of the privileged few, but that 'the common lump of men', as they put it, were 'more civilized than those of any country we have seen'.[88]

There was one 'blot' on Japanese society which the Webbs openly criticized. The blatant exploitation of the industrial labour force was, they admitted, undeniable and unfortunate, but even this did not trouble them unduly. Conditions were bound to improve, they believed, and progress would be made far more quickly than had been the case during Britain's Industrial Revolution, since Japan could face her 'problems with an instructed and and highly intelligent civil service and with the mass of the common people, in their own way, essentially civilized'.[89]

We can learn much about the Webbs' overall political outlook from their description of Japan. In effect, they saw there what they had come to see. They found an orderly and smoothly-run society, the government of which was in the hands of an enlightened professional élite, whose 'purpose and open-mindedness' Beatrice thought 'uncanny'.[90] From these remarks we can see more clearly the Webbian model of the benevolent bureaucracy of the future socialist state. Twenty years later, the Webbs would claim to have seen the same 'Samurai vocation for leadership' practised by the Communist Party of the Soviet Union under Stalin.[91]

What is equally illuminating is what they did not see in Japan. Their tendency to ignore or largely overlook the autocratic character of Japanese political and industrial life is striking. The society they admired so much was one in which capitalism was both thriving and unchallenged, where trade unions had no legal standing and strikes were outlawed, and where a tiny socialist movement had been crushed a few months before they had arrived in Japan. They seem to have been unaware of or unconcerned by the mass arrests and subsequent execution in January 1911 of twelve Japanese socialists, allegedly involved in an assassination plot.[92] Authoritarianism, they apparently believed, was a small enough price to pay for efficiency and order in social affairs. This élitist, illiberal aspect of the Webbs' thought is exposed just as clearly here in their euphoric appraisal of Japan as it was in their denigration of the rest of the non-white world.

When the Webbs returned to England in 1912, they incorporated in their reappraisal of socialist thought a discussion of the problem of empire which further reflects many of the views outlined above. Again we can see how exceptional was their treatment of the Japanese and how condescending was their attitude to every other coloured group. The first point they raised was that it would be foolish to ignore racial backwardness, which had been and would continue to be exploited by selfish Western interests. The more progressive Europeans, therefore, had a moral obligation to fulfil their protective, paternal role in Asia and Africa. Who could deny, they argued, that the Pacific Islanders, the Malays, the Arabs, the Kaffirs, the Negroes, and 'all the indigenous inhabitants of the Asiatic mainland' were, in their 'capacity for corporate self-defence and self-government, *Non-adult races*'?[93] It followed therefore, that:[94]

These weaker races are, at least in respect of power to defend themselves, virtually in the position of children in a universe of grown men; and in such a position the grown men have duties and responsibilities toward the children which they ought not to ignore.

The Webbs thus posited the need for what they called the 'Collective Guardianship' of these peoples, 'in their own interest, as far as we can discern it, and in the interests of humanity as a whole'.[95]

The period of Western responsibility for the dark-skinned races was of indefinite length. Indeed, the Webbs believed that[96]

as regards many parts of the British Empire, it would be idle to pretend that anything like effective self-government, even as regards strictly local affairs, can be introduced for many generations to come – in some cases, conceivably never.

Benevolent tutelage must replace exploitative domination the Webbs believed, as the basis of Western policy. And the former was producing results. 'The child is growing up,' they wrote in 1913. 'Whereas it used to be only seven years old, it is now fourteen.'[97] Of course, adolescence raised as many problems as did childhood, and the road ahead would not be an easy one.

We can see the Webbs' racialism expressed even more explicitly elsewhere in their pre-war writings. Of far greater danger to the future of socialism than the burdens of empire, they felt, was the possibility of 'race deterioration, if not race suicide' posed by the decline in European fertility rates. This issue had been raised by the Webbs before their Asian visit,[98] and they returned to it again in the days immediately prior to the First World War.

Beatrice pointed to the USA, as other racialists do today, as an example of what Europe had to avoid at all costs. She was horrified by what she believed were the implications of the decline in birthrate among American white Anglo-Saxons and of racial intermarriage. She prophesied darkly in July 1914 that 'the United States will in the course of a century be inhabited, in the main, by a coloured population ruled over by Jews with a fringe of Celtic Catholics'.[99] The lesson for Western Europe was clear, in her opinion. Unless the birth-rate rose among the higher strata of European society, she felt that 'we are within measurable distance of the collapse of our own civilization – it may be for the benefit of the Chinese or the Africans!'[100]

In Europe, Beatrice noted, it appeared that the French were in most danger from this threat to white civilization. Even after the assassination of Franz Ferdinand, when rumours of war were heard, Beatrice Webb still saw an 'impending catastrophe' by racial invasion 'by outcasts from Southern Europe, mongrels from Algeria, and coolies from China'. Such an occurrence, she wrote, 'seems to me a bigger tragedy than any hypothetical defeat by an army of Germany'.[101] After all, Germany was efficient, cultured, and white.

There was one further refinement in the Webbs' thoughts about racial character. They held that only parts of the Anglo-Saxon race possessed those qualities most conducive to the development of socialism. The birth-rate had to rise, first and foremost, among educated Northern and Western Europeans. If it did not, they would be overrun sooner or later by 'the offspring of the less thrifty, the less intellectual, the less foreseeing races or classes – the unskilled casual labourers of our great cities, the races of Eastern or Southern Europe, the negroes, the Chinese'.[102]

The result, 'as already in parts of the United States', was bound to be 'such a heterogeneous and mongrel population, that democratic self-government or even the effective application of the policy of a national minimum of civilized life will become increasingly unattainable'.[103]

The Webbs' version of socialism was, at least in the foreseeable future, undoubtedly the prosperous white man's affair. In August 1913 they wrote that if the 'higher races' were to lose their predominance in world affairs by sheer weight of numbers

> it is difficult to avoid the melancholy conclusion that, in some cataclysm that it is impossible for us to foresee, the civilization characteristic of the Western European races may go the way of the half a dozen civilizations that have within historic times preceded it; to be succeeded by a new social order developed by one or other of the coloured races, the negro, the Kaffir, or the Chinese![104]

Such a catastrophe would make socialism impossible, the Webbs believed, in Britain, as in the rest of the Western world.

The Webbs were not alone in voicing this 'racialism of the left'. E. D. Morel, for example, who worked tirelessly before the First World War to expose the brutality of Belgian rule in the Congo, also held similar, if not more extreme, opinions. His post-war campaign against the use of African troops in the occupation of Germany, replete with all the stereotypical charges of black sexuality and violence, found support in many quarters of the left.[105] Similarly, throughout the century, opposition within the Labour movement to Jewish and more recently, to Commonwealth, immigration, has not been based solely on fears of job competition. It may not have been a complete accident, then, that Oswald Mosley, the Fascist leader, emerged not from the Conservative, but rather from the Labour Party.

Within this context, the Webbs' ideas illustrate something more than their personal idiosyncracies.[106] Their views on race amply demonstrate how ineffectively their socialism provided an antidote to the common prejudices of their day. Indeed, their racialism may be seen as the natural outcome both of their paternalism, with which they approached the British working class as well as 'lower races', and of their failure to make of the concept of equality an integral part of their socialist position.

Webbian socialism

The Webbs' pre-war restatement of their ideas reflects a number of assumptions which separate their views at the outset from Marxism and indeed from most other varieties of socialist thought. In the Webbs' political theory, men are considered first of all as 'consumers', and only secondarily as 'producers'. They never systematically examined this distinction, but it is at the heart of their position. They recognized that men developed a trade or professional outlook and shared strong ties with those with whom they worked. But they argued that the first interest of all inhabitants of any geographical unit is the satisfaction of what they called 'consumer needs'. Since this is what men have in common, the function of any government, the Webbs asserted, is always to represent and to serve such interests. These are the premises which underlay their definition of the state as the 'national association of consumers'.

The major defect of the capitalist state, they held, was that it represented only some consumers rather than the nation as a whole. State ownership and management of industry and essential services would remedy this difficulty, even though it would not necessarily change the conditions of work for the labouring population. That is why trade unions would be necessary in the future: precisely to balance the consumer-state.

The paternalism of this theory is perhaps its most dominant

feature. The Webbs pictured the nation as a family which in future would be headed by a benign service state, the first function of which, as in all families, would be to see that all are fed, clothed and housed. Then the more important aspects of national life, the spiritual and intellectual heritage, could be cultivated and disseminated. All this would be possible only if the state took on the character of a gigantic co-operative society, which would become less and less coercive the more it engaged in the tasks of 'national housekeeping'. Social conflict would not disappear, since producer-consumer antagonism would remain. But disputes would be resolved in an atmosphere of consensus, based on a generally-accepted notion of higher purpose in social life.

In this context, we can understand why they rejected the views of those who saw class divisions as irremediable. Their mistake, in the Webbs' opinion, was to deny the identity of (consumer) interests which capitalism obscured and upon which the foundations of socialist society would rest. Throughout their writings they argued that the tenor of political life would change as the instruments of social administration were re-aligned to suit national rather than class or parochial needs. For this reason, the capture of the state by what they took to be 'narrow working-class interests' would be no improvement. Syndicalism was thus of concern to the Webbs mainly as a symptom of the social disease which capitalism bred. In their view, the militants demonstrated how much the workers shared the infectious selfishness of the capitalist. It was precisely this temper of conflict the Webbs hoped to replace.

The difficulties of this theory are apparent. The Webbs' socialism grew out of their belief that somehow men who had always thought in terms of social conflict would be led to a commitment to social integration. They never proposed, however, a remedy for the spirit of aggressiveness and domination which is the heaviest legacy of capitalism. The Owenite charge, stated in modern form, that 'Repressive men would carry their repression into the new society'[107] was never met by the Webbs. There is little reason, therefore, to accept their view that the more the state engaged in consumer services, the less coercive would it become. On the other hand, there is even less reason to assume that contact with government would improve the values or morals of the population. Surely the Webbs knew that most men and women would find it difficult to adopt their own peculiar brand of ascetic self-denial. If men were unlike the Webbs, if they were unable to control themselves, would the state perform the task for them? Paternalism and punishment usually go together. Why not in a Webbian state?

Paternalism and racialism are equally compatible, as the Webbs themselves illustrated in their writings on the non-white world. This time they pictured a family of races, composed of coloured children and adolescents, and presided over beneficently by the mature Western European Caucasians. Their thoughts on race serve as a sombre reminder of the inconsistency and shallowness of a socialist position devoid of a belief in equality.

Equally striking is their paternalistic attitude to the working class at home. Their belief in government from above is demonstrated clearly in their treatment of workers as spectators in the process of building the socialist state. The key work in the Webbian experiment would be done by a selfless, professional, intellectual élite; that is, by men and women very much like the Webbs themselves. Such people would set out the guidelines of social policy and train the functionaries of the future. They would be unconcerned with power or other rewards, content to preside over the transition to a stable and just society. Strikingly similar to Leninist views at this point, the Webbs' ideas also share the same dangers and contradictions. Here again the doubts remain about the effectiveness of the Webbian antidote to social conflict under capitalism.

TACTICS: THE WEBBS AND THE PRE-WAR LABOUR PARTY

The impact of the 'labour unrest' may be seen as much in the clarification of the Webbs' tactical views as in the exposition of their political ideas. There are always political gains to be derived from discontent, and on their return to England, the Webbs detected in the industrial ferment evidence of the existence of an emerging popular base upon which an effective socialist party could be built. The strikes had demonstrated to them that there were large sections of the working class who were more politically advanced than previously had been thought. Their conclusion was that the political tactics of British socialism had to be revised in the light of what they took to be a significant development in working-class attitudes to capitalism.

Beatrice Webb also believed that the women's movement was a concurrent advance in the formation of the political base for British socialism. In her opinion, the suffrage campaign was not mere feminism. It was 'one of three simultaneous world-movements towards a more equal partnership among human beings in human affairs'.[108] The movement of European political affairs was, she held, away from domination by class, nationality, and sex, each of which was based only on sheer physical force and/or immense economic power. Like the 'labour unrest', the suffrage agitation was a useful irritant. In both cases, the friction of social conflict generated sparks which illuminated the central problems of society.

She was disposed to dissociate herself from what she saw as the excesses of militant violence, but she also insisted on a balanced view of the situations which bred extremism. 'All violence and disorder,' she observed:[109]

> set back the movement with which they are associated. We realise, indeed, that it is one of the sorrowful reactions of the world that the denial of justice always evokes, somewhere and at some point, a wild exasperation in the oppressed. We are not called upon to condemn an exasperation which, equally with the injustice, we deplore. We condemn rather those in positions of power who themselves appeal to a physical force domination as the only possible basis of efficient government and social life.

And again, just as in the case of the 'labour unrest', those in power were, by ignoring very real grievances, unintentionally contributing to their own demise. The refusal of both major parties to deal with women's suffrage was likened by Beatrice Webb to 'the hardening of the heart of Pharaoh'. This situation, she noted, was most fortunate for British socialism and should be 'welcomed'. As a direct result of their disenfranchisement, 'British womanhood, taken as a whole, is being transformed, under our eyes, from a passively conservative into an actively revolutionary force.'[110] This reversal in the attitudes of women toward politics was, in her view, traceable directly to their exclusion from the two major parties. Hence, she concluded: 'the whole of the women's movement finds itself side-slipping, almost unintentionally, into Labour and Socialist politics'.[111] And through close comradeship with social-ists, the four million salaried female wage-earners were developing that ' "class consciousness" of the proletariat eager not merely for political but economic "enfranchisement" '.[112] Indeed, 'the vote-lessness of women' was another factor contributing to the pre-war spread of socialism 'from one end of Great Britain to the other'.[113]

The Webbs' view that the pre-war social unrest forcibly demonstrated the existence of a potential popular base for British socialism, still left two questions unanswered: how was this latent force to be converted into political power? And how was that political power to be effectively directed towards the achievement of socialist aims? The political performance of organized Labour in this period provided the Webbs with few easy answers.

On the one hand they had to contend with MacDonald's opportunistic leadership of the Labour Party and his periodic flirtations with the idea of coalition politics. The Webbs were among the many socialists who both recognized the need for a truly independent parliamentary Labour contingent, and completely disagreed with MacDonald's idea of what the party should be or how it ought to operate.

Some of the problems of parliamentary tactics were beyond Labour's control, but there were numerous instances of shortsightedness, clumsiness and ineptitude for which the party leadership was clearly responsible. The acquiescence of MacDonald in most Liberal policies was unmistakable. The party's action (or rather inaction) in dealing with the National Insurance Act of 1911 epitomized for the Webbs the futile side of Labour's record in Parliament. The fact that the contributory principle was accepted by the party's leadership demonstrated how far its outlook was from one which could be described as socialist. The conclusion Sidney drew was that 'the working class is being in this matter abandoned by those in whom it ought to rely for advice. There seems no one in the Labour Party able to watch its interests in any complicated matter.'[114]

At the same time, the trade unionists in the party were, in Webb's view, too busy with their own affairs and not sufficiently intelligent to do their job properly. He complained to Beatrice in late 1912 that, one year after the passage of the National Insurance Act, the union leaders still had no idea about its operation or necessary amendments. In fact, he added: 'they are terribly slow to understand anything at all.'[115] Beatrice repeated this appraisal in her diary while attending the 1912 Trades Union Congress at Newport. She haughtily observed: 'The bulk of the delegates are the same solid stupid folk they have always been,' uninterested in any new ideas. She did note, though, that happily, after twenty years: 'The ordinary Trade Unionist has got the National Minimum theory well fixed in his slow solid head.'[116]

Plate 3 'Labour and Capital: The Miners' Federation of Great Britain, representing over 600,000 men, has announced the intention of declaring a General Strike, unless a living wage is paid to all workers in mines.'

Labour Leader, 13 October 1911

Plate 4   'THE SUGAR TRADE [Mr. MacDonald recently denied in emphatic terms the presence of any Liberal ingredient in the Labour Sugar.] "Let not your right hand know—"'

Daily Herald, 17 April 1914

With such limited human material, it was little surprise to the Webbs that the Labour Party had made so little impact in Parliament before 1914. Beatrice ascribed the causes of political impotence to the personal shortcomings of particular M.P.s and to the 'enervating' effect of 'the atmosphere of the House', compounded by 'MacDonald's astute but over-cautious and sceptical leadership – sceptical of all the reforms he is supposed to believe in'.[117] But whatever the reason, Beatrice was explicit about the result. 'The Parliamentary Labour Party, has, in fact,' she wrote in July 1913, 'not justified its existence either by character or by intelligence, and it is doubtful whether it will hold the Trade Unions.'[118]

The myopia and timidity of the party continually exasperated the Webbs in the pre-war years. After a meeting with various Labour members in December 1912, Beatrice was particularly incensed 'by their almost instinctive dislike of any kind of agitation for fear that it would "raise expectations",' which she thought to be an odd attitude 'for the Labour Party to take up when they are assumed to be in opposition to the present Government'. If socialism meant anything at all, she believed, it meant raising expectations. She held that the party's hesitations further complicated the difficulties with which socialists were faced before 1914. In fact, Beatrice feared that, without constant prodding, the Labour Party would become 'milder than the mildest of Liberals and more timid than the Liberal Whip'.[119]

After having attended the 1913 Labour Party Conference, she was even less light-hearted. She condemned the whole party for its 'lack of consistent thought and action' and its consequent 'irresponsibility'. Finally she admitted that she had even 'wondered whether this Conference was really "adult", whether the Labour and Socialist Party meant business and not talk?' The community of feeling which the party generated was admirable, she noted, but it would continue to be superficial and ineffective until it had attained 'unity in practical purpose', that is, through a socialist outlook and a socialist programme.[120] The Webbs were fully aware of the fact that the Labour Party was far from such a commitment in 1914.

What then did British socialists gain by their membership in and support of the pre-war Labour Party? There were times when Beatrice had no positive answer to this question. In early 1914 she was despondent enough to charge that socialists were 'by their adhesion to the present Parliamentary Party bolstering up a fraud

– pretending to the outside world that these respectable but reactionary Trade Union officials are the leaders of the Social Revolution'. However, she added: 'to go back on the creation of a Labour Party would be to admit failure', which the Webbs were unprepared to do.[121]

Instead, they decided before the First World War to move closer to the centre of the party, in the hope of partially filling the vacuum of political and intellectual leadership in it. The decision was made with some reluctance. Previously the Webbs had hoped that someone else in the Labour Party, the Fabian Society, or even in the Liberal Party would emerge who had both 'the conviction and the knowledge' for effective guidance of the socialist movement. But until August 1914, the call remained unanswered. As early as 1911, Beatrice had noted: 'I am afraid we are doomed to offer ourselves as officers of the larger crusade to conquer the land of Promise.'[122] That fear turned into conviction at the time of the outbreak of war in 1914.

Their commitment to the Labour Party gave a new unity to their varied activities in the pre-war period. Their re-examination of socialist ideas was one part of the Webbs' attempt to provide intellectual leadership for the Labour movement. Another part was the establishment of the *New Statesman* 'as the organ of the young intellectual Fabians', in 1913.[123] The launching of the Fabian Research Department[124] was similarly inspired to provide the material from which the 'completely worked out philosophy and very detailed programme'[125] of a socialist Labour Party would emerge. The Fabian Summer Schools provided another point of contact for socialists in search of a coherent policy before the war.

To further the socialist cause within the Labour Party, the Webbs decided as well to work more closely with the Independent Labour Party after 1912. Beatrice Webb was elected a member of the City of London branch of the ILP on 28 November 1912.[126] She attended the 1913 ILP conference in Manchester as a delegate from the Westminster branch, and unsuccessfully stood for election to the party's National Administrative Council.[127] Sidney too was certain that co-operation between the Fabian Society and the ILP was essential for the maintenance of socialist pressure in the parent body. He insisted that there was 'much promise in the ILP generally'. But the trouble was 'that they don't produce Parliamentary leaders'.[128] Beatrice was obviously there to cultivate such future spokesmen. She was also entrusted by Sidney with the task of preventing disaffiliation on account of MacDonald's conservative policies. Fragmentation would only worsen the situation.

The Webbs knew that one of the major problems for the socialist reconstruction of the Labour Party was that MacDonald was right in assuming that the mass of his party was politically backward and ill-equipped with any coherent ideas. The cultivation of socialist ideas and policies within the Labour Party itself was still a crucial task. In this sense, disaffiliation over differences in principle would be disastrous, in the Webbs' view. Sidney urged Beatrice[129]

to make the I.L.P. realize that *their* business is still mainly educational and propagandistic among the rank and file, and the Trade Union Executives and officials. You will have to stand up against a movement to *come out* of the Labour Party, as utterly unsatisfactory.

Socialist co-operation was essential in the Webbs' pre-war strategy. Beatrice furthered the cause as one of the thirteen members of a joint committee of the Labour Party, the Parliamentary Labour Party, the ILP, the Fabian Society, and the Women's Labour League. This group first met at the House of Commons on 23 April 1913 to co-ordinate national propaganda on political and industrial questions.[130]

Although the Webbs firmly opposed restriction of the work of the Fabian Society to Labour Party channels alone,[131] they were more emphatic in their rejection of two attempts by militant Fabians to dissociate from the Labour Party. On 14 March 1913 H. J. Gillespie, a guild socialist who was Honorary Secretary of the Fabian Research Department, proposed that 'the Fabian Society disaffiliate from the Labour Party forthwith'. G. D. H. Cole seconded the motion, which was supported by other young militants including William Mellor and Harold Laski. Sidney Webb and W. S. Sanders spoke for the Executive in opposition to the resolution, which was defeated by 92 to 48.[132] Undaunted, the rebels decided to try to detach the society from the Labour Party by limiting the former's work solely to research. Sidney Webb countered with an amendment describing research as only one of its primary functions. The Webb amendment was passed by a single vote, 41 to 40. The original motion, moved by G. D. H. Cole, was defeated by the same margin, 44 to 43.[133]

Such disputes among socialists hardly contributed, in the Webbs' opinion, to the strengthening of the Labour movement. Indeed,

Beatrice noted caustically: 'judged by their capacity to work together, and respect each other', socialists were somewhat 'depressing'.[134] She repeatedly reminded the militants that any chance for socialist unity 'would be imperilled by even a discussion of secession from the Labour Party'. Of course 'those who believe in direct action can devote themselves to strengthening Trade Unions'; but she insisted that 'a condition of their work must be loyalty to the Labour Party'.[135]

In fact, the failure to co-ordinate the strike and the vote, Beatrice told the City of London ILP in 1913, was one of the greatest political weaknesses of the Labour movement. While she believed that strikes alone were insufficient to generate political change, she held that they could raise important and neglected issues. At such times, the working class had to learn to use the weapon of public opinion, through the vote, to achieve its object-ives.[136] By 1914, the Webbs believed that such electoral action had to be in support of the Labour Party. Therefore on many grounds the party could hardly be ignored, they argued, in the formulation of socialist strategy.

At the same time, they believed before August 1914 that the formation of a Labour government in Britain was a very remote prospect, only possible after generations of work. Sidney certainly did not envisage a Labour Party majority in Parliament in his lifetime. He even admitted in August 1913:[137]

I am not sure it would be desirable. After all there must be a division of labour, even in government. A certain number of labour members [is] very useful. But it does not follow that the House should be predominantly composed of them.

This statement clearly shows the conservatism of the Webbs' pre-war view of the development of socialism in Britain. It was the First World War which converted their distant hopes into real possibilities.

Nevertheless, by the summer of 1914, the Webbs were firmly committed to the Labour Party. But it is important to note that they saw their political role as a temporary one, limited by the fact of advancing years. They looked forward to their retirement, but they also realized that the time for rest had not yet come. There were immediate political objectives which remained unfulfilled at the time of the outbreak of the First World War. Beatrice wrote to

George Bernard Shaw on 13 June 1914, and noted regretfully:[138]

> I am afraid that we shall have to remain in harness within the Socialist movement for some years longer. If we could safely steer the Fabians into a united Socialist Party, and have it provided with a philosophy and a programme, and a Research Department and an organ issuing out of the Research Department, we could comfortably retire into our old age.

Another task also tied the Webbs to politics. There were still the theoretical problems of socialism to work out. Beatrice suggested to Shaw a simple division of labour. In the coming years, she wrote:[139]

> Sidney and I will do our best to work out the distribution of power among persons and classes of persons. You must work out the distribution of wealth – or of the pleasures of consumption, and the effect of this on such eternal institutions as the family, religion, etc.

The outbreak of war, though, was not the end, but rather the beginning of years of new work for the Webbs in both the theory and practice of British socialism.

NOTES

1 Sharp graduated from the anti-Poor Law journal *Crusade* to its progeny *New Statesman* which he edited until 1930. Cf. E. Hyams, *The New Statesman*, 1963, ch. 2; and Kingsley Martin, *Father Figures*, 1966, ch. 10.

2 The title of an edition of William Braithwaite's diary on the passage of the Insurance Act, ed. Sir Henry Bunbury, 1957; cf. also B. Gilbert, *The Evolution of National Insurance in Great Britain*, 1966; Mrs Jose Harris, *Unemployment and Politics, A Study in English Social Policy, 1880–1914*, Oxford, 1972; and, M. E. Rose, *The Relief of Poverty 1834–1914*, 1972.

3 British Library of Political and Economic Science, Passfield Papers, General Correspondence, 2.4.f., Sharp to Beatrice Webb, 29 March 1912.

4 Passfield Papers, General Correspondence, 2.4.f., Sharp to Beatrice Webb, 24 February 1912.

5 *Ibid.*

6 *Ibid.*

7 *Ibid.*

8 See above, p. 13.

9 *Crusade*, 3, 7, July 1912, p. 116.
10 *Ibid.*
11 *Ibid.*
12 *Ibid.*
13 Beatrice and Sidney Webb, *Industrial Democracy*, 2 vols., 1897.
14 *Crusade*, 3, 7, July 1912, p. 116. For another statement of the same point, see also the report of Sidney Webb's lecture on 'The Control of Industry', in *Christian Commonwealth*, 6 November 1912: 'He returned from the East to find England in a state of unrest, and had been struck by the amount of universal unrest, in spite of the fact that the country was enjoying enormous prosperity.' Webb went on to list the causes of the unrest as: dissatisfaction with wages at times of increasing prices; the growth in the public consciousness of the unequal distribution of wealth; the realization that trade unions represented only a small number of workers; and the knowledge that workers were being used as tools in a system of industrial tyranny.
15 Passfield Papers, General Correspondence, 2.4.f., Beatrice to her sister Kate Courtney, April 1912: 'From all one hears, things have changed remarkably and I am very sorry to have been away'.
16 Passfield Papers, General Correspondence, 2.4.f., Beatrice to Sharp, 7 April 1912.
17 'A Campaign and an Inquiry', *Christian Commonwealth*, 4 September 1912.
18 *Ibid.*
19 Nuffield College, Oxford, Cole Papers, Box 7, Folder 81, Beatrice Webb, 'Memorandum on "The Committee of Inquiry on the Control of Industry" ', p. 1. The Fabian Research Department undertook this inquiry as its first major project. In fact it owed its existence to the 'labour unrest'. Three sub-committees undertook the research and made interim reports, but the Webbs wrote the resulting articles which appeared as special supplements to the *New Statesman*, on three separate occasions: 'Special supplement on co-operative production and profit-sharing', 14 February 1914; 'Special supplement on the co-operative movement', 30 May 1914; 'Special supplement on state and municipal enterprises', 8 May 1915. The third report was written after the outbreak of war, but it embodies the Webbs' pre-war position. On the 'FRD', as it was known, cf. R. P. Arnot, *History of the Labour Research Department*, 1926; Margaret Cole, *Beatrice Webb*, 1945, pp. 118–22; and her contribution to the second volume of essays in honour of G. D. H. Cole, A. Briggs and J. Saville (eds), *Essays in Labour History 1886–1923*, 1971.
20 Beatrice Webb, 'Memorandum', p. 1. This document will be cited as 'Memorandum' throughout.
21 *Ibid.*
22 Sidney and Beatrice Webb, 'National housekeeping', *New Statesman*, 31 May 1913.
23 *Ibid.*
24 H. H. Gerth and C. W. Mills (eds), *From Max Weber: Essays in Sociology*, 1948, p. 78.

25 'Special supplement on state and municipal enterprises', *New Statesman*, 8 May 1915.
26 *Ibid.*
27 'The expansion of local government', *New Statesman*, 24 May 1913. Beatrice Webb's early affection for the Co-operative movement is unmistakable throughout.
28 Beatrice and Sidney Webb, *Industrial Democracy*, 2nd ed., 1902, pp. vi, 849, 850.
29 'The expansion of local government', *New Statesman*, 24 May 1913. My italics.
30 *Ibid.*
31 *Ibid.*, p. 204.
32 'National housekeeping', *New Statesman*, 31 May 1913.
33 *Ibid.*
34 'Special supplement on state and municipal enterprises', *New Statesman*, 8 May 1915.
35 Beatrice Webb, 'Memorandum', p. 5.
36 'The expansion of local government', *New Statesman*, 24 May 1913.
37 'Special supplement on state and municipal enterprises', *New Statesman*, 8 May 1915.
38 'National housekeeping', *New Statesman*, 31 May 1913; and 'The great alternative (2) the optimist view', *New Statesman*, 6 September 1913.
39 'National housekeeping', *New Statesman*, 31 May 1913.
40 'Special supplement on state and municipal enterprises', *New Statesman*, 8 May 1915, ch. 3; and 'The expansion of local government', *New Statesman*, 24 May 1913.
41 'Special supplement on state and municipal enterprises', *New Statesman*, 8 May 1915, p. 30.
42 *Ibid.*, pp. 15, 30, and 'Special supplement on co-operative production and profit-sharing', *New Statesman*, 30 May 1914.
43 'Special supplement on state and municipal enterprises', *New Statesman*, 8 May 1915, ch. 4.
44 'Special supplement on co-operative production and profit-sharing', *New Statesman*, 14 February 1914, *passim*.
45 *Ibid.*
46 Beatrice Webb, 'Memorandum', p. 5. Syndicalists were, in their view: 'Such professional associations of manual wage-earners or of salaried brain-workers as have for their declared purpose the expropriation of the capitalist employer and the forcible taking over of the instruments of production by the persons now working as employers'. The Webbs took as the syndicalists' strategy these three points: continuous class war with capitalism; use of the irritation strike, which would disrupt trade and also lower the quality of work; and the eventual use of the general strike for the seizure of political power. Cf. 'What syndicalism means', *Crusade*, 3, 8, August 1912, pp. 140-1.
47 'What syndicalism means', *Crusade*, 3, 8, August 1912, pp. 145-8.
48 Beatrice Webb, 'Memorandum', p. 3.
49 Nuffield College, Oxford, Fabian Society Papers, Sidney Webb

Letters, Webb to E. R. Pease from Niigata, Japan, 7 September 1911.
50 'What syndicalism means', *Crusade*, 3, 8, August 1912, p. 144.
51 *Ibid.*, p. 151.
52 *Ibid.*, p. 144.
53 *Ibid.*, p. 145.
54 *Ibid.*
55 *Ibid.*, p. 150.
56 *Ibid.*, p. 149.
57 *Ibid.*, pp. 148–9.
58 *Ibid.*, p. 145.
59 *Ibid.*, p. 150.
60 'The great alternative (1) the answer of pessimism', *New Statesman*, 30 August 1913.
61 *Ibid.* Their italics.
62 *Ibid.*
63 'The great alternative (2) the optimist view', *New Statesman*, 6 September 1913.
64 'The great alternative (1) the answer of pessimism', *New Statesman*, 30 August 1913.
65 Cf. the discussion of the Fabian justification of Empire in A. M. McBriar, *Fabian Socialism and English Politics 1884–1918*, Cambridge, 1962, pp. 124–30.
66 For other reactions to the non-European world, cf. V. G. Kiernan, *The Lords of Human Kind*, 1969; C. Bolt, *Victorian Attitudes to Race*, 1971; and M. I. Biddiss, 'Racial ideas and the politics of prejudice', *Historical Journal*, 15, 3, September 1972, pp. 570–82.
67 Cf. Sidney's own comments in Fabian Tract 131, *The Decline in the Birth-Rate*, 1907; for a discussion of its causes, cf. H. J. Habakkuk, *Population Growth and Economic Development since 1750*, Leicester, 1971, ch. 3.
68 The same complaint is made by the editor of the diary they kept during their visit to Australia in 1898. He claims that since they were 'bereft of any real historical understanding of the institutions and events they were "investigating" they were deprived of the very method of approach on which they had always relied'. A. G. Austin (ed.), *The Webbs' Australian Diary 1898*, Melbourne, 1965, p. 16. His criticism is a valid one, but is much more applicable to their reactions to China.
69 Sidney and Beatrice Webb, 'China in revolution', *Crusade*, 3, 3, March 1912, p. 43.
70 Passfield Papers, Beatrice Webb's unpublished diaries, vol. 30, 6 November 1911.
71 Passfield Papers, Personal Correspondence, 2.4.e., Beatrice to Kate Courtney, 4 November 1911.
72 *Ibid.*
73 Passfield Papers, 2.4.e., Beatrice to Mrs Kirkwood, 20–3 November 1911.
74 Passfield Papers, 2.4.e., Beatrice to Clifford Sharp, 8 November 1911.

75 Sidney and Beatrice Webb, 'China in Revolution', *Crusade*, 3, 3, March 1912, p. 54.
76 *Ibid.*
77 Passfield Papers, Beatrice Webb's Unpublished diaries, vols 29 and 30 *passim;* 2.4.e., especially on the Koreans as a 'horrid race'; Beatrice to Clifford Sharp, 18 October 1911 and Beatrice to Kate Courtney, 18 October 1911.
78 G. R. Searle, *The Quest for National Efficiency*, Oxford, 1971, pp. 57–60. Cf. also Col. Repington's despatches for *The Times*, and his collected writings on the Russo-Japanese War, *The War in the Far East*, 1905.
79 B. Webb, *Our Partnership*, 1948, p. 299, entry for 22 December 1904.
80 *Ibid.*
81 *Ibid.*
82 Passfield Papers, 2.4.c., Beatrice to Mary Playne, 2 September 1905.
83 B. Webb, *Our Partnership*, p. 299.
84 Passfield Papers, 2.4.c., Beatrice to Mary Playne, 2 September 1905.
85 B. Webb, *Our Partnership*, p. 300.
86 Passfield Papers, Beatrice Webb's unpublished diaries, vol. 30, 16–25 April 1912.
87 At a dinner in Tokyo, Beatrice met the Foreign Secretary, Uchida Yasuya, whose wit and sophistication charmed her completely. As the highest of praise, she described him as 'a Japanese Arthur Balfour . . . equally at home in Metaphysics and Art and Political Science – talked perfect English and was completely detached from any prejudice'. Passfield Papers, 2.4.e., Beatrice to Clifford Sharp, 12 October 1911.
88 Sidney and Beatrice Webb, 'The social crisis in Japan', *Crusade*, 3, 1, January 1912, p. 3.
89 *Ibid.*, p. 19.
90 Passfield Papers, 2.4.e., Beatrice to Mary Playne, 28 October 1911. Beatrice here was describing the Japanese administration of Korea, which had been annexed the previous year.
91 Cf. Sidney and Beatrice Webb, *Soviet Communism: A New Civilization*, 3rd ed., 1944, p. 909.
92 Dr Ben-Ami Shiloni of the Hebrew University kindly drew my attention to this point. That the Webbs were totally ignorant of the incident is unlikely, since the Labour Party Annual Conference in 1911 passed a resolution protesting against the executions. Cf. A. M. McBriar, *Fabian Socialism and English Politics 1884–1918*, p. 337n.
93 Beatrice and Sidney Webb, 'The guardianship of the non-adult races', *New Statesman*, 2 August 1913, p. 525. Their italics.
94 *Ibid.*
95 *Ibid.*
96 *Ibid.*, p. 526.
97 *Ibid.*
98 Sidney Webb, *The Decline in the Birth-Rate*, Fabian Tract no. 131, 1907, pp. 16–17, 19. Here we can see many of the same phrases about 'degeneration of type', or the 'country gradually

C*

falling to the Irish and the Jews', or 'The ultimate future of these islands may be to the Chinese!' which Beatrice used in her later articles.

99 Beatrice Webb, 'Personal rights and the women's movement: II The falling birth-rate', *New Statesman*, 11 July 1914, p. 429.

100 *Ibid.*

101 *Ibid.*

102 Beatrice and Sidney Webb, 'The great alternative (1) the answer of pessimism', *New Statesman*, 30 August 1913, p. 654

103 *Ibid.*

104 *Ibid.*

105 R. Reinders, 'Racialism on the Rhine', *International Review of Social History*, 13, 1, 1968, pp. 1–28.

106 Mrs Margaret Cole recalled in an interview both the Webbs' racialism and how unexceptional it was in the Labour movement sixty years ago.

107 Herbert Marcuse, 'Liberation from the affluent society', in D. Cooper (ed.), *The Dialectics of Liberation*, 1968, p. 186.

108 Beatrice Webb, p. ii of the introduction to 'The awakening of woman', a special supplement to *New Statesman*, 1 November 1913. The similarity to Dangerfield's treatment (without Freud) of the women's revolt, the 'labour unrest', and Irish affairs is unmistakable. Beatrice even added: 'To future historical philosophers we may leave the analysis of how far these three simultaneous movements all over the world are parts one of another', p. iii.

109 *Ibid.*, p. iv.

110 Beatrice Webb, 'Voteless woman and the social revolution', *New Statesman*, 14 February 1914.

111 *Ibid.*

112 *Ibid.*, p. 586.

113 *Ibid.*

114 Fabian Society Papers, Webb Correspondence, Webb to W. S. Sanders, 17 May 1911.

115 Passfield Papers, Webb Correspondence, 2.3.i., Sidney to Beatrice, 30 November 1912.

116 M. I. Cole (ed.), *Beatrice Webb's Diaries 1912–1924*, 1952, p. 5, 5 September 1912. Mrs Cole's edition is rather arbitrary at times. Omissions are not always noted. When they do occur, they usually serve to soften Beatrice's often trenchant criticism of her fellow socialists, including G. D. H. Cole. I shall refer to the published diaries only when they correspond to the typescript in the Passfield Papers.

117 *Ibid.*, 'Xmas' 1912, p. 10.

118 *Ibid.*, 5 July 1913, p. 13.

119 Fabian Society Papers, Beatrice Webb Letters, Beatrice to E. R. Pease, 17 December 1912.

120 Beatrice Webb, 'Some impressions of the Labour Party Conference', *Fabian News*, 24, 4, March 1913, p. 29.

121 M. I. Cole (ed.), *Beatrice Webb's Diaries 1912–1924*, p. 19, 12 February 1914.

122 Passfield Papers, Beatrice Webbs' unpublished diaries, vol. 28, 12 March 1911.

123 British Museum, Shaw Papers, Add. MSS. 50553, Beatrice Webb to George Bernard Shaw, 13 June 1914. Cf. also entry in published diaries for 11 October 1912, p. 6, and Hyams, *The New Statesman*, chs 1–3.

124 Further information on the Fabian Research Department may be found in the Fabian Society Executive minutes for 27 June 1913, which lists all sixty-six members of the department and discusses its work; in Fabian Society Papers.

125 Cf. also Passfield Papers, Beatrice Webb's unpublished diaries, vol. 29, 7 March 1911.

126 British Library of Political and Economic Science, City of London ILP Papers. City of London ILP Executive Minutes, entry for 28 November 1912.

127 *ILP Annual Report 1913*, p. 76. She came in sixth out of six candidates, behind W. C. Anderson, J. B. Glasier, F. W. Jowett, Miss Margaret Bondfield, Dr Marion Phillips. She stood again for the fourth N.A.C. seat, but again came in third to Miss Bondfield and Dr Phillips.

128 Passfield Papers, Webb Correspondence, 2.3.c., Sidney to Beatrice, 9 December 1913.

129 Passfield Papers, Webb Correspondence, 2.3.c., Sidney to Beatrice, 30 January 1914. His italics.

130 The other members were W. C. Anderson, chairman, C. M. Lloyd, and Francis Johnson of the ILP; Arthur Henderson, A. Cameron and J. S. Middleton, for the Labour Party; George Roberts for the Parliamentary Labour Party; Dr Bentham, Dr Phillips, and Mrs Salter for the Women's Labour League; and W. S. Sanders and H. H. Schloesser for the Fabian Society. Fabian Society Executive Minutes for 23 April 1913. Beatrice Webb also attended a Socialist Unity Conference on behalf of the British Section of the Socialist International on 13 December 1913.

131 H. H. Schloesser and Clifford Allen had circulated a 'Manifesto on Fabian Policy' on 28 November 1911 and had formed a Fabian Reform Committee, with the express viewpoint that 'if Fabians do take part in politics, they should only do so as supporters of the Labour Party'. A copy of the Manifesto is in the Shaw Papers, Add. MSS. 50681. On 13 July 1912, the Fabian Society rejected the Reform Committee's proposals by a vote of 122 to 27. Cf. Fabian Society Executive Minutes for that date. The Webbs were opposed to official orthodoxy of all kinds. Hence they objected to the Labour Party's ostracism of George Lansbury when he insisted on standing at Bow and Bromley as a Labour and Socialist candidate. For the Webbs' attitude cf. Beatrice's 'Some impressions of the Labour Party Conference', *Fabian News*, 24, 4, March 1913, p. 28.

132 Fabian Society Papers, Fabian Society Executive Minutes, 14 March 1913; and *Fabian News*, 24, 5, April 1913, p. 35.

133 Fabian Society Executive Minutes, 20 March 1914.

134 Beatrice Webb, 'The minimum wage and how to get it', *Fabian News*, 24, 2, January 1913, p. 11. Report of 20 December 1912 lecture.
135 *Ibid.*
136 Beatrice Webb, 'Weapons of Socialism', *Christian Commonwealth*, 26 February 1913. A copy was inserted in the City of London ILP Executive Minutes.
137 Comment cited in R. H. Tawney's Commonplace Book, entry for 31 July–1 August 1913. In papers in the possession of Mr Michael Vyvyan of Trinity College, Cambridge.
138 Shaw Papers, Add. MSS. 50553, Beatrice to Shaw, 13 June 1914.
139 *Ibid.*

3

R. H. Tawney's Early Political Thought

R. H. Tawney's early political thought was a profound critique of the Webbs' ideas and of the Fabian tradition in British socialist thought. Conflict in society was, in Tawney's view, a reflection of collective moral disorder, rather than primarily a function of class or political antagonism. Social unrest was traceable to the absence of a guiding moral standard by reference to which a nation should order its affairs to approach, if not to achieve, social peace. Tawney's social theory was derived from his examination of the problems of capitalist society in the light of Christian ethics. His analysis of capitalism probed beneath the surface of social institutions to the ideas and assumptions which gave them form and which underlay their development.

His work and thought illustrate his belief that socialism was a stage in human development towards greater maturity and morality in social affairs. Not only was a coherent set of political ideas essential to socialism, but just as important was the education of the men who would live and act by them. Political organizations alone, without an intellectual base in the popular ideas which inform political behaviour, could not effect significant social change.

The Webbs could take exception to none of these points, but Tawney still believed that their institutional socialism was an inadequate and insufficient challenge to the assumptions which underlay capitalism. He felt that they did not understand the causes of social conflict and thereby mistakenly prescribed administrative remedies for moral disorders. They dealt with committees and parties rather than with the individual men and women who must make socialism a reality. By concentrating their attention on the state and its institutional powers, they neglected the fact that the key to social change lay in ideas and not in organizations. In the years prior to the First World War, Tawney therefore began to develop a socialist philosophy which would explore more fully the underlying causes of discontent. The primary point of departure for his pre-war thought was, as in the case of the Webbs, the 'labour unrest'.

INTRODUCTION

Tawney was thirty years old at the time of the 1911 strikes. He lived in Manchester and Oxford where he worked as a tutor in economic and social history for the Workers' Educational Association, which he helped to build as 'an experiment in democratic education'.[1] The WEA, as it was and is known, was founded in 1903 as a challenge to the class bias in British education, of which Tawney had had personal experience while at Rugby and Balliol. He was determined in his early work to help to extend to the working class the educational privileges which he had obtained as the son of a member of the Indian civil service.

One must look to Tawney's undergraduate years to find some of the sources of his moral commitments. Oxford at the turn of the century was alive with the ideas of those who saw, as Tawney came to see, a natural link between socialism and Christianity. Prominent among them was the senior tutor of St John's College, Sidney Ball, who was in those years, according to G. D. H. Cole, 'the recognized head of University Socialism'.[2] In an article published during Tawney's first term at Balliol in 1899, Ball outlined a position strikingly similar to the one Tawney adopted in the years prior to the outbreak of war in 1914. 'No Socialism can stand,' Ball argued, 'whether in theory or practice, that will not bear the test of moral criticisms.' It was the duty of socialists, therefore, to make their economic ideas 'direct deduction[s] from [an] ethical and social ideal' or, in other words, to work to make democracy '*real* by embodying it in the industrial relationships between man and man'. Their aim was, then, to see that the state's actions should be determined in future, 'not by class interests, but by moral ideas – that it [the state] should be distinctly and consciously ethical'.[3] These statements are in the best traditions of Christian socialism, and find many reflections in Tawney's later writing.[4]

Tawney's socialist ideas were not fully crystallized until after he had completed his undergraduate degree and had tried his hand at a number of jobs which brought him into direct contact with working men and their problems. His first exposure to educational work was at the University Settlement House at Toynbee Hall in Whitechapel, where he lived prior to and in the three years after his leaving Oxford with a B.A. in *Literae Humaniores* (Greats) in 1903. William (later Lord) Beveridge, who was a contemporary of Tawney at Balliol, commented in later years on the influence of the Master of Balliol in directing the attention of many socially-conscious students to social work in London. Tawney and Beveridge were both[5]

anxious to join, by way of carrying out Edward Caird's desire expressed to us at Balliol, that when we had done with Oxford studies, some of us should go to Poplar to discover why with so much wealth, there was also so much poverty in London. This advice was the decisive factor in taking both of us to Toynbee Hall, under Canon Barnett.

Canon S. A. Barnett was Warden of Toynbee Hall from its foundation in memory of Arnold Toynbee in 1884 until 1906. His thoughts on the moral basis of social problems undoubtedly helped Tawney and many others to form their early political opinions. Tawney often sought Canon Barnett's advice and highly valued his friendship, which extended until the latter's death in 1914.[6]

Canon Barnett's influence was important in Tawney's choice of profession. Having failed to get a first-class honours degree, he was thankful thereby to have escaped a career in the Civil Service. He contemplated joining the Charity Organization Society (COS) in August 1903[7] but was uncertain where his real vocation lay. An extended visit to Germany in late 1903 helped him to clarify his thoughts about his future, and he finally rejected Charles Loch's offer of a post with the COS, whose methods he dismissed as too 'inquisitorial'.[8] Instead, he became secretary to the Children's Country Holiday Fund, one of Canon Barnett's benevolent organizations, through which he got to know his future wife Jeanette, the sister of William Beveridge.

After a year in London, Tawney was most impressed by the decline in working-class religious observance in the East End. He remarked that 'one of the great social forces of history is gradually and reluctantly drifting out of the lives of no inconsiderable part of society'. The cause of this phenomenon was to be found, in his view, in the city's 'permanent ethical atmosphere, which develops . . . poverty, crime, and overcrowding . . . and which they in their turn tend to develop'.[9] The moralist's outlook is already apparent in this early social analysis.

Charity work, however, was never a real substitute for his interest in education. Tawney admitted to Beveridge in 1906 that 'teaching economics in an industrial town is just what I want ultimately to do',[10] but he was hesitant about taking a formal university post. He eventually overcame doubts about the adequacy of his preparation, and accepted a position as assistant in economics at Glasgow University, under Professor William Smart, who was then preoccupied as a member (with Beatrice Webb among others) of the Royal Commission on the Poor Laws and the Relief of Distress. Smart signed the Commission's Majority Report in 1909. Tawney had no prior training in economics, but with the recommendation of Edward Caird, he began to teach the subject which formed his life-work. As in Arnold Toynbee's case, a second-class degree was not a bar to an academic career. At the University, he shared teaching assignments with Tom Jones, later Assistant Secretary of the Cabinet under Lloyd George and Baldwin.[11] Tawney also wrote radical leaders for the Glasgow *Herald*, that is, until the public response forced the paper, in Tawney's words, to hold up 'its hands in horror at my depravity', and to restrict his contributions to signed articles.[12]

But Tawney's commitment to education found a more permanent embodiment in the newly-formed WEA. He became a member of its executive committee in 1905, and two years later accepted the tutorship of two experimental adult classes at Rochdale and Longton, both sponsored by Oxford University and funded in part by All Souls College.[13] Both met for the first time in late January 1908.[14] After his marriage in 1909, Tawney settled in Manchester, where he was able to teach and to pursue his own historical work under the powerful influence of Professor George Unwin.[15] In 1910–11, Tawney taught courses in social and economic problems, economic and constitutional history and economic theories at Littleborough, Longton, Wrexham and Rochdale. By 1914 he added courses at Stoke on the French Revolution, at Toynbee Hall on modern European history and at Longton on the secession of the American colonies.[16] Like that of so many other teachers, Tawney's self-education accompanied his teaching responsibilities. His students were of various trades. For instance, his class at Stoke in 1912 included six miners, two potters, three ironworkers, six clerks, one librarian, three teachers, two printers, and a warehouseman. As one might have expected, his Longton tutorial class had a higher number of potters, eleven out of thirty-three in 1913. Nine of the same group attended tutorial classes since they had begun five years earlier.[17]

The close personal relationships in these extra-mural classes profoundly affected Tawney. His pre-war view of the working man's limitations and potential for improvement was largely a product of his tutorial experience with what was undoubtedly an unrepresentative sample of the working class. But more importantly, his WEA classes came to represent a microcosm of the type of community of belief and common work which he envisaged in his socialist writings. These classes were voluntary groupings of men and women who came together out of their belief in a moral principle – the pursuit of knowledge, which was in Tawney's view, one of the gifts of God. Not all his students need have been Christians or socialists, but in adult education they joined a society of equals in the widest sense of the term. In the Commonplace Book which he kept at Manchester from 1912–14, Tawney stated this idea in simple terms. His work in the WEA was an expression of his belief that men should 'think of knowledge, like religion, as transcending all differences of class, and wealth'; since 'in the eye of learning, as in the eye of God, all men are equal, because all are infinitely small'.[18]

It was clear to Tawney that a class-ridden system of education, catering for the more fortunate citizens, was a reflection of, as well as an important cause of, that society's social problems. In other words, English education was corrupt to the extent that it was bound by the values of society, which is to say, the values of capitalist materialism. 'To sell education for money is the next thing to selling the gifts of God for money', and just as intolerable, in Tawney's view.[19]

But education was really a long-term solution to problems which required more immediate action. Here Tawney came to support several specific suggestions. He was interested in Beveridge's work on labour exchanges for the Board of Trade, and suggested that they travel together to Germany to compare the labour policy of the two countries. Still, he was not completely convinced that labour exchange schemes went to the heart of the problem, since the pattern of working-class life, with few hopes and fewer chances, had already been firmly set by the time a man joined the adult labour force. 'Personally,' he wrote to Beveridge,[20] 'when I survey the class of man who applies here,' that is, to the Glasgow labour exchanges,

> and his appalling multitudes, I am rather hopeless about doing anything with them now that they have grown up, unless the law compels employers to use the exchanges. I think it would be swamped otherwise by a crowd of men ready to work at any price or under any system.

Not all working men, Tawney knew, had the motivation or the ability to profit from such assistance. Other steps were necessary to guard the labouring population, especially during 'the years of adolescence against the dangers of modern industry'.[21]

Tawney's work in London and, more particularly, his visits to Germany in 1908–10, convinced him that much could be done to prevent distress by treating one of its major causes – the misuse of boy and girl labour. In 1911, he recalled a discussion he had had with the manager of a German labour exchange. Tawney had asked the man what he did about the casual labourers who applied to his office for work. 'We don't let boys become casual labourers' was the sense of the reply, which summed up the approach Tawney hoped England would adopt.[22]

After one of his first-hand explorations of German social policy, Tawney gave evidence to the Poor Law Commission in which he advanced his interpretation of the relationship between adolescent labour and chronic unemployment. In his three years at White-chapel and his six months at Glasgow, he had observed boy labour 'in occupations within which there will be no demand for them as men, from which they obtain no industrial qualifications likely to fit them to other occupations; and out of which they are thrust at manhood into the unskilled labour market'. Here was the source, Tawney argued, of the reserve army of casual labourers: the over-supply of unskilled men. Here too was the point at which action had to be taken. The remedies he suggested at this time were, first, to raise the school-leaving age to fifteen and then to require by law employees' attendance at a trade school during part of the work-week as a condition of their employment.[23] These acts, in Tawney's view, would help to end the use of adolescents 'simply as instruments of production which are scrapped when they are no longer remunerative' and would go a long way to improving the position of 'probably the most neglected class in the community'.[24]

Tawney's testimony before the Poor Law Commission in 1908 is marked by the admiration he felt for the German approach to problems of poverty.[25] He even went out of his way to praise[26]

> the German view of unemployment as an industrial disease, not primarily an affair of individual character [which] prevents the community from leaving the workless individual to himself, in the expectation that as soon as he starts to look for work he will find it, and leads it to insist that he shall, at all events, be saved from deteriorating through involuntary want of work.

When Tawney had visited Strasbourg, he saw no workhouse since none existed. Out-of-work benefits were paid to trade unions which distributed the money themselves. There was no test of the character of the unemployed, but rather 'a test of the flexibility of the labour market'. All these features of the German system of *Arbeitsamt* or labour exchanges convinced him that England could learn much from their advanced methods of social administration.[27] In the articles he contributed to the *Morning Post* six months later, he tried to bolster his case for policy changes along German lines by the claim that they had 'at least the merit of being actually practised by a great European nation'.[28] And in his continuing advocacy of mandatory trade school attendance, he returned to the Continental precedent. 'If this can be done in Germany,' he asked rhetorically, 'why can't it be done in England?'[29]

In a sense, Tawney knew very well why this plan and other progressive policies could not be adopted in pre-war England. Programmes are built on ideas, he held, and it is the latter which have to change before law can give form to a new consensus about the proper treatment of the poor.[30] Hence he returned to his work in education in an attempt to help cultivate the ground in which new ideas could take root.

After just a few years' teaching, Tawney could claim some success in his work, both in the response from his students and in his own intellectual development. In April 1912 he published his first major historical work, *The Agrarian Problem in the Sixteenth Century*. He dedicated the book to his friend and contemporary at Rugby and Balliol, William Temple (later Archbishop of Canterbury) and to Alfred Mansbridge, respectively President and Secretary of the WEA. In his preface, he thanked the members of his tutorial classes for their assistance. He admitted that 'the friendly smitings of weavers, potters, miners, and engineers, have taught me much about problems of political and economic science which cannot easily be learned from books'.[31] In terms of his thought on contemporary society, his sense of personal debt was even more pronounced. 'My views,' he wrote in 1912 or 1913, 'such as they are, have been formed by intercourse with working people.'[32]

THE LABOUR UNREST

Tawney's contact with and involvement in working men's lives rather than the political manoevrings of their leaders, his rejection of mechanical solutions to problems which involve the deepest of human values, and his underlying religious faith, led him to a distinctive interpretation of contemporary events. Nevertheless, Tawney shared the view of the Webbs and other socialists that the pre-war 'labour unrest' was a crucial step in the development of the British working-class movement. 'The period of acute industrial conflict from 1910 to 1914,' he wrote in later years, 'was marked by the emergence of issues which, if not novel in principle, had not previously been formulated with equal sharpness.'[33] On immediate reflection at the time of the strikes, he was still more emphatic. Indeed, he saw the discontent as but the outward manifestation of an inner revolution in British politics. He shared with the Webbs the sense of a profound change in political ideas, in 'the conception which men take of themselves and their place in society'.[34] Here as always, Tawney's eyes were firmly fixed on the world of ideas, in which he saw, much more than the Webbs, the causes and remedies of social conflict. Tawney wrote in 1914 that[35]

> the minds of an ever-growing number of men and women are passing through one of those mysterious bursts of activity which make some years as decisive as generations, and of which measurable changes in the world of fact are the consequence rather than the cause.

The political implications which followed were far less clear to Tawney than to Sidney Webb. The impact of the pre-war discontent on trade union or party politics was not its most interesting aspect. Tawney was convinced, characteristically, that the 'labour unrest' presented, rather, striking evidence of the growth of a

widespread 'determination that there shall be a radical reconstruction of human relationships',[36] a renewal of[37]

> the human associations, loyalties, affections, pious bonds
> between man and man which express a man's personality and
> become at once a sheltering nest for his spirit and a kind of
> watch-tower from which he may see visions of a more spacious
> and bountiful land.

Not class relationships, not political relationships, but rather
human relationships – the encounter of moral beings in a world
which ought to be based not upon domination, but upon the
principles of service and human dignity – are at the heart of
Tawney's pre-war vision of socialism. Ideas were real things to
Tawney, powerful factors the neglect of which distorts any true
idea of historical change and conflict.

He saw the 'labour unrest' with the eyes of an idealist. He was
convinced that the 'dominant motif' of the 'first two turbulent
decades of the twentieth century' were to be found[38]

> less in the world of political and economic effort than in the
> revival among the large masses of men of an Idea . . . of the
> sacredness of human personality . . . which is a kind of lamp
> by which a host of squalid oppressions are being examined.

These oppressions had existed for generations. What had changed
in the pre-war years was not the material world, but rather the way
men approached political issues. The consciousness of injustice
was growing apace.

Before the First World War, the public conscience was beginning to awaken, in Tawney's view, to the contradiction between
the dominant pattern of social and economic organization and
'what men feel to be morally right'.[39] Here was the underlying
cause of the 'labour unrest'. Men had come to 'believe that these
external arrangements are not (like a bad harvest) the action of
natural causes, but due to human action and capable of being
altered'.[40] Discontent grew as men continued to awaken to the
wide gap between social practice and their sense of justice and
became more and more determined to act on the basis of their
beliefs.

The strikes were concerned only superficially with wages and
hours. Principles were at stake. The discontent was an inevitable
outcome of the growing 'consciousness of a moral wrong, an out-

rage on what is sacred in man',[41] and this crime – wage slavery – seemed to be intimately related to the very organization of capitalist society. What had happened in the pre-war years was that Englishmen were beginning to extend their 'conception of slavery from legal rightlessness to practical helplessness, from property in human beings to property in the labour of human beings, and to feel the same moral abhorrence at the latter as we do of the former'.[42] A mere increment in wages would not meet this fundamental point. Men had come to see that where one man is oppressed, the freedom of all is diminished. 'This is why thousands of men strike in order that justice may be done to a few, when they have everything to lose, and nothing to gain by striking.'[43]

Tawney believed that the workers were no longer prepared to accept a social system which reduced them to 'cogs in a devouring machine which grinds material wealth out of immortal spirits'.[44] It took years for this 'corroding discovery' to move the industrial population. The realization of the dimensions of the problem of 'economic privilege and economic serfdom' had not come easily. No man likes to admit that he is a slave. But that conclusion had been reached, with 'silent despair in some', and with 'what bitterness of heart and angry determination in others, let him who has not seen imagine'. Tawney urged no man to underestimate 'the mine' which had been dug 'beneath economic arrangements' by this popular awakening which was reflected in the 'labour unrest'. For 'it is in relation to economic affairs that the objective order of society is most violently in contradiction to man's conception of right.'[45]

Tawney's views rested on his belief in the progressive character of social thought. He held that the 'spiritual level of society' is not fixed and immutable. It changed as 'the view which [society] takes of man and his claim to the universe'[46] changed. Discontent reflects such movements of thought. Thus slavery was abolished when men came to see that legal bondage violated any belief in the intrinsic value of human life. As in the case of chattel slavery, it had taken years for the abolition of wage slavery to acquire a popular base. What had finally broken down was the society's willingness to tolerate the existence of widespread exploitation.

Hence it was with excitement and hope that Tawney greeted the pre-war militancy. He further believed that the working-class rebels had distinguished ancestors, whose struggles served as the focal point of Tawney's scholarly interest. In *The Agrarian*

Problem in the Sixteenth Century, published in 1912, he similarly applauded the rebellious spirit of the protests against enclosures. There he found 'the last great literary expression of the appeal to the average conscience . . ., the cry of a spirit which is departing, and which, in its agony, utters words that are a shining light for all periods of change,'[47] especially the contemporary period, of course. There too he noted that 'Discontent travelled across the enclosing counties as it does today in a Welsh mining valley, outcoursing oppression itself', and ending with a characteristically Biblical touch, 'like Elijah running before Ahab into Jezreel'.[48]

Three centuries later, the moral issues retained the same force and urgency. The spread of political education accounted for the fact in Tawney's opinion, that men were becoming more responsive to arguments about the causes of social conflict. The rhetoric of radical politics, socialist and non-socialist alike, stressed the interconnection of issues and the need for action. He believed that the furor over the reform of the House of Lords would lead to consequences quite unforeseen by the Liberal ministers. They were unwittingly contributing to an atmosphere of political debate in which their own assumptions would be examined and ultimately found wanting. Political enlightenment was not a process which one could suspend like an ordinance, at will. It often embarrassed the forces which set it in motion in the first place. Hence Tawney's appraisal of the course which political affairs appeared to be taking was optimistic. On 29 April 1912 he wrote:[49]

This has been a wonderful year. I think the cause of the unrest is mainly that the street corner preaching is at length beginning to have effect. And the Tories are right in saying that Lloyd George's speeches have contributed to it. A man who doesn't pay attention to a socialist orator is caught by the Chancellor of the Exchequer.

But at the same time, Tawney held that the strikes were a rejection of mechanical remedies to labour problems. The 'labour unrest' completely overshadowed the passage of the National Insurance Act of 1911, and the continued militancy in 1912 stamped Lloyd George's reforms as irrelevant to the real demands of Labour. He believed that the working class opposed an increase in state intervention in the form of inspectors whose sole purpose seemed to be to interfere in other people's lives.[50] The Minimum Wage Act of 1912 for the miners was too little and too late. By then Labour thought had turned from questions of poverty and state regulation to the control of industry. On 22 October 1913, in his inaugural address as director of the Ratan Tata Foundation, endowed by an Indian steel and electricity magnate for an 'inquiry into the problem of destitution',[51] Tawney commented:[52] 'The most conspicuous result of the general restatement of problems which has taken place within recent years has been the diversion to questions of social organization of much of the attention which, a generation ago, was spent on relief.' Indeed, between the time of the Poor Law Commissions' Reports of 1834 and 1909, the central concern of those interested in the condition of the people had shifted steadily from pauperism to poverty, then to the distribution of wealth, and finally, to the control of industry. The Poor Law Report of 1909 explicitly demonstrated the need of a new attitude to poverty, but, in Tawney's view, neither the Majority nor the Minority Report formulated the basis for this new approach.[53] So much for the Webbs' Crusade against Destitution. As analysis, it was useful; as synthesis, it failed to break any new ground.

The title of his Ratan Tata lecture, 'Poverty as an Industrial Problem', reflected his belief that the causes of distress were implicit in the private ownership of the means of production and the oligarchic control of industry. Reform of the Poor Law, insurance schemes, or training programmes would do very little to change the wider and defining problem. Despite their protests to the contrary, Tawney believed that Mrs Webb and the other Minority Commissioners still dealt with symptoms rather than causes just as much as the Liberals whom they attacked.

The causes of widespread suffering and oppression were rooted, Tawney argued, in the development of British industrial society. He hoped to show in his future work with the Ratan Tata Foundation that the penalties which the working class paid for the capitalist organization of society were not inevitable. He intended to refute the view, in his words, that[54]

> economic classes and institutions had stepped out of a kind of political Noah's Ark, sharply defined, highly coloured, with an unalterable destiny graven upon each wooden feature, and once the English upper classes had, like Shem, Ham and Japhet, divided the world between them, their inferiors were to accept the misfortunes of subordination as the dispensation of Providence itself.

Without the aura of historical determinism, capitalism would be shown to be as transitory an arrangement of social affairs as any other. Thereby one of the major obstacles to social change would be overcome. Thus the scholar and the striker both applied themselves to the solution of the same problems. But the practical application of the results of his research were not the direct concern of the economic historian, in Tawney's view. He did hope that 'by changing the pre-suppositions by which such conclusions are tried', such work would cause 'a silent evacuation of many fortresses which long resisted a direct attack'.[55] In the next two years he conducted detailed investigations into the operation of the Trade Boards Act of 1909 in the chain-making industry and in the tailoring trade.[56] In both cases he systematically refuted the objections brought up against the establishment of legally-enforceable minimum rates, and concluded from the testimony of employers themselves that invariably 'legislative interference with an industry' had led employers 'to introduce improvements in organisation and equipment which would not otherwise have been made'.[57] His detailed study of 'the social and economic effects produced by the intervention of a public body' in the problems of industry was the best challenge to those who could not conceive of any practicable alternative to unregulated capitalism.

Legislative interference as a principle of political strategy, however, was only a superficial step. Laws can prevent worse things from happening, and they can encourage some improvements, but in and of themselves, they are artificial and powerless. Only when large-scale movements of opinion took place, such as Tawney saw in the 'labour unrest', could statutes change society or, rather, register a change which had already occurred. 'A good law', in his view, 'is a rule which makes binding objectively conduct which most individuals already recognise to be binding subjectively.'[58]

Ethical perceptions had as well to harness the energy released in periods of discontent. Protest for its own sake, conflict without moral justification, was indefensible and pointless. This is why Tawney insisted that the rage which must follow from a deepened social consciousness needed guidance from an objective morality, or in other words, from a political (and by definition, moral) philosophy. The 'labour unrest' did raise real issues of the utmost importance, but its effect was in doubt, precisely because the working-class movement lacked an ideological base. In 1914 he wrote:[59]

> At present the agitation of the workers is like the struggles of a man who feels that he hears a message of tremendous significance, but who cannot find words in which to express it. He gesticulates, he struggles with himself, he is borne by the spirit. But the fire within him finds no expression in speech, and consumes himself instead of quickening others.

Despite the fact that, in the pre-war decade, 'economic struggles have occurred on a scale unprecedented since the birth of Chartism', Tawney noted that 'neither among the rebellious working classes nor among the half-repentent middle classes has there been produced any body of ideas sufficiently general and coherent to crystallise their uneasiness or to focus their efforts at reconstruction.'[60] He cautiously commented that 'whether Syndicalism will furnish the labour movement with a philosophy, it is yet too early to say'.[61] But certainly he did not reject it after brief reflection, as the Webbs had done. He was prepared to consider all efforts to question the basis of capitalist society, and then to draw the valid critical judgments together to form a philosophy of British socialism.

TAWNEY'S POLITICAL THEORY

Social conflict arose, in Tawney's view, when men saw oppression in the same way that they saw sin, that is, as a violation of moral standards which applied to groups as well as to individuals. His model of conflict is a classical one: 'Just as [the] individual suffers (Fox, Bunyan) when his habits of conduct are in contradiction to the conscience within him, so society suffers when its objective institutions outrage the best ideals of the age.'[62] Injustice and oppression are collective moral failures, in Tawney's view, for which all members of society must share responsibility. Here again his thought is Platonic, in the sense that men innately know what is just and must be shaken out of their slumber to see and act on what is right. Implicit in this view, as is the case in most Christian thought, is the assumption that 'Truth' exists and can be known.[63] Similarly Tawney never questioned his belief in the existence of God. On 12 July 1914 he wrote in the Commonplace Book of the imminence of Deity:

That fact, in my view, is a fact of experience, by which I mean that consciousness of contact with a personality, or with a source of thought and emotion, is a fact of direct experience infinitely more immediate than reflection on an absent but existing person, and analogous to the consciousness of the presence of the person in the same room as oneself, whom one is not a[t] the moment looking at, and with whom one communicates nonetheless easily on that account.

And, in Tawney's view, if Christianity does not speak to men in their social and economic conditions, its message is pointless. He was perfectly prepared to admit that his standard of personal and social behaviour was 'really a transcendental, religious, or mystical one'.[64]

The analogy with individual conduct, which is central to Tawney's political thought, was derived from his religious beliefs. His faith also accounts for the extent to which the component of personal guilt for the problems and failure of his society informed his thought. In a sense he judged himself by indicting his society. Indeed, Tawney's sense of ethical conflict in society is related to his own very intense feeling of sin, the belief that 'what goodness we have reached is a house built on piles driven into black slime and always slipping down into it unless we are building day and night'.[65]

The Pilgrim's Progress, the spiritual journey of the individual Christian, was his model of social as well as personal conflict. The 'labour unrest' was one indication, as Tawney saw it, that the day was nearer when arguments about expediency would no longer be a substitute for a sense of sin, and concern for social welfare an alternative to conscience, when the world would come to behave like 'a miserable sinner, flying from the city of Destruction' and come to establish 'rules of life which are approved as just by the conscience of mankind'.[66] Personal and collective moral conflict; personal and collective salvation: these are the terms of reference in Tawney's pre-war social philosophy.

Through his Christianity, he came to understand that conflict is a given factor in human and social relationships, incapable of relief through mechanical changes. At best strife could be regulated, never fully resolved, as long as men (and by analogy, institutions) remained imperfect. Since Tawney believed in original sin, he would not construct a vision of utopia or accept the vision of others.[67]

But it did not follow that men must tolerate abuses even in this imperfect world. God had given men moral judgment which, Tawney believed, must be applied to all aspects of life. Hence he was predisposed to see the socialist challenge as more philosophical than specifically political, more concerned with the development of ethical premises than social organizations. It followed easily, therefore, that the crucial task for socialists in pre-war England was, in Tawney's words, to 'deepen our individual sense of sin' and to 'objectify our morality'.[68]

On these premises, Tawney attempted to construct a coherent political theory before the outbreak of the First World War. The main axiom of his position was that a set of ideas was the only possible foundation for institutional action. Without a socialist philosophy to unite progressive thought both in Westminster and in the nation as a whole, Tawney believed, little could be expected of Parliament. The true seat of power was fixed in the ideas which control men in their daily lives, and the real task for British socialism was to develop a theory of society which went beyond politics to express the moral vision without which socialism was hollow and misconceived. On 16 June 1914, he elaborated these views:[69]

> What I mean by a society needing a philosophy is this. No machinery, whether of the state or minor corporations, can apply ideas which do not exist in society. They must always act at second hand. They must always be fed from without. All that a statute can do is to reduce a philosophy (important or trivial) into sections which are sufficiently clear to be understood even by lawyers. Hence the great days of a Parliament are when there is outside Parliament and in society a general body of ideas which Parlt. can apply. It has no *creative force*. There *is* no creative force outside the ideas which control men in their ordinary actions. There is no *deus ex machina* which can be involved though men are always trying to discover one. Nor is the modern futility of Parliament due to mechanical difficulties, which can be removed by mechanical remedies, such as revolution. It is due to the absence of any general accepted philosophy of life. Our principal task is to create one.

A *coup d'état*, a change in the ruling élite, a rash of new faces or new offices in government: why should anyone expect any alteration in the pattern of domination and oppression from these actions or from any political movement which left ideas untouched? Here is Tawney's challenge. A revolution only deserves the name if it leads to a 'new conception of human possibilities'. Indeed, a revolution is only possible, in Tawney's view, if prior to it, there exists, as in 1789 in France, 'a new system of ideas . . . based on new standards, without which material injustice would not have been revealed as so intolerable'.[70]

Tawney rejected the view that 'the necessary changes' in social arrangements 'can be brought about without any serious alteration in the structure of society and without any violent disturbance of vested interests'.[71] This acceptance of conflict, possibly violent, as a necessary factor in social change, clearly distinguishes Tawney's position from that of the Webbs. Indeed, he believed that their political orientation reflected the widespread 'anti-revolutionary character' of contemporary political thought.[72] Tawney's conflict theory could not accept the Webbs' view of the approach to social peace through state intervention.

On the other hand, Tawney rejected the Marxist theory of social conflict on the grounds that it was as materialistic as the capitalist system it opposed. His critique is in line with the tone of Marx's early philosophical manuscripts, but not with later versions of his thought. What was wrong with all types of materialism, Tawney contended, was its reduction of human behaviour into mechanical units of value and use. Marxism was therefore no advance at all in its denial of the importance of ideas as the motive force for social change. Indeed, 'Marxian socialists are not revolutionary enough', he wrote on 10 September 1913:[73]

They say that capitalist society is condemned because the worker does not get the equivalent of what he produces. He does not. But then why should he? The real condemnation of the capitalist spirit is contained in the suggestion that men should get only what they produced. As though we were shareholders in a goldmine to be paid according to our holding of stock! A barbarous, inhuman, sordid doctrine that wld weigh immortal souls and scale them down because they are not economically useful. God forbid that they shld be! This doctrine means that wealth should go to those who care for nothing *but* wealth, and are therefore least fit to have it.

Marxism over-emphasized and over-valued the material aspects of life, against which Tawney's Christian idealism naturally rebelled.

To the obvious Marxist challenge that he only dealt with the superstructure of society and that he ignored the fact that ideas are merely functions of economic relationships or the interests of the ruling élite, Tawney would be unrepentant. He did not deny that the facts of industrial life induced men to produce a system of ideas which legitimized their exercise of power as inevitable and just. And no Marxist could have objected to Tawney's acceptance of the theory of surplus value as the best explanation of what set capitalism apart 'from earlier methods of production'.[74] Where they would have differed was on the question of the autonomy of changes in ideas before the redistribution of power over the means of production.

Tawney believed that 'fundamental human claims', and not class relationships, were 'prior to government in logical order' and importance, 'though posterior to them in time'.[75] The phenomenon of class resulted, in his view, from systems of thought based on the timeless urge of some men to dominate others. Class struggle, therefore, was merely one type of moral conflict, in which 'fundamental human claims' were demanded, not because they were historically necessary or socially useful, but because they were just.

The neglect of ethical principles was one of Tawney's major criticisms of all contemporary writers on economic questions, Marxist and non-Marxist alike. Too many studies of the social substructure ultimately missed the most crucial aspects of social conflicts:[76]

> Too much time is spent today upon outworks, by writers who pile up statistics and facts, but never get to the heart of the problem. That heart is not economic. It is a question of *moral relationships*. This is the citadel which must be attacked – the immoral philosophy which underlies much of modern industry.

The way out of economic and political strife was to develop a set of ideas to which all men could subscribe regardless of work or wealth. Politicians in particular had to realize that 'As long as one remains in the sphere of interests no reconciliation of conflicting claims is possible.'[77] A test of relative strength, of political power or leverage, was the modern politician's standard of right and wrong, Tawney observed, and as long as this amoral view was maintained, the roots of social problems would remain and fester. Moral myopia was particularly noticeable in the Fabian approach to politics. Fabians, like Marxists, were caught up in the difficulties of materialism just as much as those they attacked. Their strategy as well as their philosophy was flawed in Tawney's view. They urged reform 'by explaining that justice (in moderate amounts) really pays, and that what is wrong with the world is not that it is too much guided by selfishness, but that its selfishness is not sufficiently enlightened'. That justice '*does* pay I believe is true', Tawney continued. 'Yet to put the matter in this way is to sell the things of God for gold.'[78]

Similarly, by over-emphasizing the role of political influence in social change, their strategy of permeation contained the seeds of an obsession with power rather than with right. Doubtless, the Fabians would exercise power more benevolently, but with as little concern as the present leaders of England for the real sources of social conflict. Tawney indicted the Webbs and those who shared their political orientation, in these succinct terms:[79]

> Modern politics are concerned with the manipulation of forces and interest. Modern society is sick through the absence of a moral ideal. To try to cure this by politics is like mak[ing] surgical experiments on a man who is dying of starvation or who is poisoned by foul air.

Tawney feared that British socialism, under the influence of the Webbs, in the years prior to the First World War had become merely 'a series of minute readjustments of social arrangements in the interests of the working classes'. Instead, what was really needed was 'a new conception of social justice', which was the strength of the early socialist movement.[80]

Thus the political theory of socialism had to avoid at all costs the pattern of materialist thought which capitalism itself embodied and of which Tawney saw reflections in the Webbs' ideas. He could heartily agree with Beatrice Webb when she summarized her belief in a conversation with Tawney that 'the essence of socialism was the substitution of the ideal of service for that of getting on'.[81] But how this transformation was to come about was far from obvious when one examined the Webbs' political strategy. Sidney Webb's thoughts were even less helpful in Tawney's estimation. Webb remarked to him in the summer of 1912 that 'if only one gets rid of the 3 or 4 millions at the bottom, the social problem wld be almost solved'.[82] There could hardly be a more materialistic statement, which, in Tawney's view, totally ignored the ideological (and in his terms, the spiritual) dimensions of the problem.

The Webbs countered in language closer to Tawney's own. They suggested that the abolition of economic privilege is necessary in order to provide the wealth for all to live decently and to lead a spiritual life, if they so chose. But Tawney insisted that this argument was still beside the point. Economic privilege had to be abolished because it produced wickedness, not because it produced poverty. And without a widespread change in ideas, the same attitude of selfishness would remain even with the collective ownership of industry. Again, socialism is here defined as a shift in human attitudes or no change at all. His argument is simply phrased. To the collectivist socialist, he asked: 'supposing unearned incomes, rents, etc. are pooled, will not the world, with its present philosophy, do anything but gobble them up and look up with an impatient grunt for more? That is the real question.' And he added pessimistically:[83]

> It will not be faced in my lifetime [since] as long as the working classes believe, and believe rightly, that their mentors rob them, so long will they look on the restoration of the booty as *the* great reform, and will impatiently waive aside more fundamental issues, as a traveller robbed by a highwayman declines to be comforted by being told that money, after all, does not buy happiness.

The fixation with money and the power it buys would not be remedied by collective ownership. Indeed, he flirted with the ascetic view that if the only way 'to overcome the power of the wealthy is to despise wealth'; if the just society was a poor one, then so be it. But he concluded that 'It cannot be the will of God that we should lay down the power and resources which we have amassed . . . We cannot recover from our economic position merely by surrendering it',[84] but rather by seeing wealth in a different light.

Tawney summarized his argument with the Webbs and 'state socialism' in his reflections on the development of his early political ideas. When he sketched 'the stages of thought about social affairs through which I, and I suppose other people, have passed', he approached Fabianism as but one preliminary step in his intellectual growth. Again, it was the materialist assumptions implicit in the emphasis on state action which turned Tawney from the Webbs' position. Tawney began, he believed, along with many others, by seeing poverty as individual misfortune, unconnected 'with the main institutions of society'.[85] Since, in this first stage of social thought, social and economic conditions were not seen as reflections of political relationships, there was no point in turning to the state for redress of situations beyond its control. This ideology, which Tawney identified with the Charity Organization Society, was soon superseded as he began to see the[86]

> unity underlying the individual cases of poverty; that they are connected with social institutions, specimens of a type, pieces of a system, and that this sytem is, in the first instance, the work of the state and can be altered by an alteration of the law.

This 'is the stage of the theoretical socialist',[87] Tawney commented, or in other words, the stage of the Webbs' political thought.

But Tawney had advanced from this view to a third stage of social thought, in which he had come to realize 'that the attitude of the state is just the attitude of countless individuals'.[88] The state, in Tawney's pre-war political theory, was as mechanical and inert as any other institution. As a collective entity, it was no greater than the sum of its parts. Tawney's political (and moral) units always remained life-size, and consequently the orientation of his socialist thought remained fixed on the individual. This is not to say that he neglected the social nature of individual action and thought; on the contrary. But he did insist that political action was one type of human behaviour subject to the same rules and ethical requirements as any other human activity.

Tawney believed as fervently as any other socialist that 'the attitude of governments to social questions is wrong, profoundly wrong.' But he went on to argue that

> it is wrong because the attitude of individuals to each other is wrong, because we in our present society are living on certain false and universal assumptions; and that even when statesmen honestly mean to do [?good] they will often do harm (apart from bad luck, miscalculations etc.) merely because all their actions, good and bad, proceed from a character based on those assumptions.

Thus he could not approve the Webbs' political strategy:[89]

D

What we have got to do *first* of all is to change those assumptions or principles. This is where I think the Fabians are inclined to go wrong. They seem to think that you can trick statesmen into a good course of action, without changing their principles, and that by taking sufficient thought society can add several cubits to its stature. It can't, as long as it lives on the same spiritual diet.

Tawney hoped that his political ideas would help to cure this moral malaise and lead to the construction and application of a 'principle of justice upon which human association for the production of wealth can be founded'.[90]

The primary ideological basis for Tawney's political theory was his belief in equality. And 'In order to believe in human equality,' he asserted, 'it is necessary to believe in God.'[91] Here we see the explicit connection between his religious and his social thought. Briefly, the outline of Tawney's pre-war socialist position may be summarized in the following terms: to emphasize differences between and among men and to base a hierarchical structure of society on the assumption of these arbitrary differences, such as race or class, are wrong and immoral judgments, since all men are insignificant in the eyes of the Lord and equally children of sin. In the light of the infinitely great, surely human differences appear infinitely small. It is only without a belief in God, then, that men turned to raising false distinctions between their fellows and came to erect artificial standards of moral and political behaviour.[92]

A belief in equality, Tawney went on, was the only possible basis for a stable and just social order. It implied that the seeds of social obligation lay in the recognition of the identity of human nature. It led to the assertion that the conviction of the individual conscience rather than 'wealth or power or numbers or learning is the standard by which conduct must be judged'. It required the rejection of the immoral use of men as tools for whatever ends, however noble they might be, and finally it meant that 'of all revolutionary schemes there is one awful criterion: "It were better that a millstone were hung about your neck and that you were cast into the sea than that you should offend one of these little ones" '.[93] This last statement seriously qualified Tawney's support for a violent disruption of vested interests if that were the only means available to bring about equality. Apparently he hoped that the re-ordering of society would be specific enough to avoid the danger of damaging the innocent. But since Tawney also believed that the whole society was responsible for its evils, it would be impossible to avoid drawing the entire population into the conflict. No answer to this difficulty appeared in Tawney's pre-war writing.

But however it was brought about, equality would be a stabilizing element in social and political life. Contrary to the opinion of reactionary critics, equality was not, Tawney pointed out, the equivalent of anarchy. Rather 'it is the one foundation of human subordination, of order, authority and justice, and it might more reasonably be attacked by those who love license than by those who fear [?for] liberty.'[94] Compulsion alone is not the basis of society or even the beginning of political order. Where there is mere compulsion, disorder naturally follows and leads, in extreme cases, to revolution. On the other hand, where there is true order, social constraints – law and the violence which is its ultimate sanction – are the generalization of the individual's sense of right.[95]

Such a situation was impossible under capitalism. Indeed inequality was institutionalized and perpetuated in modern industrial society by the system of economic privilege which conferred 'payment' whether in money or in social position, without corresponding services', and produced 'economic power over the lives of others'.[96] An elaborate set of social norms and expectations supported the power of wealth and transformed it into the sole determinant of authority and ultimately the social measure of human value. Economic domination was not a capitalist invention, but its close connection with the all-inclusive modern state created a new form of absolutism, a form of total social control, whereby he who employed, governed as he saw fit, as the modern equivalent of the feudal lord. And even the medieval baron was obliged to recognize the rights of his inferiors and was their protector and servant in certain matters. The modern capitalist, on the other hand, did not see his role in society as 'a post, an office' based on public trust. His behaviour need be guided by the demands of private gain alone. Hence, Tawney concluded, 'economic privileges must be abolished, not, primarily, because they hinder the production of wealth, but because they produce wickedness.'[97]

Since the opinions of the vast majority of men about the justice of their social and political relationships counted for nothing, and since there was little choice for millions but to submit to a pattern of life over which they had no real control, it made very little sense to Tawney to speak of 'liberty' under capitalism. To those who would call this analysis an exaggeration and refer to the worker's right of contract and his corresponding right to withdraw his labour if he saw fit, as examples of 'freedom', Tawney answered:[98]

> The truth is that the sharp antithesis drawn by modern commercial societies between serfs and the free labourers on whose slowly straightening backs our civilisation is uneasily poised, and emphasised as though it marked a line between hopeless oppression and unqualified liberty, requires to be supplemented by categories derived from a wider and more tragic range of human experience than was open to our forefathers. There are more ways of living 'at the will of a Lord' than were known to Glanvill and Bracton, and the utility of the contrast in the sphere of legal analysis does not save it from being but a thin abstraction of the countless forms of tyranny which spring from the world-old power of one human being to use another as his tool. That dependence on the uncontrolled caprice of a master whom one hates to obey and dare not abandon, which, by whatever draperies it may be veiled, is still the bitter core of serfdom, is compatible with the most diverse legal arrangements; with wage labour as with forced services, with tenure by a competitive money rent as well as tenure by personal obligations, with freedom of contract as well as with inherited status, with protection by the national courts as well as with its absence.

Furthermore, under capitalism, rights were supported by sanctions only when the claimant possessed wealth and the social status which accompanied it.

The key to the capitalist social system lay, in Tawney's view, in the complex status relationships which accompanied wealth. In other words, capitalism was based on the material valuation of social roles which leads to an improper distribution of authority in industry, politics, and social life. Authority implies both domination and subjection, no less in industry than in politics. In this sense, it was the absolute sovereignty of the capitalist in the nation's industrial life which Tawney challenged.

The quest for economic liberty involved a limitation of that sovereignty, in the same way that the 'paternal monarchy' was checked in the seventeenth century. The absolute dictator was undoubtedly the most efficient leader of the complex mechanism of the state, now as then, but such considerations did not make tyranny less oppressive, Tawney countered. And just as the political disruption of the seventeenth century led to the 'inefficiency and incompetence' of politics in the eighteenth, so also the overthrow of economic absolution was likely to interfere with the ordered accumulation of wealth. That was not a valid objection, in Tawney's view. He wrote that[99]

when we cut off the heads of our industrial Lauds and Straffords, we shall probably for a century or so have to put up with political jobbery and ineptitude.... But if one is asked 'Was the Great Rebellion worth while?' there are few decent Englishmen who would not say 'Yes'. And if I am asked whether it is wise to depose the economic oligarchy which rules most of us today at the risk of facing a generation of disorder and inefficiency before the new régime has made its traditions, I answer, 'Yes. This too is worthwhile.'

Indeed, since England had led the world 'into the moral labyrinth of capitalist industry', it was incumbent upon Englishmen to teach the world the meaning of economic liberty in the twentieth century, just as they had 'upheld constitutional liberty when all other nations were passing under absolutism'.[100] Tawney did not underestimate the difficulties of the task. As a student of the Reformation, he drew the following comparison: 'It took men 150 years and two revolutions to arrive at some working conception of religious liberty. It may take us as long to work out our idea of economic liberty.'[101]

CONCLUSIONS

R. H. Tawney's political theory was incomplete at the time of the outbreak of the First World War. His early views were far more useful as a critique of contemporary social thought and policy than as a basis for programmatic action. In a sense, the major weakness of much of his pre-war thought – its abstract nature – reflects Tawney's view that the preliminary work which would prepare the way for the socialist society had yet to be done. His preoccupation with the intellectual assumptions behind political behaviour was a matter of choice, not of neglect or selective distortion.

The political implications of his early writing were unspecified on the whole. He favoured the public ownership of land, the limitation of profits and bequests, and the ending of the class monopoly in higher education.[102] But Tawney failed on the whole to work out the practical organization of the attack on social problems which he advocated so eloquently.[103] While he had joined the Fabian Society in 1906 and the ILP in 1909, he did not play an active part, it appears, in pre-war Labour politics. When he told George Lansbury, Labour M.P. for Bow and Bromley, that the party 'ought to get and train its young men', it must have been clear that he did not see himself as one of their number.[104] In addition, he rarely mentioned trade unions in his pre-war writing. The fact of strikes was more important, it would seem, than the groups which led them. Indeed, the only institutional foci for his programme of moral revival were the university and the disestablished Church.[105] But why educated men or the educated society should be more aware of moral claims or more willing to submit to them was never fully explained. Before the outbreak of war in 1914, Tawney's only direct answer to the Russian populists' question, 'What is to be done?' seems to have been to live and think and act like a Christian. No socialist could take exception to Tawney's claim that:[106]

> The great problem of our day is to ennoble industry by so arranging it that every man may feel that his work, however humble, is dignified by the fact that he is a free man giving freely to the needs of society, and to humanise culture by making those who teach and study feel that education is not something which separates them from their fellows, but that they, too, are the brothers of those who labour in forge and factory and mine.

But the process by which rhetoric, however moving, turns into political action was neglected in Tawney's pre-war work. In a sense, his politics of morality makes sense only by personal example, in the pattern of the exceptional individual's life, which few men are strong enough to follow. The strength of Tawney's own idealism and his personal sincerity were unquestioned. But the real problem in his pre-war thought is whether the ethical demands of his socialism are hopelessly beyond the reach of all but a handful of men who are unlikely to reach the pinnacle of political power. Politics, in Namier's classic phrase, 'cannot wait for the humanization of mankind'.[107]

Furthermore, the complex ethical problems implicit in all political action are obscured in Tawney's political thought. He was a Puritan abolitionist who stopped somewhat short of declaring in the language of what Max Weber disapprovingly called 'the ethic of ultimate ends', that 'The Christian does rightly and leaves the results with the Lord'.[108] Tawney did see social conflict in absolute terms, as a 'war of beliefs',[109] in which right and wrong could be objectively distinguished, but he never went so far that he accepted any means as justifiable in the eradication of evil.

Still, he never met Weber's powerful objection to the tradition of Christian moralism, phrased in the following question: 'Should it really matter so little for the ethical demands on politics that politics operates with very special means, namely, power backed up by *violence?*'[110] The equation of individual and collective behaviour is not as simple as Tawney would have had it. Weber insisted with justification that the reference to physical force as the ultimate sanction of political action made politics ethically 'irrational',[111] a situation which a moralist cannot confront. Weber correctly held that politics rests on moral ambiguity and ultimately on ethical contradictions in the use of violence, the recognition of which raises serious difficulties about Tawney's attempt to construct an 'objective' political morality. Tawney's Christian social philosophy never successfully met Weber's profound challenge that 'He who seeks the salvation of the soul, of his own and of others, should not seek it along the avenue of politics, for the quite different tasks of politics can only be solved by violence'.[112] Perhaps Tawney's concentration on ideas rather than institutions and the sanctions which give them force reflects his uneasiness when confronted with this dilemma. But it is more likely that Tawney believed that conflict was inevitable in society, and that to ignore politics because it involved violence was tantamount to turning from life because it involved suffering and pain. No one ever claimed that the Pilgrim's Progress was an easy journey, but it was infinitely preferable, in Tawney's view, to abandoning politics to men who could face violence, but cared nothing for justice and human values.

NOTES

1 R. H. Tawney, *An Experiment in Democratic Education*, 1914, a pamplet reprinted by the WEA from the article in *Political Quarterly*, 1, 2, May 1914, pp. 62–84.
2 O. H. Ball, *Sidney Ball*, Oxford, 1923, p. 228.
3 Sidney Ball, 'The socialist ideal', *Economic Review*, 9, 4, October 1899, 425–9.
4 Cf. Tawney's review of Charles Raven's *Christian Socialism*, in the *Athenaeum & Nation* of 12 March 1921. The Christian Socialists 'began the task of breaking the evil tradition which divorced industry from the life of the spirit. Since their day the Church of England has never been quite without leaders – though they have been few – who refuse to be terrified by talk of economic expediency into denying the social application of the faith which they profess.'
5 British Library of Political and Economic Science, Beveridge Papers, Box LI 211. Beveridge's notes for a radio broadcast, attached to Tawney's early letters to him, are undated. On Oxford at the turn of the century, cf. M. P. Ashley and C. T. Saunders, *Red Oxford*, 1933; F. A. Iremonger, *William Temple*, 1948; Adam Ulam, *Philosophical Foundations of English Socialism*, Cambridge, Mass., 1951. On Beveridge, cf. Janet Beveridge, *Beveridge and His Plan*, 1954, and the forthcoming life by Mrs Jose Harris.
6 On Canon Barnett, cf. Mrs H. O. Barnett: *Canon Barnett: his life, work and friends*, 2 vols, 1918; J. A. R. Pimlott, *Toynbee Hall, 1884–1934*, 1935; and these two of Canon Barnett's many articles: 'Practicable Socialism', *Nineteenth Century*, 63, 74, April 1883, pp. 554–60, and 'Our present discontents', *Nineteenth Century*, 73, 432, February, 1913, pp. 328–37.
7 Beveridge Papers, LI 211, Tawney to Beveridge, August 1903, impishly addressed, 'Dear Drink'. On the COS, cf. C. L. Mowat, *The Charity Organization Society 1869–1913*, 1961.
8 'Inquisitorial' is T. S. Ashton's term, which he used in his obituary notice of Tawney for the British Academy, in 'Richard Henry Tawney', *Proceedings of the British Academy*, 48, 1962, p. 462.
9 R. H. Tawney, 'The *Daily News* religious census of London,' *Toynbee Record*, 16, 6, March 1904, pp. 87–8.
10 Beveridge Papers, LI 211, Tawney to Beveridge, 20 September 1906.
11 Beveridge Papers, LI 211, Tawney to Beveridge, 22 October 1906. T. S. Ashton, 'Richard Henry Tawney', *Proceedings of the British Academy*, 48, 1962, p. 462.
12 Beveridge Papers, LI 211, Tawney to Beveridge, 29 April 1907.
13 Papers in possession of Tawney's nephew, Mr Michael Vyvyan of Trinity College, Cambridge, hereafter referred to as the T–V Papers, letter of W. R. Anson, Warden of All Souls, to Tawney, 4 March 1913.
14 T. W. Price, *The Story of the Workers' Educational Association from 1903 to 1924*, 1924, p. 34.

15 On Unwin, cf. Tawney's introductory memoir in the edition of Unwin's writing which he prepared, *Studies in Economic History: the collected papers of George Unwin*, 1927.

16 *Highway*, 3, 26, November 1910, pp. 29–30; 4, 38, November 1911, pp. 27–9; 5, 50, November 1912, pp. 26–8; 6, 62, November 1913, pp. 27–8. Notes for lectures on the French Revolution to his Longton students are collected in a box under that title in the collection of Tawney's lectures at the London School of Economics.

17 From Tawney's own list in T–V Papers.

18 R. H. Tawney's Commonplace Book (hereafter cited as 'CPB') entry for 30 October 1912, in T–V Papers.

19 *Ibid.*

20 Beveridge Papers, LI 211, Tawney to Beveridge, 13 April 1907.

21 R. H. Tawney, ' "Blind alley" occupations and the way out', *Women's Industrial News*, 52, October 1910, p. 1.

22 From Tawney's review of F. Keeling, *The Labour Exchange in Relation to Boy and Girl Labour*, 1910 and A. Greenwood, *Juvenile Labour Exchanges and After-care*, 1910, *Economic Journal*, 21, December 1911, pp. 574–7.

23 Royal Commission on the Poor Laws and the Relief of Distress, 1910 Cd 5068, Appendix, 49, Minutes of Evidence, pp. 329–34, 16 March 1908. Tawney's statement is entitled, 'Unemployment and boy labour in Glasgow'.

24 *Ibid.*, p. 335. Cf. also R. H. Tawney, 'The economics of boy labour', *Economic Journal*, 19, December 1909, pp. 517–37.

25 Cf. R. H. Tawney, 'Municipal enterprise in Germany', *Economic Review*, 20, 3, October 1910, pp. 423–37; and R. H. Tawney, 'A report of a visit to Germany made by members of the Rochdale branch of the W.E.A.', *Highway*, 2, 18, March 1910, pp. 90–1.

26 1910. Cd 5068, Appendix, XLIX, Minutes of Evidence, p. 334.

27 *Ibid.*

28 R. H. Tawney, 'Unemployment and its remedies. The example of Germany IV', *Morning Post*, 31 October 1908.

29 Tawney, ' "Blind alley" occupations and the way out', *Women's Industrial News*, 52, October 1910, p. 10.

30 R. H. Tawney, 'The theory of pauperism', *Sociological Review*, 2, 4, October 1909, p. 372.

31 R. H. Tawney, *The Agrarian Problem in the Sixteenth Century*, 1912, p. ix.

32 From the draft of a speech, probably on the 'labour unrest', in the T–V papers, ff. 35–40. My numbering.

33 R. H. Tawney, *The Attack*, p. 121, from the British Academy obituary notice of Beatrice Webb.

34 Tawney, *An Experiment in Democratic Education*, p. 3.

35 *Ibid.*

36 *Ibid.*

37 CPB, 10 June 1912.

38 Tawney, *An Experiment in Democratic Education*, p. 3.

39 CPB, 6 May 1912.

D*

40 *Ibid.*
41 CPB, 10 June 1912.
42 *Ibid.*
43 *Ibid.* In the same passage he argued that most workers did not see the workers as 'Quixotic', but rather as rational men, despite the outcome of the strikes.
44 Tawney, *An Experiment in Democratic Education*, pp. 3–4.
45 *Ibid.*, p. 4.
46 *Ibid.*
47 Tawney, *The Agrarian Problem in the Sixteenth Century*, p. 348.
48 *Ibid.*, p. 321. He noted also that 'Such movements are a proof of blood and sinew and of a high and gallant spirit. . . Happy the nation whose people has not forgotten how to rebel', p. 340.
49 CPB, 29 April 1912.
50 Cf. Tawney's conversations with his WEA students, CPB 19 April 1912. He mentions reading Stephen Reynolds and Bob and Tom Woolley, *Seems So! A Working Class View of Politics*, 1911, which discusses working-class hostility to state intervention. On the same point, see Henry Pelling's essay 'The working class and the origins of the welfare state', in his *Popular Politics and Society in Late Victorian Britain*, 1968, pp. 1–18.
51 Passfield Papers, Beatrice Webb's unpublished diaries, vol. 31, 10–15 April 1912. Graham Wallas, Professor of Politics in the University of London and a founder of the Fabian Society, had put forward Tawney's name when consulted about his choice for director. Cf. Passfield Papers, Personal Correspondence, 2.4.f., Sidney Webb to Wallas, 23 July 1912
52 R. H. Tawney, *Poverty as an Industrial Problem*, 1914, p. 12.
53 *Ibid.*, p. 13.
54 *Ibid.*
55 *Ibid.* The same point was a subject of fierce debate among German sociologists at the same time. Cf. Dahrendorf, 'Values and Social Science', in his *Essays in the Theory of Society*, 1968, pp. 1–18.
56 R. H. Tawney, *The Establishment of Minimum Rates in the Chain-making Industry under the Trade Boards Act of 1909*, 1914, and *The Establishment of Minimum Rates in the Tailoring Industry under the Trade Boards Act of 1909*, 1915. A further study of the box-making industry by Tawney's secretary, Miss M. E. Bulkley was also published in 1915. But all the research was completed before the outbreak of the war.
57 Tawney, *Tailoring Industry*, p. 137.
58 CPB, 29 July 1913.
59 T–V papers, ff. 13–14.
60 *Ibid.*
61 *Ibid.*
62 CPB, 6 May 1912.
63 CPB, 30 October 1912.
64 CPB, 12 July 1914; 29 July 1913.
65 CPB, 10 June 1912.

66 CPB, 18 September 1912 and 22 June 1912.
67 CPB, 10 June 1912.
68 CPB, 6 May 1912.
69 CPB, 16 June 1914.
70 CPB, 6 July 1913.
71 T–V Papers, f.7.
72 *Ibid.*
73 CPB, 10 September 1913.
74 CPB, 6 October 1912.
75 CPB, 6 July 1913.
76 CPB, 26 March 1913.
77 CPB, 29 July 1913.
78 CPB, 6 February 1913.
79 CPB, 6 May 1912.
80 T–V Papers, f. 26.
81 CPB, 31 July to 1 August 1912.
82 *Ibid.* These are among the few examples of Tawney's public expression of his pre-war political theory. He did teach a summer course at Leeds in June 1912 on 'Some strands of modern political thought'. A year earlier he had given a similar WEA course at Oxford. Cf. R. L. Jones, 'The invasion of a university', *Highway*, 3, 35, August 1911, p. 173: 'Birkenhead, Birmingham and Swindon, Belfast, London and Longton, are at the moment grappling with R. H. Tawney upon the need for a unifying centre for ethical precept.' The religious belief upon which his views were based may have been so personal that he preferred to develop his thought privately. Tawney's wife Jeanette was often ill and convalescing in Europe while he kept the Commonplace Book.
83 CPB, 22 July 1913.
84 *Ibid.*, and 4 September 1912.
85 CPB, 2 December 1912.
86 *Ibid.*
87 *Ibid.*
88 *Ibid.*
89 *Ibid.* The resemblance to Platonic ideas on this point is clear. Cf. Martin Buber's essay, 'Plato and Isaiah', in the collection of his essays, *Israel and the World*, New York, 1963, pp. 103–12. A comparison of Tawney and Buber, both deeply religious socialists, would be a fascinating study.
90 CPB, 8 January 1914.
91 CPB, 6 March 1913.
92 *Ibid.*
93 *Ibid.* Cf. also this remark: 'One may *not* do evil that good shld come.' Entry for 29 July 1913.
94 CPB, 6 March 1913.
95 *Ibid.* Tawney discussed this point with his close friend and fellow WEA tutor, T. W. Price; cf. CPB, 10 August 1913.
96 CPB, 8 January 1914.
97 CPB, 22 July 1913; 6 October 1912; 10 June 1912.

98 Tawney, *The Agrarian Problem in the Sixteenth Century*, pp. 45–6.
99 CPB, 3 June 1912.
100 CPB, 10 June 1912.
101 CPB, 21 July 1912.
102 CPB, 16 October 1912.
103 He was, it should be added, a member of the Consultative Committee of the Board of Education from 1908–14.
104 CPB, 29 April 1912. Lansbury and Tawney were both unimpressed by the tame Parliamentary tactics of the Labour Party. Lansbury resigned his seat in 1912 to stand on the issue of woman suffrage, which the party would not press. He lost the ensuing by-election. For Tawney's mild rebuke of the Labour Party, cf. CPB, 29 June 1914.
105 For the university, CPB, 30 October 1912; for the Church, CPB, 11 December 1913.
106 R. H. Tawney, *Education and Social Progress*, Manchester, 1912, p. 11. Reprint of Tawney's speech on 28 May 1912 in connection with the Co-operative Congress held at Portsmouth.
107 L. B. Namier, *In the Margin of History*, 1939, p. 76.
108 H. H. Gerth and C. W. Mills (eds), *From Max Weber: Essays in Sociology*, 1948, p. 120. The references are all from Weber's brilliant essay 'Politics as a vocation', which he delivered at the University of Munich in 1919. The comparison between Weber and Tawney on the relationship between ethics and politics in contemporary society and the moral commitment of the historian puts into perspective the somewhat forced comparison between their views on Protestantism and capitalism. For instance, in his introduction to *The Protestant Ethic and the Spirit of Capitalism*, first published in 1904, Weber stated his methodological framework which adequately phrased his differences with Tawney: 'Fashion and the seal of the *literati* would have us think that the specialist can to-day be spared, or degraded to a position subordinate to that of the seer. Almost all sciences owe something to dilettantes, often very valuable viewpoints. But dilettantism as a leading principle would be the end of science. He who yearns for seeing should go to the cinema, though it will be offered to him copiously to-day in the present field of investigation also. Nothing is further from the intent of these thoroughly serious studies than such an attitude. And, I might add, whoever wants a sermon should go to a conventicle. The question of the relative value of the cultures which are compared here will not receive a single word. It is true that the path of human destiny cannot but appal him who surveys a section of it. But he will do well to keep his small personal commentaries to himself, as one does at the sight of the sea or of majestic mountains, unless he knows himself to be called and gifted to give them expression in artistic or prophetic form' (p. 29). Tawney's view of history was precisely the opposite of Weber's.
109 *Ibid.*, p. 126.
110 *Ibid.*, p. 119.
111 *Ibid.*, p. 122.
112 *Ibid.*, p. 126.

4

G. D. H. Cole and the Theory
of Industrial Conflict

The political strategy of the Webbs and Tawney's Christian approach to British socialism were complemented, in the pre-war period, by a theory of industrial conflict most fully expressed by G. D. H. Cole.[1] His political ideas embodied a third tactical choice open to the Labour movement before the first World War.

Cole's analysis of social conflict was based on the idea of class struggle. The correct line of development for British Labour, he believed, was to be found within the terms of the antagonism between Capital and Labour. He departed from the Marxist viewpoint, though, in his assertion that the trade unions were both the instruments for the eventual overthrow of capitalism and the embryonic form of post-capitalist organization. If Lenin had read Cole, he undoubtedly would have rejected his ideas as being tainted with the spirit of 'economism'.[2] This term, which was used to describe socialist thinking which neglected political work in favour of trade union action, may be aptly applied to G. D. H. Cole's pre-war outlook.

As in the case of the Webbs and Tawney, the 'labour unrest' served as the point of departure for the expression of his early ideas. His theoretical criticisms of political action and his opposition to the Labour Party separate his ideas from those of the Webbs and others in the Fabian Society and the ILP. Cole's pre-war thought thus represents a second line of attack, very different from that of R. H. Tawney, on the Webbian position in British socialist thought.

EARLY IDEAS

The 'labour unrest' was a decisive influence on Cole's early political ideas. Although elements of his thought antedated the strikes of

1911–12, the industrial discontent focused and channelled his youthful idealism. He had been converted to socialism, he later noted, by his reading of William Morris. Throughout his life, Cole retained the vision of *News from Nowhere* and its call for fellowship and for the need to restore to the working man 'joy in the labour of his hands'.[3] His ideas developed further at Oxford under the tutelage of A. D. Lindsay, A. J. Carlyle, and especially of Sidney Ball. His academic work was outstanding, and after four years at Balliol, he was elected in 1912 to a fellowship at Magdalen College, Oxford. In these years he was active in the Oxford University Fabian Society and fervently supported the Webbs' Poor Law Campaign. The only major objection he had to the Labour Party was its meagre appeal to the middle class. 'Otherwise,' he wrote in December 1910, the Party was an 'admirable' body.[4]

Two years later, under the impact of the strike wave, Cole's political views had changed. He was deeply affected by the spirit of revolt which both the Webbs and Tawney had noted in pre-war society, and his turn away from the Labour Party and orthodox Fabianism was meant to be part of that revolt. 'Wherever we go,' Cole noted in December 1912, 'we shall find the apostles of law and order at bay, with the rabble of all the advanced jacks of every trade laying furious siege to the citadel.'[5]

In Cole's view, the force behind the 'labour unrest' was also expressed in the pre-war 'Christian Unrest', that is, the new social concern of the Church of England, and the 'Aesthetic Unrest' in art and poetry. Indeed, the pattern of rebellion was so widespread, he observed, that it touched virtually every aspect of life and thought. The post-impressionists, the futurists, the cubists, as well as the suffragettes, the Orangemen, and of course, the syndicalists: the force and vitality of all these movements testified, he believed, to the breakdown of central authority in modern society.[6] 'Everywhere, in fact,' Cole observed, 'we are faced with the uprising of the group. Everywhere we have before us a new group-psychology, group-ideal, and group-action.'[7] Here Cole showed the influence of Graham Wallas, whose *Human Nature in Politics* was published in 1908,[8] and of J. N. Figgis, the Anglican theologian and political philosopher.[9] Here, too, we can see the affinities between Cole's ideas and those of Jean-Jacques Rousseau.

He published in 1913 a translation of *The Social Contract and Discourses* and added an introduction which shows how much he drew from the French *philosophe*. 'Rousseau,' he recalled, 'helped me to see the same underlying basis of common will as the sustaining force, not only of "the State", but of all associations and of all informal groupings.'[10] His belief in economic equality as the prerequisite of political equality and in the need to maximize the participation of men in the ordering of their social lives can also be traced to Rousseau.[11] The roots of Cole's political pluralism may be found in this early work.

Through his analysis of Rousseau and his observation of contemporary affairs, Cole came to see the need for a systematic revision of socialist thought. 'What the French call the "étatisme" of Parliamentary Socialism is again in the melting pot,' he noted in late 1912, and 'it is too early to say exactly what will emerge.'[12] Alongside the 'awakening of the fighting spirit in the ranks of organised labour' he saw in pre-war England 'an intellectual unrest which may be called the Labour movement in search of a philosophy'.[13] This search had not ended by the outbreak of war in 1914. But Cole had developed in these years a position which he believed could provide the basis for a new and revitalized working-class movement. Whichever line was chosen, though, Cole was sure that after the 'labour unrest', socialist thought could not have reverted to its old forms. Cole noted (repeating his imagery):[14]

Not for a long time has there been so much re-examination of first principles or such wide differences among socialists themselves concerning policy and ultimate aims. If socialism is not in the melting pot, at any rate many of our ideas about it are, by our own confession, undergoing considerable revision.

The Fabian Society and the Labour Party

The Fabian Society was Cole's first choice as the instrument of that revision. By 1914 he had joined forces with a number of similarly-inclined young Fabians, including William Mellor, with whom he wrote numerous articles and pamphlets critical of Webbian socialism. In fact, the Oxford University Fabian Society, under Cole's influence, turned 'the major proportion of its efforts' to 'attacks on Fabianism'.[15] Their unsuccessful efforts to detach the parent Fabian Society from its association with the Labour Party have been noted above.[16]

Even though Cole admitted that 'As a political body . . . the

Fabian Society is beneath contempt,' he did see some redeeming qualities in it. The Fabian Research Department (FRD), initiated by Beatrice Webb to collect the material for her Inquiry on the Control of Industry, was, in his opinion, a potential 'intelligence department' for Labour as well as a secondary, though important, 'justification of Fabianism'. He invited rebels to permeate the permeators and to change the society from within: 'That Labour needs an intellectual force behind it we all admit. May not the Fabian Society yet help to provide that force, for all its bad traditions? Stranger things have happened.'[17]

Cole refused to be awed by the austere and industrious Webbs. By their belligerent solidarity and overall boisterous behaviour, his group of militants succeeded, in fact, in annoying their older colleagues and in disrupting the staid atmosphere of the Society. At the 1914 Fabian Summer School, held during the last pre-war weekend, Cole's party were at their most rebellious. The young dissidents did not hide their hostility to the habits or views of official Fabianism. On the contrary, they unabashedly publicized their attempts to take over the Society. Beatrice Webb noted in her diary on 31 July 1914: 'G. D. H. Cole told me that they [Cole's group] intended to use us "as a platform" – but the platform will give way if they stamp on it too heavily.'[18] Her fears were completely unfounded. Cole's group failed to displace the 'Old Guard' or their ideas, and the clash of views which his personality and intellect made inevitable was a refreshing challenge to the Webbs. In addition Beatrice knew that a reappraisal of the hallowed dogmas of the socialist faith, which the young rebels zealously demanded and worked for, had been long overdue.

The political implications of Cole's early socialism were clear. He called for the rejection of the Labour Party's leadership of the working-class movement and for the development of a new strategy for Labour, stressing industrial militancy, solidarity and the consolidation of strength in industrial unions.

Cole's opinion of Ramsay MacDonald and most of his colleagues was far from generous. 'The present Labour Party can never become a majority,' he wrote, 'and would be sadly at a loss to know what to do if it did become one.'[19] The inability of the party to influence parliamentary affairs was, in his view, undeniable. Its working-class constituency had expected some coherent policy from their spokesmen at Westminster. But instead they had been rewarded, he argued, with a group confused about its real identity,

Plate 5   'THE PUPPETS: Being the self portrait of that master
tactician, Ramsay MacDonald, as he paints it by word of mouth for his
enthusiastic followers on every occasion upon which he addresses them.'
Daily Herald, 17 February 1914

Plate 6   'LEADERS OF A GREAT PEOPLE: They are in form for the opening of the popular Westminster Play.'

Daily Herald, 3 February 1914

Plate 7 'GUARANTEES—*TRADE UNIONISM (who has discarded what protects him that he may protect our soldiers better)*: "Remember, John, you will have won no victory if at the end that shield is not returned intact to me." '
        Herald, 26 June 1915

Plate 8   'Munitions of War—or Peace?'   *Herald*, 1 May 1915

neither independent, nor totally absorbed by its Liberal hosts. Such a party was 'doomed to ultimate extinction'. Indeed, that prospect was not completely fantastic. 'To attack the Parliamentary Labour Party nowadays may look rather like flogging a dead horse,' and an election in 1913, in Cole's view, would have decimated the ranks of the party. The remnants would have owed their survival to the good will of the Liberals.[20]

Cole did not shrink from the threat of reduced parliamentary representation for Labour. On the contrary, such a 'purge' of political Labour was precisely the course he suggested. However, he rejected scrapping the party altogether, and favoured a 'small fighting group' of socialists: Hardie, Snowden, O'Grady, Thorne, and Jowett, who had had the courage to oppose the National Insurance Act on the contributory principle, despite the official party position. Cole's new party would rely on the force of organized Labour in the country, rather than numerical strength in the House. Only then could it become the foundation for 'a real Socialist Party capable of voicing the wider aspirations of the workers in the political field'. Such a party would 'be distinguished from the capitalist parties by the fact that it is out to give expression to a theory' rather than to seek power for its own sake.[21] With this policy in mind, he believed that 'Instead of the reformist Labour Party, there is hope that some day we shall have a revolutionary party imbued, not with the spirit of blind revolt, but with a real consciousness of what the State must be made.'[22]

Cole saw no alternative to the acceptance in socialist thought of the predominance of the industrial wing of the Labour movement. Since 'Labour cannot hope within a measurable space of time to command a majority: it is condemned to perpetual opposition, and consequently has to rely on the weapon of organised protest',[23] that is to say, on industrial action. And ultimately, it had to be admitted, in his view, that 'The Labour Party, that sad failure of Socialism . . . cannot perform any functions in the industrial sphere.'[24] Here he reduced the role of political Labour from the negligible to the non-existent.

With such a shift in the perspectives and priorities of the Labour movement in mind, Cole moved in exactly the opposite direction to the Webbs in the period immediately prior to the outbreak of the First World War. Socialism in his view had 'taken a wrong turning'[25] in its reliance on political action in general and on the Labour Party in particular. His advocacy of a theory of industrial conflict was an attempt to modify the assumptions which underlay Labour thought and to provide a way out of the intellectual confusion of the pre-war period.

THE THEORY OF INDUSTRIAL CONFLICT

Marxist leanings

In his early political thought, Cole shared the orthodox Marxist view that the organization of the means of production, that is, the society's economic substructure, determined its political super-structure. Socialism was concerned primarily, in his view, with 'the complete transformation of the productive processes of the present economic system, and a complete transvaluation of all the factors that enter into wealth production'.[26] Similar Marxist views were expressed by Cole and Mellor in an article entitled 'The World for the Workers' in the *Daily Herald* of 30 June 1914, two days after the assassination of Archduke Franz Ferdinand in Sarajevo. The political crisis which grew out of this event was of little interest to Cole at this time. Political quarrels were merely the 'shadow' rather than the 'substance' of historical reality, in his opinion.[27] Political murder, and all other political acts for that matter, were unrelated at least directly to the economic basis of society and were, therefore, relatively unimportant. But on the other hand, if ever the structure of the capitalist organization of society were changed, Cole believed that the 'political super-structure' which 'always reflects the economic basis of society . . . will change automatically with it'.[28] Thus, in the pre-war period, Cole announced that he was 'More Concerned with the Government of Machinery than with the Machinery of Government'.[29] What really mattered in modern industrial society was economic power, or 'economic sovereignty', that is to say, the power to exploit or to resist exploitation, which were the only alternatives under capitalism.[30]

In his theory, political power is derived from and therefore 'cannot be transformed into economic power'.[31] Indeed, 'as long as the class-structure survives,' Cole argued, 'political organisa-tions, in so far as they have any reality at all, will inevitably reflect that structure'.[32] The only alternative, in Cole's view, was to reject the political approach to socialism and to accept the fact that 'economic methods are essential to the achievement of economic emancipation',[33] which was the only real freedom. The aphorism, 'Economic Power Precedes Political Power', which Cole adopted from the writers of the *New Age* circle like Orage and Penty, was meant to epitomize all these points.[34]

In addition to the primacy of economic power, Cole also accepted the Marxist model of social conflict under capitalism: the class struggle. In the class war, he found the dominant historical and social fact in which 'our industrial society finds its natural and inevitable expression'.[35] Cole offered no analysis of the genesis of capitalism, but he assumed nevertheless that 'the interests of Capital and Labour are diametrically opposed', and that there was consequently 'a real class war' in which the hostile forces were in 'ceaseless' conflict. The only way to escape from this unremitting strife was by 'the overthrow of capitalist society'. Liberation from capitalism was possible, in his view, only through the organized pressure of the working class through their trade unions. Thus, the class struggle was seen as a necessary but transient historical 'phase' rather than a permanent feature of industrial life. The object of the struggle was 'the overthrow of capitalism' and 'the substitution for [capitalism] of a society dominated throughout by the producers' point of view, which is the spirit of social service'.[36]

Third, Cole shared the orthodox Marxist view that the emancipation of the workers had to be their own act. But here he diverged from Marxist revolutionary theory in his assignment to the trade unions of the role of vanguard of the social revolution. Economic action meant trade-union action to Cole. He believed that the only way to alter the capitalist system of the relations of production, that is, the wage-system, was 'through a return to a belief in economic power and building up of Trade Unions'.[37] Whereas political reform meant change from above, economic action, it was argued, would inevitably reflect change from below, which was the only possible generative force of the class struggle.[38] In 1914 Cole noted, 'Economic action, and still more economic organisation, are the need of Labour today'.[39] A better statement of 'economism' is hard to find.

The theme of liberation through struggle illustrated yet another point of contact between Cole's thought and some versions of Marxism. In his pre-war writing, he accepted the view that social conflict was a product of class society rather than a function of all social organization. This belief led him to formulate a polarized social theory, so that capitalism, conflict, and social war were interchangeable terms of reference when he described contemporary society, whereas socialism, equilibrium and social peace were equally synonymous in his vision of post-capitalist society. Cole's early political theory offers two exclusive choices, based on two ways of looking at the world. And the only way to make the transition from capitalism to socialism, was by conflict in the class struggle.[40]

Cole's conflict theory of capitalism is easily seen in his use of countless military metaphors. The 'labour unrest' was thus an 'offensive' of the workers in the class war. The wave of strikes in the pre-war period merely brought to the surface the 'suppressed war' which was the 'normal condition of the world of industry'.[41] Since he accepted the fact that 'the capitalist position must be attacked on the industrial field', it followed easily that every strike or labour dispute had to be seen as one operation in the larger 'conflict between Labour and Capital'.[42] Again, 'in the daily battles of the Unions [are] the manifestations of the one great struggle of the workers to destroy exploitation.'[43] 'The Trade Unions must fight,' Cole argued 'in order that they may control; [for] it is in warring with capitalism that they will learn to do without it'.[44]

But conflict, in Cole's political theory, was not an end in itself. It was the medium of social change as well as the school in which the workers would learn to control their own lives. This vision of future tranquillity is what Cole saw as the basis of socialist belief. Belligerence and struggle were never solely destructive, in the terms of his conflict theory, but rather represented the painful return of men to the common humanity which had been twisted and distorted by capitalism. Cole wrote in early 1914:[45]

I believe that the democracy cannot, without utter destruction, abandon the doctrine of class antagonism; but I believe equally that this antagonism itself rests upon a deeper comradeship. Love and human brotherhood must, in the society of the present express themselves in warfare – not hatred.

And again, 'it is a poor theory of society that regards industrial warfare as permanent;' Cole insisted, because 'such warfare is presumably directed to the securing of justice and will cease when justice has been secured.'[46] Social conflict and socialism were mutually exclusive events, in Cole's pre-war political theory.

The state

Cole's theory of socialism emphasized the evolution through the class struggle of both the state and the trade unions, from instruments of conflict to institutions of stability and equilibrium. In the first case, he disagreed with the orthodox Marxists, who formulated the theory of the withering away of the state under socialism. Cole did not doubt that 'In the Society of to-day, the State is a coercive power, existing for the protection of private property, and merely reflecting in its subservience to Capitalism, the economic class-structure of the modern world.'[47] But he did reject the view that the present character of the state was unalterable. Here is where both the Webbian collectivists and Marxist revolutionaries went wrong. They accepted or rejected the principle of state action on the evidence of the seriously flawed contemporary model. The state was neither in his words the 'capitalist dodge'[48] of the Marxist theory nor the repository of most if not all progressive hopes of the moderate Fabian theory. In contrast, Cole's theory was more imaginative, expansive, and perhaps romantic, in foreseeing the evolution of the state's role, once again, from coercion to equilibrium, from the arbitrator or participant in social conflict to its 'proper' sphere as 'the expression of the nation as a real person, possessing a self and will of its own, and determining, by democratic methods, what manner of life it will lead'.[49] This personification of the state was another point in Cole's thought where the influence of Figgis and Rousseau may be seen.

But prior to the realization of this distant ideal situation, Cole postulated the role of the state as that agent which would ultimately resolve class conflict by expropriating the means of production, the private ownership of which was the prime cause, in his view, of injustice and social strife. Here he was closer to the Webbs' view that the state would itself initiate the equilibrium phase of its existence, and 'preside over the process of transition' to socialism.[50]

He also accepted their idea that the state under capitalism in theory represented the consumer, but he claimed that in practice, it did so 'imperfectly indeed', and 'only in the distorting-mirror of a powerful governing class'.[51] The capitalist state did not really reflect the interests of more than a handful of its citizens who had 'captured' the state for their own ends. Since all men were consumers, both Cole and the Webbs argued, the true reflection of their interests could come about only under socialism. To this end, the state had to be captured once more and this time turned into an instrument of radical social reconstruction.

But to influence political leaders or their policies was not Cole's idea of the way to capture the state, since the economic causes of unrest would remain untouched. For this reason Cole feared that the Webbs' collectivist state would run on a slightly modified principle of capitalist corporate selfishness, where the interest of the consumer still would take precedence over that of the producer. The Webbs' state would interfere in industrial affairs to gain efficient and cheap services, moderate prices, and to avoid the dislocation of industrial disputes, regardless of the grievances of the producers. Such an example of 'social peace' was, in Cole's estimation, only the equivalent of the preservation of the *status quo*. Although the Webbs favoured the fundamental change of the ownership of production, they left unmolested the capitalist structure of the relations of production, that is, the wage system itself.[52]

The Webbs' socialist state seemed to involve, in Cole's view, a more efficient 'business proposition' rather than an alteration of social relations.[53] The quality of the producers' life and work would not necessarily be improved, in that case. Here was the real problem in the Fabian position. 'The ordinary Socialist,' Cole noted with justification,[54]

> still expects the State merely to step into the employers' shoes, and run industry, much as the private capitalist has run it, for its own profit. Better wages will no doubt be paid and better conditions secured to the workers by the omnipotent and benevolent consumer-in-chief; but otherwise there will be no change. The worker will still be a 'cog in the machine'; the State will merely take the master's place as skilled machine-minder. . . . The State may not be, in M. Lagardelle's phrase, 'a tyrannical master'; but in the eyes of many advocates of nationalisation, it is certainly to be a 'master'; and a 'master', however benevolent, is not what the producer wants.

The real antagonism would continue if the state merely 'steps into the capitalists' shoes',[55] Cole continued, repeating the same metaphor. Thus Cole was very sceptical of the view that 'the mere extension of the State's sphere of action would bring all other blessings in its train'. Rather he feared that 'extension of the powers of the State may be merely a transference of authority from the capitalist to the bureaucrat'.[56]

But Cole did accept the Webbs' view that the only way that the producers could hope to gain control over industry was through municipalization and nationalization. And 'Expropriation is the State's business; and the development of the new forms of industrial control must be under State guidance and direction.'[57] It was perfectly understandable, Cole argued, that the workers' hostility was directed to the contemporary state, which had 'come to represent merely a "justice" which either holds its hands or miscarries'. But it was still 'the State that, in the end, will set [the workers] free'.[58]

Thus Cole favoured nationalization as the only method through which the state could begin to approach its rightful role, which he defined in these terms: 'to liberate and stimulate energy, to give the worker the fullest measure of control that he is capable of, in order that he may be got to desire more'. Then the state could turn to its more important task 'not merely to supply, but to stimulate the demand, for the "good life"'.[59]

State control would thereby politically and spiritually revitalize the working class, which would play a far more important part in the life of the nation than they had demanded or enjoyed previously under capitalism. The state would preside, in Cole's view, over the alteration of the relations of production, whereby the commodity theory of labour would be rejected. But the real change had to come from within, that is, in the attitude of the workers themselves.[60] Only then could the state shed its form as 'the centralised bureaucratic mechanism of today' to become in the future socialist society 'the alert and flexible instrument of the General Will'.[61]

The trade unions

The conflict-equilibrium model which underlay G. D. H. Cole's socialist thought is best illustrated in his theory of trade unionism. Under capitalism the function of producers' organizations was active warfare, in his view. With the advent of socialism, the unions would turn from their necessarily destructive behaviour to become the productive agent of a free society. They would then share power on equal terms with a state purged of its capitalist and coercive character. Unions were thus both military units which prepared men for their future peace-time work and the agents of that participatory democracy at which Cole's plans were aimed.[62]

Cole asserted in the pre-war period that the trade unions existed 'to carry on the class-struggle'. Indeed, 'it is their first business to attack and overthrow Capitalism'.[63] The unions could not avoid their role as the vanguard of social conflict; if they did, socialism would be unattainable. Only[64]

> By the force exercised by the Unions, by the development of working-class intelligence and pugnacity, and not by the charity or benevolence of a dominant bureaucracy will the Industrial Commonwealth be brought about. The emancipation of the workers must be their own act; in the State of the future they will reap the benefits of their class consciousness far more securely than if the Control of Industry were conceded them without a hard and bitter struggle.

The state which presented workers their freedom as a gift or out of guilt for past injustice, would retain by that act, Cole believed, supremacy over those it liberated. Freedom had to be earned in order to be lasting, and in his view, the unions would evolve through this 'war of liberation' into the organs of a stable society:[65]

> From fighting bodies, organised against capitalism, they [the Unions] must develop into controlling bodies, capable of carrying on production. All the same, they must not, during the period of transition, lose their fighting strength, or there will be no transition at all.

Thus Cole opposed the growth of trade unionism through legislative enactment or any contact, other than an adversary one, with the contemporary state. 'Bodies created artificially by the State,' he argued, 'would be so much material in its hands, to mould as it might think fitting.'[66] It was time, in Cole's view, for the producers to do the moulding of social institutions, through their own efforts:[67]

> The control secured by the Trade Union (or Guild) as against the Collectivity (or State) will be determined largely by its power. I believe that the State will find it more effective to concede regular control of industrial processes to the Unions;

the Unions will have to protect themselves against isolated or recurrent acts of aggression on the part of the State by the exercise of their corporate bargaining power.

This process was unavoidable. The unions were locked in a struggle with capitalism, from which neither side could disengage. It would depend on the strength of the unions, he warned, whether 'Labour will expropriate or itself be spoliated'.[68] There was no middle ground. At times, he lapsed into an optimistic determinism about the outcome of the struggle, which is also reflected in the *Communist Manifesto*. Cole traced back the conflict to the repeal of the Combination Acts, the consequences of which were irreversible:[69]

The State had conceded the right to combine, and when that is granted, in the end everything follows. The workers have 'nothing to lose but their chains, and a world to win'; and, finally, they cannot help winning it.

As has been noted above, Cole believed that shifts in ideas were caused by shifts in social structure, and this case was no exception. The assertion of the workers' viewpoint in political theory, and especially in Cole's contribution to it, followed from the vastly increased social and economic power of the trade unions, which was shown in the 'labour unrest'.[70]

But he did not completely idealize trade-union altruism. Just as 'Collectivism which is not supported by strong Trade Unions will be merely state bureaucracy on a colossal scale,' so Cole believed that 'Trade Unions not confronted by a strong and purified State will relapse into group anarchism and collective profiteering.'[71] Here is his key objection to French syndicalism and its British counterparts. Their 'new "Droit Ouvrier",' he argued, '. . . is the right of Nietzsche's superman in a new form',[72] and equally pernicious. Functional differentiation, devolution, and balance, rather than domination by force, were the major aspects of Cole's pre-war social theory. He was completely in favour of self-governing unions in control of industry, as long as they did not 'menace' the state in its external affairs.[73] The unions and the State each had to keep the other's power to check. Imbalance led to the two alternatives which he rejected: Collectivism, or when the state was more powerful than the workers' organizations, and Syndicalism, which was the opposite case. Neither situation, Cole argued, would solve the problem of authoritarianism and sub-servience in social affairs. Therefore he aimed at a mixture of both theories which would avoid the pitfalls of each.

Here we see the implications of Cole's pluralism. In the capitalist or conflict phase, he supported the development of self-governing 'lesser social democracies within the State' which would grow in power and authority as they gained a greater role in the deter-mination of industrial and social policy.[74] But as time passed, and the class struggle was superseded during the transition to socialism, these lesser institutions (the unions or guilds) eventually would achieve the same status and power as the state itself. It was true, Cole noted, that in the future 'the force of the State' would still be 'needed to balance contending interests among producers as well as the representatives of the non-producing part of the community'. And he did grant that some strife would occur. For their own protection:[75]

> The Union must preserve the right and the economic resource to withdraw its labour; the State must rely to check unjust demands, on the organised opinion of the community as a whole. As a last resort, disputes must be settled by conflict, but it is hard to imagine that in a democratic society, such a method would often be necessary.

Then without the need for constant coercion of its members, the state would be, ideally, an association of men like any other in society. This view was the prime tenet of pluralism.

It is clear that the demystification of the state was one of Cole's major aims in attributing 'a wholly new importance to Trade Unions' in British socialist thought. It appeared logical enough that a disarmed, pacified, and purified state would be more prone to accept other associations as its equal. This prospect was very attractive to Cole. It justified a change in the socialist approach to both the state and the unions. In this light, the unions were no longer 'a passing phase due to the abuses of Capitalism,' but rather 'corporations which are destined not to extinction, but to a con-tinual growth and extension of capacity'.[76]

This radical change in the function and nature of trade unions was the key to the development of Cole's society of equilibrium and balance. On their growth depended the fate of socialism. With the overthrow of capitalism, which need not be 'violent and catastrophic', the unions would be regarded 'no longer as a mere fighting organisation, existing only because the employer is there to combat, but as a self-governing independent corporation, with [productive] functions of its own, the successor of Capitalism as well as its destroyer'.[77] In the conflict phase, what was required was 'the conscription of workers for the class-war'. But in the equilibrium phase of social relations, Cole foresaw 'the enrolment of the workers in the industrial army which exists fundamentally not to foment revolution, but to produce wealth'.[78]

CONCLUSIONS

Cole was aware of the utopian nature of his thought. Nevertheless he believed that until the present 'industrial system lies in ruins, it is hopeless to think of detailed methods of reconstruction'.[79] What was needed was a new social vision, a marriage of what was best in Collectivism, Syndicalism, and Marxism, adjusted to British conditions. This new theory would replace the outdated and exhausted inspiration of Fabian thought which, although 'too fruitful to be allowed to die', was at the same time 'too narrow to be the whole truth'. Similarly he saw in syndicalism 'the germ of the political philosophy of the future'. Yet in its contemporary embryonic form, it was 'too narrow a base' for a complete socialist theory.[80] Its three major limitations – that it took the producer as the sole socially significant factor (which was as much of a distortion as the Collectivists' concentration on the consumer), that it regarded 'society as a federation of loosely connected trades', and its denial of the state – required its rejection as 'a theory of politics'.[81] Third, while he recognized that 'Marx has left us in his heritage much that is valuable and great', Cole saw the dangers in the infectious 'economic fatalism' of his thought. In Cole's view, government of the future socialist state ought not to be in the hands of the dictatorship of the proletariat.[82] Above all, Cole was determined to avoid the mere substitution of one type of authoritarianism by another.

So G. D. H. Cole was left, at the outbreak of the First World War, with a position composed of fragments of the European socialist tradition. In his later work he attempted to fuse these components together into a new and comprehensive socialist philosophy. His theory of social change was, at this time, the fundamentally Marxist one of the supercession of capitalism through class conflict, which held the promise at its end of a stable and peaceful society. 'Social peace is an ideal,' he admitted, 'as Socialism is an ideal; and the two will come together, if they come at all'.[83] In this aphorism, is the key to Cole's pre-war socialist political thought.

NOTES

1 Mrs Margaret Cole kindly offered her comments and criticisms of many points raised in this chapter. Cf. her biography, *The Life of G. D. H. Cole*, 1971.
2 V. I. Lenin, *What Is To Be Done?*, trans. by S. V. and P. Utechin, Oxford, 1963, ch. 3.
3 G. D. H. Cole, *William Morris as a Socialist*, 1960.
4 G. D. H. Cole, 'Oxford socialism from within', *Socialist Review*, 6, 34, December 1910, p. 284.
5 Nuffield College, Oxford, Cole Papers, Box 7, Folder 84. Paper entitled 'The New Romantic Movement', pp. 2–3.
6 *Ibid.*, p. 3; G. D. H. Cole, *The World of Labour*, 1913, p. 5.
7 Cole, *The World of Labour*, p. 19.
8 G. D. H. Cole, 'Loyalties', in *Studies in World Economics*, 1934, p. 271. On Wallas, cf. M. Wiener, *Between Two Worlds*, Oxford, 1971.
9 Cf. J. N. Figgis, *Churches in the Modern State*, 1913, p. 8. 'The real problem is the relation of smaller communities to that "*Communitas communitatum*" we call the State, and whether they have an existence of their own or are the mere creatures of the sovereign.' On Figgis, cf. D. G. Nicholls, 'Authority in Church and State', Cambridge Ph.D. dissertation, 1962.
10 J. J. Rousseau, *The Social Contract and Discourses*, trans. G. D. H. Cole, 1913; and Cole, *Studies in World Economics*, 1934, p. 270.
11 Cf. C. Pateman, *Participation and Democratic Theory*, Cambridge, 1970, pp. 35–44.
12 Cole Papers, 'The New Romantic Movement', p. 6.
13 Cole, *The World of Labour*, p. 1.
14 Cole Papers, Box 8, Sequence A, 'The Principles of Socialism'.
15 M. B. Reckitt, *As It Happened*, 1941, pp. 121–6.
16 See above, p. 57. Mellor undoubtedly followed Cole's intellectual lead, and although some of the phrasing of their joint articles may have been Mellor's, the ideas were certainly Cole's. On Mellor, cf. the personal note and evaluation by Beatrice Webb in her unpublished diaries, vol. 32, f. 50.
17 G. D. H. Cole, 'Fabian excursions', *Daily Herald*, 10 December 1913.
18 Passfield Papers, Beatrice Webb's unpublished diaries, vol. 32, 31 July 1914.
19 Cole, *The World of Labour*, p. 15.
20 *Ibid.*, pp. 395–9. Cf. also Cole's report for the Fabian Committee on the Control of Industry, entitled, 'Syndicalism: What validity does our inquiry show it to possess? Its influence on English Trade Unionism and the Labour Party.' Cole's reports as chairman of the sub-

committee on 'Associations of Wage Earners' may be found in the British Library of Political and Economic Science.

21 Cole, *The World of Labour*, pp. 398–9, 394.
22 *Ibid.*, p. 422.
23 *Ibid.*, p. 401.
24 *Ibid.*, pp. 242–3.
25 Cole Papers, Box 7, Folder 81, 'Notes', 2 May 1912.
26 *Ibid.*
27 Cole Papers, 'Notes', 27 June 1912.
28 G. D. H. Cole and William Mellor, 'The world for the workers: guild socialism and syndicalism', *Daily Herald*, 30 June 1914.
29 Cole and Mellor, 'The bondage of iron', *Daily Herald*, 12 May 1914.
30 Cole Papers, 'Notes', 13 June 1912; *The World of Labour*, pp. 16, 44, 286, 393.
31 Cole Papers, 'Notes', 13 June 1912.
32 Cole, *The World of Labour*, p. 394.
33 Cole Papers, 'Notes', 27 June 1912.
34 *Ibid.*, 9 May and 13 June 1912; Cf. also a typed draft of a paper on Labour policy in Cole's pre-war files, hereafter referred to as 'Economic Power'. On the New Age Circle, cf. P. Selver, *Orage and the New Age Circle*, 1959. On the use of 'EPPPP' see A. J. Penty, 'Collectivist Ghosts', *Daily Herald*, 18 March 1914. Cole himself admitted in a letter to the *New Statesman*, printed on 10 January 1914 that 'the New Age proposals have all along been a very real inspiration'. He did add that he differed in part from the guild socialism of the *New Age*, but he did not elaborate the points of contention. In 'The wage system and the way out', *Daily Herald*, 26 May 1914, Cole and Mellor repeated their faith in 'EPPPP' and called the *New Age* writings 'the starting-point of all constructive political thought in the world of Labour'. The work of S. G. Hobson was of particular interest to them.
35 G. D. H. Cole, 'The free state of the future, II', *Labour Leader*, 26 March 1914.
36 Cole, *The World of Labour*, pp. 288, 392.
37 'Economic Power', p. 1.
38 Cole and Mellor, *The Greater Unionism*, Manchester, 1913, p. 19.
39 Cole and Mellor, 'The wage system and the way out II: guild socialism or social bureaucracy', *Daily Herald*, 28 May 1914.
40 My construction of Cole's political theory has been strongly influenced by the work of Ralf Dahrendorf, especially his *Class and Class Conflict in Industrial Society*, 1964.
41 Cole, *The World of Labour*, pp. 286, 289, 329–30.
42 Cole Papers, 'Notes', 22 August 1912; Cole's letter to the *New Statesman*, printed on 20 December 1913.
43 Cole and Mellor, 'The need for Greater Unionism. Lessons of the fight at Chipping Norton', *Daily Herald*, 24 February 1914.
44 Cole, *The World of Labour*, p. 392.
45 Cole's letter to the *New Statesman*, printed on 31 January 1914.
46 Cole, *The World of Labour*, p. 392.
47 Cole, 'The free state of the future, II', *Labour Leader*, 26 March 1914;

G. D. H. Cole and W. Mellor, 'The class war and the state', *Daily Herald*, 3 March 1914: 'the whole attitude of the State is essentially capitalistic.'

48 Cole, *The World of Labour*, p. 389.

49 Cole, 'The free state of the future II', *Labour Leader*, 26 March 1914. He added: 'The proper sphere of the State is the expression of the common needs, strivings, aspirations, which stand in a democratic Society for national solidarity in face of external societies and of particular associations within itself. It represents the general will of the community, those interests which all the members have in common, whatever interests they may have through their special function in Society.'

50 Cole, *The World of Labour*, p. 400.

51 *Ibid.*, pp. 389-90.

52 *Ibid.*, p. 416.

53 *Ibid.*, pp. 346-7.

54 *Ibid.*, pp. 378-9.

55 Cole Papers, 'Notes', 2 May 1912.

56 Cole, *The World of Labour*, pp. 347-8; 381-2; 305.

57 *Ibid.*, pp. 391; 381-2.

58 *Ibid.*, pp. 25, 392.

59 *Ibid.*, pp. 381-2.

60 Cole Papers, Box 7, Folder 84, Paper entitled 'Means and Ends', in Cole's hand, dated April 1912.

61 Cole, *The World of Labour*, p. 421.

62 Pateman, *Participation and Democratic Theory*, ch. 2.

63 *Ibid.*, p. 370; Cole and Mellor, 'Industrial unionism and the guild system', *New Age*, 25 June 1914.

64 Cole and Mellor, 'The class war and the state', *Daily Herald*, 3 March 1914.

65 Cole and Mellor, 'The wage system and the way out', *Daily Herald*, 26 May 1914.

66 Cole, *The World of Labour*, pp. 373, 385-6; G. D. H. Cole and W. Mellor, 'Miners and the rights of minorities', *Daily Herald*, 24 March 1914: 'As their forces grow, they [the Unions] will learn to rely more on themselves, and less on acts of Parliament; they will legislate on their own behalf, dictating to the owners up to the highest limits of their economic power.'

67 Cole's letter to the *New Statesman*, printed on 10 January 1914.

68 Cole, *The World of Labour*, p. 16.

69 *Ibid.*, p. 20.

70 *Ibid.*

71 Cole, 'The free state of the future II,' *Labour Leader*, 26 March 1914.

72 Cole Papers, Box 7, Folder 84, 'The New Romantic Movement'.

73 Cole Papers, Box 7, Folder 84, 'Means and Ends'.

74 Cole Papers, Box 7, Folder 84, 'Means and Ends'.

75 Cole, 'The free state of the future II', *Labour Leader*, 26 March 1914.

76 Cole, *The World of Labour*, pp. 368-9.

77 *Ibid.*, pp. 39, 369.

78 Cole and Mellor, *The Greater Unionism*, p. 20; Cole, *The World of Labour*, p. 392.
79 Cole and Mellor, 'Industrial unionism and the guild system', *New Age*, 25 June 1914.
80 Cole, *The World of Labour*, pp. 3–4, 54, 22.
81 *Ibid.*, pp. 25, 126, 367, 391; Cole Papers, Box 7, Folder 84, 'Means and Ends'; Cole, 'Syndicalism: What Validity does our inquiry show it to possess?'
82 Cole Papers, Box 7, Folder 84, 'Means and Ends'. Whether Cole completely avoided this economic fatalism is another question entirely. In addition Cole was *not* an internationalist. Cf. *The World of Labour*, p. 185.
83 Cole, *The World of Labour*, p. 318.

Plate 9 'POSTER APPEAL TO PROFITEERS* [If Mr. Asquith will not use force with the food and other profiteers, why does he not APPEAL to their patriotism? This is done with the working classes, whose native patriotism is not so much in need of goods as that of the profiteers. We suggest another wide Poster Campaign on the part of the War Office—directed to awakening the decency of the War Hogs, and offer the above suggested poster as our contribution to the idea.]'

Herald, 20 February 1915

Plate *10* 'THE AIM OF THE CONSCRIPTIONISTS—*Jeames Morning Post:* "A Lawful Monster, young lady. A most Insupportable Monster, but there is a danger it may be killed before us Hinglish have got a like one of our own to put in its place." '

Herald, 14 November 1914

II

THE IMPACT OF THE FIRST WORLD WAR

One thing is certain. It is a foolish delusion to believe that we need only live through the war, as a rabbit hides under the bush to await the end of a thunderstorm, to trot merrily off in his old accustomed gait when all is over. The world war has changed the conditions of our struggle, and has changed *us* most of all.

Rosa Luxemburg
The Junius Pamphlet, 1915

5

G. D. H. Cole, Guild Socialism and the First World War

G. D. H. Cole's theory of industrial conflict broke down under the stress of the First World War. At first, he tried to maintain his belief in the primacy of class struggle despite the war. But by 1917, he was forced to reconstruct a theory of action and social change which was far more moderate and reformist than his earlier views would have allowed.

The militant

The outbreak of war did not alter Cole's view that all social problems under capitalism were reflections primarily of class, rather than political or moral, conflict. He saw the war as additional evidence of the breakdown of capitalism in Europe, but he was not prepared to try to seize the opportunity to challenge the social order which had spawned the conflict.[1] Rather, he attempted at the outset to re-assert the class analysis of British society and to urge the preservation of as much as possible of the gains made by the working class in the pre-war years.

The workers did not bring about the war, Cole asserted, but nevertheless they would have to live with the terrible consequences of it. Everyone expected widespread distress in the first months of the conflict, and Cole looked not to the state, but to working-class institutions to provide for their own. He urged co-operators to develop during the war a new sense of their proper function which was, in his view, to help 'their class to become class-conscious and imbued with the spirit of the class-war'.[2] By highlighting the need for mutual defence, Cole and William Mellor pointed out in August 1914, the war had provided 'the opportunity to bring home to the workers the great lesson of solidarity in face of the capitalist system'.[3]

The fact that that lesson had yet to be learned was evident in the overwhelming support for the war effort among the working class. The only explanation to Cole was that nothing had really changed and that the primary industrial struggle had merely been postponed for a time. From this viewpoint then, the workers were holding their breath, as it were, until that day when they would begin to function normally again as the antagonists of the same men they now had joined in arms. Cole called on the Labour movement in August 1914, in terms he agreed to use throughout the first years of the war, 'to show that, even in the midst of a great European conflagration, it still recognises that some day it will again be called upon to wage its war – the only war that really matters – against wage-slavery'.[4] Two years later, his stated position was very similar. 'It is no use,' he and Mellor argued, 'comforting oneself with the reflection that once Germany is beaten all will be well. Underneath the surface the class war still goes on.'[5] And in terms of the essentials of class struggle, 'The war has made no moral difference'.[6]

The need of Cole and his associates to deny the importance if not the very existence of the European war is clear throughout their early war writing. One salient example is the language in which Cole and Mellor advised the engineers in September 1914 to concentrate on the broad questions of the organization of industry rather than on narrow wage issues. They insisted that it was above all the workers' 'first business to attack and overthrow Capitalism, and that, till our industrial system lies in ruins, it is hopeless to think of detailed methods of reconstruction'.[7] It would seem that nothing had changed since they had used the same words in an article in the *New Age* in June 1914.[8]

Cole repeatedly insisted during the first years of the war that it was 'absurd to suppose that the class-struggle can be altogether eclipsed by any national crisis'.[9] On the contrary, he wished that the class struggle would somehow succeed in eclipsing the war itself, so that the workers would be able to rediscover their true interests and to resume their historical role as the 'aggressor' in the war with capitalism.[10] In the meantime he hoped that the two conflicts would be waged simultaneously, and without prejudice to the belligerent status and power of Labour.[11]

But unfortunately, such was not the case. In the first year of the war, Cole reflected, 'Surely at all costs the forces of Labour should have preserved their identity'.[12] Instead, they had joined the recruiting campaign, submitted to the Treasury Agreement of March 1915 proscribing strikes and 'relaxing' trade practices in industries supplying war goods, accepted state control without demanding management responsibility for the workers, and even had entered the Coalition Government. From Cole's point of view, the year was a time of unmitigated disaster. 'The first phase of the class-struggle under war conditions,' he noted sadly in 1915, 'ended in the rout of the Labour forces.'[13]

Still, Cole did not abandon hope for the future. He continued to point out that the war had solved none of the old problems, but instead had added a new dimension to industrial strife. Thus he remarked in April 1915:[14]

If it is true, as our statesmen do not weary of telling us, that the European war will be lost and won in the engineering shops, it is no less true that there Labour also is fighting its battles. . . . It is indeed not too much to say that during the last few months the engineers have been sustaining the double burden of war and class war.

With a proper perspective, Cole argued, Labour could fight both wars and still maintain enough strength to face the renewal of normal industrial conflict which was bound to come after the armistice.[15]

Cole's initial position was that Labour in wartime had to have a dual commitment and a dual outlook. He hoped that the unpleasant tasks of war would be carried out by the workers with little enthusiasm, maximum suspicion, and complete hostility. Since he knew that the workers were unprepared to deny the tools of war to their fellow-citizens in uniform, he urged that Labour should occupy the borderline of protest. In time, perhaps the 'pent-up discontent' of service to 'the double tyranny of masters and Government' would 'burst forth',[16] to what end he never specified. But until then, Cole's initial advice to Labour was to develop tactical schizophrenia: support the war effort reluctantly with your muscles and yet at the same time oppose with your minds the class who ran the war and whose interests it really served. Compliance, but not respect; assistance, but not subservience: these were the proper attitudes of Labour in wartime, Cole insisted in the first years of the war.

The moderate

Cole tried hard to retain the coherence of his class theory under the enormous difficulties of war, but by 1917, his position began to fall apart. First, Cole revised his views on the appropriate tactics of class war. In late 1917 he published a book, *Self-Government in Industry*, as a belated sequel to his pre-war *World of Labour*.[17] In this new study he contradicted the position cited above which he and William Mellor twice had advocated in print in 1914 both before and after the outbreak of war. Now he repudiated the view of those who 'feel that it is their first business to attack and overthrow Capitalism, and that, till our industrial system lies in ruins, it is hopeless to think of detailed methods of reconstruction'. Three years after he had co-authored these very words, Cole concluded, 'This is certainly a short-sighted view'.[18]

His break with Mellor coincided with the latter's fight against induction into the British Army. Cole had received an exemption from military service from the Oxford Tribunal as a trade union official attached to the Amalgamated Society of Engineers (ASE). Beatrice Webb speculated that the Oxford authorities were reluctant to embarrass a Fellow of Magdalen College and indirectly the University itself.[19] Mellor had no such support. His appeals were denied, and both he and Page Arnot were in gaol at various times in 1916 and 1917. On one such occasion, just before his arrest, Mellor wrote to Cole to ask him to take over the joint articles they had written for the *Herald*. 'Despite certain rather acute differences of opinion between us, I make this request.'[20]

These differences were publicly aired early in 1917. Cautiousness and preparation rather than boldness and attack were the lessons which Cole appears to have learned after three years of the First World War. This shift caused a serious split in the ranks of the guild socialists, who in 1915 had formed the National Guilds League (NGL) to propagate their views.[21] At the 1917 annual conference of this body, Cole moved that

> all schemes of industrial reconstruction, from whatever source they come, should be considered on their merits and action taken according as they further or retard the development of industrial self-government by the organised workers in the interests of all.

Mellor and others objected to the phrase 'on their merits' as reformist rather than revolutionary, and the offending words were struck from the resolution.[22] Cole saw no difficulty in his position. While still opposing measures which would make the existing order more 'tolerable', he characterized the views he claimed to share with other guildsmen in these terms:[23]

> We are, if you will, 'revolutionary' in purpose, and for the time being, 'reformist' in tactics. We are out for 'la victoire intégrale' and nothing less; but at the moment we are conducting a war of attrition and of preparation. The Big Push will come in its due time; but there is much work to be done before it can go hopefully forward.

Apparently, the experience of men like Mellor and Page Arnot as war resisters had made them more sensitive to matters of principle than their more fortunate colleagues like Cole.[24]

Cole's adoption of the classical revisionist position in tactics paralleled the striking reversal late in the war of his views on the pervasiveness of class conflict. He was prepared in 1918 to compartmentalize social affairs in a way which not only undercut much of his previous class theory, but also allowed for a new and sympathetic interpretation of the behaviour of the same men whom he had denounced in 1914 for renouncing class war and defending their country, or in Cole's phrase, 'the Commonwealth'. Thus Cole had discovered a national identity which superseded that of class, and may have thereby revealed latent patriotism which was difficult to express earlier in the war. If one granted his new premise that 'although the class-struggle tends to dominate social groupings in modern industrial Commonwealths, it dominates at most only the organized part of the lives of men', it was clearly only a short logical step to the following position. 'In times of crisis,' Cole now presumed[25]

> it is not to the State in the sense of the machinery of government that men offer their support, it is to the Commonwealth that underlies all forms of government and of voluntary association. The unorganised part of men's lives, which is still by far the greatest part, is compact of sentiments, customs and traditions; and these customs, sentiments and traditions attach themselves intimately to the person of the Commonwealth.

Since collective representation really existed outside the world of class, Cole could now explain why an exclusively class theory of social action was inadequate to deal with war: 'The class-struggle is suspended, or largely suspended, in times of external strife, not because the State is greater than the Trade Unions, but because the individuals in such times transcend the groups through which they ordinarily act.'[26] Cole's implicit admission in this statement of the inability of his own class analysis to deal with the problem of war is turned into the highly disputable claim that no class theory could explain it.

The implications of Cole's decision to consider political proposals 'on their merits' now becomes clear. Granted that there were legitimate and competing sources of social obligation other than class, there were also principles of action other than class struggle by which one had to evaluate all political issues. With this modification, Cole's class theory of social change, while retaining all the military metaphors and much of the language of industrial conflict, becomes completely ambiguous. For instance, Cole reprinted in *Self-Government in Industry* an article which appeared in the *New Age* of 26 November 1914, in which he asserted:[27]

If Capitalism is to be overthrown, the workers must not only be animated by a common spirit of class-consciousness; they must present a solid front. They must organise again *la grande armée* of the Revolution, and, whatever sub-divisions it may contain, it must be one army, marching under the impulse of a common idea, against the common enemy.

But what this army was to do when it was finally prepared for its fateful encounter with capitalism did not easily emerge from Cole's argument. He stated elsewhere in the same book that the control of production and exchange must be 'wrested'[28] from the capitalists. But by the end of the war the mechanism of such a fundamental social transformation had to take into account the protection of other valuable elements in society which were granted by Cole an existence independent of class.

Cole's emphasis of the constructive tasks of socialism provided a partial answer to these difficulties in his theoretical position which the war exposed. Function rather than dysfunction was given a new priority in his social theory towards the end of the war. The important task was to make the capitalist socially functionless, by developing the capacity of workers' organizations to manage industrial affairs in the interests of the entire community.[29] But now overt and destructive class conflict was not at all in Cole's view the only or indeed the necessary means whereby this displacement of social roles had to occur. Social change by organic functional growth or 'encroaching control'[30] was Cole's main prescription by the end of the war. To this end some co-operation with the capitalists would be necessary, but this drawback hardly outweighed the fact that moderation on both sides would protect the Commonwealth from the unavoidable and ugly scars of an open and violent class war.

THE STATE IN THEORY: PLURALISM AND PACIFISM

Cole remarked in September 1915, that 'Every attempt to answer the question: "What is the fundamental principle of social obligation?" is coloured by the circumstances of the time in which it was made.'[31] His own political theory was no exception. As a reaction to the First World War, the pluralist aspects of his thought, elements of which certainly antedate the war, became explicit and central after 1914. At the very time that the power and authority of the British state had reached unparalleled heights, Cole emphatically rejected the concept of state sovereignty as incompatible with the 'republic of obligations'[32] which he proposed as the philosophical basis of guild socialism. In addition, the theory of pluralism and group personality, which he derived from J. N. Figgis among others, provided Cole with a theoretical basis for the gradual modification in his class analysis which was noted above.

The war undoubtedly had accelerated the movement towards unbridled state power to which Cole had objected before 1914. The direction of events was all the more reason, Cole believed, why the theoretical basis of state sovereignty had to be exposed, examined, and refuted. In early 1915, Cole admitted that he had 'lost the illusion of an inevitable democratic political progress', but precisely because of this new-found pessimism, he speculated that 'we may reasonably hope to reach', at least in theory, 'a more inclusive conception of social action, and a better idea of the relation of particular associations to the State'.[33]

The mere existence of such associations which had arisen independently of the state was sufficient proof to Cole, in a 1915 paper on 'Conflicting Social Obligations', 'that the State cannot

127

fully express the associative will of man'. And since 'these associations are the work of human volition', they had to be credited 'with all the attributes of collective personality' which were granted to the state. Once that was done, he asked rhetorically, 'what superior claim has the State to the allegiance of the individual as against some particular association to which he belonged?'[34] Clearly no inherent claim at all. It was not his view 'that associative acts are wholly social', but rather 'that State acts are not'. 'The State,' Cole contended, 'even if it includes everybody, is still only an association among others, because it cannot include the whole of everybody.'[35]

He accepted that the state, as the 'geographical grouping', had the right to final authority over these problems where the interests of men are determined solely by where they live.[36] But he refused to admit its jurisdiction over other 'spheres of action' such as religion or industrial affairs which, he claimed, affected men unequally or in different ways. It was also true, he added that 'In so far as any privileged order retains governmental rights or functions', this inequality of treatment was bound to occur. At such times, it could hardly be argued that the state was 'purely geographical in its basis'.[37]

But even in an ideal situation, he argued: 'Not only cannot an electorate gathered together on a geographical basis alone be fitted to deal with special questions which do not affect them all, or all alike, but also the persons whom they elect cannot possess this fitness.'[38] The only possible step which followed from this view was 'the withdrawal, therefore, of some class of action from the sphere of the State', an adjustment which was 'simply a denial,' he claimed, 'that the State is the right mechanism for the execution of certain types of social purpose'.[39] The governmental body that was left would become merely 'an association among others . . . at the most *primus inter pares*',[40] 'elder brother, if you will, but certainly in no sense father of the rest'.[41] Each member of the social family would then perform the tasks most appropriate to it. Functional devolution was the key phrase in the development of Cole's war-time theory of the state.

Cole admitted in 1916 at the height of the conscription controversy that 'The denial that the State is an end in itself', which underlay his rejection of its absolute sovereignty, 'carries with it great consequences.'[42] Not the least was a theoretical justification for pacifism. He held that the recognition that[43] no State can use, in its external any more than its internal relations, the whole organisable force of its citizens without regard to other loyalties that have a claim upon them . . . sets men free to assign limits to the duties which they owe to their State, and to follow the path of those duties which they owe to other associations or to their own consciences.

Furthermore, 'the citizen's obligation to serve the State is dependent,' he asserted, 'upon the extent to which the State fulfils the will of the citizens', that is, the extent to which it is democratic in all social affairs.[44] And the fact that 'States are, in their external relations, even less democratic than in their internal administration' seemed to Cole 'to lessen the obligation which they impose'.[45]

Even in wartime, therefore, loyalty to one's state was a far more complex question than most patriots would have recognized. But while he admitted that 'war furnishes the most obvious illustration of the difficulty' of conflicting obligations, the resolution of this problem was left ambiguous in his argument. 'Even if the State has not the right to compel a man to perform a particular act which conflicts with some other obligation,' he claimed:[46]

it may still have the right to demand of him some equivalent service to which no such objection can be raised. The right of the democratic State is limited, not as to the amount of service which it can require, but as to the kind of service.

Cole never specified how one tested whether an objection to acts of state coercion, such as conscription, was really based on conflicting loyalties. Only the denial of any social obligation was clearly rejected here, and few pacifists ever took that position.

It is apparent, therefore, why guild socialism took on added appeal among dissenters during the First World War. Cole's theoretical defiance of the state was taken to be part of the same struggle which pacifists like Bertrand Russell and Clifford Allen waged in practice. Both Russell and Allen were drawn to guild theory because it made the problem of state power central to socialist thought. Their adoption of guild socialism by 1918 was part of a wider movement of opinion during the war which brought many very different men to the position which Cole and others had developed.

In an unpublished manuscript which Allen wrote in 1919 about his war experiences, he commented: 'I would wish that this book might develop the close association between the ideas that led to

resistance to Conscription, and those that inspire wider movements towards industrial and civil liberty.'[47] Earlier, at a meeting
of the City of London Branch of the ILP, of which Cole was also
a member, Allen had moved the following resolution for submission to the Party's Regional Conference:[48]

> That this Conference having regard to the hazardous experi-
> ments in the national direction and bureaucratic control of
> industry since the beginning of the war, and seeing that the
> Treasury Conference between Trade Unions and the Govern-
> ment preceding the Munitions Act marked the beginning of
> a new era of State recognition of Trade Unionism, hereby
> declares that no scheme of nationalisation will be deemed
> satisfactory which does not provide democratic control by the
> workers in the industry affected, and affirms the belief that the
> Socialist Society of the future can only be founded on the
> principle of joint control of industry by Trade Unions and
> the State.

Russell, like Allen, was imprisoned during the war, and just before
one such occasion, the former in April 1918 finished a book on
Roads to Freedom, in which he advocated guild socialism, modified
by a touch of anarchism.[49] But in another wartime study, *Political
Ideals*, written in 1917, no such qualification was made. Freedom
in their working lives for the population, he argued, 'can be
secured by guild socialism, by industrial self-government subject
to state control as regards the relations of a trade to the rest of the
community. So far as I know, they cannot be secured in any other
way.'[50] Even Ramsay MacDonald had come to see that by 1917.[51]

> The war has given a new significance to some of the later
> movements within Trade Unionism and Socialism, especially
> to that known as the Guild movement . . . no doubt should
> be left regarding the fact that the guild must play a character-
> istic part in the Socialist industrial State. It is required to
> guard against the deadly evil of over-centralisation in a political
> servile state, of a community the material comforts of which
> will stifle spiritual spontaneity, of a working class deprived of
> the stimulus of freedom by legal arrangements of a mechanical
> nature.

This statement was inconceivable before the war, when for
instance, MacDonald had supported the National Insurance Act

and had argued in its favour on the collectivist side in a debate with Hilaire Belloc on 'Socialism and the Servile State'.[52] After three years of war, the state was seen to be a very different and far more dangerous creature by even a moderate socialist like Mac-Donald.

During the war, though, Cole was careful to avoid too close an identification of pacifism and guild socialism, so that the growing strength of guild ideas among trade unionists would not be endangered by a patriotic backlash. Although Cole had joined the No Conscription Fellowship and the City of London ILP, a centre for pacifists like Allen, and although he had urged the ILP in January 1916 to be 'quite open' about its pacifist position,[53] he still felt that it was essential to keep guild propaganda and war resistance apart, if not in theory, at least in practice.

There was some basis for his concern. A series of four lectures on national guilds to be delivered at Central Hall, Westminster, in late 1917, was cancelled at the last moment because, Cole said, the management 'had received letters threatening to break up the meetings if held'.[54] Cole's complaint to Arthur Henderson on this matter is most revealing. The fact that the lectures had been prevented because men like W. H. Massingham, editor of *Nation*, George Lansbury, and Cole himself were associated with them, 'raises', he pointed out, 'an important question of principle'.[55]

> The National Guilds League has no attitude to the war, being a purely economic body with no views on war and peace. I personally have kept out of all war propaganda, and have made no public pronouncement on the war except a public protest with Massingham and others against the violation of Belgium in 1914. The lectures had not the remotest connection with the war, and the speakers included A. G. Walkden and G. K. Chesterton, whose patriotism is surely not suspect. The only explanation seems to be that now not only pacifism, but also industrial propaganda is to be forcibly prevented. It is not a far cry from this to an attack on any attempt to oppose the worst excesses of our Jingoes at home. . . . Of course, we do not intend to take this lying down. For one thing, *after keeping the N.G.L. strictly apart from pacifism for three years, I do not want to have it dragged into disrepute in this way.*

Cole wanted to have it both ways: the support of pacifists without the public censure which inevitably accompanied it during the war. The opportunism which Beatrice Webb detected in Cole's political behaviour[56] had no better illustration.

THE STATE IN PRACTICE: NATIONALIZATION

' "Cole is a young Karl Marx",' Page Arnot remarked to Beatrice Webb in 1916. ' "He is going to work out the philosophy of the Functional State." ' Beatrice was not unduly impressed by this boast, and suggested typically, 'He will have to work out the practical [side] too.'[57] After 1914 that task involved above all coming to terms with the state's actual control of the lives and livelihood of millions of men and the implications of the war experience for the future.

Cole was perfectly aware that war collectivism raised issues of the greatest concern for all socialists. It challenged many of his hopes and confirmed most of his fears. The practice of state power during the First World War was as repugnant to him as the theory which lay behind it. He claimed to be among the many people who 'have seen the State monster at work, and . . . know what State Sovereignty means in an oligarchical society'.[58] He also knew that the key issue of the nationalization of industry had to be re-examined in terms of that recognition.

His pre-war view that it was 'the State that, in the end, will set [the workers] free'[59] clearly would no longer do. War control had changed the entire picture. 'Instead of the old collectivist idea of the State nationalising industry,' Cole noted in December 1916, 'we have the new Capitalist coup of capital taking over the State.'[60] And what was a war necessity then could very easily become a capitalist's convenience after the war.[61] Because of the war, he argued, 'it may prove easy enough to nationalise', but at the same time, 'it will be no such child's play to socialise industry. National management is one thing, but national ownership, which all socialists unite in desiring, is quite another.'[62] In this context, 'national ownership' meant democratic control, the demand for which had met with as little sympathy from the public employer as from his private counterpart.

Such hostility and reactionary behaviour was not at all surprising to Cole and other guildsmen. The workers could testify to the fact that 'The State and the municipality as employers have turned out not to differ essentially from the private capitalist.'[63] The social role of management by oligarchy was the same in both cases, and the struggle for control had to be waged against either adversary. The evidence was abundant, Cole insisted, that during the war the state 'has served Mammon as it served him in peace'.[64] And the most subtle service it offered capitalism was to take over the control of industry before the workers were ready for it, the very reason, Cole argued, why nationalization would come, prematurely, as the 'capitalists' last card'.[65] 'State-run industry', from this point of view, was revealed early in the war as 'only concentrated Capitalism to the nth power'.[66] Therefore 'It is no use,' Cole concluded, 'for the workers to look to the State for salvation: the State responds to economic pressure, and the salvation that will be got from it will be strictly in proportion to the economic pressure applied.'[67] In well-organized trades, such as mining and the railways, the pressure for control could be maintained regardless of state ownership of industry. But where trade unionism was weak, 'Nationalisation is dangerous', Cole declared, and to be resisted.[68]

The ferment of ideas about reconstruction forced Cole to further clarify his attitude to the state. Overall, he considered four approaches to the problem of the organization of industry after the war: (1) decontrol and reversion to the industrial *status quo ante bellum*, which he rejected, while still insisting on the restoration of trade union customs suspended for the duration; (2) continuation of war control, without a change in ownership, which he immediately dismissed as tyranny by bureaucracy; (3) nationalization, and (4) joint management of industry by workers' and employers' associations unrestricted by state interference where possible.[69] He was prepared to accept alternative 3 if necessary, but he worked to promote alternative 4 as the optimal road to democracy in industry.

Cole's ambivalence about the state is apparent in his treatment of these alternatives. On one hand, he was a realist, who saw the growth of state power as an evil though inevitable consequence of the war. From this standpoint, the only question left was which one of the plans for government control presented the fewest obstacles to the growth of revolutionary trade unionism. The answer by 1917 seemed to be joint control, but as an alternative to the system instituted during the war, Cole was reluctantly willing then to accept the collectivism which he had previously ridiculed so frequently. At an industrial symposium sponsored by the *New Age* in early 1917, he admitted:[70]

To me it seems that the whole problem of nationalisation has radically altered as a result of the war. Some Guildsmen have always been opposed to nationalisation. I have never taken that view; and perhaps I can best define my past attitude as one of half-benevolent neutrality. Today, my position is different. We are faced with two immediate alternatives in industry – the continuance of private ownership backed by State protection under the guise of control or nationalisation. Of the two I vastly prefer nationalisation. Under either system, the power of the State is arrayed on the side of the wage-system; but the chance of developing the Guild idea and the Guild demand among the workers seems to me very much greater under national ownership than under State Capitalism. By it we at least secure that great step towards our ideal – unified management; . . . Collectivism is to be preferred to State Capitalism.

But not, it seemed, to joint control.

This distinction became clear when Cole shifted his attention from the immediate situation to a broader perspective, at which time he expressed a somewhat different attitude to the state. In April 1917, at the NGL conference, he declared that his entire position was based on his 'intense hostility to the State'. He continued:[71]

I feel at the moment that the State is more dangerous than the employer . . . that the biggest danger we are up against is the danger that the State will assume a new and important function in industry, and that the State will take over far more than it has before, regimenting all men in connexion with their industries. That fear of what the State is going to do leads me to desire very much to play off the capitalist against the State.

Nationalization would be very difficult to defend in terms of this argument. Indeed, Cole reminded his colleagues that it was[72]

necessary to appreciate the change which the war has introduced, because that change has been made in the new strength it has brought to capitalism, and in the new alliance it has created in the larger form of capitalism and the State.

For that reason, 'I want to dish the State,' he announced, 'and I want the trade unions to enter into joint control with the employers over the labour exchanges' and all other issues of industrial management.[73]

JOINT CONTROL

Cole recognized that joint control had it own drawbacks. But the spectre of defection or co-optation through contact with employers did not frighten him. In fact he welcomed the opportunity to expose the true character of the many prominent men in the Labour movement whose allegiance to the working class was, in his opinion, somewhat suspect. By 1917, he insisted:[74]

We want to get rid of [these] trade union leaders, to get them out of the movement. We have got to reckon with the fact that at least fifty per cent of the men at the top of the trade union movement will go over to the capitalists' side. The sooner they go the better. I do not think the fact that they will go over to the other side is any reason for objecting to some form of co-operation. You may have at the start trade union leaders who will play the employers' card, but I can think of no better way of clearing those men out of the movement than of giving them a real rope to hang themselves.

After three years of war, Cole was prepared to expect the worst. His pessimism was based on what he took to be the uniformly dismal record of most trade union leaders during the war. And it was precisely because so many union leaders had meekly joined the state machine in wartime and had ensured thereby that industrial autocracy would be maintained that he was convinced about the necessity for joint control. The important task was to get the government out of industrial affairs, to counteract the state's almost mystical power to intimidate and make humble all kinds of men.

One such notorious occasion, Cole believed, was acquiescence in the Treasury Agreement of 1915, as noted above. As technical adviser to the Amalgamated Society of Engineers, Cole's major dilemma was what to do about the Munitions Act, which gave legal sanction to the agreement. At first he considered obstructionist tactics such as just not working its provisions to force its repeal. But he quickly recognized that both he and the ASE had to live with the Act, whether they liked it or not.[75] Hence he concentrated on amending it to provide a framework for workers' participation in management. In October 1915, he suggested an alternative to the centralized direction of munitions production on the principle of joint control. He urged that local production committees be established whose members would be elected half by the local employers and half by the trade unions. This group would be empowered to rule on any alteration in workshop rules and customs, to regulate the supply of labour in each locality and the granting of leaving certificates, and to hear all grievances instead of the Munitions Tribunals. A central joint committee, independent of the Civil Service or other political controls, would supervise the whole system. The 'essence' of this plan, Cole noted in October 1915, was that 'it seeks to replace bureaucracy by democracy, and that in place of the centralised control of Government officials, it would set self-government in industry by employers and employed'.[76]

Cole intended this scheme to be a model for post-war industrial relations. 'Even now,' he wrote in December 1915, despite the setbacks of the past year, 'the establishment of the principle of Joint Control' was within the workers' grasp.[77] The shop stewards' movement later in the war gave Cole additional reason to press for the enactment of this proposal, but like so many of his other suggestions, it remained just an interesting idea.[78] 'In the labour movement,' Cole knew all too well, 'men grow used to disappointment.'[79]

Nevertheless, Cole continued to search for a practicable way out of the dead end he saw in the choice between government control and unregulated capitalism. His hopes were raised by the appearance of an embryonic, though promising, plan for joint control, the outline of which was published in March 1917 in the interim Report of the Reconstruction Committee on Joint Standing Industrial Councils, popularly known, after the chairman's name, as the Whitley Report.[80]

The Whitley Committee was appointed in October 1916 to consider 'suggestions for securing a permanent improvement in the relations between employers and workmen'. Its major finding was in support of the formation of Joint Industrial Councils, supplemented by Works Committees and District Councils, in which representatives of employers and workers would meet on equal terms to discuss all aspects of industrial relations.[81] A second report appeared in 1918 which advocated the classification of industries in three categories according to the organization of both labour and management, and concluded that state participation in these councils should vary inversely with the degree of consolidated leadership in each industry.[82] The state's proper role was therefore to assist in the formation of structures which would eventually eliminate any governmental presence in the internal affairs of industry.

The resemblance to Cole's developing views on joint control was not at all a coincidence. Beatrice Webb noted that in 1916 'Cole was busy with [Arthur] Greenwood (the secretary of the Whitley Committee) devising the Councils and persuading the representatives of labour on the Committee to accept them'.[83] When the first interim report appeared, Cole's response was predictably sympathetic. He saw it as a 'concession to Labour's growing demand for control' and applauded both the fact that it would help to disenfranchise the non-unionist and more importantly, that it would keep the state out of industry as much as possible. Because he believed that 'The State of today is the *alter ego* of capitalism' Cole supported the Whitley Report as an alternative to 'a Triple Alliance of Capital, Labour and the State [which] would merely grind Labour to powder between the upper and nether millstone'.[84] Furthermore, since the Whitley scheme provided the machinery through which the workers could learn to share and ultimately to control the management of industry, these Joint Standing Industrial Councils could very well be, Cole speculated in July 1917, the 'training ground for a new Trade Unionism'.[85]

Other guildsmen were not so easily convinced that the transition to guild socialism lay in the provisions of the Whitley Report, since it seemed to leave the wage system intact. In fact, Cole had to moderate his views in the following months in response to the nearly uniform hostility of his associates to the committee's report. On the very day that one of his articles appeared in the *Herald* cautiously praising the report, Cole signed a violently hostile critique of it as a member of the NGL Vigilance Committee on After-War Problems. The argument advanced in this public paper, which was printed as a mock official document 'presented to the Trade Union movement on command by the National Guilds League', flatly contradicted many of Cole's contemporary statements. 'No scheme of so-called "joint control",' the report affirmed, 'can meet the demand of the workers; and . . . no such scheme can give in any way, or under any circumstances any real control. Labour cannot secure the control of industrial affairs through the agency of a composite body.'[86] And 'From the very fact of their inherent antagonism', the two sides could not possibly 'control jointly. The very first essential of a controlling body is that its members shall have – not, indeed, identical views – but a certain community of purpose, and a certain identity of point of view'. Since that could not be the case in the foreseeable future between workers and employers, the Whitley Report was, they concluded, 'in no real sense a step towards control'.[87]

In late 1917 Cole continued to defend the Whitley Report in discussion and at the same time to sign published denunciations of it.[88] However by the middle of the following year he had given up any hopes of reconciling his colleagues to the principle of joint control or its specific embodiment in the Whitley proposals. 'By its prompt repudiation of the principles upon which the Whitley Report is explicitly based,' Cole disingenuously claimed in June 1918, 'the National Guilds League put itself in the forefront of advanced industrial organisations.'[89]

Cole's conflict with his fellow guildsmen on this issue was undoubtedly very disturbing to him. It was probably the cause of the extraordinary remark he made to Sidney Webb in November 1917 that he, Cole, 'hated the name of National Guilds'. Sidney speculated after the difficulties of the past year, 'It seems to me that Cole is retreating more and more to mere Trade Unionism of the older type.'[90] Webb was premature in his judgment, but his comment throws some light on the reasons for Cole's turn towards politics of the 'older type' in the last year of the war. Since the NGL was more intent on ideological purity than political influence, the reconstructed Labour Party seemed to be a more promising vehicle for the propagation of his own views.

POLITICS

G. D. H. Cole's attitude to political action changed drastically towards the end of the First World War. Previously he had been instrumental in the formation of the NGL in 1915 as a body dedicated to the 'rescue' of socialism 'from the position of a purely political creed'.[91] Throughout the war he repeatedly castigated the Webbs and other Fabians for their obsession with political and administrative change. He even resigned from the Fabian Society in 1915 when it rejected his proposal to divert the work of the group to the tasks of research rather than politics.[92] Even though he returned to the society in short order, he continued to believe that both the ILP and the Fabian Society worked on a mistaken theory which[93]

> was exclusively political; they tended to regard all social questions almost entirely from the point of view of legislation and administration; in their eyes the cure of all social evils seemed to lie in the passing of the right law by Parliament, and their administration in the right way.

Because of this one-sidedness, Cole told Beatrice Webb in March 1917, 'I do not like being regarded as a Fabian or having anything I do mixed up with the Fabian Society.'[94]

At the same time, he dissociated himself from the views of those revolutionaries who were convinced, especially after the February Revolution in Russia, that the primary aim of socialism was the seizure of power. In April 1917 he speculated:[95]

> Suppose we have a revolution tomorrow with the fullest success, we should still not have established National Guilds. We should still have to pass through a series of stages before we can reach National Guilds. Even if the economic power of the workers were sufficient to create a revolution to oust the capitalist class, the workers are not yet prepared to pass through transitional stages. Whether your policy is revolutionary or reformist you have got to pass through this series of stages.

This critical preparatory work was still industrial rather than political and would remain so, he believed in April 1917, in the immediate future. The 'revolution in the industrial system' which he advocated here did not depend primarily on political action.[96] He wrote in the same year:[97]

> In politics, democracy can nibble, but it may not bite; and it will not be able to bite until the balance of economic power has been so changed as to threaten the economic dominance of capitalism. Then, *maybe*, politics will become a real battleground instead of an arena of sham fights; but the power of the disputants will be still the economic power which stands at their back.

At the 1917 NGL conference, a resolution was defeated which

proposed to make the league a specifically socialist body. The designation 'socialist' was rejected, in Mrs Emily Townshend's words, 'because that word has at present a political signification, and I think it is very important that the National Guilds League should steer clear of politics for years to come'.[98] George Lansbury ridiculed this argument but without success. He asked his colleagues this pointed question:[99]

> I should like to know what we all are? Any one would think that a socialist was a species of leper. I don't understand it at all, and further I don't understand all this holy horror of politics. Most of you seem to be taking part in some sort of politics, and how do we propose to get national ownership without politics? I do not at all subscribe to this horror of political action.

By the end of 1917, neither did Cole. After the departure of Arthur Henderson from the Cabinet in the summer of that year to supervise the subsequent formulation of plans to reconstruct the Labour Party and after the heated debates and conflicts within the NGL, Cole was willing to work within and for a political party, but not necessarily for exclusively political ends.

As early as February 1915, Beatrice Webb reported that Cole had moderated his attitude to politics since the outbreak of war 'and is now willing to work with the Labour Party in order to get into closer touch with the Trade Unions'.[100] But his use of the party for his own purposes did not at all imply commitment to it. Certainly access to the Labour leadership was useful to Cole, and he took advantage of the fact that his sponsor at the ASE, W. H. Hutchinson, was elected to the Labour Party Executive as Arthur Henderson's replacement on 28 June 1915.[101] By the middle of the following year, Cole agreed to work with an offshoot of the Labour Party office, the War Emergency Committee,[102] to help formulate a programme for labour after the war. He served on the WEC's advisory group on the restoration of trade union conditions, along with prominent Labour leaders such as J. R. Clynes, George Wardle, and W. A. Appleton.[103]

These associations, though valuable in their own right, were really peripheral to Cole's primary interest in industrial organization at this time. But when the new constitution of the Labour Party was being drafted in late 1917 and after it was ratified in February 1918, he became more directly involved in policy plan-ning and later in electoral propaganda. First, in September and October 1917, Cole joined Henderson, Webb and others in discussions on the programme and structure of the new party.[104] Then, on 13 March 1918, nine advisory committees to the Labour Party were established.[105] Cole served on both the international affairs and industrial policy groups.[106] At the second meeting of the former, he joined Sidney Webb, R. H. Tawney, Leonard Woolf, G. L. Dickinson, R. C. K. Ensor and Camille Huysmans in an examination of the plans for a League of Nations. They agreed that its establishment should be postponed until the end of the war so that all the belligerents could join it.[107] In July 1918, Cole signed a memorandum written by H. N. Brailsford against Allied intervention in Russia. Webb and Ensor drafted their own memorandum in favour of military action against the Bolsheviks, and both papers were submitted to the Labour Party Executive, where they were inserted in the minutes.[108] No action was taken on this matter, but such a memorandum cannot be found in the executive minutes before that date. The importance of the advice of specialists, that is, intellectuals, had been admitted.

A few weeks later, Cole accepted the invitation of the Labour Party to house the FRD free of cost and to support it financially. Cole himself was paid under the new arrangement £150 a year as the chief official of the newly-christened Labour Research Department. An auxiliary of 'brain-workers' was thereby added to the hard-pressed Labour Party staff. Beatrice Webb favoured this move, and commented acutely: 'Henderson has shown a certain breadth of vision in risking having turbulent elements inside the party office, and Cole has sacrificed some of his rebellious morals and manners to the opportunity for influence.'[109]

Cole was convinced that the new Labour Party recognized the value and accepted the services of intellectuals in a way which was previously inconceivable.[110] He observed that 'soldiers of the middle class', managers and other professionals, were 'sick and tired of the old parties and are seeking for a new allegiance'.[111] The Labour Party, he affirmed in September 1918, could provide it. Cole believed that, just as the NGL attempted to construct a common economic platform for co-operation between manual workers and professionals, that is, the middle class, so 'The widened and reorganised Labour Party is an attempt to find for these two sections a common political platform'.[112]

The capitalists too, he argued, had consolidated their forces during the war and had developed a new unity, which was reflected in the membership and actions of the Coalition Government. This fact was a boon to Labour in that it could organize in 1918 a real opposition to capitalism in what Cole and Massingham called 'The People's Party'.[113] In an electoral pamphlet reprinted from the *Herald* in November 1918, Cole wrote anonymously:[114]

> Never before has there been in politics a perfectly clear and sharp distinction between the Haves and the Have-nots. The Coalition of Capitalist Parties presents Labour with a matchless opportunity. Labour has become *the* opposition, and it is not a long step from being the opposition to becoming the Government. No longer can the old parties continue to play the game of Tweedledum and Tweedledee. In their panic at the rise of the workers they have combined into a single party of reaction, and in doing this they have enabled Labour to find its soul. They have made the class-struggle *the* political issue of the future, and gladly does the Labour Party accept a challenge which can only result in the catastrophic overthrow of privilege and the complete realisation of democracy in industry and in politics. Capitalism has thrown down the glove, and in cutting free from the Coalition, Labour has once for all asserted its independence and its claim to full political and economic power.

At the last stages of the election campaign Cole publicly admitted his firm commitment to the Labour Party. But what was most significant about his statement of support was the parallel and equivalent importance he now granted to political action in socialist strategy. 'In politics,' he wrote, 'the workers' aim must be nothing less than the complete capture of the political machine, and its use for the establishment of the Social democracy.' In industry, he added, 'Their aim . . . cannot be less ambitious; it must include the capture of the industrial machine and the establishment of workers' control in industry.'[115]

Cole was prepared to assist the post-war Labour Party in its political tasks and to ensure at the same time that they did not obscure the significance of the industrial struggle which accompanied them. There was no assurance, however, that the new political power of Labour would ever be put to the uses which he envisaged. His commitment to the party was more a reflection of the contemporary mood of buoyant optimism than of rational calculation. But the fact that Cole and other socialist intellectuals were by the end of the war trusted and intimate advisers rather than the often hostile and unwelcome critics of old was an important change in Labour politics which could not be ignored.

In the last year of the war, G. D. H. Cole moved closer to the political mainstream. At the same time he abandoned many of his pre-war views. The socialist position which he had begun to build before August 1914 was scarcely recognizable four years later. In this sense, he was probably typical of the many socialists throughout Europe whose ideas did not survive the conflict. There were others, however, who lived through the First World War and whose thought retained its force and coherence despite the ordeal. One man who experienced the worst of war and who emerged from it with his deepest beliefs intact was R. H. Tawney.

NOTES

1 Oral information from Mrs M. I. Cole. She said that Cole never seriously contemplated the consequences for the working class or the socialist movement of a German victory. But M. B. Reckitt, who had met Cole at Oxford in 1914 wrote that, during the war, Cole 'had much too much common sense to doubt that a German victory would be a disaster for Europe', *As it Happened*, 1941, p. 121. Reckitt was one of the most ardent patriots among the guild socialists during the First World War, so his statement may be, from his point of view, flattering to Cole. Still he (Cole) did admit in *Labour in Wartime*, 1915, pp. 3–4, that 'the individual to whatever groups besides he may feel an attachment, cannot see with indifference the defeat or downfall of the nation to which he belongs'. But since Cole preferred to ignore the explicit issues of commitment to the war effort, at least in his theoretical and journalistic work, and since so little of his correspondence exists, it is impossible to deal with his attitude to the war in the same way that one would approach Tawney's views or the Webbs'.
2 G. D. H. Cole and William Mellor, 'Co-operators and the war', *Daily Herald*, 13 August 1914.
3 *Ibid.* Mr R. Page Arnot informed me that Mellor drafted the articles they wrote together, Cole amended them and submitted them under both their names. I shall assume that Cole's signature on an article or a letter signifies his approval for the sentiments stated therein.
4 Cole and Mellor, 'Playing capital's game', *Daily Herald*, 20 August 1914. Cf. also the following articles they wrote jointly in the *Herald*: 'Trade unions in war-time', 2 January 1915; 'Compulsory arbitration', 27 March 1915; 'Thrift for some people', 11 December 1915.
5 Cole and Mellor, 'Labour after the war', *Daily Herald*, 4 March 1916.

6 Cole and Mellor, 'Labour after the war: the problem – the class struggle', *Daily Herald*, 11 March 1916.

7 Cole and Mellor, 'Industrial unionism and the guild system', *Amalgamated Engineers Monthly Journal and Report*, 9, September 1914, p. 51.

8 Cf. above, ch. 4, note 79. This is but one of many examples of what Page Arnot called the guildsmen's 'personal boycott' of the war. *History of the Labour Research Department*, 1926, p. 9.

9 Cole, *Labour in Wartime*, p. 36.

10 *Ibid.*, pp. 19, 46.

11 Cole and Mellor, 'A second open letter to the Trades Union Congress', *New Age*, 2 September 1915, pp. 421–2.

12 Cole, *Labour in Wartime*, p. 36.

13 *Ibid.*, p. 80.

14 Cole, 'The state and the engineers', *Amalgamated Engineers Monthly Journal and Report*, 4, April 1915, p. 75.

15 Cole, *Labour in Wartime*, p. 291.

16 Cole and Mellor, 'Rumours of class war', *Herald*, 13 March 1915.

17 G. D. H. Cole, *Self-government in Industry*, 1917, is a collection of the occasional pieces Cole contributed to various Labour journals during the war. Articles which appeared in the *Church Socialist* and the *New Age* in 1914 appear verbatim side by side with essays written two and a half years later. None of the essays is dated, so that the reader must conclude that many of the views Cole held in late 1914 were retained in 1917, which is further evidence of Cole's attempt to ignore the war. It appears that Cole's shift in views did not convince him that his earlier writing needed revision.

18 *Ibid.*, pp. 132–3.

19 Passfield Papers, Beatrice Webb's unpublished diary, vol. 33, entry for 18 March 1916. Cf. also entries for 9 March, 8 April, and 13 September on the problems of Cole, Mellor, and Arnot over conscription.

20 Cole Papers, Box 8, Item 8, Mellor to Cole, undated, late 1916. Cf. also M. I. Cole, *Growing Up Into Revolution*, 1949, p. 77. Her brother, Raymond Postgate, was also imprisoned as a conscientious objector.

21 The Cole Papers at Nuffield College contain the minute books and correspondence of the National Guilds League, under the headings: Cole collection on Guild Socialism and the J. P. Bedford Papers. About 200 people joined by 1916.

22 Cole Collection on Guild Socialism, Transcript of 1917 Annual Conference of National Guilds League, p. 29. Cole's resolution was defeated by 20 to 19 votes. Cf. also 'National Guilds League Conference', *Guildsmen*, May 1917, and an article under the same title in *Herald* of 14 April 1917.

23 Cole and W. N. Ewer letter to *Nation*, printed on 16 March 1918.

24 Arnot commented in an interview with the author that after he had emerged from prison in 1918, he was convinced that Cole's views had shifted sharply to the right.

25 G. D. H. Cole, *Labour in the Commonwealth*, 1918, pp. 49–50. This

book was intended for younger readers of the middle class. The title of the new study specifically shows how Cole's interests had shifted from the narrower, more parochial *World of Labour* to the wider question of the place of labour as one constituent element in society. Still, *The World of Labour*, 1913, was reprinted in 1915 and 1917.

26 *Ibid.*, p. 50. Somehow Cole failed to notice the contradiction between this statement and his claim on p. 47 that 'Internally, then, the Commonwealth to-day can only express itself in terms of the class-struggle.'

27 Cole, *Self-government in Industry*, pp. 246–7.

28 *Ibid.*, p. 174.

29 Cf. these passages in *ibid.*: 'The power of any class at any stage of human society rests ultimately upon the performance of functions . . . we, in our day and generation, shall succeed in overthrowing capitalism only if we first make it socially functionless' (p. 173). And, 'It is my contention that without economic functions, social or anti-social, they [the capitalist class] cannot long sustain their economic power' (p. 182).

30 *Ibid.*, pp. 161–2; Cole, *An Introduction to Trade Unionism*, 1918, pp. 103–8.

31 Cole, 'At the sign of the book', *Highway*, 7, 84, September 1915, p. 205.

32 Cole, 'Conflicting social obligations', *Proceedings of the Aristotelian Society*, 15, 1914–15, p. 155.

33 *Ibid.*, p. 149.

34 *Ibid.*, pp. 149–50. Many of these views were repeated later in the war. Cf. *Self-government in Industry*, pp. 73, 81–2. At the same time as Cole was developing these ideas, Harold Laski was also exploring pluralist theory in Canada and the United States. Laski told Oliver Wendell Holmes on 1 January 1918 that he had read *Self-government in Industry*, and called it 'a most able book'. He also reviewed it favourably in the *New Republic* in April 1918. M. de W. Howe (ed.), *Holmes–Laski Letters*, 1953, vol. 1, p. 123. On Laski's thought at this time, cf. his *Studies in the Problem of Sovereignty*, New Haven, Conn., 1917, and his *Authority in the Modern State*, New Haven, Conn., 1919, and Bernard Zylstra, *From Pluralism to Collectivism, The Development of Harold Laski's Political Thought*, Assen, 1968. I am grateful to Professor Ralph Miliband for bringing this study to my attention.

35 Cole, 'Conflicting social obligations', p. 154.

36 Cole meant consumer problems. Cf. Cole Papers, Box 6, Folder 81, letter of Cole to Mr Ellingham, 5 November 1914: 'The State is only all the consumers.' Box 8, Item 2, Draft of the Storrington Document, drafted in December 1914 by Cole and others as a guild socialist programme, p. 1. The state as the consumers, which he had postulated before the war, is a definition repeated throughout this period. Cf. *Self-government in Industry*, p. 79, for example: 'the State only represents the individual in his particular aspect of "neighbour", "user" and "enjoyer".'

37 Cole, 'Conflicting social obligations', p. 151.

38 *Ibid.*, p. 153.

39 *Ibid.*, pp. 153-4. Cf. the same argument in Cole Papers, Box 3, Folder 40, handwritten draft of paper c. 1917 on 'The state in theory'.

40 Cole, 'Conflicting social obligations', p. 154.

41 *Ibid.*, p. 157.

42 Cole *et al.*, 'Symposium: the nature of the state in view of its external arrangements', *Proceedings of the Aristotelian Society*, 16, 1915-16, p. 315.

43 *Ibid.*, pp. 313, 316.

44 *Ibid.*, p. 320.

45 *Ibid.*, p. 321.

46 *Ibid.*, p. 323.

47 I am grateful to Mr Martin Gilbert for drawing my attention to this manuscript, which is part of the Allen papers in his possession.

48 City of London ILP minutes, 9 December 1915.

49 Bertrand Russell, *Roads to Freedom*, 1918, pp. 141-2, 13.

50 Bertrand Russell, *Political Ideals*, 1917, p. 59.

51 J. Ramsay MacDonald, *Socialism after the War*, 1917, pp. 20, 23. Cf. also this statement in his article, 'Socialism and the State', in the *Labour Leader*, 5 July 1917: British socialism 'opposes the cruder Syndicalism of the Sorel school', but 'it need not oppose National Guilds especially if they will supplement their industrial programme by recognising that the State must exist to regulate national industrial interests in a general way'. This was precisely Cole's position.

52 H. Belloc and J. R. MacDonald, *Socialism and the Servile State*, 1911.

53 R. Page Arnot probably brought Cole along to the City of London Branch of the ILP, where the latter was elected a member along with William Mellor on 25 March 1915. Cf. Minutes for that date. And Beatrice Webb's unpublished diary, vol. 33, entry for 8 April 1916. She accused Cole of being 'careful not to appear at the [NCF] convention'. And Cole, 'The Labour Party Conference', *Nation*, 29 January 1916.

54 Labour Party Library, War Emergency: Workers' National Committee Papers, Box 11, From Milk to Miscellaneous, letter of Cole to Henderson, 6 November 1917.

55 *Ibid.* Italics mine. The lectures were re-scheduled for Kingsway Hall, London on 18 December 1917, but this time a German air raid interrupted the first lecture, which was finally delivered by W. N. Ewer on 'The State' in March 1918. Cf. reports in the *Guildsman*, December 1917, March 1918.

56 Passfield Papers, Beatrice Webb's unpublished diary, vol. 32, 14 February 1915. This perceptive comment was deleted by Margaret Cole in the published diaries: 'Cole indulges in a long list of personal hatreds. The weak point of his outlook is that there is no one that he does like except as a temporary tool – he resents anyone who is not a follower and has a contempt for all leaders other than himself.' In 1921 Beatrice criticized Cole's opportunism with much deeper bitterness. The issue was Cole's agreement to accept £6,000 a year

from the Russian Trade Delegation to keep the Labour Research Department financially solvent. This decision was condemned by Beatrice as 'idiotic' since Cole once more wanted support without the consequences. The result was to Beatrice a disaster: 'The Fabian Research Department – a promising child of ours – ends in a lunatic asylum.' vol. 36, entry for 7 October 1921.

57 Passfield Papers, Beatrice Webb's unpublished diaries, vol. 33, entry for 13 September 1916.

58 Cole, 'The ILP and trade unionism', *Labour Leader*, 18 January 1917.

59 Cf. ch. 4, note 58.

60 Cole, 'The busy rich class', *Herald*, 23 December 1916.

61 Cole, *Self-government in Industry*, p. 211, reprinted from *New Age*, 1 October 1914.

62 Cole papers, Box 6, Folder 81, October 1914, London Fabian Lecture, handwritten draft.

63 *National Guilds. An Appeal to Trade Unionists*, Pamphlets of the National Guilds League, no. 1, October 1915. I am grateful to Mr M. B. Reckitt for the loan of his collection of pamphlets and other documents related to guild socialism.

64 Cole, *Self-government in Industry*, p. 16.

65 *Ibid.*, p. 203, reprinted from *New Age*, 17 September 1914.

66 *Ibid.*, p. 212.

67 *Ibid.*, p. 16.

68 *Ibid.*, p. 206, reprinted from *New Age*, 24 September 1914, and p. 22. Cf. also *Towards a Miners' Guild*, National Guilds Pamphlet no. 3, January 1917, p. 7 and *Towards a National Railway Guild*, National Guilds Pamphlet no. 4, June 1917, pp. 3, 16 for the same point.

69 Cole, *Self-government in Industry*, pp. 165, 169, 179–180; Cole and Mellor, *The Meaning of Industrial Freedom*, 1918, p. 4; and the following articles they both wrote for the *Herald*: 'What of the state?', 13 November 1915; 'The need for unity', 4 December 1915; 'Labour after the war: the problem', 4 March 1916; 'Labour after the war: state control of industry', 8 July 1916.

70 Cole, *Self-government in Industry*, p. 326, reprinted from *New Age*, 11 January 1917.

71 Cole Collection on Guild Socialism, 1917 conference transcript, p. 67.

72 *Ibid.*, pp. 69–70.

73 *Ibid.*, p. 71.

74 *Ibid.*, p. 72.

75 M. I. Cole, *Growing Up Into Revolution*, p. 60 and oral information from Mrs Cole.

76 G. D. H. Cole, 'The Munitions Act: A plea for reconsideration', *Nation*, 16 October 1915.

77 Cole and Mellor, 'The price of dilution to labour', *Amalgamated Engineers Monthly Journal and Report*, January 1916, which is an open letter to the members of the ASE conference signed 30 December 1915.

78 On the shop stewards, cf. Cole, *An Introduction to Trade Unionism*, 1918, pp. 53–6, and *Labour in the Commonwealth*, p. 133.

79 Cole, 'The meaning of the Trades Union Congress', *Nation*, 11 September 1915.

80 The best analysis of the Whitley report is still to be found in Élie Halévy's two essays, 'The policy of social peace in England' and 'The problem of worker control', both of which appear in the collection *The Era of Tyrannies*. A slightly histrionic, though complete, account of the work of all the reconstruction committees may be found in P. B. Johnson, *Land Fit for Heroes*, 1968. For a radical critique of the Whitley idea, cf. J. T. Murphy, *Compromise or Independence?*, Sheffield, 1918.

81 1917–18 Cd 8606, xviii, 415. A useful summary may be found in P. and G. Ford, *A Breviate of Parliamentary Papers 1917–1939*, Oxford, 1961, pp. 319–21.

82 1918 Cd 9002, x, 659; Ford and Ford, *A Breviate of Parliamentary Papers 1917–1939*, p. 320.

83 Passfield Papers, Beatrice Webb's unpublished diaries, vol. 34, f. 32 Note of May 1918.

84 Cole and W. N. Ewer, 'The Whitley Report I, *Herald*, 7 July 1917.

85 Cole and Ewer, 'The Whitley Report II its uses and abuses', *Herald*, 14 July 1917; Cole and Ewer, 'The Whitley Report III is it control?', *Herald*, 28 July 1917.

86 Bedford Papers, Box 1, National Guilds League Vigilance Committee on After-War Problems, *Observations on the Interim Report of the Reconstruction Committee on Joint Industrial Councils*, 1918, a copy of which in Cole's hand may be found in his collection at Nuffield on Guild Socialism, in a file labelled 'NGL–Whitley'. Besides Cole, A. E. Baker, Monica Ewer, W. N. Ewer, M. B. Reckitt, and Mrs Emily Townshend signed the report dated 14 July 1917, the same date as the Cole and Ewer article cited in note 85.

87 *Ibid.*

88 Bedford Papers, Box 5, Folder 34, 'Notes for Trade Unionists in Connection with the Adoption by the War Cabinet of the Interim Report of the Reconstruction Committee on Joint Standing Industrial Councils Known as the Whitley Report', dated December 1917, signed by Cole and eleven others. Cf. also 'Conference on the Whitley Report', *Fabian News*, 29, 2, January 1918, pp. 7–8, and 'Workshop committees', *Guildsman*, January 1918, for reports of a conference on the Whitley Report arranged by the FRD and held in the Fabian Hall on 28 November 1917. The two pamphlets on the Whitley Report were consolidated in a pamphlet issued by the NGL in October 1918 under the title, *National Guilds or Whitely Councils?*

89 Cole, 'The Whitley Councils', *Guildsman*, June 1918, and *Labour in the Commonwealth*, pp. 130–1.

90 Passfield Papers, Webb Correspondence, Sidney to Beatrice Webb, 24 November 1917.

91 Bedford Papers, Box 1, File 1, Circular on 'A Guild Socialist League', 1915.

92 Fabian Society Papers, Executive Minutes, 14 May 1915.

93 Cole, 'Recent developments in the British Labour movement',

American Economic Review, 8, 3, September 1918, p. 492.
94 Passfield Papers, General Correspondence, Cole to Beatrice Webb, 14 March 1917.
95 Cole collection on Guild Socialism, transcript of 1917 NGL conference, p. 33.
96 *Ibid.*
97 Cole, *Self-government in Industry*, p. 76. Italics mine.
98 Transcript of 1917 NGL conference, p. 8.
99 *Ibid.*, pp. 8–9.
100 Passfield Papers, Beatrice Webb's unpublished diaries, vol. 32, entry for 14 February 1915.
101 LPEC, 28 June 1915.
102 For which, see below, ch. 7.
103 War Emergency: Workers' National Committee Papers, Box 30, From Labour after the War to Legal, Cole to Middleton, 6 August 1916. Box 8, Labour after the War, Draft of agenda of meeting of 27 July 1916 with lists of proposed members of sub-committees.
104 Tom Jones, *Whitehall Diary*, ed. K. Middlemas, 1969, vol. 1, pp. 37, 38, entries for 10 September and 30 October 1917.
105 LPEC, 13 March 1918.
106 Unfortunately the papers of the Industrial Policy sub-committee have not survived.
107 Labour Party, Library, International Advisory Committee minutes, 14 June 1918.
108 International Advisory Committee minutes, 15 July 1918. LPEC, 24 July 1918.
109 Passfield Papers, Beatrice Webb's unpublished diaries, vol. 34, entry for 1 July 1918; 'Research department', *Fabian News*, 29, 9, August 1918, p. 33.
110 Cole, 'Recent developments in the British Labour movement', p. 494.
111 *Ibid.*, p. 495.
112 Cole, *Labour in the Commonwealth*, p. 84.
113 Passfield Papers, Beatrice Webb's unpublished diaries, vol. 34, entry for 7 June 1917.
114 Cole, *Why Labour Left the Coalition*, 1918. The pamphlet is unsigned but is included in bound volumes of Cole's pamphlets at Nuffield College. Italics are Cole's.
115 Cole, 'A call to industrial Labour', *Herald*, 23 November 1918. Cf. also an interview with Cole under the title 'Democracy in industry', *Christian Commonwealth*, 26 June 1918 for his views on the Labour Party.

6

R. H. Tawney and the
First World War

The true front runs through the licentious soldiery, the true
front runs through the revolution, the true front runs through
the heart of the soldier, the true front runs through the heart
of the revolutionary. The true front runs through each party,
each group and each member of a group. On the true front
each fights against his fellows and against himself, and only
through the decisions of these battles is he given full power
for other decisions.

Martin Buber[1]

R. H. Tawney lived through the 'world crisis'[2] of the First World
War as a socialist, as a soldier, and above all, as a Christian. He
was a witness to a conflict which he believed to be a reflection of
the same moral disorders which were the fundamental cause of
the pre-war social strife. His philosophical approach to the war
added depth and coherence to his views on its significance and
consequences. Tawney's deepest beliefs were unshaken by the
war and his ordeal on the Western Front, but because of the war,
his political thought changed. After 1914 he was able to accept
institutional reform as the central tactic of British socialism.

INTRODUCTION

On 25 November 1914, Tawney volunteered for military service
with the Manchester Regiment as a private.[3] It is said that he was
offered a commission, but turned it down, since he believed it had
been given to him for all the wrong reasons, meaning Rugby and
Balliol.[4] He left his job as lecturer for the WEA and suspended
the research in economic history in which he had been engaged

Plate 11
R. H. Tawney (seated 2nd row, 5th from right) as a corporal in the Manchester City Battalion, 1915

Plate 12
Cartoon of R. H. Tawney by Jabo, *New Standards*, 1924

in association with Professor George Unwin. Tawney also terminated his work as director of the Ratan Tata Foundation, which had brought him formally to the London School of Economics in 1913. By volunteering for the army, he also left a wife who was chronically ill, but whose family could be relied on to watch over her for the duration.[5]

Tawney was often on weekend leaves from Salisbury Plain, where he underwent most of his basic training. In short order he was promoted to lance-corporal, then corporal. By mid-1915 he was a full sergeant.[6] In July 1915 he was in Belgium for the first time as a combatant, and by November, he had had his first experience in trench warfare near the Somme. It was, he noted, a 'tamish affair'. He wrote home to his wife of the problems of 'trench vermin' (lice) and mud, and once contracted influenza, which secured him a three weeks' leave in June 1916.[7] Then he returned to his regiment, at times fulfilling the role of interpreter, since he was one of the few men in the regiment who spoke French fluently.[8] At headquarters at St Omer, he once met four Fabians who drafted a soldiers' manifesto from trade unionists at the Front to the striking Clyde munitions workers.[9] Of the four, Tawney, W. S. Sanders, C. M. Lloyd, and Frederick Keeling, only Sanders survived the Battle of the Somme unscathed. Keeling was killed in August 1916; both Tawney and Lloyd were wounded on 1 July 1916.[10]

On the first day of the Battle of the Somme, at a salient at Fricourt near Albert, Tawney led a platoon on an assault of German lines and was hit in the abdomen by shell fragments. He was briefly treated, but since medical aid was unavailable, he remained in no-man's-land for about a day. Tawney's survival was attributed to his 'wonderful constitution' by his doctor. His wife told her family that 'He lay out twenty-four hours and then got back to the trench on his own feet.'[11] It was remarkable that he did not bleed to death. His company suffered 55 per cent casualties on the first day. After a few days, fifty-four men were left, out of a company of 820. No advance was made in this sector.[12]

Tawney was on the critical list for two weeks, and when he was out of danger, he was sent back to England.[13] He was given odd secretarial jobs while recuperating, and was not discharged until September 1917, and then only after an appeal to the War Office by Beveridge that Tawney's educational work was important to the war effort.[14] While still in uniform in late 1916, he was appointed a member of the Archbishop of Canterbury's Fifth Committee of Inquiry into Christianity and Industrial Problems, and spent several months with another member of the Commission, Bishop Charles Gore, in Oxford.[15] The report was published in 1918. By that year he was a lecturer at both Balliol (until 1921) and LSE, which became his academic home for the next forty years. He accepted the Balliol fellowship on condition that he would 'be free to contest a Labour seat, if asked and able to do so'.[16] He served on the Labour Party Advisory Committees on Education and on International Affairs in 1918. In the 'khaki election' at the end of the war, Tawney stood unsuccessfully as the ILP candidate at Rochdale. By the armistice, his turn to the Labour Party was complete.

THE DECISION TO FIGHT

Tawney arrived at his decision to support the Allied cause and to enlist in the British Army after careful reflection. His friends took opposing views on the justice of British entry into the war. P. A. Brown, a fellow WEA tutor, who shared Tawney's interest in the French Revolution and with whom he collaborated on an edition of documents on economic history, enlisted in early November 1914. He was later killed in action.[17] Another friend, and Tawney's contemporary at Balliol, R. D. Denman, on the other hand, held that Britain was not at all obliged to go to war over Belgium. He did not regard himself as a pacifist, but he was sickened in particular by the 'hypocrisy and intellectual dishonesty of the Churches', which were 'a revelation' of 'how deep and far-reaching is the debasement caused by militarist passion'. He identified his position with that of Keir Hardie and George Lansbury, and Denman congratulated the latter on his 'clearer vision' of the issues of the war.[18] Tawney's brother-in-law William Beveridge had little difficulty in supporting the war, but the two men shared few beliefs or prejudices.

Tawney was more likely to consider seriously the views of George Unwin, undoubtedly one of the major influences on his life. Unwin's views on the war were clear, and although Tawney sympathized with them, he nevertheless rejected their implications. Unwin was horrified by the vision of destruction which the war presented. He wrote to his friend and colleague J. L. Hammond on 10 August 1914:[19]

This war is an unspeakable crime and blemish of Western Civilisation. But in a few months it will and must pull Europe up sharply. The Western World will rise against the infamy and plain facts will have destroyed Jingoism. But there will be a new world to build up and we shall be wanted. Now is the time to think it out.

The two men spent many days in the autumn of 1914 going over the problems which the war raised. In fact they were together on the last night before Tawney left for active service.[20] We can gather something of their exchange from the introductory memoir to Unwin's collected papers which Tawney published in 1927. During the war,[21]

[Unwin] felt that his business was to serve the cause, neither of England nor of Germany, but of a world of spiritual values which both were destroying. 'We are entangled,' he said in some notes for a lecture, 'in an implicit theory that State force has built up Society. We didn't avow this; but we, like the Germans acted on it, and so made ourselves responsible for the dilemma. If the State made our civilization, we owe it our lives, and we can rightly die to maintain it. What is made by force must be maintained by force. But, if civilization was made by a European society – by Gothic churches, Shakespeare, Kant, Beethoven, Rousseau, Tolstoi and the spiritual life of unknown Christian souls – then England made Germany, Germany made England, and France made both.'

He further believed like Elijah, Tawney recalled, that

'there is a still small voice to be heard amid all this earthquake, tempest and fire,' and that in time it would command attention. His sympathies were with those who, by intellectual labour, or the life of fellowship, or by silent faith and endurance in sorrow, were making possible the growth of a temper of love and fruitful cooperation in the future.

Tawney accepted the force of Unwin's argument. He too saw that his task was to serve a world of spiritual values, but he thought that only by the defeat of Germany could the principles upon which both he and Unwin agreed, have had any chance of survival. But Tawney's position was far from jingoism. The violation of Belgium was a crime, but this was only one stage of analysis. The extraordinary fact about his reactions to the war was that he saw the struggle being fought out on so many levels at once. Germany was not only a political entity to Tawney, but also a state of mind, a way of approaching human affairs in both war and peace, against which he was to fight in one way or another throughout his life. At the outset, the war did not raise new issues for Tawney. It merely heightened all the old conflicts and presented them in a new and stronger light. The struggle against Germany was thus a continuation of and another form of the struggle against tendencies within English industrial society, and indeed, if one may speculate, within Tawney's own character. As always, he had a strong sense of the conflicting and unresolved alternatives which live, as he later wrote, 'in vigorous incompatibility together'[22] and are present in every human dilemma. He could not accept the pacifist alternative, since he felt the temper of conflict too strongly within himself to deny the validity of its expression to others. Yet he could not accept war as conflict alone. He needed to adhere to a set of principles which justified the sacrifices of war. His socialist beliefs provided that justification. As he wrote two years later, the 'moral quality of war' is like 'the moral quality of man's economic activities and institutions', since both depend 'on the spirit which directs them, not on the tools which they direct'.[23]

Tawney was convinced that there was a striking resemblance between the nature of the strife in European society before 1914 and the character of the war. On 28 December 1914, after he had enlisted, but before reporting for active service, Tawney wrote:

> If one takes a broad view of the nature of this war, and ceases the futile discussion 'who began it?' one sees that to a considerable extent [it] is the natural outcome of the ideals and standards which govern Western Europe, especially Germany and England, in its ordinary every day social and economic life.

Tawney's war ultimately was a struggle between ideas which were personified as nations. Hence he argued that:[24]

> The scale of values which horrifies us, when it appears in the claim of some Prussians to have a right to determine the future of 'weaker' or 'inferior' nations, which identifies might with power, and recognizes no obligation which cannot be enforced on them by superior force, that conception of human affairs is only too similar to that which a cool observer would consider to be realized in our industrial system.

Indeed the types of men which war brings to the fore are not unlike the scions of industry:

They must have energy, self-control, foresight, a willingness to take risks. They must be undisturbed by pity for the weak, by doubts as to the value of the immediate ends at which they aim, by reverence for the finer and more delicate human qualities and achievements, by humility or consciousness of personal deficiencies. They are essentially a conquering race.

As always, Tawney saw the dual nature of their role:

Like other conquerors, they confer great benefits which are usually no part of their design: system and organisation, order, facilities for accumulating vast material resources, power to conquer natural obstacles, a field for splendid careers for the bold, the energetic, the unscrupulous. Like other conquerors they leave a trail of wreckage, consisting of the weak, the exceptionally scrupulous and honourable, the unconventional, the merely gentle and kindly who 'dare not have the lives of others on their conscience.'

Such men who live and thrive on domination existed and always will exist. The problem remained, if one were committed to change society, could one avoid fighting against such men by the very tools which they use? For Tawney, a real desire to change society had to be based on the recognition of conflict, armed or otherwise, as the major means for resolving the issues which divided society and the world into hostile camps. Merely to avoid the problem and to throw up one's hands and say that the world is too stupid or base for what one had to offer[25] – this pose was utterly impossible for a man as deeply involved as was Tawney in his society and its problems. He could not 'opt out', to use a modern phrase, and commitment to his set of values meant joining the British Army in November 1914.

But he never ceased to view the war as only one skirmish in the larger battle for men's spirits. The last entry in his commonplace book sums up this view, with disturbing contemporary relevance. He wrote:[26]

So I say again: War is not the reversal of the habits and ideals we cultivate in peace. It is their concentration by a whole nation with all resources on an end as to which a whole nation can agree. As long as mankind believe that the normal order of society should be one in which the strong win their way to power over the ruin of the weak, so long will it find nothing fundamentally abhorrent in the intensification of that struggle to the point at which 'peace' ceases, and 'war' begins.

And here the socialist inserts his final plea:

If we are to end the horrors of war, we must first end the horrors of peace. There are no mechanical arrangements by which men who regard society as a struggle for existence can be prevented from fighting. There is one way and one only: to abandon the standards of good and bad, success and failure which are expressed in the existing arrangements of industry, property and social life, and to seek to make society, when it is at peace, a field in which mere power, ruthlessness, ambition can *not* override the merciful and gentle.

Tawney's insight into the similarity between internal and international conflict, not at all surprising in the light of his interest in the French revolutionary period and of his deep Christian beliefs, gave a coherence to his views on the war. And because he had a sense of the unity of political phenomena, he was able to avoid both the shock which the outbreak of the war produced in many men and their subsequent misunderstanding of the causes and significance of the conflict.

No nation could shirk responsibility, Tawney insisted, for the crime of complacence, which led to the tacit acceptance of both 'the armed peace between nations' and 'the armed peace between classes' as 'inevitable and durable' parts 'of the system of mundane affairs'. Indeed:

So bound is each generation by its inheritance of unstated assumptions, so rare in man is the steady eye which can detect the slow accumulation of forces towards the crash, that the world was still discussing the minutiae of policy when the foundations were undermined.

Many men compared human affairs to a 'see-saw', he remarked.[27]

But the see-saw is balanced on a bridge hung above a torrent and while we are labouring to prevent our rivals mounting at the expense of our own depression, the bridge breaks and precipitates friends and enemies into the gulf together.

It took a 'catastrophe' like the First World War to bring men to see that peace depended 'not upon maintaining an uneasy equilibrium by accumulating safe-guards against a collapse'. There could be no better time to convince people that 'the state system of Europe' had to be rebuilt 'upon foundations which correspond with the permanent instincts, ideals and interests of its members'.[28] This international reconstruction, which Tawney left in this vague outline in 1914, depended, in the first place, on the prevention of a German victory.

At the same time, the very nature of that struggle reflected back on the equally important tasks of social reconstruction. Men who supported the war as a conflict of ideas had to confront 'domestic problems with a similar desire to consider principles, to escape from the conventional formulae of our generation, and to revise with an open mind the tacit presuppositions upon which our social order is established'. This intellectual revision was no luxury to be casually attended to in peace-time. It was, he believed, a necessary part of the war effort and would give essential strength to the Allied cause. Tawney admitted in the autumn of 1914 that 'To speak in the Europe of today of the domestic problems which faced European countries three months ago seems a kind of profanity, like the discussion of household accounts in the presence of a corpse'. Still, he argued, 'we must speak of them, if only to be worthy of ourselves. For the justification of a war consists in the [moral] character of the civilization which is victorious.'[29]

It was right, Tawney felt, to fight against Germany 'in order that the spiritual personality of nations may not be over-ridden by a machine'.[30] But it was just as necessary to correct the moral defects of British society which, if left alone, would make a mockery of the sacrifices men were freely making for their country. The war crisis had to be, therefore, the time not for 'recovery but for advance and alteration' of the nation's social organization. Here, the aims of the socialist and the soldier combined in pursuit of a common goal, which was what Tawney called 'the free development of the ancient pieties of Europe', those human, and for him Christian, values, in defence of which 'what remains in Europe of mercy and reverence has taken arms'.[31]

WAR SERVICE

Tawney's military service, culminating in the Battle of the Somme, was an important step in the development of his socialist thought.

In combat his beliefs were tested severely, and the fact that he emerged from the war unbroken, but tempered in his views, strengthened Tawney's socialism and his desire to apply his ideas to the reconstruction of British society.

The force of his idealism sustained him during his army training in 1915. When he surveyed his fellow volunteers in February 1915, he commented that 'they are marked, however faintly, with the stamp of the man who once in his life regarded himself and his future as something worth throwing away'. He estimated 'that nearly all of us joined because we felt that the larger the number of men in training, the sooner the war was likely to be ended'.[32] 'Kitchener's Army' was an unusual group of men whose spirit, in his opinion, distinguished it from the regular army. Still the former group was far from 'democratic', since by its very nature[33]

> an army reproduces everything and originates nothing. It is a petrified model of the society in which it is born. . . . Till the Revolution arrives in England no English army will be democratic, because the customs of the army are simply the customs of English society crystallised.

Class barriers were very strong in the army, and Tawney's remarks in the *Nation* were particularly telling, since he was one of the few men who wrote from the standpoint of the private soldier.

Military training or 'the conversion of a mob into an army' reminded Tawney 'of the process of organising an unorganised body of workers'. This transformation was bound to be somewhat incomplete because the volunteers, by virtue of their reasons for enlisting, were 'for good or evil, incurably civilian'. Still, their common purpose and sense of a mission were the real strength of the men in the ranks.[34]

Tawney shared the time-honoured disrespect of enlisted men for staff officers and their failings. He wrote to Beveridge after a year's training that 'What is called discipline is mainly – after a few very elementary matters have been learned – a code of rules for preventing any sort of new idea struggling into the august presence of the Authorities.' He added that 'What is really wrong [with the staff officers] is just stupidity and conceit, conceit and stupidity, with of course, a good deal of idleness thrown in.' 'I have never met anyone who has been at the game for a year or so who did not damn the staff . . . the men who make the really big blunders. . . . They escape Scot free, or with nothing worse than a Peerage.'[35]

By the end of a year's training, however, he also admitted that he had learned as much about the men in the ranks as about the officers, and the new-found knowledge was somewhat sobering. The wartime moderation of his views may have dated from this early period of the war. Tawney had taught workers before, but he had never really lived among them, except at Toynbee Hall. Now that he had spent a year in his regiment, a good deal of his idealization of the working man as yeoman, which marks his pre-war study, *The Agrarian Problem in the Sixteenth Century*, was gone. At the end of 1915, he admitted that:[36]

> [the] problem of making the [British] Workman and Employer decently public-spirited and less totally selfish can't, I fancy, be handled under a generation or two. A year with the former has taught me a good deal – among other things that his philosophy, as much as that of his masters, is 'Get as much and give as little as you can'. He has been brought up in that creed – although of course very many rise above it – and one can't change the habits of four or five generations in a year or two. It is like the old game of decasualizing the man who has been carefully taught to be a casual.

Tawney did not stop idealizing, though. He found a pleasing alternative to the British workman in the French peasant, who accepted the war with such 'placid resignation'. His picture of the peasant reflected a stage of disenchantment with England, or rather, one suspects, with those elements of English life which Tawney recognized in himself. He remarked to Beveridge about France:[37]

> I don't mean to be killed if I can help it, but if I am it will be a small consolation to be killed here, and on the whole I prefer to think of myself as fighting for this country than for England. If I survive and can scrape together enough cash, I should like to settle down in France a bit. They have not 'made a bargain with fate' to the same extent as we have.

He believed that the French could appreciate the issues which the war raised and could see the conflict in a much fuller sense than could the English. But in addition, he expressed here his ambivalence of fighting *for* England. He was clear what he was fighting *against* – the assertion of unadulterated power in social, political and international relations – which Germany symbolized for him and of which the German attack on Belgium was a prime example. But what could he be fighting for, aside from the men who stood by his side? Surely not the structure of English society and politics before the war. Surely not for the way of life based on aggressiveness, self-assertion, and pugnacity which he found disturbingly pervasive in English society and at times, present in his own character. Tawney fought for an England which did not exist and may never exist. The point of fighting, ultimately, was to survive, and by surviving to achieve what he saw as a moral authority that could be applied positively to the re-making of English society.[38] The point of fighting, for Tawney, was also to die in part, and through suffering to purge oneself of the weaknesses which prevented concentration on the truly important tasks of one's life.

These remarks only make sense in terms of a religious vision, and it was precisely this aspect of his experience at the Battle of the Somme which Tawney emphasized in the recollections which he wrote soon after the event. His account of the battle is one of the classic pieces of expository prose to come out of the First World War. It is a remarkable portrait of an anguished Christian, and helps reveal the extent to which Tawney's beliefs were exposed to the most severe tests on the Western Front.

Tawney began his recollection of the battle with a priest giving communion in a wooden shanty, with the communicants kneeling in ranks outside. And with the support of prayer, Tawney himself approached the spiritual problems of war. His description of the scene the night before the battle could be taken directly from the *Iliad* or from *Pilgrim's Progress*:[39]

It was a perfect evening, and the immense overwhelming tranquillity of sky and down, uniting us and millions of enemies and allies in its solemn, unavoidable embrace, dwarfed into insignificance the wrath of man and his feverish energy of destruction. One forgot the object for which we were marching to the trenches. One felt as though one were on the verge of some new and tremendous discovery; ...

In Tawney's mind, gigantic forces were present on the Somme, but also very real human beings who, more often than not, were killed at his side.

He was an actor in a gigantic drama, an insignificant ant; yet this realization did not diminish the shock and revulsion he felt as he watched the suffering of those around him. Tawney introduced to the reader all but one of his comrades in arms to describe their human qualities, and then to remark on their death. After crossing the first line of trenches rather easily, he recalled:[40]

'If it's all like this it's a cake-walk,' said a little man beside me, the kindest and bravest of friends, whom no weariness could discourage or danger daunt, a brick-layer by trade, but one who would turn his hand to anything, the man whom of all others I would choose to have beside me at a pinch; but he's dead.

The shock was repeated later in the action:[41]

Just in front of me lay a boy who had been my batman till I sacked him for slackness. I had cursed him the day before for being drunk. He lay quite flat, and might have been resting, except for a big ragged hole at the base of his skull where a bullet had come out. His closest friend, also a bit of a scallywag, was dead beside him.

But the startling abruptness of death evoked only one level of emotional reaction to the battle. The turmoil he felt was deepened by Tawney's natural compassion – and revulsion – for the men half-killed and maimed. He approached a man shot through the stomach:[42]

I went to him, and he grunted, as if to say, 'I am in terrible pain; you must do something for me; you must do something for me.' I hate touching wounded men – moral cowardice, I suppose. One hurts them so much and there's so little to be done. I tried, without much success, to ease his equipment, and then thought of getting him into the trench. But it was crowded with men and there was no place to put him. So I left him. He grunted again angrily, and looked at me with hatred as well as pain in his eyes. It was horrible. It was as though he cursed me for being alive and strong when he was in torture.

Again in no-man's-land, he was confronted with this macabre scene. Tawney saw his men[43]

staring stupidly, like calves smelling blood, at two figures. One was doubled over his stomach, hugging himself and frowning. The other was holding his hand out and looking at it with a puzzled expression. It was covered with blood – the fingers, I fancy, were blown off – and he seemed to be saying: 'Well, this is a funny kind of thing to have for a hand.'

Such bizarre events were all too familiar to millions of men who shared the damp squalor of the trenches. Tawney felt the need to tell the yet unknowing world of these casual slaughters, and his ironic tone brings out well the surrealistic nature of battle.

But how ironic could he be about his relationship to the third party to this comic, yet all too human drama: not the metaphorical or metaphysical German idea, but the enemy troops who were being killed and maimed just as surely as were his own men? His statement about confronting the Germans is the most revealing of Tawney's descriptions of his reactions to the Battle of the Somme: [44]

> For the moment the sight of the Germans drove everything else out of my head. Most men, I suppose, have a palaeolithic savage somewhere in them, a beast that occasionally shouts to be given a chance of showing his joyful cunning in destruction. I have, anyway, and from the age of catapults to that of shot-guns always enjoyed aiming at anything that moved, though since manhood the pleasure has been sneaking and shamefaced.

The civilized veneer was stripped from Tawney during the battle, and it was on this level of the instinctive, destructive, and capricious animal that he did his duty. His targets were easy and very human: [45]

> For the Germans were brave men, as brave as lions. Some of them actually knelt – one for a moment even stood – on the top of their parapet, to shoot, within not much more than a hundred yards of us. It was insane. It seemed one couldn't miss them. Every man I fired at dropped, except one. Him, the boldest of the lot, I missed more than once. I was puzzled and angry. Three hundred years ago I should have tried a silver bullet. Not that I wanted to hurt him or anyone else. It was missing I hated. That's the beastliest thing in war, the damnable frivolity. One's like a merry, mischievous ape tearing up the image of God. . . . God forgive us all! But then it was as I say.

The beastly, the childish, the frivolous, the urge to destroy mechanically, acts drained of all human sentiment: Tawney was guilty of all these and had to confess these sins to the reader.

At the same time other men had to pay the price for Tawney's mistakes in the battle. Having lost contact with the unit on his right, and having forgotten that that was the purpose of one of his crawling forays along the trench, Tawney told a man near him[46]

> to take an order to establish contact, if there was anyone with whom to make it. Like a brave fellow he at once left the comparative safety of his shell-hole; but I'd hardly turned my head when a man said, 'He's hit.' That hurt me. It was as if I'd condemned him to death.

But so far, he was an observer to all these scenes of butchery and casual slaughter, and indeed here was his last defence. His own position was secure as a witness to the ordeal. Tawney thought his position was safe. Indeed, he recalled, 'I knew I shouldn't be hurt; knew it positively, much more positively than I know most things I'm paid for knowing.'[47] And again:[48]

> One couldn't believe that the air a foot or two above one's head was deadly. The weather was so fine and bright that the thought of death, if it had occurred to me, which it didn't, would have seemed absurd.

But then Tawney was brought down to earth – literally. He felt that he had been[49]

> hit by a tremendous iron hammer, swung by a giant of inconceivable strength, and then twisted with a sickening sort of wrench so that my head and back banged on the ground, and my feet struggled as though they didn't belong to me. For a moment or two my breath wouldn't come. I thought – if that's the right word – 'This is death,' and hoped it wouldn't take long.

Yet he did not die so quickly. That would have been too easy. Finally, he had been struck down, not only by a German shell, but also, he may have felt, by the gigantic forces which swirled above his head. And as Tawney lay in no-man's-land, no longer able to remain detached from the pain or suffering which was all around him, he experienced the last and most difficult stage of his ordeal: spiritual isolation. He remembered that 'being cut off from human beings' was the worst part of it all.[50] He was bleeding profusely, without his men or any man to comfort him, with only the noise and tumult of the powers above him, as in the sound of heavy cannons 'starting a long way off, and sweeping towards one with a glorious rush', and Milton is writ large over his words, 'like the swift rustling of enormous and incredibly powerful pinions'.[51]

He was hit in the stomach after about the thirtieth round of cannon fire, and hoped his suffering was over. But 'it was only an extra heavy sod of earth' which had temporarily taken his breath. All he could do was wait and stare at the sky to divert himself by telling time by the sun.[52] Tawney wrote with unmistakable Biblical reference: the sun 'stood straight overhead in an enormous arch of blue. After an age I looked again. It stood in the same place, as though performing a miracle to plague me.'[53] The divine forces were still around as they had been throughout the battle.

But there were limits to his strength. Finally all Tawney's restraint broke. He wrote that he had lost his self-respect, cried out for men to come to help him, although he knew it was asking people to commit suicide. And he could not even faint. He felt 'as though the world had spun him off into a desert of unpeopled space'.[54] Pain, helplessness, abandonment, the nearness of death, the scent of blood: Tawney described and intended to describe the experience of the cross.

And as if by a miracle, he was resurrected by a doctor who thought that Tawney would die, and that there was really very little to be done for him. Nevertheless Tawney had felt the presence of another human being. He wrote:[55]

I did so want to be spoken kindly to, and I began to whimper, partly to myself, partly aloud. But they came back, and, directly the doctor spoke to his orderly, I knew he was one of the best men I had ever met. He can't have been more than twenty-six or twenty-seven; but his face seemed to shine with love and comprehension, not of one's body only, but of one's soul, and with the joy of spending freely a wisdom and good-ness drawn from inexhaustible sources. He listened like an angel. . .

Tawney was back where he started: in the presence of a priest, a man of God, who had brought him back to life. He wrote that at that moment:[56]

after I had felt that divine compassion flow over me, I didn't care. I was like a dog kicked and bullied by everyone that's at last found a kind master, and in a grovelling kind of way I worshipped him.

The ordeal was over, and Tawney had survived physically, and more importantly to him, spiritually. He had covered only a few hundred yards of French soil, but it would be unreasonable to estimate how far he had gone in his 'spiritual journey', which was the way he saw it. The important fact was that he had come back from the dead with his belief in God intact. Thus he could write in October 1916 that 'in suffering, as in knowledge, there is something that transcends personal emotion and unites the soul to the suffering and wisdom of God'.[57]

The next step for Tawney was to relate his ordeal to the development of his society. During his convalescence in the months after the battle, he was forcefully struck by what he saw as the spiritual distance between the men who had fought and the men who had stayed at home. The difference in experience was obvious, but the age-old problem of the psychological, social, and moral reintegration of the soldier into civilian life remained. Was it the veterans' task to forget, to reduce the intensity of his experience in order to be able to live in the everyday world, to go through an emotional decompression chamber, as it were? Tawney's answer was no. Rather, it was the soldiers' task to help remake society to meet the demands of the vision of sacrifice which the war had provided. If the combatants' standard of fellowship in a common purpose could be brought to bear on internal political issues, this would constitute, Tawney felt, a revolution in political thought, a profound change in the way people approached social questions. Here was the soldiers' legacy as well as the social justification for their ordeal.

But he was afraid that the civilian population would find these issues utterly foreign, because of the spiritual and intellectual gap, the differences in 'modes of thought'[58] between England and the Front. Tawney believed that the people at home were incapable of seeing the moral problems of the war, of seeing war as a 'state of existence' shared by both sides. One cause of this incomprehension was the journalistic description of trench life which sickened him. They presented war as a spectacle, 'a work of art', a second-rate novel with villains, the Huns, and heroes, the Tommies. Tawney angrily asked, in an article in the *Nation* in October 1916:[59]

Do you not see that we regard these men who have sat opposite us in mud – 'square-headed bastards', as we called them – as the victims of the same catastrophe as ourselves, as our comrades in misery much more truly than you are?

What was missing was the awareness of the moral difficulties which every soldier in each army faced. And without this awareness, all the pictures of men at war were caricatures or obscene jokes. Tawney had returned home to find that:[60]

Of your soldiers' internal life, the constant collision of contradictory moral standards, the liability of the soul to be crushed by mechanical monotony, the difficulty of keeping hold of sources of refreshment, the sensation of taking a profitless part in a game played by monkeys and organised by lunatics, you realise, I think, nothing.

And when he realized that few men knew or wanted to know of the pathetic nature of war, he saw all the effort, energy, and real idealism of the men who had fought evaporate. And most were not even aware of the loss. After seeing various accounts in the press, he was at his most despairing:[61]

As I read them, I reflect upon the friends who, after suffering various degrees of torture, died in the illusion that war was not the last word of Christian wisdom. And I have a sensation as of pointed ears and hairy paws and a hideous ape-face grinning into mine – sin upon sin, misery upon misery, to the end of the world.

The only way out of this hideous vision, the only way to avoid losing control of one's mind during war and one's sense of perspective about it, Tawney believed, was to establish and act on an idea of what was to follow the conflict. This was the importance of the idealism of the summer of 1914: that it would lead to the demand for a new world to be built through 'fellowship in a moral idea or purpose'.[62] Tawney's desire to translate that vision into concrete form led to the readjustment of his political thought in the last two years of the war.

THE WAR AND TAWNEY'S POLITICAL THOUGHT

Tawney's war experience deeply affected his socialist thought. The fact that the nation virtually with one voice had committed its material and human resources to the prosecution of a just cause convinced him that the conflict had altered the internal development of British political and social affairs in a positive way. He saw in the national mobilization for war the faint outline of a future stable society in which men were bound together for the moral and physical betterment of all. This spiritual unity which the conflict generated in its first months fulfilled what Tawney defined as the necessary preconditions for institutional action. All political associations were, in his opinion, inherently mechanical bodies, which were capable of effective action only when animated by a body of opinion which existed outside and grew independently of them. He was convinced that the First World War had uncovered and developed such a progressive movement in mass political and social attitudes. Accordingly during the war he adjusted his ideas about the state, the Anglican Church, and the Labour Party.

The state in wartime

Tawney was still recuperating from his wounds when he was asked in November 1916 by the Assistant Cabinet Secretary, Tom Jones, to help draft a memorandum on 'the need for a new spirit in government and the conduct of the war'.[63] Also invited to exchange views on this subject were J. J. Mallon, a labour adviser at the Board of Trade and a friend of Tawney, A. E. Zimmern, the Oxford classical historian, and a former member of Milner's 'Kindergarten' in Egypt, the industrialist Lionel Hichens. Lloyd George wanted the finished document within twenty-four hours of his request on 28 November.[64] It was clearly part of his attempt to under-score the need for new and dynamic national leadership, which, of course, only he could provide. Apparently, Tawney was able to overlook Lloyd George's unscrupulousness in the hope that he would be better able than Asquith to reassert the authority required to win the war.[65]

The overall theme of the memorandum was the need for universal submission to the state in wartime. Tawney and his colleagues stated that Britain had to develop 'a form of national concentration' as effective as German efforts and at the same time 'consistent with our highest traditions and compatible with the ideals which led us into the struggle'. What had to be combated at home was 'the surviving poison of social prejudice and class interests', which led to the taking of unjustified profits and 'advances in wages beyond what may reasonably be required to meet the increased cost of necessaries' by well-paid workers 'when the weakest members of the community are not far from starvation'.[66] Sections of the Labour movement were not immune from the indictment which Tawney among others supported. 'It is detestable,' they felt, 'that the conduct of industry, any more than the manning of a fire-trench, should be the subject of haggling over the division of financial spoils wrung from the country in its hour of need.'[67] Tawney's hand may be seen in the further admonition that:[68]

> The soldier at the front expects from the civilian and from the Government a sense of obedience to duty and an enforcement of discipline as severe and as exacting as that to which he is himself accustomed. The call of duty should be imposed on all alike.

The key words in this appeal: concentration, obedience, discipline, duty, took on a new and specific meaning for Tawney during the First World War. Their religious as well as military reference reveal his belief in the need to transform the wartime state into a church militant.

In that spirit, Tawney advocated the following measures (1) 'That obedience to the considered decision of the Government should be rigidly enforced upon all sections of the Community'; (2) that state control had to be extended over shipping and food importation, production and distribution, regardless of property rights; (3) 'That in order to liberate labour and capital for more fruitful employment, the State should prohibit the manufacture of certain commodities', and encourage the export trade by selective supply of raw materials; (4) that more industries should be nationalized with 'provision for adequate representation of the workers' or at least that limitation of profits should be enforced in all trades; and (5) 'That the age of liability to national service be raised to 60.'[69] Lloyd George was explicitly told by Tom Jones that the last point was a call for industrial conscription. Only on the question of coloured labour coming to Britain to help fill the manpower shortage did Tawney and his colleagues fail to agree.[70]

Tawney's support for these proposals showed his willingness to sanction the erection of a vast wartime state with unparalleled powers and authority. The claims of lesser associations, such as trade unions, had to be overlooked during the national emergency.

It is difficult to see the place of dissent, let alone an anti-war movement, in the political structure which he helped outline. But Tawney's war was a struggle for survival, and therefore groups of people opposed to the war at least had to be prevented from interfering with the national effort.

At the same time, he was fully aware that the consent of the working population was crucial to prevent the transformation of national direction into dictatorship. He repeatedly insisted, Tom Jones noted, 'that some way of getting the Labour leaders to "lead" must be found, and of making the working men feel how much is at stake for them'.[71] Tawney therefore wrote in December 1916 that in order to win the war, England[72]

> must sound a call that can stir the blood of men who do not chatter in lobbies or lounge in clubs, but who sweat half-naked in the mine and at the forge, and who will not be so quick to hear it because they have not heard it for so long.

Repeating his argument at the outbreak of the war, he insisted two years later that the only way to mobilize the support of those men was to 'make victory in this war a symbol of the victory of the social aspirations of the mass of Englishmen', by applying 'the principles which united the nation for a few months in 1914 . . . to the purpose of social organisation for war'.[73]

One important step which Tawney specifically advocated was that the state should accept the partnership of the trade unions 'as the industrial organs of England at war'. The fact that they were not recognized earlier, he reasoned, accounted in part for the hostility of some trade unionists to the war and for the fact that others 'have tended to drop merely into the position of critics, when they should have insisted that it was for democracy to plan the economic and social organisation, by which a war for democracy is to be carried on'.[74] The entire Labour movement had to be shown, Tawney believed, that the war could be a powerful vehicle for social change, but only if they asserted the workers' right to manage their contribution to the war effort. Such a shift in political power would amount to an 'internal revolution', the only alternative to which was to make peace because the purpose of the war had been lost. The choice, in Tawney's words, was between 'Democracy or Defeat'.[75]

There was a third alternative of which Tawney became aware in the next year of the war. It was the continuation of the war for no better reason than sheer inertia. This loss of purpose was partly due to the lack of 'intellectual direction and leadership'. He agreed with the Master of Balliol, A. L. Smith, that there was a 'want of single-mindedness in the nation' in December 1917, which had 'grown as different classes became less assured of the moral issues involved in the war'. 'Three years ago,' Tawney recalled.[76]

> the war was popular, a thing for which people were glad to make sacrifices. At present, as far as I can see, it is not. I doubt if one could get a hearing at a working-class meeting if one spoke on the principles at stake. One would get laughed down.

Even an 'authoritative statement' of the Government's objects 'would not take us very far now. Suspicion has gone too deep. The whole governing class, and its appendages, is disturbed, including, with one or two exceptions, the Labour members who have joined the Government.'[77] Tawney flirted with the idea of a new Coalition in which Labour would serve on its own terms, and with stronger representatives, not just those who were 'manageable'. The 'result might be a new confidence and spirit of unity' and 'the support of the vociferous forces whose inertia and silent opposition is an obstacle to winning the war'. But he stepped back from political manoeuvre. He was against the views of those who, without regard for the war effort, would 'use this "occasion" to grind the Labour or any other axe'.[78] The real problem was still the mobilization of popular attitudes. Tawney concluded, therefore, that:[79]

> The war seems to have caught us halfway in a transition to Democracy. We have not the kind of strength Germany has. Nor have we the kind of strength which we should have if the mass of the working people felt that this war was their war, not an enterprise for which their rulers want their arms but not their minds and hearts.

Again, Tawney put his ideas into print in an attempt to bring attention to the 'degeneration of national purpose' which he believed to be the greatest threat to the war effort. Echoing some of the sentiments which Lord Lansdowne had expressed in the controversial letter which was published on 29 November 1917 in the *Daily Telegraph*, Tawney complained bitterly in the December 1917 *Athenaeum* that, by then,[80]

> the loyalty which was given to the cause for which the war was undertaken is transferred to the war itself. It becomes an

article of faith whose character and objects it is heresy to question. ... Peace itself is no longer thought of as the reconciliation of enemies through the victory of a principle. It is the last trick to be snatched by the winner of a game of bluff and cunning.

The Russian Revolution, and its progressively more hostile reception in the West, and the withdrawal of Arthur Henderson from the government in August 1917 may have contributed to Tawney's progressive disillusionment with the war. 'A year ago,' Tawney recalled, the soldiers[81]

> discussed one thing and one thing alone: How long will it last? Today the question is turning into another: Why does it go on? They have some right to an answer, the right of men who are waiting for death.

Yet, he did not go as far as Lord Lansdowne and say that the war had to end before all that was valuable in Western civilization was destroyed. All Tawney demanded here was a statement of war aims and an indication of the point at which negotiations could begin to end the conflict. Then he believed the whole nation could 'more effectively wage war, by waging it with our minds as well as with our bodies'.[82] All aspects of political life and state policy were still, in his view, components of the military victory for which he was prepared to, and nearly did, give his life.

But regardless of the outcome, Tawney believed that institutional relationships within the state would never be the same after the war. His work for the radical reform of the Anglican Church, through the Archbishop's Committee of Inquiry on Christianity and Industrial Problems and the Life and Liberty Movement, organized by his contemporary at Rugby and Balliol, William Temple, and his contribution to the reconstruction of the Labour Party were reflections of his belief, as stated in 1918, 'that the social and political existence of the majority of Englishmen now living will be dominated by the forces which the war has released'. He further asserted that:[83]

> The England of 1920 will differ from that of 1914, not merely because it has passed through an Industrial Revolution, but because of a new quality in its moral and intellectual atmosphere. Partly as the culmination of movements at work in all European countries before 1914, partly as the result of the development of thought in the forcing-house of war, the world

has been prepared side by side with the practical innovations in its industrial organisation, for a revolution in the standards by which industrial and social life are judged. Not merely the facts, but the minds which appraise them have been profoundly modified.

Surely, the war did not create 'the problems which reform must solve, it has only been the lightning which revealed' their existence to the nation as a whole.[84] Thus because of the war the Church and the Labour Party could act, Tawney believed, in ways which were inconceivable before 1914. Their leaders owed no less than a new beginning to the war's countless casualties. 'A little less than five hundred years ago,' Tawney wrote in February 1917:[85]

> a great man desired to commemorate the end of one of the most futile and miserable of wars in which the English nation was ever engaged. He endowed a college 'to pray for the souls of all those who fell in the grievous wars between France and England.' We stand for a moment where Chichele stood, because we stand upon a world of graves. With a nobler cause we ought not to be content with a memorial less noble.

This eloquent argument for the reconstruction of educational institutions applied with equal force to all others as well. Reform would come, Tawney believed, because 'the war has forced thousands of Englishmen to look, as they never looked before, into their own souls'.[86]

The Church of England

In that spirit, Tawney collaborated from late 1916 until 1918 with Bishop Gore, the Reverend G. K. A. Bell, later Bishop of Chichester, A. L. Smith, George Lansbury, Albert Mansbridge of the WEA, Lionel Hichens, with whom he drafted the memorandum for Lloyd George, and nineteen others in an effort, in the words of Bishop Talbot of Winchester, 'to search out and lay to heart in definite and practical form, the lessons which through the War, God had taught to us'.[87] This remarkable report was based upon 'the belief that the time requires a new beginning on the part of the Church in defining its attitude to the economic and social life of the nation'. And:[88]

> To admit the necessity of a new beginning is to imply that something has been wrong in the past, and to acknowledge a

need for repentance . . . for an undue subservience of the Church to the possessing, employing and governing classes of the past.

Penitence was often a response to military defeat, such as in the most recent case of France after 1871, but it was very unusual in a nation whose armies were still intact. The authors of the report expressed 'a desire that a call as of a trumpet should go forth to the Church to reconsider its moral and social meaning and bearing of its faith'.[89] 'The lamentable failure of the Church's recent witness' was to be seen in its exclusive concentration on charity and personal character, which neglected the social determinants of the latter.[90] What the Church had consistently failed to see or deliberately ignored was the fact that the industrial 'system itself makes it exceedingly difficult to carry into practice the principles of Christianity'.[91] Tawney's style may be seen in the extension of this argument:[92]

We cannot believe in the stability of any society, however imposing its economic triumphs, if it cripples the personality of its workers, or if it deprives them of that control over the material conditions of their own lives which is the essence of practical freedom.

And again in the insistence 'that industry is before all things, a social function',[93] which had to be based upon 'that common principle of public service which, as we have already suggested, receives in modern industry, no emphasis sufficiently obvious and unmistakable to make it of cogent authority'.[94]

The commission was unable to agree on a specific call for the nationalization of certain industries, as Tawney would have preferred, but it did go so far as to endorse his view that 'industrial autocracy'[95] must be ended and that:[96]

the organisation of industry must be such as not merely to yield a life of security and comfort to all engaged in it, but to admit of their exercising a genuine and increasing control over the conditions upon which their livelihood depends and over industrial policy and organisation, in so far as those conditions are affected by them.

'What is required is some change of status' of the worker, the report went on, so 'that his position should be that, not of a hand, but of a citizen of industry'.[97]

At the same time, the educational views of Tawney, Mansbridge, and A. L. Smith, all of whom were dedicated to the WEA, were endorsed by the commission. The Report stated that 'After the Church, education is the most formal and public recognition of the claims of the spirit which the world has allowed.'[98] It also urged the increase of expenditure on all related services, including adult education.

'We believe,' the report concluded, 'that in a "day of fire" like the present, much that has been wrong and worldly in the past will be burned away.'[99] It followed that the organization as well as the policy of the Church had to be modernized to meet the crisis, or in its original meaning, the judgment, of the day. To secure a new freedom of action for the Church, and to loosen the tight control of the worldly state, Tawney joined William Temple and others in the spring of 1917 to form the Life and Liberty Movement.[100]

Temple accepted the argument of the Archbishop's commission that the war was a time of crisis for the Church of England as for the rest of European civilization. But even though the task of reform was accepted, 'When the Church, realising the presence of Judgment, sets itself to remedy the fault' of indifference to 'the moral demands of Christianity' in social and industrial life, it could do little, since 'even so far as concerns administrative machinery and the appointed order of worship, it finds its hands tied' by parliamentary control.[101] All Temple asked for the Church was the 'full power to manage its own affairs through representative and responsible assemblies'.[102] The exact form of the new Church and its relation to the state were left unspecified at this time, though, since Temple believed it was more important to convince Christians of the 'intolerable hindrance' to the Church's 'spiritual activity' than to make concrete proposals.[103]

Above all, the need to re-think and re-structure all aspects of social life under the impact of war was at the heart of the Life and Liberty movement and Tawney's work for it. Lansbury classed him and Temple as the two leaders of the movement.[104] For both men, it was precisely during war that a new spiritual purpose had to be found to revitalize all associations. At a meeting to launch the movement on 18 July 1917, at which Tawney was a prominent speaker, the following resolution was carried:[105]

Revolutionary changes are taking effect in other departments of national life: our industrial system is passing from the despotic or oligarchic stage to the democratic; our educational system is being extended in a way that two years ago would have seemed incredible. Is the Church alone to be condemned to immobility so long as the war lasts, though it is in the sphere of the spiritual that the changes of our time go deepest?

Temple reiterated this view in his note to his parishioners, on his resignation from St James's, Piccadilly, in order to devote all his efforts to Life and Liberty in November 1917. The war was the occasion for institutional reform, he believed, precisely because 'Men's minds are open now to large ideas. The world has to be rebuilt. Now is the time for tracing the lines of the new building.'[106]

The Labour Party

The same analysis applied to the Labour Party, the reconstruction of which was made inevitable by the war. By 1917, Tawney was prepared to give his whole-hearted support to the efforts of Henderson and Webb to revise the party's structure and programme. But even before the former left the Coalition over the Stockholm affair in the summer of 1917, Tawney told Tom Jones that they and their friends, such as Mallon and Arthur Greenwood, 'ought to stand [for Parliament] at the end of the war and help on reconstruction'.[107] By October 1917, Tawney joined a group of Labour intellectuals, including Mallon, Greenwood, and G. D. H. Cole, who gathered to 'discuss the programme of the new Labour Party' with Henderson and Webb.[108]

Tawney's acceptance of the tactical primacy of parliamentary socialism was a major shift from his pre-war political thought. His move to the centre of Labour politics was partly a result of the party's wartime turn to the left. It was also a reflection of his belief that 'This is a war after which there will be no Restoration.'[109] New political structures were needed to wage war and were found. Similarly, a new Labour Party was called forth to act on the 'revelation of the possibilities of social transformation' which the war occasioned.[110] In 1918, socialists like Tawney could point to the fact that 'the economic mechanism, which seemed so ponderous and rigid' before the war, had been radically altered 'by a collective act of will, because there was a strong enough motive, which was not an economic motive to transform it'.[111] It was their task to see a similar motive applied to post-war social problems.

Tawney was instrumental in the preparation of some aspects of party policy in 1918. He was the dominant figure on the Education Advisory Committee which the party established as one of nine on 13 March 1918.[112] He also attended the meetings of the International Advisory Committee at irregular intervals,[113] but it was on the former group that his influence was most significant.

The official chairman of the committee, Frank Goldstone, M.P., agreed to head the group on condition that he did not have to attend its fortnightly meetings.[114] His absence resulted in an invitation to Sidney Webb to replace Goldstone, but even then, Webb merely seconded the proposals which Tawney drafted.[115] The latter prepared numerous memoranda on the Education Bill of 1918, which provided continued education for all children aged fourteen to sixteen, and after 1925, to age eighteen.[116] Tawney wanted to impress upon the Labour Party that 'The young men and women of the future will be very largely what the continuation schools make them'. Since the vast majority of working-class children would pass through these schools 'at the most plastic period of their development' it was not an exaggeration to say that 'Upon the quality of the schools ... will depend not only the physical and intellectual development of the next generation, but their outlook upon life, their conception of society, and their capacity for citizenship'.[117] As in his Memoranda on nursery schools, maintenance scholarships, and juvenile labour as affected by the war, Tawney's educational ideas had not changed.[118] What was new was his influential role in the formulation of Labour Party policy.

The final aspect of his work for the Labour Party during the First World War was his unsuccessful fight as parliamentary candidate for Rochdale in the 1918 election. Tawney agreed to contest Rochdale, with the approval of the ILP, on 26 October 1918, only after the initial choice of the Rochdale Trades and Labour Council, E. C. Fairchild of the British Socialist Party, chose conscientious objection as an alternative to military service. J. J. Mallon was considered by the Council before Tawney, but the former was placed at Saffron Waldon, so Tawney was finally adopted.[119]

His opponents were: Vivian Philips, who had been private secretary to Asquith for the previous twenty months; the Conservative, A. J. Law, J.P. who eventually got the 'coupon', or official support of the Coalition; Joe Terrett of the British Workers' League, a trade-union group hostile to the ILP and what it thought to be the disproportionate influence of pacifists in the Labour Party; and Major Fitzgerald Jones of the National Party.[120]

In one of his campaign addresses, Tawney 'expressed himself in favour of the principles of the labour movement', but also spoke to potential middle-class supporters in asserting that 'he did not base his appeal on sectional interests'.[121] In the interests of all, he urged the continuation of public ownership in all the industries taken over by the government in wartime. He also complained about Lloyd George's hurry in calling the election, resulting in the disenfranchisement of about half the men in uniform. He attributed the rush to the fact that 'The ruling classes knew that if the people had time to reflect they would demand real and fundamental changes'.[122]

On one specific point, he revealed that his idea of the wartime state would not, in part, outlive the conflict. The new Labour Party, he argued, had to recover the liberties which were suspended during the previous four years. 'To save Europe,' he reasoned, 'we acquiesced in the introduction of compulsory military service; [the Labour Party] must see that that temporary measure did not become a permanent institution.' He admitted that although some conscientious objectors may have been foolish and misguided, they had been badly treated. Furthermore, it was true that during the war, 'Parliament had surrendered the right to criticise and control the executive.' But he opposed the Coalition precisely because he believed that it 'endeavoured to subvert the Parliamentary system' by trying 'to return tied members' to the House of Commons.[123]

Tawney angered some of his audience in his election address of 8 December by insisting: 'I am in favour of making Germany pay full reparation to the countries she has ravaged. I am not in favour of imposing on Germany the cost of the war.'[124] Even from a former soldier, this statement sounded too pro-German in the heady days after the armistice. Allegiance to Lloyd George as the man who had won the war was the order of the day, and consequently Tawney received 4,956 votes, which placed him third on the poll behind the Coalition Unionist, who was elected, and the Liberal candidate, who was not.[125] For the present, Tawney's role in the Labour Party had to remain that of an adviser and theoretician.

The party he now supported had been through a very severe test during the war. While his beliefs had brought him to enlist and serve in uniform, others were engaged in the work which made it possible by 1918 for socialists as different as Cole and Tawney and thousands of others to commit themselves to what was really a new political party. Arthur Henderson and Ramsay MacDonald are the public figures most closely associated with this transformation. But the man who did most to enable the Labour movement to weather the storm of war and to emerge from the conflict in a much strengthened position was Sidney Webb. Like Cole and Tawney, his attitude to the world crisis and to Labour's role in the war effort grew directly out of his socialist ideas. The story of Webb's war experience is, to a large extent, to be found in the history of a group known as the War Emergency: Workers' National Committee.

NOTES

1 M. Buber, *Pointing the Way*, 1957, pp. 119–20, in memory of the German socialist, Gustave Landauer.

2 The phrase is that of the title of Élie Halévy's 1929 Rhodes Memorial Lectures given at Oxford. They are reprinted in *The Era of Tyrannies*, trans. by R. K. Webb, 1967, pp. 161–90. Tawney attended these lectures and was profoundly moved by them. He repeatedly stated that Halévy's interpretation, stressing the disturbing effect of the war on the precarious social equilibrium of each combatant nation, coincided with his own views. Cf. Tawney, *Why Britain Fights*, New York, 1941, p. 32; his article, 'Social Democracy in Britain', in W. Scarlett (ed.), *The Christian Demand for Social Justice*, New York, 1949, p. 96; and, his pamphlet, *The Workers' Educational Association and Adult Education*, 1953, p. 6. The same reference to Halévy's thesis on the war appears in a number of Tawney's unpublished lectures, collected in a box labelled 'War and Contemporary Post-War Politics', which may be found at the London School of Economics. Professor M. M. Postan, who also attended the lectures, confirmed that Tawney's views on the war are best understood in terms of Halévy's thesis.

3 Beveridge Papers, LI 210 additional (a), Jeanette Tawney to her family, 26 November 1914.

4 J. R. Williams, R. M. Titmuss and F. J. Fisher, *R. H. Tawney*, 1960, p. 7.

5 Jeanette Tawney's correspondence in the Beveridge Papers continually records her illnesses. Prior to the First World War, she frequently convalesced in Malta for increasingly longer periods at the suggestion of her doctor. The long list of maladies she repeatedly described to her brother included a number of physical impossibilities. One could speculate about the financial burden involved in her treatment, since she constantly asked her brother for money to help make ends meet. Cf. Jeanette Tawney to her family, 19 October 1910, 15 January 1911, 11 February 1911, etc. in L210, Box 2; also Tawney to Mrs Beveridge

on his wife's financial support during the war, 31 May 1916, Box
LI 210 additional (b): all in the Beveridge Papers. Jeanette worked
as a factory inspector during the war.

6 Beveridge Papers, LI 210 additional (a), Jeanette to her family,
5 February 1915, 3 March 1915; 25 April 1915; 24 May 1915;
7 August 1915; 23 September 1915.

7 Beveridge Papers, LI 210 additional (a), Jeanette to William Beveridge, 23 February 1916; Jeanette to her family, 12 October 1915;
10 November 1915; LI 210 additional (a), Tawney to William
Beveridge, 1 December 1915.

8 Beveridge Papers, LI 210 additional (a), Tawney to Beveridge,
22 December 1915. On Tawney's regiment, cf. G. L. Campbell,
The Manchesters, Manchester, 1916, pp. 73–4; and F. Kemster and
H. C. E. Westropp (eds), *Manchester City Battalions*, Manchester,
1916, p. 318, for a picture of Tawney in uniform as corporal 20328
in Platoon V, B Company, 22nd Service Battalion, 91st Infantry
Brigade, 7th Army Division, 13th Corps, 3rd Army. See Plate 11.

9 Beatrice Webb recorded this extraordinary meeting in her unpublished diary, vol. 33, 22 February 1916. I have not been able to find
a copy of this manifesto.

10 On Keeling, cf. E. Townshend (ed.), *Keeling Letters and Recollections*,
1918. Many of the letters published there may be found in the R. C.
K. Ensor collection at Corpus Christi College, Oxford.

11 Beveridge Papers, LI 210 additional (a), telegram of Jeanette to her
family, 6 July 1916: 'Harry wounded sunday sent base please try
ascertain particulars'; letter of Jeanette to William Beveridge, 6 July
1916; postcard from Jeanette to her family, 17 July 1916.

12 Tawney, 'The Attack', in *The Attack and other papers*, 1953, p. 20.
Cf. also, A. Gleason, *What the Workers Want*, 1920, p. 36, for this
description of Tawney in 1919: 'No one seeing the care-free, lovable
young person would guess that two years ago he lay for thirty-six
hours in No Man's Land, bleeding his life away. What saved him
was the fact that he had previously drunk his canteen of water, and,
being parched, the blood so thickened as to form its own protective
clot.' The war diary of Tawney's regiment described the attack as
partially successful, since B company and one other occupied the
first German line. The main objective, 'Fritz trench', was not
reached. PRO, War Office Papers, 95.1669.

13 Beveridge Papers, LI 210 additional (a), card of Jeanette to William
Beveridge, 13 July 1916.

14 Beveridge Papers, LI 210 additional (a), card of Jeanette to William
Beveridge, 24 September 1917; LIII 227, Beveridge to Brigadier-
General Geddes, 11 November 1916.

15 British Library of Political and Economic Science, Lansbury Papers,
vol. 7, Gore to Lansbury, 23 December 1916.

16 Bodleian Library, The Hammond Papers, Mss. 17, Tawney to
Hammond, 3 May 1918.

17 P. A. Brown, *The French Revolution in English History*, ed. J. L.
Hammond, 1918.

18 Lansbury Papers, vol. 7, Denman to Lansbury, 13 June 1915; cf. also Denman, *Political Sketches*, Carlyle, 1948.
19 Hammond Papers, Mss. 17, Unwin to Hammond, 10 August 1914. Unwin was a victim of social ostracism for his pacifist view. Barbara Hammond wrote to her husband, who was a cavalry instructor in Scotland, that at the mention of Unwin's name, Professor Tait 'began to exclaim that Mr. Unwin's wild and absurd views on the war made it impossible for his colleagues to see anything of him'. Letter of 11 September 1916.
20 T. S. Ashton, 'Richard Henry Tawney', *Proceedings of the British Academy*, 48, 1962, p. 463.
21 Unwin, *Studies in Economic History*, 1927, pp. lii–liii.
22 Tawney, *Religion and the Rise of Capitalism*, 1926, p. 212.
23 Tawney, 'The philosophy of power I', *Athenaeum*, April 1917, p. 169.
24 CPB, 28 December 1914. For the stability of Tawney's position during the war, cf. this statement made thirty months later: 'The War has revealed the logical conclusion of a certain temper and spirit in public affairs, and that conclusion is applicable far beyond the immediate range of military policy and international law to which its application is most obvious.' Tawney, 'The philosophy of power I', *Athenaeum*, April 1917, p. 168.
25 The phrase is Max Weber's, from his essay 'Politics as a Vocation', in H. H. Gerth and C. W. Mills (eds), *From Max Weber: Essays in Sociology*, 1948, p. 127.
26 CPB, 28 December 1914.
27 T–V Papers, ff. 11–12.
28 *Ibid.*, f. 12.
29 *Ibid.*, f. 30.
30 *Ibid.*
31 *Ibid.*, f. 31.
32 Lance-corporal, 'The *personnel* of the new armies', *Nation*, 27 February 1915. Identified from Jeanette Tawney's letter to her parents, LI 210 additional (a), 3 March 1915.
33 *Ibid.* cf. also this comment in Tawney's article, 'The army and religion', *Challenge*, 10 October 1919: 'What civilians appear often to forget is that (except in the peculiar case of long-serving regulars) an army is what a nation is. It reproduces the shades of civilian thought, social distinctions, and etiquette with monotonous accuracy, only it reproduces them more or less petrified and systematised.'
34 *Ibid.*
35 Beveridge Papers, LI 210 additional (a), Tawney to Beveridge, 22 December 1915.
36 *Ibid.*
37 *Ibid.*
38 His friend, J. L. Hammond made the same point six months after the end of the war. He wrote: 'The soldier who returns has broken through the strongest force in our nature, the customary standard, the habit of accepting the world as he finds it. . . . This is a new moral force in our society: the presence of a great mass of men, conscious

of sacrifices and services, who look at the world with new eyes.'
Hammond, 'The war and the mind of Great Britain', *Atlantic
Monthly*, 123, 4, March 1919, p. 356. Hammond, too, was a soldier.

39 Tawney, *The Attack and other papers*, p. 11. The title essay was
written in late July 1916 and was first published in *Westminster
Gazette* in August 1916. It later appeared in the 1937 edition of Guy
Chapman's anthology of writing on the First World War, *Vain
Glory*, which has recently been reprinted. I have been fortunate in
having had the opportunity to discuss Tawney's views on the war
with Dr John Bowlby, who knew Tawney and wrote a very influential book, *Personal Aggressiveness and War*, 1939, with another
friend of Tawney's, E. M. F. Durbin.

40 *Ibid.*, p. 14.
41 *Ibid.*, p. 16.
42 *Ibid.*, pp. 14–15.
43 *Ibid.*, p. 15.
44 *Ibid.*, pp. 15–16.
45 *Ibid.*, p. 16.
46 *Ibid.*, p. 17.
47 *Ibid.*, p. 14.
48 *Ibid.*, p. 17.
49 *Ibid.*, p. 18.
50 *Ibid.*
51 *Ibid.*
52 *Ibid.*, p. 19.
53 *Ibid.* He refers to the story of Joshua in the valley of Ajalon.
54 *Ibid.*
55 *Ibid.*
56 *Ibid.*, p. 20.
57 Tawney, 'Some reflections of a soldier', in *The Attack and other
papers*, p. 27. This essay was reprinted by the WEA from the
original article in the *Nation* in October 1916.
58 *Ibid.*, p. 21.
59 *Ibid.*, p. 25.
60 *Ibid.*
61 *Ibid.*, p. 26.
62 *Ibid.*, p. 27.
63 Tom Jones, *Whitehall Diary*, ed. K. Middlemas, 1969, vol. 1, p. 3,
December 1916. The editor has informed me that the original
manuscript has been reprinted virtually verbatim.
64 *Ibid.*, p. 2, 28 November 1916. Most of the entries are in the form of
notes from Jones to his wife.
65 *Ibid.*, pp. 7–8, 7 December 1916.
66 *Ibid.*, p. 3.
67 *Ibid.*, p. 4.
68 *Ibid.*
69 *Ibid.*, pp. 4–5.
70 *Ibid.*, p. 3, 28 November 1916.
71 Ibid., p. 8, 7 December 1916.

72 Tawney, *Democracy or Defeat*, 1917, p. 8, reprinted by the WEA from the *Welsh Outlook* of January 1917. Cf. Tom Jones's note in his *Whitehall Diary*, vol. 1, p. 16, 16 December 1916: 'I have just written a line to the P.M. for tomorrow Sunday and have sent with it a typed copy of Tawney's article for the next 'Outlook' on 'Democracy and Defeat', on the chance of L.G. reading it. For I think in his heart, L.G. agrees with our position, that the people themselves must realise more and more that it is democracy that is at stake.'

73 Tawney, *Democracy or Defeat*, pp. 8–9, 10.

74 *Ibid.*, p. 8.

75 *Ibid.*, pp. 9, 10.

76 Balliol College, Oxford, A. L. Smith Papers, Tawney to Smith, 27 December 1917.

77 *Ibid.*

78 *Ibid.*

79 *Ibid.*

80 Tawney, *The Sword of the Spirit*, pp. 4–5, from the *Athenaeum*, December 1917, reprinted by the Athenaeum Literary Department in 1918.

81 *Ibid.*, p. 15.

82 *Ibid.*, p. 8.

83 *Labour and Capital after the War*, ed. S. J. Chapman, 1918, pp. 93–4. Chapter 5 of this book was written by Tawney and has been reprinted under the title, 'The conditions of economic liberty' in R. Hinden (ed.), *The Radical Tradition*, 1964, pp. 97–117.

84 *Ibid.*

85 'A national college of All Souls', *Times Educational Supplement*, 22 February 1917, reprinted in *The Attack and other papers*, p. 29.

86 Tawney, 'Educational programme', *Manchester Guardian*, 10 March 1917.

87 W. Talbot *et al.*, *Christianity and Industrial Problems*, 1918, p. vii.

88 *Ibid.*, p. xix.

89 *Ibid.*, p. 1.

90 *Ibid.*, p. 2.

91 *Ibid.*, pp. 80–1.

92 *Ibid.*, p. 87.

93 *Ibid.*, p. 92.

94 *Ibid.*, p. 107.

95 *Ibid.*, p. 138.

96 *Ibid.*, p. 137.

97 *Ibid.*, pp. 138–9.

98 *Ibid.*, p. 174.

99 *Ibid.*, p. 212.

100 William Temple, 'The Life and Liberty movement', *Contemporary Review*, 113, February 1918, p. 163. On Temple and the war cf. his article 'The spiritual call of the war', *Christian Commonwealth*, 26 January 1916. There is also a rather sketchy file on the movement in the library of Lambeth Palace, which includes the interesting letter of 1 July 1917 from eight chaplains at the Front to Temple,

urging that the war had to be a time for new ways for the Church, and a letter of Temple to J. H. Roberts, 7 February 1918, which describes Life and Liberty as part of the necessary return to the 'supernatural element in religion' by the diminution of worldly ties.

101 Temple, 'The Life and Liberty movement', *Contemporary Review*, 113, February 1918, p. 163.

102 *Ibid.*, pp. 165–6.

103 Temple, 'Life and Liberty for the Church', *Christian Commonwealth*, 18 July 1917, which is a report of the Queen's Hall meeting of the movement.

104 George Lansbury, 'Life and Liberty', *Herald*, 20 July 1918. Lansbury paraphrased: 'The Church, as R. H. Tawney says, must make the choice we must all make: "Be Pagan and wealthy or Christian and Poor." '

105 Temple, 'Life and Liberty for the Church', *Christian Commonwealth*, 18 July 1917.

106 Unfortunately, for Tawney, 'Life and Liberty' did not alter the structure of the Church or the nature of its mission in any major way. Cf. F. A. Iremonger, *William Temple*, 1948, pp. 220–81; and St James's Piccadilly *Parish Magazine*, November 1917, in the file on Life and Liberty in Lambeth Palace Library.

107 Tom Jones, *Whitehall Diary*, vol. 1, p. 26, March 1917.

108 *Ibid.*, p. 38, 30 October 1917.

109 S. J. Chapman (ed.), *Labour and Capital after the War*, p. 93.

110 *Ibid.*, p. 97.

111 *Ibid.*, p. 96.

112 LPEC, 13 March 1918.

113 Labour Party Library, Labour Party International Advisory Committee minutes, 14 June 1918.

114 Labour Party Library, Labour Party Education Advisory Committee Minutes, 15 May 1918.

115 *Ibid.*, 12 September 1918.

116 Labour Party Education Advisory Committee Memorandum 6b, 'Continued education under the new Act', November 1918; 6c, a revised version of the first; 6d 'The curriculum of the schools'.

117 Memorandum 6c. Cf. also his address to the Federation of Master Cotton Spinners in Manchester on 16 February 1918, reported in *The Times Educational Supplement*, 21 February 1918.

118 Memoranda 1, 4, 5, 9.

119 *Rochdale Observer*, 5, 19, 26 and 30 October. The *Observer* was a Liberal paper.

120 *Ibid.*, 16 November 1918. On the British Workers' League, cf. Roy Douglas, 'The National Democratic party and the British Workers' League', *Historical Journal*, 15, 3, September 1972, pp. 532–52.

121 *Rochdale Observer*, 23 November 1918.

122 *Ibid.*, 27 November 1918.

123 *Ibid.*

124 *Ibid.*, 11 December 1918.

125 *Ibid.*, 1 January 1919.

7

Sidney Webb and the
War Emergency Committee

The War Emergency: Workers' National Committee,[1] the only independent voice of the united British Labour movement after August 1914, was the primary institutional focus for the Webbs' socialist thought until 1918. Through his work on the committee, Sidney Webb became the guiding figure in the formulation of the only consistent and coherent wartime Labour programme. Under his unquestioned intellectual leadership, this body provided a firm foundation for the reorganization of the Labour Party in the last year of the war.

FORMATION AND MEMBERSHIP

The formation of the War Emergency Committee was an historical accident. On 4 August 1914, Arthur Henderson, as the secretary of the Labour Party, wrote to the members of the NEC to call a special meeting at 10 a.m. the next day 'to consider what action should be taken in the very serious crisis in Europe and any other business that may arise'. He also suggested that a conference of Labour leaders be convened at the House of Commons at 2 p.m. the same day 'for the purpose of considering the formation of a National Peace Emergency Committee'.[2] The objects of this proposed group were to be:

1 To urge the strictest neutrality possible in the present crisis.
2 To take all necessary steps to secure a permanent peace.
3 To render all possible assistance to necessitous citizens by the provision of food, etc.
4 To conduct such propaganda in London and the Provinces as shall assist in furthering any or all of these objects.

5 To publish articles and leaflets giving effect to the objects of the Committee.
6 To raise funds for giving effect to the objects of the Committee.[3]

Henderson envisaged an organization of unprecedented size and representation, which virtually would have constituted a Parliament of Labour. Besides the full Labour Party NEC and Parliamentary Committee of the Trades Union Congress (PCTUC), and the entire management committee of the General Federation of Trade Unions (GFTU), the Peace Emergency Committee would also have included three members each from fifteen major Labour and socialist bodies.[4]

However, Henderson's idea of a Labour peace group did not even outlive the day of its inception. The invasion of Belgium and the subsequent British declaration of war on Germany abruptly ended all attempts to promote neutrality. From that moment on the success of the war effort came before all other considerations. When the Labour Party NEC met during the afternoon of 5 August, it approved by a majority vote its support for British entry into the war, while at the same time declaring its opposition to the policy of the balance of power which produced it.[5] The war resolution pledged the party leadership to the task of working 'to secure peace at the earliest possible moment', but with this major and ambiguous qualification: 'on such conditions as will provide the best opportunities for the re-establishment of the amicable feelings between the workers of Europe'.[6] Any number of interpretations from jingoist to pacifist could be and were placed on the wording and sense of this statement. The fact that it aimed to satisfy everyone hardly obscured the fact that the war resolution really committed the Labour Party to no specific policy at all. By the evening of 5 August, Labour had placed its fate in the hands of the Asquith government.

This wartime renunciation of political independence put the Labour leadership in an extremely awkward position, which caused it considerable difficulty and embarrassment throughout the war. The policy of Labour was that of the nation: to obtain a lasting peace. But at what cost? Suffering and loss were inevitable, but what was not at all clear was the part Labour ought to play in the determination of its particular contribution to the war effort.

However, any attempt to establish a distinct position after

August 1914 involved the extraordinarily difficult task of balancing the rights and interests of Labour against the requirements of national unity and the war. This classic dilemma – hardly confined to the First World War – underlay the ambivalence which was shared by all but the most vehement of the war's supporters. It also helps to explain the function and evolution of the War Emergency Committee.

Aside from pacifism, only one course of action was available to British Labour at the outbreak of the First World War: to defend the rights and interests of the working class from unreasonable encroachment or unnecessary sacrifice. But even such defensive tactics were hopelessly limited, since any attempt to mobilize mass action as a tool of protest even by those who supported the war effort undoubtedly would have split the Labour movement into violently hostile factions. A direct challenge to the state on virtually any issue to arise out of the war, therefore, was politically impossible if not legally dangerous.

Furthermore, since Labour never controlled policy, results could only be achieved if civil servants, administrators and friendly members of the government were prepared to listen to reason. The First World War therefore gave a new lease of life to the old Webbian policy of permeation. And to give effect to this Fabian strategy of investigation, deputation, and vigilance, the War Emergency Committee was formed.

The task at hand at this time was, Henderson stated, 'to mitigate the destitution which will inevitably overtake our working people whilst the state of war lasts'.[7] The government realized the urgency of action here and authorized the formation of local Citizens' Committees to help counter the disruption of civilian life on account of the war. At the same meeting at which the war resolution was passed, the Labour Party Executive requested 'all affiliated Labour and Socialist organisations to give whole-hearted assistance' in the work of these committees, so that they would be able 'to watch carefully the exploitation of the people by the increase of prices' and to urge the government 'to take all means to minimize the risk of such exploitation'.[8] To co-ordinate this effort and future initiatives was the initial purpose of the War Emergency Committee.

The meeting at which Arthur Henderson intended to launch his Peace Emergency Committee was in fact held on the afternoon of 5 August at the House of Commons. There in his capacity as chairman of the Joint Board of the NEC and the PCTUC, Henderson presided, as he had originally planned, over a group of more than one hundred Labour, socialist, and co-operative delegates. The object of this meeting was 'to consider the industrial and social position of the working classes as affected by the war'. The Conference then officially constituted itself as the War Emergency: Workers' National Committee and appointed an executive of fifteen. Besides three members each from the Labour Party Executive, the PCTUC, and the management committee of the General Federation of Trade Unions (GFTU), six individual members were elected, including Robert Smillie, President of the Miners' Federation of Great Britain (MFGB) and Sidney Webb.[9]

On Wednesday 6 August, the executive of the War Emergency Committee (WEC) met for the first time at the Commons. Henderson was made chairman; J. A. Seddon of the Shop Assistants' Union and the PCTUC, vice-chairman; and W. A. Appleton of the Lacemakers' Union and the GFTU, Treasurer. The first act of the committee was to enlarge itself by inviting the Co-operative Union and the Co-operative Wholesale Society to appoint two members each. Invitations were also extended to six new independent members, including J. Ramsay MacDonald.[10] The policy of co-optation was continued throughout the war, allowing the committee to absorb representatives and financial support from the Miners' Federation, the Scottish TUC, the Textile Workers' Association, the National Union of Railwaymen, the Transport Workers' Federation, the Independent Labour Party, the British Socialist Party and its pro-war offspring, the National Socialist Party, the Fabian Society, and the National Union of Teachers.[11]

Affiliation to the WEC was theoretically open to any organization affiliated or eligible to affiliate to the Labour Party.[12] However, the need to keep down the size of the committee precluded strict adherence to this principle, and numerous local groups were refused representation.[13] A total of fifty men and women intermittently served on the WEC throughout the war.[14] Henderson served as chairman until he joined the Coalition in June 1915. He was replaced as chairman by J. A. Seddon until the latter lost his place on the PCTUC. On 23 September 1915 Robert Smillie assumed the chairmanship which he held for the remainder of the war.[15]

The heterogeneous membership of the committee ought not

obscure the fact that it was really an extension of the Labour Party's national office. Here the dominant role becomes apparent of J. S. Middleton, assistant secretary of the Labour Party who also served as secretary of the WEC. The son of a printer and telegrapher, Middleton's experience as a reporter on the Workington *Star* and his work as a printer for a North London newspaper, brought him to the attention of MacDonald in 1904, when the latter was looking for an assistant to help him to carry on the work of the Labour Representation Committee. Middleton appeared to be the right man for the job, and this initial association developed into a deep and lasting friendship.[16]

Middleton's work on the WEC and his subsequent career can only be understood in terms of his identification with MacDonald. The two men held very similar views on the war at its outbreak. 'It seemed a little unreal,' Middleton wrote in retrospect, of the anti-war demonstration in Trafalgar Square,[17]

> to stand on the plinth of Nelson's Column and, knowing full well that peace was impossible, listen to Hardie, Lansbury, Henderson and our other stalwarts denouncing war on this second day of August, when Germany had already declared war against Russia.

Middleton waited at MacDonald's flat in Lincoln's Inn Fields after the demonstration to hear the results of the latter's conversations at Downing Street on the crisis. MacDonald brought his friends 'the depressing news they had feared', that war was inevitable. He also made quite clear 'that he was having nothing to do with war, and that he would continue his opposition to it inside and outside the party'.[18]

As chairman of the PLP, MacDonald had to reply on 6 August to the Prime Minister's request for war credits of £100,000,000. He had the choice of a change in his views on the war or a change in his role in the party. He chose the latter. Although he was under intense pressure to alter his anti-war 'theme', it was evident to Middleton 'as it must have been to the others that MacDonald was not going to budge from his pacifist line'. The meeting of the PLP before the war credits debate was an 'emotional' one, Middleton recalled, 'and it would be ridiculous to say that tempers were not lost'. The opposition to MacDonald at that meeting was 'so bitter and powerful that he resigned there and then as leader of the Party'.[19]

The fact that 'The party and the movement were split from end to end', in Middleton's words, was the primary concern of the Labour leadership at the time of the formation of the WEC. 'Its one collective object' was 'to hold the forces of labour together',[20] and no one worked harder at that task than Middleton himself. Though his views on the war were not shared by the majority of the NEC, he still believed, as did MacDonald, that those opposed to the war must not desert the Labour Party. Middleton kept in close touch with the younger, more radical and consistently anti-war members of the movement, such as Clifford Allen and R. Page Arnot, with whom he joined the City of London branch of the ILP in 1915.[21] Middleton was also associated with the unsuccessful attempt of Allen, Cole and other rebels to transform the Fabian Society into a body dedicated solely to research.[22] Nevertheless his main desire during the war was to prevent a witch-hunt in the ranks of Labour to purge the heretics of either right or left.

The centre of the committee's work was Middleton's office at Labour Party headquarters on Victoria Street in London. The party's staff was engaged virtually full-time in handling the voluminous correspondence of the WEC. Indeed, aside from its sponsorship of this group, the Labour Party hardly existed as a national organization until late in the war. The political truce had suspended all electoral activities, and anyway the national agent, Peters, was preoccupied with the recruiting campaign. Also since MacDonald and Henderson, especially after mid-1915, were rarely at the party office, the national Labour Party was often reduced in size to Middleton himself.[23] On his shoulders rested the responsibility for all the daily work of the WEC. Only a physical breakdown in February 1918 interrupted his efforts on behalf of the committee throughout the First World War.[24]

But Middleton's role was the application of policy rather than its formulation, which to a large extent was left to Sidney Webb. Webb's work on this committee provides a key to the development of his socialist thought and his influence in the Labour movement after 1914.

The war came as a shock for which the Webbs were totally unprepared. In the autumn of 1914, they refused on very revealing grounds to sign a manifesto of British intellectuals in favour of the war. In reply to the request of Gilbert Murray, the Oxford classicist, Beatrice pleaded ignorance:[25]

We have both of us a rooted disinclination to sign statements on questions about which we have no special information or enlightenment. . . . How to end this state of affairs I don't know, and I feel personally quite helpless in the face of it. I am not sure whether the best solution of the present gigantic struggle would not be the complete collapse of all the parties concerned. . . . But as we are of no account on all these questions of international relations, and have neither knowledge nor philosophy about them we feel inclined to be scrupulous.

No other choice was available, the Webbs reasoned, but to adjust to the war as to any other natural calamity which men were still unable to prevent.

This adaptation to the war was easier for Sidney, since he did not share his wife's doubts about the Allied cause or her introspective nature. In reply to a request from a Swedish professor, he developed his thoughts on the causes of the conflagration and Britain's attitude to it. Webb observed calmly:

My own belief is that the war, like the smaller Transvaal War of fifteen years ago, had, as a result of evil thought, gradually become inevitable. It is the outcome of long continued national pride and ambition, coupled with a belief in irresistible power, and a willingness to use that power ruthlessly in pursuit of national aims.

Noting parenthetically, 'How very imperfectly human nature is yet moralised, and how prone it is to take whenever it feels the power to take,' Webb concluded that 'the clash of Germany's ambitions, aspirations and natural self-complacency, with the very position of the British empire in the world . . . made a life and death struggle inevitable'. In this conflict, Webb shared the nearly unanimous opposition of his nation to Prussian aggression.[26] From that point on, Sidney Webb never questioned his support for the British war effort.

At the same time, though, he regarded the war as a 'setback' to all his hopes of social reconstruction. At the beginning of August 1914, the Webbs believed that they could only prepare for that time when their work could be resumed.[27] However, Sidney gradually abandoned this defensive attitude. His shift was probably unconscious, but none the less real. In a rare moment of personal reflection, Sidney later remarked: 'Things impinge on me, and I react to the impact, occasionally, with ideas and suggestions that prove interesting.'[28] The First World War was one such occasion, and the institutional framework which he chose to give form to his reactions was the War Emergency Committee. Webb's talents and temperament perfectly suited him for the leadership of the committee. His unparalleled knowledge of social administration and his persistent dedication to the minutiae of labour problems were indispensable. His organizational ability, procedural tact and draftsmanship made him the complete committeeman. And most importantly, his unselfishness and lack of personal ambition disarmed those who would mistake the advocacy of policy for the pursuit of political power. Avoiding the tendency to brood over the fearful losses of the war, which at times immobilized his wife,[29] Sidney Webb turned back to the task of social reconstruction after the initial shock of the war had worn off.

THE WAR EMERGENCY COMMITTEE
AND THE DEFENSIVE STRATEGY OF LABOUR

The producer in wartime

The initial policy of the War Emergency Committee centred on the role of the producer and the effect of the war on the wage-earner in his working life. In the same way it developed a parallel line of work which emphasized the worker's role as consumer and the effect of the war on his home life. But at the earliest stages of its work, the problems which the committee confronted involved working-class incomes rather than the cost of living.

Employment Sidney Webb provided the WEC with a consistent approach to the industrial dislocation which everyone feared in the autumn of 1914. Webb was convinced that private industry could not hope to adjust to a war economy without throwing thousands of men out of work. The state therefore had either to provide jobs for these workers or else face the prospect of enormous expenditure for relief and maintenance and a social situation which was bound to breed unrest. To forestall this disaster, which in turn might seriously imperil the war effort, Webb drafted certain proposals which were adopted by the committee.[30] The WEC called on the government[31] to appoint a standing Departmental Committee to stimulate and coordinate the efforts of Government Departments, local Authorities, and other employers to maintain the aggregate volume of employment by keeping their staffs at the fullest possible strength and if circumstances allow to undertake additional enterprises in order to prevent the occurrence of as much unemployment as possible.

Furthermore, the government was strongly urged to exercise its powers under the Development Commission and Road Board, as well as under the Unemployed Workmen Act to 'expedite . . . works of public utility'.[32] The committee also decided to make immediate representations to the appropriate government offices and the London County Council to oppose any policy of systematic overtime and any reduction in services.[33]

Webb's proposals were based on principles which he had advocated long before August 1914. The right to subsistence and the social organization of the labour market were demands which took on a new urgency during the war. This was a far more persuasive point in their favour than the fact that these measures were inherently just.

Webb repeatedly emphasized his view that continuity in production and subsequent high employment were the highest priorities for Labour at the beginning of the war. He was far more concerned about maintaining incomes than in stabilizing prices. The sacrifice of consumer interests was of secondary importance at that time. Hence he vigorously opposed all deflationary policies even in the face of a rise in the cost of living. 'High prices are not to be feared like unemployment,' Webb commented on 6 August 1914, and added patronizingly, 'To a certain extent they might do good by teaching the people to economise. They would mean the cutting down of wastefulness in food, and other things.' And in any event, he asked: 'What is the use of having food cheap if the people have not the money to buy it? Make sure that people go on getting their wages. Keep people from being thrown out of employment. That is the vital thing.'[34]

In the next few months, the WEC repeatedly supported Webb's position on employment. By participating on the various Cabinet committees, numerous members of the WEC advanced these views and brought into operation on one front its policy of investigation and protest. Although Beatrice Webb was not formally a member of the WEC, her work on the London sub-committee on the prevention and relief of distress supplemented Sidney's findings as a member of the group engaged on the statistical enquiry into London unemployment. Combined with information obtained by the WEC's women's representatives on the Central Committee for women's employment, the factual basis for the WEC's policy dealing with the producer was formidable indeed. On these government bodies, the members of the committee kept a constant watch on any fluctuation in the pattern of employment.[35]

Throughout August 1914, the Webbs and others studied the returns and reports of these governmental bodies, and were relieved to find that they showed 'surprisingly little distress'.[36] However, their optimism was qualified by two factors. The Webbs believed first that the mass enlistment at the outbreak of war was an artificial support for the labour market. And second, they were concerned that the position of the four million women workers, especially in the sweated trades, still remained precarious.

Therefore the WEC was quick to point out the counter-productive tendencies of the rash of 'Lady Bountiful' proposals to make and donate clothing and necessities to the British Army and the poor. In a resolution drafted by Webb, the committee urged those 'benevolent persons' to 'avoid doing positive harm by confining themselves to many duties and services that are performed only by volunteers and of which more will be provided'. At the same time, the WEC called upon the local education authorities to 'withdraw from the labour market as many girls as possible by affording temporary maintenance scholarships for girls as well as boys'.[37] Here was another of Webb's old ideas which took on added attractiveness as a contribution to the Allied cause.

In September 1914, forebodings of industrial doom on account of the war still marked the committee's position on public employment. The WEC therefore urged Labour representatives on municipal and government bodies to find for those who would otherwise be unemployed:[38]

regular wage-earning employment in their own trades – not necessarily for the production of 'profit' or indeed anything to be sold in the market, but for the many purposes of public usefulness that are still quite inadequately supplied, such as the execution of all sorts of work of repairing, painting, cleaning, and improving; the provision of additional houses, schools, hospitals etc.; of more roads, parks, bridges, etc.; and ever so many things that could advantageously be done by public bodies with a view – to use the Government's own phrase – 'to maintain the volume of employment.'

On the same grounds the committee urged the government to take advantage of the slack in the building trade to 'relax' the conditions for building grants for educational projects, 'so as to enable the whole cost to be met without raising the rates'.[39] Again we see the view that war could provide the occasion if not the cause of the completion of useful social tasks.

Sidney Webb gave this aspect of the committee's work his particular attention.[40] Hence it was natural that he presented the committee's views on employment in a deputation to Lloyd George on 6 October 1914 to protest against the Chancellor's speech on the 'necessity of economising resources'. Webb thought that the choice of words was unfortunate at best and misleading and pernicious at worst. He pointed out:[41]

> I cannot help thinking that the word thrift is better than 'economy'. Economy is understood to mean not to spend; thrift means taking the wisest use of your resources. We want to be thrifty, but I do not know that we want to be economical in that bad sense.... Unless something is done to reassure municipalities and disabuse them of the impression that it was not the wish of the Government that they should start works, it will be very bad.

To wait until distress became 'acute and insistent'[42] before acting at all was the height of foolishness, in Webb's view. Prevention rather than relief was the old theme that he emphasized here and throughout the war.

Relief The guidelines of government policy on relief set at the beginning of the war were applauded by the WEC. The Prime Minister's commitment that 'no one in distress due to the war is to be driven to the Poor Law', as Middleton paraphrased it, was taken by the WEC to be a complete vindication of the 'Right to Work' policy of the Labour Party.[43] It was also a major step forward in the Webbs' old campaign to modernize the administration of relief. Here was another point at which the war provided an opportunity for the advance of Webbian ideas.

The establishment of a National Relief Fund in the name of the Prince of Wales provided a source of financial support for what the Webbs saw as a new approach to relief. The formation of this fund was a recognition, in their view, that the war was being fought on two fronts. Surely, Sidney pointed out, 'we can no more escape casualties on the industrial front,' that is, unemployment, 'than on the firing line itself.'[44] This new sense of the unity of the war's social consequences both at home and abroad was, they believed, a profound advance. Unemployment or distress was no longer shameful and relief need not be ignominious in wartime, since, at least until the armistice, the welfare of every citizen was the welfare of all.

Here the Webbs appealed to all those who wanted to see the war won. 'It is useless for Lord Kitchener to think he can repel the invader,' Beatrice stated, 'if the working class is starving behind his line of troops.'[45] And in Sidney's more telling phrase: 'Absolute hunger knows no law and will not long continue patriotic.'[46] In the interests of the war effort, Webb led the WEC's effort to help ensure 'that the nation shall be fed'.[47]

Hence it was all important to ensure the proper administration of the Prince of Wales Fund. The committee demanded repeatedly that the fund had to be used solely for the relief of civilian distress, that is, for those who were not involved in military service. Provision for 'military distress', in Webb's phrase, had to be met out of the War Office and Admiralty estimates.

When attempts were made to 'raid' the Prince of Wales Fund to provide allowances for soldiers' and sailors' families, Webb naturally drafted a very strong protest on behalf of the WEC. He pointed out that this maladministration had dire consequences. It was wrong to allow industrial relief, he argued, once again to lapse into its old subordinate position as a social issue.[48] And if enough money were spent on objects for which the fund never had been intended to promote, civil distress could go completely unrelieved; except, of course, by Poor Law provision, which was completely unacceptable to Webb and the rest of the WEC. Furthermore, since most of the fund was earmarked for post-war demobilization problems, Webb felt that it was all the more important to protect the financial base for relief during the war.[49] As usual, it would be the poor who would suffer for political and administrative mistakes.

When the Cabinet Committee first announced its proposed

scales of relief in September 1914, Sidney's prediction seemed to have come true. Acting under the fear that the Prince of Wales Fund was 'in danger of being prematurely exhausted', Webb commented, the government had set guidelines for maximum allowances which were morally and politically indefensible. He drafted the WEC's emphatic protest which argued that the government scales 'would, at present prices, suffice for far less food than the minimum physiologically required for the maintenance of health, according to even the lowest scientific standards, and considerably less than is allowed either in prison or in the workhouse.' This treatment of the industrial casualties of the war 'actually worse than paupers or criminals' amounted 'to a sentence of slow starvation'.[50] The noble words of social unity apparently had been more rhetorical than real. Therefore Webb took it upon himself to remind the Liberals of two crucial points: first, that 'the needs of the poor are not to be measured by the sums the rich choose to spare'; and second, that 'the relief of the suffering caused by the War is a national concern, and has to be met by the nation as a whole out of national resources'.[51]

A short-sighted and parsimonious policy would justifiably, Webb believed, 'produce the fiercest resentment among the whole wage-earning class'.[52] The implication was clear. To promote the war effort it was in the government's interest to 'buy off' discontent. The consequences of failure to meet Labour's demands were never publicly specified. Apparently Webb believed that the mixture of expediency and social justice which the WEC, under his lead, offered as the basis of government policy, would prove irresistible. In this case, some upward adjustment in the scales of relief was made, although they were still far from WEC standards.[53] The committee probably helped to bring about this change. But more important than its tangible results was the style of defensive protest which marked the first phase of the WEC's work.

Trade union work and related problems The initial policy of the WEC was to defend the entire working class, not just the organized minority. This outlook undoubtedly increased the number of people whom the committee could reach. But it also led concurrently to one of the major restrictions of its effectiveness: isolation from the trade union movement at the very time of its steady growth in membership and power.[54] Contributing to this problem was the resentment of the PCTUC to the incursion of the

WEC on its privileged position as defender of the organized wage-earners. They were particularly sensitive on this point since their main rivals, the GFTU, were also represented on the WEC. Friction between these two groups was bound to cause difficulties. Also, later in the war, hostility to the 'pacifist' views of Smillie and Middleton made any real co-operation between most union leaders and the committee almost impossible.

Nevertheless, the WEC took various steps to help protect the trade unions during the war. Industrial dislocation, Henderson pointed out, meant financial hardship for many unions. He noted that by the end of August 1914 some unions were already at the point of bankruptcy. Since they had served the state by providing unemployment, sickness and death benefits, and[55]

> in view of the assistance which has been already rendered by the Government to the banks and financiers of the country, it is only fair that Trade Unions, who have done so much in the past should receive some [financial] considerations.

Henderson personally put his case to the government in a deputation on 27 August 1914. The result was agreement to make grants to unions paying unemployment benefits whose funds were likely to be reduced by expenditure for war relief.

Another approach to the insurance problem was taken by Sidney Webb. It was clear that trade-union membership fees and insurance contributions together presented problems for some workers. A state subsidy for individual payments would probably help prevent a decrease in union membership. It would also counter the fact that 'literally millions of workers' who were 'being placed on short time' instead of being discharged still had to pay full insurance contributions. As a remedy, Webb proposed that these deductions from wages constituted a hardship attributable to the war. He urged 'as a measure of national war emergency' that arrears in insurance payments should not count during the war and that no deductions be made from low-paid or casual workers.[56] He argued this case in a deputation to the Treasury on 16 September 1914, but with little effect.[57]

More significant help was given to the trade unions by the legal advice which the WEC provided, mainly through the work of the Fabian barrister, H. H. Slesser.[58] He offered his services as legal adviser to the committee on 11 September 1914 and was immediately instructed to write a précis of the emergency legislation as it affected Labour.[59] His opinion on the legal rights of trade unions, which he submitted on 25 February 1915,[60] formed the basis of Labour's official industrial policy until the Treasury agreements of March 1915.[61] But until the union leaders voluntarily renounced their rights, Slesser's view held that a strike was only 'wrongful if it threatens the safety of ships, communications, docks, harbour, railways, etc., or is a specific jeopardising of the defence of public safety of the realm'. No legal action could be taken against the organizer of a strike 'unless the official or workman has caused disaffection among His Majesty's subjects or has obstructed or procured the obstruction of work ordered by the military authority'.[62] Here the WEC provided a justification for industrial independence and a policy for the defence of trade-union privileges which most of the unions themselves chose to ignore. Only Smillie's Miners' Federation kept aloof from Lloyd George's blandishments, which Smillie knew hid 'a serious interference with the rights of the Trade Union movement'.[63]

But soon after March 1915, the WEC served the unions by acting as a clearing-house for complaints about the employment policy and conditions of labour in firms which received government contracts. To this end the committee demanded successfully the publication of the names of these firms. Thereafter, the committee could bring to the attention of the government any irregularities brought to the WEC's attention by the trade unions.[64] To a large extent this is precisely what did happen.[65]

In addition complaints were registered throughout the war with the committee about the treatment of women workers and agricultural workers. The WEC passed resolutions in favour of equal pay for the former,[66] and a minimum wage for the latter.[67]

The WEC also seconded trade-union protests on the employment of Belgian refugees instead of British workers on the docks.[68] The committee was even more emphatic in its rejection of the introduction of coloured labour into Great Britain. The Transport Workers' Federation leader, Robert Williams, saw in this immigration 'a menace to Western civilisation' with serious moral as well as economic consequences.[69] His resolution to this effect was passed without discussion by the WEC mid-way through the war.[70] The Webbs later praised this action as part of its 'valuable work done throughout the war, not in the interests of Trade Unionism only, but in those of the wage-earning class, and of the community as a whole'.[71]

Finally, for the first two years of the war, the WEC supported the trade-union campaign to raise old age pensions from five shillings to seven and sixpence per week.[72] This half-crown maximum increase was granted as from 31 August 1916.[73] Disabled soldiers presented related though separate pension problems, for which the WEC advocated the establishment of a separate ministry, run with trade-union assistance.[74] The formation of a government pensions sub-committee on which Harry Gosling of the London County Council, the M.P. George Barnes and Beatrice Webb served, and the creation of a Ministry of Pensions in December 1916 seemed to meet the WEC's request. However, both these bodies ignored the committee in favour of the PCTUC. The latter group was asked to recommend Labour representatives for the local pensions committees, which Middleton had hoped would be the prerogative of the WEC. He was aware that both the committee and its secretary were 'already regarded with a good deal of suspicion', and reiterated that 'we have no desire to overlap in any way with other bodies' on pensions or any other issue.[75] At least in this case, it had little chance to overlap. The stated reason for the government's snub was that the WEC was a 'semi-political' body 'without proper standing as a channel of official labour communications'.[76] But the organizational jealousy of the PCTUC was undoubtedly more to blame.

The consumer in wartime

After the spectre of mass unemployment failed to materialize in the early months of the war, the War Emergency Committee devoted greater attention to the problems of the working-class consumer. Food, fuel, and rent were the three main items of consumption with which the committee was concerned.

Food The food policy of the WEC was outlined at the initial meeting of 5 August 1914.[77] First the committee registered its support for the municipal and government control of '(a) the purchase and storage of food, (b) the fixing of maximum prices of food and trade necessities, (c) the distribution of food'.[78] Three administrative recommendations were also adopted in the interests of the consumer, that is to say, primarily the family unit. The local citizen committees, in close association with borough, district, and county councils, were designated by the WEC specifically to guard against 'exploitation' of the consumer by high prices.[79] Membership on these local committees, Sidney Webb suggested with the committee's approval, had to include not only representatives of the trade unions, but also of the Co-operative Societies and the working women's organizations in each district.[80] Secondly, pressure was to be exerted on the Board of Education to put into operation the provisions of the Education (Provision of Meals) Act for the free feeding of school-children. In addition the Local Government Board was to be persuaded to direct the local health committees to arrange for the supply of milk to nursing mothers, infants, young children and sick people.[81] Each of these proposals aimed to protect home life from wartime distress.

These problems affected the middle class almost as much as the working class. Hence the WEC addressed its propaganda about food prices to a wider audience than it had done when dealing with specifically producers' issues. For example, the committee early in the war urged that the home-grown supply of wheat be commandeered to prevent food profiteering by farmers and merchants if possible and at least to interfere with it. To this end a resolution was adopted which stated:[82]

> The Workers' Committee believe that in this emergency all British subjects should be prepared to share in bearing the burden imposed on the nation. We see large numbers of the working and middle classes responding nobly to the call of duty, sacrificing useful careers in industry and commerce and even life itself on behalf of their country. On the other hand, we find already well-to-do people who appear to be prepared to take advantage of the opportunity presented by the emergency to raise the price of food so that they make extra profits for themselves.

The response of the Board of Agriculture to this suggestion was predictable in 1914: 'The Board think that so long as the price of wheat remains moderate it would be unwise to interfere with the free play of competition.'[83]

By the end of 1916, these liberal sentiments were rarely heard. The 'free play' of the market had resulted in approximately a seventy per cent rise in the cost of living. The purchasing power of a pound spent on food in August 1914 had been reduced in twenty-four months to ten shillings and eightpence.[84]

In the interim the WEC brought forward a battery of suggestions to help restrain the price rise. To protect the sixpenny quartern bread loaf, the committee urged the control of shipping to keep down the price of wheat imports,[85] as well as the compulsory purchase of the home-grown wheat supply.[86] As the food shortage became more acute, stronger measures were urged. The nationalization of four million acres of arable and unused land was proposed to provide more bread and other foodstuffs for the nation.[87] The committee also organized numerous district conferences on food prices in February and March 1915 and December 1916. In all cases the maintenance of maximum prices for food was supported.[88]

The establishment of the Ministries of Food Control and Shipping which accompanied Lloyd George's accession to power in December 1916 was a validation of the principle of control which underlay the food policy of the WEC. But as in the case of the Prince of Wales Fund, the committee were perfectly aware that the acceptance of government responsibility did not necessarily lead to effective action. The committee were particularly offended by the Corn Production Bill of 1917 which gave bounties to farmers who had good harvests. An alternative policy was brought forward. The WEC insisted that:[89]

the aims of labour should be to give every support to arable cultivation on condition that the assistance given by the State should be used to secure the complete social ownership and control of the land of the country, so that it will be used to supply national needs and not to provide rents and profits and pander to social prejudice and pleasure.

This was one of H. M. Hyndman's pet formulae, which he believed could be translated into fact on account of the war. He was to press this demand as the key to Labour policy when the WEC came to formulate its Conscription of Riches proposals.

Hyndman's enthusiastic support for total food controls was an important contribution to the committee's consumer work. His position was acknowledged in early 1918 when he was appointed with two other WEC members to the newly-formed advisory Consumer Council on which he served until after the end of the war.[90] Both on this body and on the WEC, Hyndman repeatedly complained in 1917 that 'the food difficulty in many working class districts is becoming acute and a very grave crisis is approaching'. In this emergency, he argued, equality of consumption had to be enforced to prevent the rich from 'consuming more than their share'.[91] There was some disagreement over the form of food supply in the last year of the war, either as a rationing system of coupons which the co-operators favoured or as a money subsidy which the WEC favoured. However there was complete agreement by 1918 that the total control of the food market was essential to prevent widespread famine and the social unrest which would inevitably accompany it. Here the Webb-Hyndman pro-war line determined the committee's policy. But in any event, no one at any time on the WEC was prepared to use hunger as a political weapon with which to disrupt the war effort.[92]

The committee's work on consumer issues was more a nuisance than an inspiration to the government. Still, it was effective enough, so that when a replacement was sought for the first Food Controller, Lord Devonport, in the spring of 1917, Lloyd George turned to Robert Smillie. This offer was an indirect recognition of the work the committee had done to promote the organization of the food supply. It was also an undisguised attempt to absorb Smillie into the Coalition, which would have effectively silenced one of its most forceful critics. The miners' leader looked very much like a political threat to Lloyd George, especially after Smillie had agreed to chair the meeting at Leeds on 3 June 1917 which welcomed the Russian Revolution and purported to establish Workers' and Soldiers' Councils in England. Before he went to Leeds, Smillie told the Prime Minister that he wanted nothing to do with the Coalition and returned to his work for the Miners' Federation and the WEC. The assertion of an independent line on labour problems was far more important, in Smillie's opinion, than administrative responsibility.[93] In a sense, this gesture symbolized the committee's real purpose. As Henderson corroborated a few weeks later, a policy of unfettered protest was far more valuable to Labour than a mere taste of political power.

Coal Smillie and the other miners' representatives on the WEC brought special knowledge of the coal industry which was most useful in the committee's work on fuel consumption. Its policy was clear throughout the war. It never varied from 'the firm conviction that prices to consumers can only be kept at a reasonable level by the coordinated action of the State and Municipalities in taking over the entire national supply [of coal] in the public interest'.[94] But if 'the control of the output of collieries during the continuance of the war' proved to be politically impracticable for the Coalition, at least, the committee argued, they could fix 'both the pit-head and retail prices'.[95] Also advocated as checks on costs were the nationalization of the distribution of coal[96] or just as appropriate, distribution through the Co-operative Societies.[97]

In July 1915, the Committee went on record in support of the miners' strike, but concurred with the Miners' Federation that the men should go back to work 'from day to day' until their grievances were met. Again the WEC avoided a direct commitment to mass action in wartime, in favour of an expression of sympathy with the strikers' cause.[98] The committee was more emphatic in its rejection of the half-crown per ton increase in the pit-head price of coal which had contributed to the dispute. 'Ultimately,' the WEC argued, 'the charges will fall upon the over-charged consumer,'[99] whose plight steadily worsened as the war went on.

As in the case of food, the appointment of a coal controller in December 1916 did not end the committee's agitation. But it was then able to press more effectively its earlier protests against what it saw as excess profits in the coal industry.[100]

Rent The WEC, in conjunction with other Labour groups, was most helpful to the working-class consumer in relation to the question of wartime rents. When he first wrote to Henderson to offer his legal services to the WEC, Slesser had raised the question of liability for rent as one of the issues on which the committee could act.[101] In 1915 he advised the committee that an increase in rent did legally constitute a hardship due to the war.[102] Immediately thereafter Middleton wrote to the Prime Minister on behalf of the WEC to ask for legislative remedy. Once again his reasoning combined the arguments of social justice and expediency. He called the government's attention to:[103]

the very grave problem that is arising as a result of many landlords increasing the house rents of their tenants. From the reports that this committee is daily receiving from many different parts, it is convinced that this raising of rents is not only inflicting great hardship likely to affect adversely both the public health and infantile mortality, but it is also (a) arousing ill-feeling and resentment against the war; (b) seriously interfering with recruitment; and (c) hindering the increase of output of munitions.

Continuing in the tone of loyal outrage, the committee recommended that the Prime Minister declare that 'any increase in rent in war time, where the house remains unchanged, is an unpatriotic act, which no landlord ought to commit'.[104] The government's response to Labour Party pressure was favourable, and the Rent Restrictions Bill was passed in December 1915.

Unfortunately, this measure did not end the rent problem. Many landlords continued to demand an increase in rent which was too often paid by people unaware of their rights. Some tenants later deducted these excess payments from subsequent rent payments. This practice became the subject of test litigation. The Birmingham Trades Council took up one particular case, that of Sharp Brothers and Knight, timber merchants, against Harry Chant to collect five shillings in back rent. The County Court judge decided for the defendant on 4 May 1916.[105] The landlords then appealed against this decision in the High Court, where the earlier ruling was upheld. But in the Court of Appeal, the verdict was reversed and such deductions rendered illegal.[106]

It was at this point that the WEC entered the case. Dan Rider, secretary of the War Rents League, spoke to Middleton about the case, which the committee promptly took up.[107] On this issue the alternatives were either to appeal to the House of Lords or seek legislative remedy. Slesser urged the latter course on financial grounds. Therefore, W. C. Anderson of the ILP introduced a measure in the Commons on behalf of the Labour Party which would give the tenant the right to deduct excess payments. This measure was enacted as an amendment to the Courts (Emergency) Powers Bill, which received the Royal Assent on 10 July 1917. All extra rents could then be legally recovered until January 1918. It was obviously unnecessary to pursue the case of Sharp versus Chant.[108]

The WEC agreed to collect money to allay the £300 legal fees in the rent appeals case. By 10 October 1918, the costs were settled through the contributions of sixteen societies affiliated to the committee.[109] For once, the WEC could claim credit for an important contribution to a successful campaign.[110] Here was one occasion on which a parent body and the committee were able to work together without friction.

Less successful were the WEC's efforts in favour of a rent subsidy for soldiers' families. In May 1916 the committee urged that such rent be divided equally between the householder, landlord and Treasury.[111] Ramsay MacDonald went even further and suggested that the state should pay all the rent for conscripted married men.[112] And towards the end of the war, the committee took the view that the post-war rent problem was bound to be even more serious. On this point Sidney Webb argued for the extension of the Rent Restrictions Act at least six months beyond the armistice. A free rent market before new housing was built would lead, Webb was convinced, to a 'most dangerous upheaval, and should be decisively negatived'.[113] Although all war restriction continued until after the war, the failure of the Coalition to provide enough homes 'fit for heroes', let alone the million which Webb demanded, once again made scarcity the only real determinant of rent.

The Co-operatives   One index of the effectiveness of the WEC was the fact that by 1917 the Co-operative Societies believed that the committee was becoming too well recognized as Labour's voice on consumer issues. Therefore, at the very time that all Labour groups were beginning to rediscover their independence, in mid-1917, the Co-operative Societies decided to withdraw from the WEC.

The major reason given was 'to secure the united action of the central organisations of the Movement', which the co-operators had come to believe to be incompatible with association with the committee.[114] This view was disputed by the Co-operative representatives on the WEC who strongly disapproved of the action of their organizations.[115] Mrs Gasson of the Co-operative Union, for example, condemned this 'retrograde' step on these grounds:[116]

Personally I am extremely sorry, because I am certain that this Committee has had a greater influence upon the Government and the country in calling attention to and suggesting remedies for many of the evils brought into existence through war conditions, than any committee I know.

Perhaps that was just the point.

It was true that the policies of the two groups did conflict on some points, such as the sixpenny loaf and food rationing, but there was agreement on most other issues. However, it was undeniable that, as the *Co-operative News* noted, 'the two committees were crossing each other's lines in their work'.[117]

Middleton expressed 'surprise' at the co-operators' action, since in his opinion there had been 'no cause of disagreement between the committee and the Co-operative section'. He undoubtedly overstated his case when he said that 'in no single instance has there been any conflict of interest pointed out to us'.[118] But he was still prepared to try to persuade them to change their minds.

The WEC appointed a delegation of Smillie, Ben Turner of the Textile Workers' Union, Webb and Middleton to look into the affair and take appropriate action. Webb and Middleton met the Parliamentary Committee of the Co-operative Congress on 13 November 1917, and Turner and Middleton attended a meeting of the United Board of the Co-operative Union on 24 November.[119] Middleton told the latter group that their withdrawal 'was a great disappointment and quite a blow to the members of the Committee'. His greatest fear was that 'we [on the WEC] shall lose our link with the big consuming public' which the Co-operatives represented. As in the case of the conflict with the PCTUC over pensions, the issue was still whether the committee would be crippled by the organizational suspicion of other Labour groups.

The two major criticisms advanced by the co-operators were that the WEC was self-appointed and not responsible to any electorate and, second, that members of the committee were known to be pacifists. But more relevant was the opinion of one co-operator that their organizations 'were a little jealous of other people representing their views before the various Ministers'.[120] In any event, both executives refused to alter their decisions at that time.[121]

The separation was not universally popular among co-operators. Numerous people shared the views of the *Co-operative News* that[122]

> the Committee has worked together in a very amicable fashion and its conclusions have set the pace for united action on the part of the workers that had hitherto seemed impossible. . . .
> There has been no other body that has done so much to lead the Government into paths of righteousness towards the man and woman of low degree.

After a few months of persuasion, the Co-operative Societies re-affiliated in the interests of Labour unity.[123] But the affair clearly showed the resistance in its own ranks with which the WEC had to deal and pointed to the unlikelihood of its survival after the war.

LABOUR'S NEW INITIATIVE

The introduction of compulsory military service in 1916 brought about a fundamental change in the strategy of the WEC and its contribution to the Labour movement. Until that year the committee had reacted defensively to the effect of the war on the workers. Thereafter, the War Emergency Committee took the lead in forcing Labour to regain the initiative it had lost by its voluntary subservience to the war effort.

The manpower needs of the army which made conscription inevitable had political consequences which the military and their political superiors could never have known. The opposition that this issue aroused was not formidable enough to alter the course of war policy. But it did eventually undermine the wartime political truce, and more importantly, it gave a new life to those who looked to Labour as the party of dissent, as the only political group not discredited by the machinations which brought about the war or the incompetence of its prosecution. The War Emergency Committee was instrumental in adapting Labour policy to this new political function.

On conscription, the WEC was closer to the Independent Labour Party than to the other, more powerful organizations affiliated to it. The committee repeatedly stated its firm opposition to the Derby scheme of voluntary attestation introduced in late 1915 and to the Military Service Acts of 1916. However, it shared both the inability and the unwillingness of every other Labour group to organize anything more than a rhetorical challenge to the government on this issue. Instead an oblique course was charted by the WEC. If Labour could not deflect the Coalition from its recruitment policy, so the argument ran, at least it could try to obtain the highest possible price for the sacrifices which conscription involved. The committee therefore developed a campaign for the Conscription of Riches as a *quid pro quo* for Labour's compulsory contribution of manpower for the trenches.

This appeal was far from an ultimatum, since the committee expected neither government compliance with its demands nor a subsequent Labour revolt. The real significance of this policy lay elsewhere: in the internal development of Labour and socialist politics.

Here Sidney Webb's influence was decisive. Although he was

not opposed to conscription on principle, as were Smillie and Middleton, he still saw that this issue would prepare the ground for Labour's emergence from its wartime political role. After 1916, both on the WEC and the Labour Party Executive, he worked to formulate a position upon which to build the policy of the post-war Labour movement.

The Conscription of Riches campaign and the Labour After the War programme, which the WEC also initiated in 1916, were the forerunners of the socialist commitment which Webb outlined in the Labour Party's 1918 constitution and in its policy statement 'Labour and the New Social Order'. On all four, Webb's signature is clear. The principles upon which his policies were based clearly ante-dated the First World War. But it is to the political challenges of war and his ability to meet them that we must turn for the reasons for the dissemination of his ideas and their adoption by the Labour movement.

Conscription

At the same time that the government's intention to introduce conscription became apparent in September 1915, Robert Smillie became chairman of the WEC. His criticism of the war and its consequences was much more radical than that of either of the two previous chairmen, Arthur Henderson or J. A. Seddon. At the beginning of the war, Smillie rejected the views of those who saw the conflict as a solvent of class barriers. The war-time industrial truce was a superficial event in his view:[124]

> When the nightmare of slaughter passes, when Satan is satisfied that enough devilment for the time being has been accomplished, then the tacit agreement will have run its course and the struggle between Capital and Labour all over Europe will be resumed with increased intensity because of the destruction of wealth which is presently going on.

His attitude to the impact of the war on the Labour movement was far more pessimistic than Webb's. Not only did he ignore the Treasury agreements and oppose Labour's entry into the Coalition but he also defied the government by organizing a strike of the Welsh miners in response to industrial restrictions.[125] The war was an unmitigated disaster in his view, and it left behind a field strewn with the wreckage of the rights of the individual and Labour as a whole.[126] Conscription was the culmination, Smillie believed, of this trend towards authoritarian control. He urged the Labour Party to oppose it with all the means at its disposal:[127]

Once admit, even by acquiescence, the claim of the State to compulsory military service from any class of men, and you cannot logically defend the voluntary principle in industry. If military conscription is right, upon what solid ground can munition workers, transport workers, railwaymen, miners, or those engaged in any vital industry, claim to be exempt from industrial compulsion? Unless you resist compulsion now, you will be left without a case against industrial compulsion when this Government, or its successor, demands it. . . . Compulsion is a fundamental issue on which we must take a stand, if we are not to surrender every argument – moral, intellectual or legal – that we have ever advanced in support of civil and industrial liberty.

Middleton shared Smillie's opposition to conscription, and the two men decided to put the WEC on record in support of the campaign against it.[128] Two resolutions were immediately passed to this effect, stressing the dangers to trade unionism.[129] This point was the chief subject of a pamphlet which the committee had previously issued in the autumn of 1915 on 'Compulsory Military Service and Industrial Conscription'. We see here the same argument which Smillie used at the Labour Party conference a few months later. The 'special peril' of conscription 'for the British wage-earning class' was that it would be used to meet the really urgent demand not for men, but for munitions. The committee argued that through conscription men might well be forced into factory work in industry for private profit and without trade unionism to protect them. 'This is what is meant by Industrial Conscription. It is an attempt to make use of the present war to get Servile Labour.'[130] It was not that the 'workers are against national service – but they are against enforced conditions of work', the pamphlet continued.[131]

On the other hand, the proponents of conscription ought to have considered 'the real shirkers', the WEC suggested, who were 'the owners of property and unearned incomes'.[132] Here was an urgent task for state action, since

it is money that furnishes the sinews of war; and the experts are looking more to financial exhaustion to bring the war to a close than to any dramatic military achievement. Yet our Government is not seizing the wealth of the nation.

Why was it 'only the lives of men' that the conscriptionists asked 'the Government to commandeer. . . . Is it fair to take men before taking motor-cars, to commandeer people before commandeering property?'[133] Six months later when compulsion became a reality, this question turned into a demand for the conscription of riches.

Sidney Webb supported this proposition from an entirely different set of assumptions. He believed that there was a 'proper system' of universal military service, but it would take years 'to mature'. If time were available, he told Shaw:[134]

> What could be advocated is Compulsory Training for all youth from fourteen to twenty-one, not in Military drill only but in *everything* needed for citizenship (including drill and the use of arms) – not of the physically fit only but of everyone especially those who are below par physically.

But such a plan could not apply to the present war, he admitted. Still, he accepted the fact that since extreme steps were required to win the war, only total organization would do. Webb conjectured in August 1915:[135]

> If I were in power, and were driven by urgent military needs or political pressure to do something drastic, I should decree *Universal Submission* to the national need – not young men for the trenches only, but everyone for what he was fitted; and not persons only, but also property and possessions – everything to be placed at the disposal of the Government against a mere receipt on paper, and then let the Government Departments organise what they could in each branch, preparing plans for Munitions, Aircraft, Ships, Transport, and what not with the materials in persons, things and cash thus placed at their disposal.

In the case of the First World War, the conscription of riches at least would be a step in the right direction.

However, this policy alone was not enough. What was really needed in Webb's view was not mere 'fighting men' or munitions, but rather 'organising ability and determination, and half a million additional food for powder won't augment this'.[136] Conscription of property would make sense as a tactic with which to win the war only if the government were prepared to accept the burdens under which it would have to operate. Since that situation was far from the case in 1916, the demand for the conscription of riches had to be modified, Webb believed, to fit the limited capacity of the state. Here again we see the administrative principle which underlay Webb's political thought, which enabled him here to reduce the issue of conscription from a moral question to a purely technical one. However, it was Webb's approach to the problem which channelled the outrage of Smillie and others into a campaign which British Labour could wholeheartedly support.

The decision of the TUC to oppose conscription on 6 January 1916 convinced Middleton that the time was right for the assertion of the WEC's new policy. He confided to Hyndman his 'considerable surprise' at this overwhelming rejection of the government's recruitment policy. He noted on 10 January 1916:[137]

> It indicates the deep distrust of our own particular class of British Junker and is likely to give pause to them in their campaign. That they will come again I have no shadow of doubt, but their measure is being taken and their success will be very dearly bought.

He anticipated correctly that the miners would also come 'down pretty strongly on our side' in their vote the same week. And most importantly, he concluded, 'It does seem to me that the conscription agitation gives us an opportunity of reducing to concrete terms the "conscription of wealth" alternative.'[138]

Three weeks later the WEC pledged itself 'to render all possible assistance to those actively opposing the [Conscription] Bill'.[139] However, they were powerless in the face of the view of both the Labour Party Executive and the PCTUC that 'the Government's recruiting proposals are essential to winning the war'.[140] To challenge this surrender, the WEC decided on 25 May 1916 to organize a national conference on conscription, to discuss the effects of this measure on trade-union organization and administration, the danger of industrial conscription, and the conscription of riches.[141] Middleton urged C. W. Bowerman of the TUC to convene this conference 'despite differences that may exist as to the principle of the conscription legislation'. He added that if the TUC did not act, 'several of the larger Trade Unions would consider taking action for themselves, with a view to focusing the opinions of the movement as a whole on these various subjects'.[142]

Bowerman reluctantly agreed, and the conference was held in London on 30 June 1916.[143] The following resolution was then adopted:[144]

> In view of acts now having been passed to impose Conscription for Military Service upon all males in Great Britain between the ages of eighteen and forty-one without any mandate from the constituencies or any reference to the people at large, this Conference demands that an Act shall be passed enforcing the conscription of accumulated riches for the service of the nation.

The precise formulation of this demand did not arise though, until another year had gone by; a year during which the appalling casualties of the Somme and the first Russian Revolution had completely changed the character of the war. By 1917 the built-in inertia of institutions seemed to be overcome for a time. Labour came to realize that a wider vision than patriotism was required to see what could be rebuilt over the ruins of the pre-war world. The conscription of riches alternative emerged in this changed political atmosphere.

At the height of the controversy in the summer of 1917 over whether British Labour ought to attend the proposed international conference at Stockholm, H. M. Hyndman brought forward in the executive of the WEC a resolution on the conscription of riches. The timing of this motion ensured the fact that it would be considered as part of the overall review of the war policy of the Labour movement. The resolution read:[145]

> Since practically the whole adult male population of Great Britain is liable to Conscription for active service in the field, thus being compelled to risk life and limb for the defence of a country which they do not own; since more than eighty per cent of the soldiers conscripted are of the wage-earning class, since the munitions of death and the munitions of life are produced or obtained by the labour of the same class, the War Emergency Workers National Committee demands that the entire riches of this Island be conscripted and placed at the disposal of the community at large, in order to meet all the enormous costs of the war and the expenses of thorough social reconstruction after the Peace.

Here Hyndman adopted the Webbian war necessity argument in

support of his proposal. Contrary to what Hyndman wrote to an American socialist friend, this resolution was not carried at this meeting, but rather referred to a sub-committee of Webb, Mac-Donald, Anderson, Susan Lawrence, the co-operator B. Williams and Hyndman himself.[146]

In the discussion which followed, Hyndman enumerated the steps he advocated. According to his plan, the following measures were to be enacted as of 1 January 1918: the conscription, presumably without compensation, of:

(1) Homes and foreign bonds and all shares and debentures in public or private companies, with interest earned and payable thereon: thus giving the Community entire control for the purposes mentioned over all Mines, Factories, Workshops, Railways, Shipping, Tramways, Waterways, etc.
(2) All deposits in Banks.
(3) All insurance companies: the welfare of actual insurers and annuitants being safeguarded by the community.
(4) All land in town and in country with all buildings to be held and dealt with as public property.

In addition, Hyndman proposed that:[147]

(5) The whole adult population to be liable to conscription for productive and distributive labour as may be decreed by a Constituent Assembly elected under proportional representation, all adults having the right to vote.
(6) All members of the Community to have an equal right to a high standard of life in food, clothing, habitation, leisure and general opportunities for full intellectual, moral and physical education and enjoyment.
(7) A registry of ownership, prior to the Conscription of Riches, to be made and kept.

This scheme was not accepted in its original form, mainly because of the criticisms of Sidney Webb. He told Middleton in September 1917 that he would 'try to prepare a draft resolution' for the WEC which would avoid Hyndman's 'impossibilities'.[148] The detailed memorandum which Webb drafted ultimately formed the basis of the committee's policy.

Webb pointed out that Hyndman's plan for the conscription of riches really involved two propositions:[149]

(i) the transfer to the Government for public purposes of wealth now in private ownership, whether what is transferred is capital value or annual income; and

(ii) the transfer to the Government for use for public objects of the control over certain essential instruments of production, such as land, mines, railways, docks, factories, plant etc.

Webb argued that 'It is possible, and, indeed, usual to attain these two purposes separately.' Nationalization need not imply the transfer of wealth, nor did taxation involve administrative control. 'The Committee,' Webb reasoned, 'may wish to recommend action along both lines, and along both simultaneously. Experience points however, to the desirability of putting one at a time.'[150]

Webb's choice of priorities was based upon his views on the incomplete administrative development of the state, about which he had previously written to Shaw. On the same grounds, he commented that government control of industry 'without at all adequately conscripting wealth' was so vastly accelerated by the war, that the state was acting 'probably as fast as it knows how to organise the necessary public administration'. Therefore, Webb concluded:[151]

It does not seem desirable to urge that the *present* Ministry should take over, in addition the administration of all the 300,000 farms, or to press the existing Town and District Councils to take over the management of the half-a-million retail shops.

He looked upon the conscription of riches as a war proposal which had to take account of institutions as they were rather than as they ought to be. He did not explicitly rule out the desirability of a Labour Ministry taking such steps as Hyndman proposed. But until that future date, Webb believed, 'What is more urgent is to press for the "Conscription of Wealth", irrespective of "nationalisation" or "municipalisation" of production.'[152]

Webb suggested three lines of action to effect his policy:

(1) to double the yield on the Income Tax and Supertax 'so as to "confiscate" annually an additional £150 million, almost from the (estimated) 70,000 family incomes in excess of £1,000'.

(2) to establish a Capital Tax of up to 20 per cent on all estates worth more than £300, which might yield £900 million;

(3) to sequester all unearned incomes, along the lines of W. C.

Plate 13 'THE COROLLARY OF MAN COMPULSION. "The question of compulsion, which is for the present in abeyance by common consent, will emerge, on the authority of the Prime Minister, as a mere matter of expediency."—*Times* on Mr. Asquith's speech. When it finally does emerge it will not emerge alone!'

Herald, 6 November 1915

Plate 14 'THE MAN BEHIND CONSCRIPTION—"Why these unfounded working-class suspicions of Conscription?"—"National Service" plaint.' *Herald*, 18 September 1914

Anderson's parliamentary resolution. Webb predicted that proposals (1) and (2) together might pay 'annually something like a quarter of the current cost of the War'. And, 'The second might pay off a sixth of the present National Debt.'[153]

On 4 October 1917, the WEC adopted Webb's conscription of wealth policy. With full Webbian pro-war logic, the committee declared its intention 'to press for the "Conscription of Wealth" as a means of carrying on the war, irrespective of the "nationalisation" or "municipalisation" of production'. At the same time, the committee recommended that those industries and munitions works then under government control ought to be taken into complete ownership, 'the capitalist interests being definitely got rid of'.[154] But, as Webb wanted, the former proposal was given more prominence and was clearly more important. And since Webb presented the WEC's proposals in the joint deputation with the Labour Party Executive, the PCTUC, and the Executive of the MFGB in November 1917,[155] we may see the complete acceptance of Webbian thought on this measure – the first independent Labour programme during the First World War.

Labour after the war

The call for a citizens' army raised one set of problems for the British Labour movement. The prospect of disbandment and the re-integration of millions of men into peace-time society raised yet another. The response of the WEC in the second case was to organize an enquiry into post-war problems which paralleled its formulation of the conscription of riches programme. The WEC saw in the first a role for itself as the chief adviser to the Labour movement on reconstruction problems. The hope was that its work here would ensure the growth of its status and its emergence as a permanent political unit. However, the prospect of another Labour group to compete with the PCTUC or Labour Party Executive after the war led those bodies to check the development of the WEC and restrict its efforts on the problem of Labour after the war.

As early as March 1915, Sidney Webb was speculating about post-war conditions. He told an audience at the Hermes Club to expect 'a great dislocation and slump' after the armistice.[156] The volunteer army then would be thrown back on to the labour market at the worst possible time. Added to this dismal picture was the uncertainty of the future of trade unionism despite Lloyd George's reassurances, after the Treasury agreement of that month.[157] A detailed study of post-war problems was obviously in order. Under Webb's influence, the WEC decided in May 1915 to consider 'the transfer of the new army to civil life at the conclusion of the war'.[158] One month later, a demobilization sub-committee of three was appointed, of which Webb was a member.[159]

However, the strong disagreements within the wartime Labour movement made any discussion of post-war problems an extremely delicate affair, of which the WEC was completely aware as it began its exploratory work in the next few months. But it was impossible to avoid severe criticism of the Coalition when the WEC surveyed the government's avoidance of the problems of demobilization. Its draft report was thus described by Hyndman as a 'startling exposition of approaching industrial chaos'. A 'more scathing indictment of our government,' he concluded, 'could not be drawn up'.[160] There was complete agreement on the WEC that 'the competition for wages on a lower standard of life in all ordinary employment will be terrible' after the war. Hyndman spoke for the committee in his comment that 'The outlook is nothing short of appalling. It is of the greatest importance that this should be brought home to all classes.'[161]

The main message of the WEC's first report on Labour after the War was that all Labour organizations had to join together to present a united voice to the government on post-war problems. Its major recommendations incorporated the earlier Webbian policy on employment and relief. In addition, the WEC urged Trades Councils and local Labour Parties to appoint local committees on Labour after the war to co-ordinate work in their particular areas.[162] It followed easily that the WEC was the proper agency to organize Labour action on this problem.

The Labour Party Executive was not at all happy with the WEC's assertion of policy or its self-projected role as Labour spokesman on post-war problems. Three days before the WEC issued its report, the Labour Party Executive set up its own sub-committee to deal with this subject.[163] Sidney Webb agreed to serve on this group, and his transfer of allegiance greatly disturbed Middleton and annoyed Smillie.[164] It appeared that Webb was undermining the committee's work which he had initiated previously. A more likely explanation was Webb's desire to strengthen the political support for his proposals and his correct opinion of the WEC's political weakness. This renunciation of support for the committee is indicative of Webb's shift of allegiance to the Labour Party. His replacement of the Fabian Society's representative on the Executive, Stephen Sanders, who had enlisted, gave Webb the opportunity to translate his work on the WEC into the basis of a much wider political programme.[165]

At the end of February 1916, the Labour Party Executive instructed its 'After the War' sub-committee to consolidate its work with the WEC. A joint meeting of the groups appointed by the Labour Party, PCTUC, GFTU, the Joint Board and the WEC, was called for 9 March 1916. The Labour Party Executive itself decided by a vote of six to five to insist that reconstruction work be taken out of the hands of the WEC and to redirect responsibility for it to a joint committee of the above-named groups.[166]

Middleton recognized this decision as an undisguised attempt to emasculate the WEC. He had already come under attack in the Labour Party Executive for having acted more like Henderson's successor than his temporary replacement while in the Coalition.[167] And his identification with MacDonald and the ILP made any of his proposals somewhat suspect to the more patriotic members of the executive. Hence he knew that his presence on the committee was less than a tactical advantage. He wrote despondently to Smillie after the meeting of the joint committee was called:[168]

The position . . . is somewhat serious and personally, I believe the whole future of the Workers' National Committee is more or less at stake. . . . The truth is that there has been a very quiet but studied attempt to undermine the work of the [committee] and it would be bad tactics on our part to stand out of the proposed conference. Our position has been clear throughout, the other bodies have been perfectly well aware of our activities on this subject and have taken a certain line of action knowing that they were duplicating the work and indeed, in most cases, duplicating the membership in several ways. It is imperative that you should be present at the Conference.

Middleton also admitted the personal aspect of the problem:[169]

Frankly, my position is an awkward one, as I explained to the full Committee last week and as far as possible I want to harmonise my allegiance as secretary of the Workers' National

Committee with that of my position on the Party staff, and at the same time take no action that will prejudice the future of the National Committee.

To balance these roles was clearly impossible.

Smillie recognized the difficulty of Middleton's dilemma, but he took a more dispassionate view of the situation. He wrote to calm Middleton's fear: 'I hear nothing but praise of the work of the War Emergency Committee, which really means your work.' And although he felt that the WEC was the group which could deal with 'the "After the War" Scheme,' he added,[170]

> I have no personal feelings in the matter at all, and would gladly give over the whole matter to any representative Committee that would undertake to do it, but I feel that with the Labour Party and the General Federation being already fully represented on the War Emergency Committee, the setting up of another joint committee is foolish, and would only lead to loss of time.

Smillie apparently had a less possessive attitude towards the WEC than did its secretary. The end result of a united Labour voice was more important to him than the means by which it was achieved. And Smillie had no need to develop an alternative political base for his activities.

Still Middleton resisted this attack on the WEC. He urged the strengthening of the committee by an increase in its membership as an alternative to joint action, but the Labour Party Executive, with Webb's approval, rejected his proposals.[171] Reluctantly, Middleton agreed to serve as secretary of the joint committee.[172] Yet he found his double role 'too much of a "Jekyll and Hyde" nature to be comfortable'. In addition he was aware that the formation of the joint committee had done little to change the minds 'of some of the members of the three national committees that the time is long past for the Workers' National Committee to shut up shop'. He feared that their financial control 'may settle the matter ultimately', to the detriment of the entire Labour movement.[173] He also knew that the WEC was not considered reliable enough to develop Labour policy on its own. Stripped of its vanguard role, the committee was thereby assured of its eventual extinction.

Nevertheless, the WEC contributed to the joint work on Labour after the war, but mainly as a very junior partner. Its helplessness when Webb shifted his attention elsewhere is explicit proof of his importance to the committee. Formally, Webb represented the WEC on the joint committee, but his position on the Labour Party Executive was clearly of greater importance to him.

On 27 July 1916, sub-committees were established on Trade Unionism, Taxation, Transport and Shipping, Land and Agriculture, Health and Insurance, Unemployment, Demobilization and Pensions, and Education. To assist the work of these groups, the Fabian Research Department agreed to supplement the hard-pressed Labour Party staff. These bodies were the embryonic form of the Labour Party Advisory Committees.[174] Although it was not as Middleton had hoped, still one year before Stockholm the Labour movement had begun to emerge from its self-imposed intellectual somnolence.

This re-awakening was not accepted without protest by those who strongly supported the war. Meetings of the Labour after the War sub-committees were therefore often frustrating for Sidney Webb. He wrote to Beatrice on 2 November 1916:[175]

> The Trade Union leaders are hopeless. Yesterday I spent two hours ... struggling with their complacent stupidity and apathy, and with the real desire of some of them to prevent anything being published that would 'arouse expectations' and lead to anything beyond what the Government is conceding.

Again, one week later, he complained about the attitude of his colleagues: 'I can't quite make out whether it is only stupidity or whether there has been a real desire to obstruct and prevent the issue of any report inconvenient to what they believe the government wish.'[176] But he really had only himself to blame, since his desertion of Middleton had made this deadlock inevitable. Reports on housing, demobilization, unemployment, and trade-union conditions were printed in the next year.[177] But little of real substance appeared until Webb himself summarized the policy towards which the WEC's work was directed in 'Labour and the New Social Order'. By the time that document and the new constitution of the Labour Party appeared, the War Emergency Committee had virtually outlived its usefulness. In the last year of the war, Webb directed its ideas and approach into more lasting channels.

SIGNIFICANCE

Towards the end of the war, Middleton reflected on the political significance of the War Emergency Committee. He wrote to one committee-man:[178]

> Our three years work on the National Committee has been a great endeavour, and has really helped to keep us sane in these mad times. I believe that we have done much more permanent work than we quite realise. The keeping together of our local forces in the constituencies, which after all, from a political point-of-view has been a great success, will make our task of re-organising the Labour Party much easier than I fear otherwise would have been.

Middleton's assessment was correct. The WEC's work was of the greatest importance in preventing the major and irreversible schism over the causes and conduct of the European war which plagued continental Labour. The fragile unity of the British movement was maintained in part by the committee's attempt to divert attention from the question of the merits of British participation and war aims to an issue on which all could agree: the high price paid by the working class, both as producers and consumers, for the maintenance of the war effort. In this defensive strategy of protest against wartime distress, the WEC adopted the pressure-group role which the Labour Party had abdicated by its unconditional acceptance of national unity. In this sense, the committee's work was in line with the non-assertive and severely confined strategy of the pre-war Labour Party. By deflecting interest from the wider issues of the war, the WEC helped to maintain the political truce which meant for British Labour symbolic partnership at best and at worst unmitigated subservience to political forces over which it had no control.

Therefore, the work of the WEC was, on one level, undeniably cautious, parochial, and short-range, albeit helpful in calling attention to popular grievances and suggesting appropriate remedies for them. In the early stages of the war, the committee was little more than a wartime crusade against destitution and distress, on the precise model of the Webbs' abortive pre-war campaign for the break-up of the Poor Law. But once the Webbs and other socialists had set aside their fears about the disruptive, if not catastrophic, immediate effects of the war on industrial and social life, a new and competing factor, which was also traceable to the Webbs, gave a new direction and significance to the committee's work.

Webb felt no compunction in approaching the war crisis as an extraordinary opportunity for the consolidation of the political Labour movement under socialist leadership. First in the WEC and later in the Labour Party Executive, he acted upon the belief that with proper guidance, the war experience could be transformed into a powerful vehicle for progressive social change. The speed of that change would be limited, however, by the slow evolution of social administration. In the WEC, Webb was supported energetically on this point by his old antagonist, H. M. Hyndman, whose total commitment to the war was unshakable.

Less optimistic about the effect of the war on the Labour movement were its last chairman and secretary. The development of the WEC becomes clear only by reference to the tension between the Middleton-Smillie defensive approach, which concentrated initially on the mitigation of wartime distress, and the Webb-Hyndman tactics of socialist advance through war. These competing tendencies were not exclusive and constantly overlapped, and their interaction provides the key to the growth of the committee's vision and its widening constituency.

The first phase of the committee's work centred on the effect of the war on the workers as producers and as consumers. The defensive character of the committee's approach predominated when it approached the first of these problems. A concentration on the questions of the welfare and conditions of labour brought the committee into contact with numerous individuals whose cause it argued, at times with positive results. However, the parallel work of the trade unions, coupled with the unwillingness of certain patriotic conservatives within the union leadership to challenge wartime unity, severely limited the committee's effectiveness and inevitably led to friction.

On the other hand, when the committee turned to consumer questions, such as food and fuel prices, rent and taxes, it tried to reach a far wider and more receptive audience. As in the case of the trade unions, there was some difficulty with the Co-operative Societies over jurisdiction. But here the WEC, with some exceptions complemented rather than contradicted the co-operators' policies. Most significantly, the WEC's protests about the cost of living applied with equal force to the middle class, which found in the WEC a Labour organization prepared to deal with issues of interest to all wage-earners. As a voice of protest for the productive nation, the WEC provided an important example which the Labour Party took up toward the end of the war.

The constituency and projected appeal of the WEC widened even further when it was confronted with the problem of conscription. This crucial issue affected the lives of all citizens. On this point we see the clear emergence of the Webb-Hyndman approach which Sidney was to bring to bear with far-reaching effect in the reconstruction of the Labour Party in 1917–18. In its protests against violations of civil liberties, its agitation against military and industrial conscription and the related Conscription of Riches campaign, and its initiation of a precise Labour after the War programme, the WEC reached out to represent the population as a whole. On these issues, the other Labour organizations followed the WEC's lead only with hesitation and annoyance at the latter's independent tactics.

In each of these areas of its work, the WEC committed the cardinal political error of forcing lethargic and more powerful bodies than itself to think and to formulate a policy to meet the crisis of war and its aftermath. Its penalty was ultimate extinction. The committee lingered on until 1920, but it effectively ceased to exist in mid-1918 as the Labour Party staff turned back to the more urgent and orthodox electoral tasks. However, the WEC's legacy of independent thought, so dangerous in wartime, was far more lasting than its immediate political fate.

In August 1917, Beatrice wrote of her husband's reaction to the prospect of the immense changes which lay ahead:[179]

> To Sidney they are exhilarating – they stimulate him – he is perpetually thinking of how to mould them in his own dear disinterested way. He refuses to dwell on the horrors of the war and he believes that through the war will come the changes he believes in.

The ultimate significance of the WEC lay in Webb's use of it during the First World War as an instrument to project his policies and to set the distinctive Webbian stamp on the ideas of the Labour movement. He was able to succeed in this mission during the war and because of the war. The 'country is "on the jump", ' he wrote in October 1917. 'Old habits of thought are broken up.'[180]

A decade after the armistice he came to the same conclusion. 'The War, with all its evils,' he wrote, 'broke up the "ice-pack", and threw the whole world open to new ideas.'[181] His work on the War Emergency: Workers' National Committee was a major contribution to the wartime transformation of British socialist politics.

NOTES

1 The papers which James Middleton accumulated while secretary of the War Emergency Committee have recently become available for research at Transport House. This collection comprises thirty-six boxes of correspondence on various subjects arranged alphabetically, but completely haphazardly. I have numbered the boxes in the order that I found them, and a complete list may be found in the Bibliography. This collection is of the greatest interest, and I am very grateful to the librarian of the Labour Party Library, Mrs Wagner, for giving me generously of her time and assistance during my research. I will refer to this collection as 'WEC, Box 8', etc. throughout.

2 WEC, Box 22, From Conference to Conference, Letter of Arthur Henderson to NEC, 4 August 1914.

3 WEC, Box 22, From Conference to Conference, text of proposed objects and membership of the Peace Emergency Committee.

4 *Ibid*. They were: the MFGB, the National Union of Railwaymen, the Women's Trade Union League, the National Union of Women's Suffrage Societies, the London Trades Council, the Transport Workers' Federation, the ILP, the Fabian Society, the BSP, the Women's Labour League, the Women's Co-operative Guild, the Textile Federation, the Amalgamated Society of Engineers, the Co-operative Movement (taken as one unit), and the PLP. This list was drawn up by Henderson. It is interesting to note the subordinate place held by the PLP.

5 LPEC, 5 August 1914. The vote was 8 to 4.

6 *Ibid*., and WEC, Box 19, From War to War Office, Circular signed by W. C. Anderson and Henderson on behalf of the Labour Party Executive, 6 August 1914. This resolution was drafted by a subcommittee of Anderson, MacDonald, Roberts and Hodge.

7 *Ibid*.

8 LPEC, 5 August 1914.

9 WEC, Box 22, From Conference to Conference. Text of statement issued by Henderson on formation of the War Emergency Committee, undated. The executive members of the parent organizations were:

PCTUC: Seddon, Gosling, Bowerman.
NEC: Henderson, Anderson, Hodge.
GFTU: Cooper, Tillett, Appleton.

The other four elected members were: Albert Bellamy of the NUR, Mary MacArthur of the Women's Trade Union League; Dr Marion

Phillips of the Women's Labour League, and H. M. Hyndman of the BSP.

10 WEC, Box 1, General, Mimeographed sheet on 'War Emergency Workers Committee'. Beside MacDonald, these people were also asked to join: Stephen Sanders of the Fabian Society, Robert Williams of the Transport Workers' Federation, Susan Lawrence of the London County Council, Margaret Bondfield of the Women's Co-operative Guild, and A. W. Golightly of the Stratford Co-operative Wholesale Society.

11 WEC, Box 1, Statement of accounts 4 August 1914 – 31 March 1916. The ILP joined officially in early 1915. *ILP Annual Report* 1915, p. 13. Probably earlier membership would have signified a tacit acceptance of the war.

12 British Library of Political and Economic Science, WEC Executive Minutes, 11 September 1914. Hence Sylvia Pankhurst's request for affiliation of the East London Suffrage Society was turned down. The Webbs apparently deposited their printed copies of the minutes in the LSE. There are scattered minutes throughout the files at Transport House, but the LSE collection is the only near-complete set. Cited as 'WEWNC'.

13 WEC, Box 11, From Milk to Miscellaneous, Numerous letters, for instance, Middleton to D. Milne of Civil Service Clerical Alliance, 16 October 1917.

14 WEC, Box 1, Attendance lists from 6 August 1914–9 January 1918.

15 WEWNC, 3 June 1915; 16 September 1915; 23 September 1915.

16 Oral information from Mrs Lucy Middleton. Cf. also J. S. Middleton, *Farewell*, 1944, which is the text of a speech he gave at a meeting to honour him at which Attlee presided.

17 Draft autobiographical sketch written by Middleton, undated, in possession of his wife, pp. 79–80.

18 *Ibid.*

19 *Ibid.*

20 *Ibid.*

21 Oral information from Mr R. Page Arnot. Cf. City of London ILP Executive Minutes, 4 February 1915.

22 'Proposal to change the constitution of the Society', *Fabian News*, 26, 5, April 1915, pp. 27–32.

23 Oral information from Mr R. Page Arnot. Cf. also WEC, Box 11, From Milk to Miscellaneous, Middleton to Harry Derbyshire of Amalgamated Union of Co-operative and Commercial Employees, 18 June 1917 and WEC, Box 27, From Executive to Food, Middleton to J. T. Abbott, 28 February 1917.

24 WEWNC, 26 February 1918.

25 Passfield Papers, Beatrice Webb's unpublished diaries, vol. 32, Letter of Beatrice to Gilbert Murray, 14 October 1914.

26 *Ibid.* Memorandum on the causes of the war, undated, in reply to Professor Gustafe Steffen of Gottenburg (*sic*) University.

27 Sidney Webb, 'The birth of the Labour Party', *St. Martin's Review*, 455, February 1929, pp. 77–8. The Webbs wrote six essays which ap-

peared from October 1928–March 1929 at the suggestion of Reverend Dick Sheppard. Sidney wrote three other articles besides the above-mentioned. They were on 'Trade unionism', 'The London County Council', and 'The London School of Economic and Political Science'. Beatrice's two essays were on 'The Consumers' Co-operative movement' and 'Science, religion and politics'.

28 Sidney Webb, 'Trade unionism', *St. Martin's Review*, 452, October 1928, p. 478. Beginning the series, Webb made this extraordinary remark: 'Let me say at once that I have no intention of writing an autobiography, I am, I believe, "not that sort". Indeed I have very little knowledge of what has happened to me internally.' Perhaps Beatrice was introspective enough for them both.

29 Beatrice suffered from repeated attacks of gloom, depression and 'neurasthenia', or sympathetic shell-shock. Cf. the numerous entries in her unpublished diaries for 21 October 1914; 25 September 1915; 12 October 1915; 2 July 1916, etc.

30 WEC, Box 29, From Food to Food Prices, Text in Webb's hand of proposals issued as a statement by Henderson on behalf of the committee and sent to the Prime Minister on 6 August 1914.

31 *Ibid.*

32 *Ibid.*

33 WEC, Box 1, General, Mimeographed sheet on the first meeting of the WEC.

34 Robert Lynd, 'Employers and the coming distress', *Daily News and Chronicle*, 6 August 1914.

35 British Library of Political and Economic Science, Sidney and Beatrice Webb, Reports and Papers on the Relief of Distress, 5 volumes. WEC, Box 20, From Acts to Agriculture, File on the appointment of Cabinet committees on the relief of distress and urban housing. Cf. also A. M. McBriar, *Fabian Socialism and English Politics 1884–1918*, p. 142.

36 Reports and Papers, vol. 1, Report on conditions of employment and distress, 15 and 22 August 1914.

37 WEC, Box 1, General, Draft in Webb's hand of resolutions moved by Mary MacArthur and seconded by Webb on 10 August 1914.

38 WEC, Box 1, General, Mimeographed text of Suggestions for Labour Members on Local Committees, September 1914.

39 WEC, Box 1, General, Resolution drafted by Webb on 10 August 1914 and report of deputation by Webb and other members of the WEC urban housing sub-committee to the Local Government Board on 8 October 1914.

40 Cf. Webb's article 'Behind the fighting line', *Daily Chronicle*, 25 August 1914.

41 WEC, Box 12, From Municipal Activity to Munitions, transcript of deputation.

42 *Ibid.*

43 WEC, Box 1, General, Suggestions for Labour members. Middleton urged the local committees to 'convert' this gain 'on paper . . . into reality'.

44 Sidney Webb, 'Behind the firing line', *Daily Chronicle*, 26 August 1914.
45 Beatrice Webb, 'Prevention – not alleviation', *Labour Leader*, 27 August 1914.
46 Sidney Webb, 'Behind the fighting line', *Daily Chronicle*, 25 August 1914.
47 *Ibid.*
48 WEC, Box 14, From Postal to Prisoners of War, Draft resolution and covering letter of Webb to Middleton, 28 August 1914: 'Here is the resolution I was asked to draft. It is strong but I think strong language is needed.' The resolution was sent to Warren Fisher of the National Relief Fund on 7 September 1914. Cf. also WEWNC, 11 September 1914.
49 WEWNC, 21 January 1915 noting assets in the Prince of Wales Fund: £4,435,000; allocated: £1,104,000; balance: £3,140,000 (*sic*), most of which to be used after the armistice.
50 WEC, Box 15, From Provision of Meals to Relief, Webb's draft of WEC resolution of 13 September 1914. Henderson and Mary Macarthur were members of the Executive of the Prince of Wales Fund.
51 *Ibid.*
52 WEC, Box 1, General, Letter of Webb to Middleton covering draft of resolution adopted on 13 September 1914.
53 WEC, Box 1, General, J. S. Middleton, 'Points on the Committee and its Work, 5 August–2 November 1914'.

First Government Proposal	WEC scale	Final scale
14/6 for family of 5	25/-	16/6
6/- for one adult	12/6	8/-
10/- for two adults	17/6	12/-
1/6 for each child	2/6	1/6

54 H. Pelling, *A History of British Trade Unionism*, 1962, p. 262.

Union Membership:	1914	4,145,000
	1915	4,359,000
	1916	4,644,000
	1917	5,499,000
	1918	6,533,000

55 WEC, Box 1, General, Letter of Henderson to W. Barber, secretary of Bradford and District Trades and Labour Council, 26 August 1914.
56 WEC, Box 8, Industrial Compulsion to Labour after the War, Draft of resolution and covering letter of Webb to Middleton, 25 August 1914.
57 WEC, Box 8, Hyndman to Middleton, 10 February 1915 asking for further action. He wanted to end all contributions. Cf. also WEC Exec. Minutes, 11 February 1915.
58 H. H. Slesser, *Judgment Reserved*, 1941, p. 80. At the outbreak of the war Slesser changed his name from Schloesser to avoid being mistaken for a German.

59 WEC, Box 30, From Labour after the War to Legal, Slesser to Middleton, 7 September 1914: 'I am anxious to offer my services gratuitously to poor people in the movement during the war with regard to their legal rights under the Courts (Emergency Powers) Act and in other ways. I don't know how this fact may best be made known; it has occurred to me that I might do so under the aegis of the Workers Emergency Committee.' Answered by Middleton on 12 September 1914 accepting his offer. Cf. WEWNC 11 September 1914.

60 WEC, Box 1, General, H. H. Slesser, 'Opinion on the effect of war emergency legislation and proclamations on the legal rights of Trade Unions'.

61 A copy of this agreement is also in WEC Box 1.

62 WEC, Box 1, General, Slesser's opinion.

63 Cf. Robert Smillie, *My Life for Labour*, 1924, pp. 156ff.

64 WEC, Box 24, From Contracts to Contracts, MacDonald to Middleton, 23 November 1914.

65 WEC, Box 19, From War to War Office, Webb to Middleton, 14 August 1914 on conditions at Deptford Navy Yard.

66 WEWNC, 15 April 1915; 18 March 1915; 17 February 1916. Women were urged to join trade unions and demand the same wages as men, at a conference organized by the WEC on 16 April 1916.

67 WEWNC, 11 March 1915; 11 January 1917; 10 May 1917.

68 WEC, Box 5, From Belgian Refugees to Coloured Labour, Ben Tillett to Henderson, 7 January 1915.

69 WEC, Box 1, General, H. Gosling and R. Williams, 'The British Transport Workers Movement during the War: A Report to Our Comrades of the International', December 1916. Cf. also the unsigned article in *Labour Leader*, 18 January 1917, 'Coloured labour and the Labour Party'. Its author complained that the 'imperialist capitalist masters' decided that 'black labour must be brought into Britain "to release" every available white man for the trenches. Our saner Trade Union leaders recognising this demand for the crime it is against the whole human race, have flatly refused to countenance any such project.'

70 WEWNC, 30 November 1916. This resolution was sent to the Prime Minister and to Henderson as Labour Adviser to the Government on 2 December 1916. A copy of Middleton's covering letter is in WEC Box 5.

71 Beatrice and Sidney Webb, *The History of Trade Unionism, 1666–1920*, 1920, p. 691n.

72 WEC, Box 34, From Pensions to Postal, on all aspects of this problem. Cf. also WEWNC, 13 January 1916; 23 March 1916; 11 May 1916; 3 August 1916.

73 WEWNC, 28 September 1916.

74 WEWNC, first proposed 30 September 1915; 3 February 1916; 12 October 1916.

75 WEC, Box 34, From Pensions to Postal, Middleton to D. R. Campbell of Belfast and District Trades and Labour Council, 17 May 1916.

76 WEC, Box 34, Middleton to W. Harris of South Wales Miners' Federation, 27 June 1916.
77 WEC, Box 29, From Food to Food Prices. Text of statement issued by Henderson on 6 August 1914.
78 *Ibid.*
79 *Ibid.*
80 WEC, Box 1, General. Text of Webb's resolution on the citizen committees which was forwarded (covering letter in WEC, Box 5) to Herbert Samuel at the Local Government Board on 6 August 1914.
81 Cf. note 77.
82 WEC, Box 5, From Belgian Refugees to Coloured Labour. Text of letter of 12 October 1914 to President of the Board of Agriculture, Lord Lucas, on behalf of the WEC. The letter was signed by Seddon and B. Williams.
83 WEC, Box 5, Reply of A. H. Rew, assistant secretary at Board of Agriculture, 24 October 1914.
84 WEC, Box 1, General, Memorandum on the Increased Cost of Living During the War, August 1914–October 1917, compiled from Board of Trade figures. The bread price index was up 78% on 1 December 1916.
85 WEC, Box 5, Pamphlet on wheat prices. WEC Exec. Minutes, 21 January 1915, 11 March 1915, and 28 September 1916.
86 WEWNC, 28 September 1916.
87 WEWNC, 30 November 1916.
88 WEC, Box 22, From Conference to Conference, Files on all conferences. Cf. also WEC Exec. Minutes, 4 February 1915 and 30 November 1916.
89 WEWNC, 26 April 1917. This statement has Hyndman's touch.
90 WEC, Box 28, From Food to Food, Webb to Middleton, 14 January 1918 turning down membership; Hyndman to Middleton, 13 January reluctantly accepting it. Middleton had his own doubts about the Council, which were expressed in February 1918: 'The Workers' National Committee will take up its share of the new Consumer Council but naturally enough it feels very much like a fire brigade called up after the blaze has got going and the task given to it almost helpless.' Hyndman agreed, but he still believed that it was always worth while to have 'a few determined persons inside the enemy battlement'. Hyndman to Middleton, 2 February 1918. Cf. also WEWNC 7 February 1918.
   One civil servant described Hyndman as 'the most picturesque figure' among the workers' representatives on the Council. F. H. Coller, *A State Trading Venture*, 1925, p. 128.
91 WEWNC, 6 December 1917; also 9 January 1918; 23 January 1918; 10 October 1918.
92 WEC, Box 1, General, As early as June 1917, the committee presented the case for the 'socialisation of the food supply' in a deputation to Lord Rhondda. Present were MacDonald, Anderson, Bramley, Williams and Phillips.
93 Smillie, *My Life for Labour*, pp. 174ff. The man who was ultimately

appointed, Lord Rhondda, was a mine owner whom Smillie knew
and respected.
94 WEC, Box 1, General, Executive Minutes of 12 August 1915,
missing in LSE file.
95 WEC, Box 5, From Belgian Refugees to Coloured Labour, Mimeographed letter signed by Middleton, 3 November 1915.
96 WEWNC, 30 September 1915.
97 WEWNC, 4 February 1915; 4 March 1915.
98 WEWNC, 15 July 1915.
99 WEWNC, 20 July 1915.
100 WEC, Box 5, Text of resolution on coal prices in Webb's hand.
Cf. also WENNC, 20 July 1916, for protests on excess profits, with
accompanying figures for South Wales, the Midlands, and Scotland.
101 WEC, Box 37, From War Savings to Women's War League, Letter
of Slesser to Hyndman, 5 September 1914.
102 WEWNC, 14 October 1915.
103 WEC, Box 16, From Relief to Rent, Letter of Middleton to Asquith,
18 October 1915.
104 *Ibid.*
105 WEC, Box 16, *Birmingham Post*, 5 May 1916 for account of case.
106 WEC, Box 16, Mimeographed letter of Middleton, 24 March 1917.
107 D. Rider, *Ten Years' Adventures among Landlords and Tenants*, 1927,
p. 105. Mrs Lucy Middleton kindly brought this book to my attention.
108 WEWNC, 14 December 1916; 15 March 1917; 29 March 1917;
26 April 1917; 19 July 1917.
109 WEWNC, 25 October 1917; 15 November 1917; 16 May 1918;
10 October 1918.
110 WEC, Box 16, Mimeographed letter of Middleton, August 1917.
111 WEWNC, 23 March 1916.
112 WEWNC, 8 March 1916.
113 WEWNC, 10 October 1918. There is surprisingly little reference in
these papers to the famous Glasgow Rent Strike of 1915, for which cf.
W. Kendall, *The Revolutionary Movement in Britain 1900–1921*, 1969.
114 WEC, Box 26, From Co-operative Representation to Enlistment.
A. Whitehead, Gen. Sec. of Co-operative Union to Middleton,
25 September 1917; and from Henry May of Co-operative Congress
to Middleton, 24 September 1917.
115 WEC, Box 26, Letter of B. Williams to Middleton, 3 October 1917.
116 WEC, Box 25, Contracts, Letter of Mrs Gasson to Middleton,
28 September 1917.
117 WEC, Box 26, *Co-operative News*, 29 September 1917.
118 WEC, Box 26, Middleton to W. R. Blair of Liverpool Co-operative
Society, 8 October 1917.
119 WEWNC, 6 December 1917; 15 November 1917. *Co-operative
Congress Annual Report*, 1918, p. 157.
120 WEC, Box 26, *Co-operative News*, 1 December 1917.
121 Cf. note 119.

122 WEC, Box 26, *Co-operative News*, 13 October 1917.
123 WEC, Box 26, Letter of May to Middleton, 12 January 1918 and Whitehead to Middleton, 21 January 1918, both rescinding earlier withdrawal.
124 Smillie, 'The future of trade unionism', *Herald*, 19 December 1914.
125 Smillie, *My Life for Labour*, pp. 159–62. Curiously enough, Smillie did not mention his work on the WEC in his discursive autobiography.
126 WEC, Box 23, From Conferences – Food to Consumer Council, Memorandum by B. N. Langdon-Davies, secretary of the National Council against Conscription, the chairmanship of which Smillie accepted on 14 January 1916. Margaret Bondfield and Robert Williams were on its executive; Mary MacArthur, Slesser, and Middleton were listed as members of the council.
127 WEC, Box 28, From Food to Food, Letter signed by Smillie and Langdon-Davies on behalf of the National Council against Conscription, which was distributed to Labour Party delegates at the January 1916 conference at Bristol.
128 Oral information from Mrs Lucy Middleton and Mr R. Page Arnot. She said that her husband would have been in a dilemma if he had been called up, but that he was granted exemption on the grounds that his work for the Labour Party was of national importance. But he was wholly sympathetic to those like Clifford Allen and Page Arnot who refused to serve, and even helped the latter in his evasion of arrest in 1917.
129 WEWNC, 16 and 23 September 1915; 13 January 1916.
130 WEC, Box 1, General, Leaflet entitled 'Compulsory Military Service and Industrial Conscription', p. 3. The inequality of army service and the class selection of officers was also condemned; p. 7.
131 *Ibid.*, p. 11.
132 *Ibid.*, p. 13.
133 *Ibid.*, p. 6.
134 Shaw Papers, Add. MSS. 50553, Webb to Shaw, 18 August 1915.
135 *Ibid.*
136 *Ibid.*
137 WEC, Box 36, From War Savings to Women's War Service, Middleton to Hyndman, 10 January 1916.
138 *Ibid.*
139 WEC, Box 28, From Food to Food, Langdon-Davies Memorandum, dated 3 February 1916.
140 WEWNC, 11 May 1916.
141 WEWNC, 25 May 1916. Ben Turner moved the resolution calling for a conference, and Webb seconded it. The urgency of a conference had previously been stated at the executive meeting of 27 April 1916.
142 WEC, Box 18, From Ships to Trades Union Congress. Middleton to Bowerman, 26 May 1916.
143 WEC, Box 18, From Ships to TUC. Bowerman to Middleton, 8 June 1916.
144 WEC, Box 2, Miscellaneous. Typed statement of conference resolutions.

145 WEWNC, 9 August 1917.
146 *Ibid.*, and the Algernon M. Simon Papers, deposited at the University of Wisconsin, on microfilm at the London School of Economics. Hyndman to Simon, 12 August 1917.
147 WEC, Box 28, From Food to Food, Mimeographed sheet entitled 'The Means for Creating and Distributing Wealth', undated. Land nationalization was one of Hyndman's favourite themes. Cf. his letter in Box 28 to Middleton, 29 July 1917.
148 WEC, Box 28, Webb to Middleton, 19 September 1917.
149 WEC, Box 28, From Food to Food, S.W., 'Notes submitted to the Sub-committee on the Conscription of Riches', undated.
150 *Ibid.*
151 *Ibid.* Italics mine.
152 *Ibid.*
153 *Ibid.*
154 WEWNC, 4 October 1917. The committee made only one alteration in this policy statement in May 1918, to include the liquidation of the expected National Debt of £10,000,000,000 due to the war as another function of the conscription of riches. Cf. WEWNC, 16 May 1918.
155 WEWNC, 15 November 1917.
156 Slesser, *Judgment Reserved*, p. 81. Slesser's version of Webb's address also included these remarks: 'After the war, he said, governments would everywhere be greatly strengthened in controlling their citizens and he also contended that pacifism in the old sense was dead and what was wanted was what he called a super-policeman to keep the nation in order.'
157 Cf. also Webb's article in *Labour Leader*, 9 November 1916 entitled 'The chains of Labour'.
158 WEWNC, 18 May 1915.
159 WEWNC, 17 June 1915. WEC, Box 8, Middleton to O'Grady, 23 November 1915. Harry Duberry and James O'Grady were the other two members.
160 WEC, Box 8, Industrial Compulsion to Labour after the War, Hyndman to Middleton, 1 February 1916.
161 *Ibid.*
162 WEC, Box 1, General, 'Labour after the War. First Report', dated 17 February 1916. Reactions to the report in the Labour press were favourable. For instance cf. 'Labour's problems and programme after the war', 1 March 1916 in *Christian Commonwealth*, which suggested that the ILP, Fabian Society, and Guild Socialists ought to work out the theoretical problems of reconstruction, and the WEC its technical details.
163 LPEC, 14 February 1916. Wardle was designated chairman and Henderson, secretary of the sub-committee. Other members were Anderson, Clynes, Hutchinson and Robinson.
164 WEC, Box 8, Smillie to Middleton, 28 February 1916.
165 LPEC, 18 November 1915, at which Webb's appointment was

confirmed. At the same time Fred Jowett took the ILP seat which had been vacant since Keir Hardie's death.

166 LPEC, 24 February 1916; 9 March 1916.
167 LPEC, 15 September 1915.
168 WEC, Box 8, Middleton to Smillie, 25 February 1916.
169 *Ibid.*
170 WEC, Box 8, Smillie to Middleton, 28 February 1916.
171 LPEC, 30 March 1916; WEWNC, 23 March 1916; 15 June 1916.
172 WEWNC, 8 March 1916. Members of the joint committee who attended its first meeting on 9 March 1916:
NEC: Wardle, Clynes, Robinson, Henderson.
PCTUC: Gosling.
GFTU: O'Grady, J. N. Bell, Ben Cooper, Appleton.
WEC: Smillie, Appleton, O'Grady, Duberry, Hyndman, MacDonald, Webb, Marion Phillips, and Middleton.
WEWNC, 11 May 1916 and 15 June 1916. Final membership of the Labour Party after the War Committee:
PCTUC: Gosling, Thorne, Bowerman.
NEC: Wardle, Clynes, MacDonald.
GFTU: O'Grady, Cooper, Appleton.
WEC: Smillie, Bellamy, Webb.
173 WEC, Box 11, From Milk to Miscellaneous, Middleton to Councillor W. Barber of Bradford and District Trades and Labour Council, 11 April 1916.
174 WEC, Box 8, Industrial Compulsion to Labour after the War, Sub-committee membership lists:
Trade Unionism: Cole, chairman, Button, MacArthur, Bellamy, Clynes, Bell, Robinson, Hill, Bramley, Bowerman.
Taxation: Snowden, Webb, MacDonald, May.
Transport and Shipping: Gosling, Wardle, Thomas, R. Williams.
Land and Agriculture: B. Williams, G. N. Roberts, Hyndman.
Health and Unemployment Insurance: Appleton, Cross, Jowett, Turner, Gosling, Bondfield, Beatrice Webb.
Unemployment: O'Grady, Hutchinson, Anderson, Stokes.
Demobilization and Pensions: Barnes, MacDonald, O'Grady, Appleton, Stuart-Bunning.
Education: Goldstone, Webb, Susan Lawrence.
Notice how the membership included external individuals like Frank Goldstone and Beatrice Webb and other WEC members like Hyndman and Cross.
175 Passfield Papers, Webb Correspondence, Sidney to Beatrice, 2 November 1916. Bowerman was particularly annoying to Webb.
176 Passfield Papers, Webb Correspondence, Sidney to Beatrice, 9 November 1916. This time it was O'Grady, Cooper and Appleton who prompted Webb's remarks.
177 These reports may be found in the general catalogue of the British Library of Political and Economic Science.
178 WEC, Box 26, From Co-operative Representation to Enlistment, Middleton to B. Williams, 11 October 1917.

179 Passfield Papers, Beatrice Webb's unpublished diaries, vol. 34, 5 August 1917.
180 Sidney Webb, 'The new constitution of the Labour Party', *Observer*, 21 October 1917.
181 Sidney Webb, 'The birth of the Labour Party', *St. Martin's Review*, 455, February 1929, p. 78.

8

Socialism and Political Independence: the Formulation of the 1918 Labour Party Constitution and Programme

Sidney Webb initiated in the War Emergency Committee the creation of an independent voice for British Labour during the First World War. By 1918 that formative task had been completed. In the formulation of a coherent programme and the establishment of a new structure for the political Labour movement, Webb's contribution was second to none. But the success of his efforts depended entirely on his alliance in the Labour Party NEC with J. Ramsay MacDonald and Arthur Henderson, two men whose views in the first years of the war were worlds apart. For very different reasons, however, by mid-1917, both men were fully prepared to join Webb in the reorganization of a national Labour Party formally committed to Webbian ideas.

MACDONALD AS POLITICAL EXILE

Ramsay MacDonald's advocacy of the reconstruction of the Labour Party was an outcome of his political isolation during the First World War. His reaction to the outbreak of the war and his subsequent relinquishment of the chairmanship of the PLP have been noted above.[1] By September 1914, he was resigned to the fact that 'Socialism in Europe at the present moment is on the shelf'.[2] He was hardly surprised, though, since he also held that among the inevitable consequences of the war were that 'Progressive political movements are set back. Socialism becomes impotent, Labour is split and is paralysed for a generation. All the bulwarks which the poor have raised to protect themselves against their exploiters fall.'[3]

MacDonald was not a pacifist and resented the charges that he was unpatriotic. He wrote in September 1914 that 'the young men of the country must for the moment, settle the immediate issue of victory'. Furthermore, he would welcome an opportunity, he told the Mayor of Leicester, to 'appeal to the pure love of country' of the working class. 'They will gather to her aid,' he predicted. 'They will protect her and when the war is over they will see to it that the policies and conditions that make it will go like the mists of a plague and the shadows of a pestilence.'[4]

His pessimism about the effects of the war was deepened, though, by the bitterness he felt about what he saw as the political capitulation of his colleagues. The culmination of their passive attitude, he believed, was the acceptance of Asquith's offer to Arthur Henderson 'to associate' in a Coalition government in May 1915. MacDonald's pre-war flirtation with coalition politics apparently ended when he became the party's most prominent dissenter. Although a majority of the PLP opposed entry into the government, MacDonald was in the minority of only three out of twelve in the NEC who were against the decision. On a joint vote, the proposal to join the Coalition was passed, seventeen to eleven.[5]

MacDonald published in the *Labour Leader* his objections to this decisive step. He reminded his colleagues that the Labour Party[6]

> went into the House of Commons knowing that taking office was not the way it was to use its influence, and convinced that being in ministries diminished its powers rather than increased them. . . . It is not today that the party is to suffer for its mistakes. It is when the time comes for us to go back to where we were last July and resume our own special work that we shall discover what we have lost and the penalties we shall have to pay.

But in the course of the following months, unfortunately, participation in the Asquith coalition did not bring home these facts to most of the party leadership. On the contrary, MacDonald noted sadly in April 1916: 'There are indications here that our Labour Party is finally burst. Men like Hodge, who were always very ignorant and Seddon and Tillett, who were lacking in character, are enjoying the companionship and the patronage of our enemies.'[7]

Predictably, therefore, the invitation to join what he saw as an even more reactionary coalition under Lloyd George in December 1916 was approved without much hesitation by the party leadership.[8] He told an audience in Blackburn:[9]

He regretted most profoundly that the Labour Party had associated itself with the new ministry. . . . It was not (as some said) a National Government that was in existence now, but just an ordinary party government. It was controlled by just the ordinary old-fashioned anti-Labour Tories who could no more change their nature than the leopard could change his spots.

Once again MacDonald intoned that to join coalitions 'jeopardised the existence of the Labour Party'.[10] Five months after Lloyd George had come to power with Arthur Henderson at his side, MacDonald warned:[11]

If you create a party and allow men who get to the top of it to be drained away into other parties or other relationships, it simply means that the Party is going to be a ladder for people to climb up. You can put men in office in order to take authority from them. You can give men honour in order to take respect from them. You can give men the badge of power in order to tie their hands behind their backs and make them ineffective for other work.

Fourteen years later, these words would return to haunt him. In 1917, he was it appears, immune to the temptations of power. And with the handicap of Labour in the Cabinet, he remarked, 'The ordinary meetings of the Party took on a character which made it a sheer waste of time.'[12] The Labour Party, he believed, had ceased to exist after three years of war.

This turn of events reinforced MacDonald's view, which he had developed early in the war, that the progressive forces in British politics had to be reorganized. As early as 24 August 1914, he wrote to E. D. Morel, who had been his friend since the 1906 agitation over Belgian atrocities in the Congo.[13] MacDonald suggested that they should 'convene a private conference of representative men', that is, those who differed from the Foreign Office interpretation of the causes of the war.[14] Out of this meeting emerged the Union of Democratic Control, an organization to which he devoted much of his time during the war.[15]

By mid-1916, MacDonald was prepared to discuss his views

about necessary future changes in political organization. His thoughts were prompted by his reading the German sociologist Robert Michels' analysis of *Political Parties*, the English translation of which appeared in 1915.[16] In an extensive and highly favourable review of this study of the contradiction between ideology and organization, especially in democratic and socialist political groups, MacDonald revealed the extent to which the war affected his political ideas.[17]

Since the outbreak of the war, MacDonald wrote in April 1916, he had come to see the dangers of the tyranny of political oligarchies, a problem illustrated so strikingly by Michels. The suppression of dissent in the interests of sustaining the organization and the 'threatening imperiousness' of the 'authority of executives' were wartime facts which made him 'so keenly aware of the truth of much of what Professor Michels has written'.[18] In fact:

> One need not try to dispute the instances and the experiences upon which Professor Michels founds his indictment. Indeed it will do us good to face them quite honestly, and perhaps to supplement and amplify them from our own experience.

The conclusion MacDonald drew from this observation was significant. He claimed that by 1916:[19]

> *The structure and the mind of the Labour Party demand careful survey*; the part it has played during the war has been a test which has left those who understand what a Labour Party should be doubtful upon many points which, two years ago, we thought we should never doubt.

He then restated his criticisms of the Labour leadership, but added a new point to this analysis. 'That I am profoundly disappointed with some of my colleagues goes without saying', MacDonald began. But now he suggested that the source of the trouble was that 'they were badly equipped for the test they had to undergo. . . . Had they ever had any conception of the industrial state they would have been guided by that during the past year and a half'.[20] Their ideological backwardness had terrible consequences. He claimed:[21]

> A war which should be the end of militarism in Europe and of the policies and diplomatic method which make war in-

evitable, is being fought and will be ended, just as all past wars have been and will be followed by sequels similar to what all past wars have had. That will be largely the fault of the Labour Party. *The failure of the Labour leaders was an intellectual one, not a moral one.*

Hence MacDonald argued that an intellectual base for a revitalized Labour Party was essential for two reasons: first, to counterbalance the oligarchical tendencies of the leadership; and, second, to avoid a recurrence of the collapse of the political movement in future times of stress.

In view of the experience of the war, he came to the conclusion as well that Labour had to look outside trade unionism, that is, to the middle class, for the men who would give the party this crucial ideological strength. It was essential, therefore that 'the Labour Party . . . open its doors to young men who have been trained to act independently and who have come to it by roads other than those of Trade Unionism'. It was also time, he added, to reduce the over-emphasis on the importance of financial contributions to the party. He held that:[22]

> One now-a-days all too frequently hears an argument by some Trade Union leaders that their influence inside the Labour Party should be in proportion to the money they put into it. Money did not make the Party, and money will not keep it going; ideas made and ideas are necessary to maintain it.

MacDonald's renewed interest in political ideas is apparent in much of his wartime writing. Because of the war, he wrote in 1916, all questions of political thought 'can now be approached with new experience and from a fresh angle of vision'.[23] Reference to his flirtation with guild socialism has already been made.[24] This phase of his thought was an outcome of his opposition to conscription, censorship, and the silencing of dissent, which, he believed, reflected a new and dangerous trend towards authoritarian government. Consider this passage from an article he wrote in 1917 as one example of the effect of the war on his attitude to the state:

> After the war we may nationalise the railways and run them as State capitalist enterprises. We may nationalise essential industries and run them in the spirit of the Munitions Act offering 'national necessity' as a justification. In form Socialism will have triumphed; in fact it will have receded, because

capitalism will be the ruling factor and will be strengthened by becoming representative, impersonal and political, instead of being individualist and unrepresentative.

He called this future organization a 'Labour Philanthropic State' which, he believed, would serve, 'not liberty, but obedience, not democracy but bureaucracy, and if a majority of Trade Union officials using the votes of their societies were to support this bureaucracy, that would not make it the duty of Social Democrats to acquiesce'. 'Before the war,' he recalled, 'I felt that what was called "the spirit of the rebel" was to a great extent a stagey pose.' By 1917 he was convinced that 'It is now required to save us.'[25]

The urgency of rethinking socialist ideas was proved beyond a doubt, MacDonald believed, by the February Revolution in Russia. At the Leeds convention of June 1917, he hailed the revolution not only because of its objective importance, but also on account of its repercussions in the West. He said:[26]

When the war broke out, organised Labour in this country lost the initiative (Hear, Hear). It became a mere echo of the old governing classes and opinions (Hear, Hear). Now the Russian Revolution has once again given you the chance to take the initiative yourselves.

The assertion of an independent foreign policy was the first step, he stated, in the process of Labour's emergence from its self-imposed 'servitude'. Previously:[27]

the great opportunity which the war gave to the Labour Party to take hold of diplomacy was thrown away, because the Labour Party never saw what the real meaning of the war was, and without the Russian Revolution, the opportunity would not have occurred.

British Labour had to join, he insisted, in the effort to end the war and to rewrite the old rules of international politics.

The necessary parallel between internal and international reconstruction was a line of argument which MacDonald and many others pursued towards the end of the war. In this view, the conflict had been a test of both diplomatic and party political machinery. On any criterion, he insisted, the old organization of the Labour Party, just like that of the Foreign Office, was a failure which could not be allowed to survive the war unchanged.[28]

In 1917 he turned to the task of providing Labour with the political structure appropriate to the new role it had to play in the years after the armistice. The reconstruction of the Labour Party, that is, giving it a new form and a new mind, in MacDonald's own phrase, was a direct outcome of the pressures of the war.

ARTHUR HENDERSON AND THE RUSSIAN REVOLUTION

Arthur Henderson came to advocate the reconstruction of the Labour Party in mid-1917 after his mission to Russia had been completed. For the first three years of the war, Henderson's faith in the justice of the Allied cause and the necessity of total victory over Germany was matched by a commitment to the old structure of the party of which he was the undisputed wartime leader. But after his six weeks' stay in Petrograd as a representative of the British Government, Henderson's approach to ending the war and his view of Labour's political identity had completely changed.

Before Petrograd

Henderson was the first Labour M.P. in a British government. He served in Asquith's reconstructed ministry as President of the Board of Education and after August 1916 as Paymaster-General with a seat in the Cabinet. In December 1916 he joined Lloyd George's War Cabinet of five as Minister without Portfolio.[29] His chief tasks were to be the government's intermediary with the trade unions and its specialist on industrial problems. His dedication to the war effort could not have been in question.

Even before he had accepted government office in May 1915, he had been instrumental in arranging the Treasury Agreement of March of that year, whereby strike action had been renounced by most of the major unions. In the following months, he spent much of his time seeing that the conflicts which arose in industry did not interfere in any important way with war production. Henderson's prestige among the organized working class did much to assure the overall success of his work as Asquith's and later as Lloyd George's chief industrial conciliator, and as such, he fulfilled a vital political mission. As valuable to the government were his efforts to quiet the outcry in the Labour movement over the introduction of conscription in 1916.[30]

Lloyd George knew that Henderson's voice commanded respect

among the industrial population, but he had no intention of granting him major responsibilities. On the other hand, Henderson was not content with his figurehead status, and in January 1917, he tried to improve his position. He submitted to the Prime Minister an outline of what he thought his powers should be. He wanted control over[31]

(1) Man Power in the widest sense, i.e., including National Service, the Ministry of Labour and the Labour Departments of the Ministries of Munitions and the Admiralty.

(2) Reconstruction, so far as Labour is concerned, i.e., Demobilization, Redemption of Pledges and Industrial Reorganization.

(3) Miscellaneous Problems of Civil Administration as they arise, e.g. Liquor Control and Pensions which especially affect the working classes.

This ambitious proposal was in no sense a demand, and its author probably knew that it had little chance of securing Lloyd George's approval. But it does show that Henderson wanted to make better use of his unprecedented political position and to try to increase Labour's share in the determination of internal policy. He failed in this aim, but he was able at least to prevent some ill-advised government actions. For example, Lloyd George asked him on the same day he submitted the memorandum cited above to estimate what would be the effect on the Labour Party conference, which was to convene in a fortnight, of the suppression of the ILP paper, the *Labour Leader*, for printing seditious articles. Henderson argued against such a step, partly because it would render his own position 'quite intolerable'. In recent weeks 'no one has come in for more criticism . . . than myself personally,' he complained, and a blatant provocation of anti-war sentiment would make it almost impossible for him to continue in office.[32] The *Labour Leader* continued to appear, without government harassment.

The strain of retaining his commitment to his party and to Lloyd George became greater as the war dragged on. While he found it increasingly difficult to cope with the growing mood of discontent within the Labour Party and many unions about the conduct of the war, he still resisted any weakening in Labour's official support for the government. He was similarly opposed to any alteration of the organization and objectives of his party which would have made it possible to challenge the Coalition as an independent force. His views on both these major issues changed after his visit to Russia.

At the Manchester conference of the Labour Party in January 1917, W. Frank Purdy of the Shipwrights' Union, the party chairman, claimed that it[33]

> has steadily, and, in my opinion, wisely, always declined to be bound by any programme, or to subscribe to any dogma, or to lay down any creed. It has refused to adopt any mechanical formulas or to submit to any regimentation either of ideas or of policy.

Henderson's line was similarly conservative. When a resolution was moved to force the party executive to remove a candidate from the official party list if he was repudiated by an affiliated organization, Henderson asked on behalf of the executive for the rejection of the proposal for the reason 'that the present was not the time for tinkering with the Constitution'.[34] He also opposed a resolution to reorganize the executive on the grounds that the party had been built up through the old constitution, and therefore he was extremely reluctant to change it. 'When organisations were invited in under a particular Constitution,' he pointed out, 'the greatest care ought to be exercised before any alteration was made in it.'[35]

The 1917 conference was also significant in the surprisingly hostile reception Henderson received during the discussion of the deportation of trade unionists on the Clyde. He was accused by one of the deportees, David Kirkwood, of having lost the confidence of Labour by his association with Lloyd George and the repressive measures he had authorized to silence dissenters.[36] While trying to defend himself despite numerous interruptions Henderson remarked that he never had been the target of such heckling, and that he knew that 'the Conference was not in that frame of mind to do justice to men like himself'. He told the irate delegates that he was fully conscious of the difficulties he faced in trying to reconcile his post as party secretary with Cabinet office, and that he had no part in the deportations. To cries of 'resign' from the government, he replied bitterly:[37]

> If he had to resign he would be resigning every day to please some of them. He was not sure he would not resign if he were to please himself, but he was not there [in the Cabinet] either to please himself or them, he was there to see the War through.

And with that patriotic assurance and a promise to look into the matter, he weathered at least that storm of criticism.[38]

Henderson was also exposed to equal pressure for loyalty from his Cabinet colleagues. One of his most important functions was to keep the government informed about the state of Labour opinion both in Britain, and when possible, on the Continent. He dutifully reported to the Cabinet his impressions of the 1917 Labour Party Conference,[39] and earlier in January, he told of his reactions to a conference of Allied socialists in Paris 'at which it was clear that there is a considerable development of pacifist feeling'. He noted optimistically, though, that the conference was 'satisfactory' since the socialists were still resolved 'to assist the Government in the prosecution of the war'.[40]

Henderson was elated at hearing the news of the February Revolution in Russia. He believed that it was an event which both changed the character of the war and made it even more essential to work for the total defeat of Germany. He greeted the fall of the Czar much more warmly than did the other members of the War Cabinet. On 19 May 1917, he told an audience in Richmond: 'We could depend upon it that of all the wonderful things that have happened during this war, there was nothing to approach the Russian Revolution.' His emotional reaction to these events became more and more apparent as his speech went on. 'Never has such a thing been seen,' he maintained, 'since the world began. There is nothing to compare with it in human experience for its completeness, its unanimity, and above all its self-control.' Claiming to speak 'as a representative of the British Socialists', he said that he 'rejoiced at the act of liberation and sent to all our fellow workers in Russia warmest greetings' and the assurance 'that if they wanted our help they could count upon us both in word and deed to the utmost of our power'. The Allied effort, he concluded, had become unambiguously the cause of democracy. The British and Russian working classes now had to work together and to redouble their efforts to defeat the common enemy and to bring a real peace, and not an armistice 'dictated by uncontrolled and unrepentant military despots'.[41]

Henderson knew that the February Revolution in Russia added a new set of problems to the Allied war effort. The foreign policy of the deposed Czar was completely acceptable to the British government, but no one could be certain that the new Provisional Government in Petrograd would maintain it. Henderson and the rest of the Cabinet were horrified by the possibility that internal disorder could lead to the collapse of the Eastern Front. Anyone could see that the consequences of an interruption of Russia's contribution to the fight against the Central Powers, let alone her unilateral withdrawal from the war, would be staggering to the Allies. Enormous additional pressure would then be brought to bear on the armies in the West. Some way had to be found in the spring of 1917 to convince the Russian socialists to continue the struggle.

The Cabinet were therefore happy to hear from Henderson in late March that he had received a note from a group of French socialists who were in England en route to Petrograd 'to persuade' the Russian Socialist Party 'to do all in its power to bring the war to a satisfactory conclusion'. Henderson was instructed to get a 'suitably composed British Labour Deputation [to] accompany the French party with the same object'.[42] W. S. Sanders, Will Thorne and James O'Grady agreed to go, and the two delegations proceeded to Russia.[43]

At about the same time, the fall of the Czar had rekindled hopes among some European socialists that they were now in a position, on account of the prestige of the Russian Revolution, and the support of its leaders, to launch a peace offensive. On 24 April 1917, Henderson received a telegram from Camille Huysmans, the Belgian secretary of the ISB, informing him that the Dutch section were going to convene at Stockholm a special meeting of the European socialist parties affiliated to it. The conference was tentatively scheduled for 15 May 1917. Henderson knew that the French Socialist Party Executive were against such a conference, which German and Austrian socialists were likely to attend. He therefore had little difficulty in persuading the Labour Party Executive on 9 May to pass a resolution 'that the British Labour Party should not be represented at the Stockholm Conference'.[44] Instead, Henderson moved 'That a Conference of the Socialist Parties in the Allied Countries (Belgium, France, Russia, Italy, the United States, and Great Britain) should be held in London as early as possible' and furthermore 'that a British Deputation be appointed to proceed to Russia for the purpose of consulting with the Russian Council of Workmen's and Soldiers' Delegates with a view to urging them to send representatives to the proposed London Conference'. The provisional date for this alternative meeting was set for the week ending 23 June 1917. Purdy, G. H.

Roberts, and Henderson agreed to go to Russia to persuade the Russians to come to London rather than Stockholm.[45]

Henderson reported these developments to the Cabinet two days later, and explained that his party executive had agreed 'to send a Mission to Petrograd to impress on the Russian Socialists the danger of a separate peace'.[46] The Cabinet expressed reluctance to let Henderson leave the country in view of the growing industrial unrest in Britain. But the Under-Secretary for Foreign Affairs, Lord Robert Cecil, convinced them on 21 May that it was essential for Henderson to go to Russia on a mission parallel to that of M. Thomas, the French socialist Minister of Munitions who had replaced the ambassador, M. Paléologue.[47] On 23 May the Cabinet decided that the British Ambassador, Sir George Buchanan, was 'no longer the ideal British representative' in Petrograd on account of his close association, like Paléologue, with the Czarist regime. It was also agreed:[48]

> that the British representative in Petrograd should be a person calculated to exercise a powerful influence on the democratic elements which now predominate in Russia to pursue the war with energy. They therefore invited Mr. Arthur Henderson to make a personal sacrifice and go to Petrograd on a similar footing to that of M. Albert Thomas.

No decision was taken on the length of his stay, only that it would be 'temporary'.[49] Henderson agreed to the proposal, and with his mind set against the Stockholm Conference, he left the next day for Russia.[50]

The impact of Russia

Henderson arrived in Russia on 1 June 1917,[51] without any idea of the magnitude of the problems which confronted the Provisional Government. His ignorance of the Russian language and his inexperience in foreign affairs left him at first completely in the hands of Sir George Buchanan, the man whom ostensibly he had been sent to replace.[52] Henderson respected his views and could not see any advantage in his departure from Petrograd. On the contrary, he wrote to Lloyd George, soon after his arrival:[53]

> It was a great satisfaction to me to find that the Government here fully share the high opinion we have formed at home of

the skill and courage shown by Sir George in dealing with the old regime. . . . There can be no comparison between his position and that of M. Paléologue who I understand, lived in complete isolation under the old regime and was wholly out of sympathy with the objects of the new.

It was true that Buchanan had been 'the object of violent attacks on the part of the extremists', but Henderson advised:

I attach much weight to an observation of Prince Lvov that the recall of the Ambassador at this moment would be regarded as a concession to popular clamour. In other words his departure, so far from strengthening our influence here would I believe actually weaken the authority of the Provisional Government, of whose desire to work in close and intimate cooperation with our own there can I think be little question.

During his stay, the relationship between the Ambassador and the Labour leader developed along lines of mutual respect and trust, and Henderson was given every assistance in his effort to begin to untangle the very complex strands of the Russian political situation.

He quickly learned of the circumstances surrounding the resignation two weeks previously of the Foreign Secretary of the first Provisional Government, Paul Miliukov, who was a leader of the Liberal Cadet Party and an exponent of both all-out war against Germany and the adoption despite the revolution of the annexationist policies of the Czarist regime. His political demise was a victory for the moderate Menshevik socialist leaders of the Petrograd Soviet of Workers' and Soldiers' Deputies, which held political power effectively but not officially after the February Revolution and whose spokesmen now dominated the Provisional Government as well. While Prince Lvov remained titular head of the new government, among the socialists, Alexander Kerensky became Minister of War and Irakli Tsereteli, Minister of Posts. The Liberals could not yet be ignored, however, and the portfolio of foreign affairs went to Michael Tereshchenko, a widely-travelled millionaire who had been Minister of Finance in the previous Coalition.[54]

The new Provisional Government adopted the two-part peace policy of the Petrograd Soviet: to press for a general peace without annexations and at the same time to defend the homeland and the revolution against the invader. This appeal to both pacifists and

Plate 15
J. Ramsay MacDonald and
J. S. Middleton

Plate 16   Arthur Henderson

patriots was popularly known as Revolutionary Defencism, the outlines of which had been prepared by Tsereteli and other Mensheviks during their pre-1917 exile.[55] In the spring of that year, this plan seemed to provide the way for Russia to begin to disengage from a war which she could not continue indefinitely.

The success of Revolutionary Defencism depended on the one hand on the participation of the Allied socialists in the proposed Stockholm Conference. The military situation was the other determinant of foreign policy at the beginning of June 1917. At that time, the Russian government hoped that this assembly of socialists would mobilize Western public opinion in such a way that the respective governments would be forced to move towards a negotiated settlement. While Henderson was en route to Petrograd, Buchanan had an interview with Tsereteli, in which the latter said:[56]

> that it was necessary that Allied Democracies should come to complete agreement on the subject of the aims of the war and of eventual Peace Terms. . . . He (further?) dwelt on necessity for maintaining closest contact between British and Russian Democracies by means of exchange of visits between representatives of the various Labour and Socialist groups in each country.

The British ambassador had further assured Tsereteli that the Russian Revolution 'was likely to bring views of British and Russian democracies into closer harmony more especially as regards the war'.[57] Thus Henderson's presence in Petrograd was an excellent opportunity to enlist the support of a powerful Western Labour leader on an issue which the Russian socialists in office rightly saw as crucial to their political survival. If the Mensheviks and their allies could not extricate their country from the war, there were others, as Lenin had made plain in his April theses, who would act to end the slaughter.[58]

In the first weeks of his mission, Henderson began to recognize the precariousness of the Russian situation, but it took him somewhat longer to decide that the Allies and in particular the Allied socialists had to act in concert to keep the regime alive. His support for the aims of the February Revolution was complete, but about a month passed before he was convinced that for the new leaders of Russia, the alternative to peace was political disaster.

His early impressions of Russia are marked by a bewilderment which was shared by many other observers. Henderson decided that the people 'are suffering from the intoxication that has followed upon their newly-won freedom'. The result was that 'Unfortunately, both in civil life and in the armies a great percentage have no desire whatever to get on with the war.' Both war-weariness and the permeation of 'pacifist theories', Henderson wrote to his agent, had taken their toll of the will to fight.[59] What was worse:[60]

> With the newly-won freedom newspapers and parties have sprung up like mushrooms and the teaching in the cheap press and the meetings you can find at almost every street corner are calculated not only to disturb but to poison the mind. . . . Indications are not lacking that much of this irresponsible propaganda has its inception, inspiration and support in German sources.

The Mensheviks clearly needed all the assistance they could get. The Petrograd correspondent of *The Times* noted in a dispatch dated 6 June 1917 that 'Mr. Henderson's visit coincides with a labour crisis here, and will certainly be helpful to the Provisional Government'.[61] At a Council of Ministers meeting in Petrograd in early June, Henderson was told by Prince Lvov that Russia was undergoing 'in industry [the] destructive stage of [the] revolution'. The Prime Minister added that his government wanted to make full use of his knowledge of industrial affairs, and to this end Skobelev, the Minister of Labour, invited him to come to his office and to consider it his headquarters.[62]

Henderson informed Lloyd George of this meeting and of Prince Lvov's view that 'as [the] Government gain in strength all classes are beginning to realize the existence of an authority in the state superior to both capital and labour'. But he learned at the same time that 'Extremist propaganda was causing [the] Government much anxiety, worst offenders being found among returning exiles'.[63]

Henderson learned that the Bolshevik danger was an important factor in an appreciation of Russian affairs. He received the report of 'an active but moderate socialist' from Moscow and passed it on as authentic to G. H. Roberts, a Labour M.P. and Parliamentary Secretary at the Board of Trade, whose own plans for a trip to Russia had to be cancelled at the last moment. The opinion of this unnamed observer was that a crisis was unavoidable.

Every day the relations between the extremists and all those Socialists who support the temporary Government are becoming more strained. In a few weeks we shall have two groups, the 'pro-Kerenskyites' and the 'pro-Leninites,' and it remains to be seen which of these groups will prevail.

'At any rate,' he warned, in the coming weeks, either 'the moderate socialists and the Coalition Government will have triumphed or we shall all be hanging from the nearest lamp-posts.'[64]

Henderson was perfectly prepared to help counter the revolutionary defeatist propaganda of the Bolsheviks and their allies. He agreed to address various groups of Russian workers in an attempt to transmit to them the enthusiasm of their British counterparts for the war effort. On 15 June he spoke to a crowd of over 5,000 workers and soldiers assembled at the People's Palace in Petrograd. We can get some idea of the intended, if not the actual, effect of Henderson's visit on public morale from the report of his speech in *The Times*:[65]

His reference to the unanimous determination of all classes in the British Empire to continue the struggle till a victorious peace had been assured evoked tremendous cheering. He spoke of his own personal share in the war. When he told the audience that his eldest son was among those who had fallen on the battlefield the whole audience rose and sang the Russian Requiem.

At the conclusion of the speech there was a scene of indescribable enthusiasm. Men and women, moved to tears, demanded a general mobilization, amid cries of: – 'We are all ready to march against the foe.'

Few have claimed that Henderson was a powerful orator, and Robert Wilton, correspondent of *The Times*, who was fiercely anti-Bolshevik,[66] was probably carried away here by his prose. But it is hardly surprising that those opposed to the continuation of the war distrusted Henderson and his mission.

The Bolsheviks did not hide their contempt both for the Stockholm idea and for Henderson himself. Lenin called the preparations for the conference a 'comedy' growing out of 'the political manoeuvres of German imperialism'. The Germans were only interested in discussing peace terms with the Allied 'social chauvinists', he claimed, because they were beginning to see by

July 1917 that 'to carry on the war now is a hopeless task'.[67] To Sukhanov, Henderson was one of the 'agents of Shylock come to demand from the Russian Revolution their pound of cannon-fodder'. A speech reported in *Pravda* repeated the charge that he was one of those deluded majority socialists who[68]

> favor the sacred union of classes, a principle wrought by the enemies of the working class who have beguiled the worker aristocracy. He who extends a hand to Henderson and Thomas, extends it at the same time to Lloyd George and Ribot, and to the French and English bankers.

On 14 June, Henderson's Petrograd apartment was ransacked and his personal documents were taken. Wilton of *The Times* concluded that the Bolsheviks were responsible. He reasoned that Henderson's statements sounded so much like British propaganda that 'The Leninists . . . stole his papers – to ascertain whether he was really a Socialist leader or merely an agent of the British Government'. He added that 'Their mermidons also took his clothes, which was excusable, in as much as the members of the Soviet were suffering from a shortage of garments due to the decreased output of the textile mills.'[69] But regardless of who was to blame in this minor incident, Henderson was aware of the Bolsheviks' hostility to him. He also knew that very little could be taken for granted in Russia, not even the personal security of a distinguished guest of state.

A visit to Moscow at the end of June did not alter Henderson's impression of the confusion and gravity of the political situation. In his public pronouncements he tried to bolster the government's position by pointing out to employers and employees that the failure of moderate socialist leadership would lead inevitably to the victory of the extremists. At a meeting of the Moscow bourse committee, he described the operation and advantages of state control of industry in wartime. The following day, he intervened successfully in an industrial dispute which had involved Welsh tinplate workers on loan to a Moscow factory.[70] He even convinced the Nevsky Thread Company, which was backed by British investors, to agree to the transfer of control of their works to the government for the duration.[71] Still, his pessimism deepened.

At the end of his visit, he cabled Lloyd George: 'I am afraid I have brought back [from Moscow] an even less cheerful view of [the] position than I had formed in Petrograd.'[72] He told the

Prime Minister of his speech to the British colony there in which he urged the 'necessity for supporting [the] Provisional Government' to prevent worse things from happening. On a brighter note, he added:[73]

I have noticed a distinctly more reasonable tone appearing in conversation with business men since I have been here. One hears less of closing down to give Socialists a lesson. Employers are beginning to realize [that the] only safeguard against control of workmen is control by [the] State. . . .

Henderson admitted being appalled, though, at the 'complete absence both of machinery of traditional (?) [sic] collective negotiation and of administrative experience in Government' and therefore ended his cable to Lloyd George with this prediction: 'You must anticipate such a reduction in productive capacity of Russia as will not far remove it from complete collapse.'[74]

His despondency was not relieved by a meeting of the Moscow Soldiers' Council, which the acting Consul-General, Bruce Lockhart, had arranged. Henderson addressed this body and learned at first hand of the suspicion in which British war aims and the Allied cause were held by many Russian socialists.[75] Their hostile reception and a subsequent discussion with the President of the Soldiers' Council, Urnof, confirmed Henderson's fears about the consequences of the failure of the friendly Provisional Government. Henderson wrote:[76]

[Urnof] explained frankly that Russia was sick of the war and industrial exhaustion. National feeling hardly existed but at the same time there was even in [the] masses a sentiment of honour which made [the] idea of a separate peace distasteful. To create out of this feeling real enthusiasm for war in the people and army was the task of his party and it was rendered very difficult by refusal of [the] Allies to accept without reserve [the] platform of Russian (?Socialists). . . . He added rather naively that what in particular made view of British Labour on war suspicious to his friends was that they seemed to coincide with those held by Russians of middle class.

Lockhart told Buchanan of Henderson's reply:[77]

that the English workers had their own point of view about the war, that they were in no way influenced by the Russian bourgeoisie, and that if the Russian bourgeoisie held the same point of view as the English workers the latter were not to blame.

The consul wryly noted that it was 'difficult to explain in a dispatch the unfortunate effect which such an answer produced'. The interview 'was certainly not one of the most striking successes of Mr. Henderson's mission', and it showed 'how far removed' his thinking was from that of moderate Russian socialists, let alone from that of Lenin and his colleagues.[78] Lockhart added that his visit did 'serve to encourage the bourgeoisie and pro-war elements. In view of the bitter class hatred which is being propagated in Russia at present, it is a matter of conjecture whether such encouragement is a real benefit or not.'[79]

Recalling that meeting in later years, Lockhart wrote of Henderson: 'The comrades in the Soviet bewildered him. He did not understand their language. He did not like their manners.' And 'Whatever its effect on the Russians', his exposure to the views of even patriotic, anti-German men like Urnof 'had the advantage of curing Mr. Henderson of any revolutionary tendencies for the rest of his life'.[80] There is some question as to whether he needed a cure in the first place, but there is no doubt that he was not only thrilled by but also appalled by the prospects of the Russian Revolution.

In any event, the turmoil which swept through Russia in mid-1917 was, in Henderson's opinion, certainly bound to diminish her contribution to the Allied war effort. On 1 July 1917, he wrote to Lloyd George:[81]

> Conclusion which I draw from a month's observation is that Russia can no longer be regarded as [an] effective Ally. . . . Therefore we must make up our minds to continue the struggle alone with France and America carrying Russia with us as an inert partner. . . .

This view did not imply that he was indifferent to the political complexion of the Petrograd government, as Lloyd George may have gathered from his consistently pessimistic dispatches. On the contrary, Henderson still believed that even a crippled partner ruled by men sympathetic to the Allied cause and liberal democracy was far preferable to a Bolshevik Russia which would sue for a separate peace at the first opportunity. To help forestall this unwelcome change, Henderson decided in early July to support the Stockholm Conference.[82]

The Stockholm question

The evolution of Henderson's stand on Stockholm paralleled his growing doubts about the industrial outlook in Russia. In the early days of his visit, he joined Thomas and the Belgian socialist Vendervelde in opposing an international conference of socialists without prior agreement on issues such as Alsace-Lorraine and reparations, which they knew the Germans could not accept.[83] Henderson wrote to the Foreign Office on 8 June that the proposed binding conference of all belligerent parties was 'most objectionable'.[84] Three days later, he told the Petrograd Soviet that a settlement of the issues of the war would be 'fully and frankly dealt with by the representatives of the Allied nations assembled at the Peace Conference' and not at Stockholm.[85] On 17 June he warned the same body:[86]

> We must be careful; because our choice to-day may be between honour and infamy; an untimely peace and years of fear; a few months of fighting and suffering and a lasting peace. These are, I think, the views of the overwhelming majority of the organised workers of Great Britain.

In fact, Henderson went further and shocked his Russian colleagues by his statement that it was British Labour and not the government or its representatives like Buchanan, which opposed Stockholm. In conversation with Tsereteli, he remarked: 'In order to understand the difference between my attitude and Buchanan's, it is necessary to remember that if we decide to go to Stockholm, then the pleasure of meeting the Germans will be mine and not Buchanan's.'[87]

By early July, however, Henderson's fears about the weakness of the Provisional Government led him to soften and then to reverse his previous opposition to participation in the Stockholm Conference. He never wavered, though, in his determination to see an Allied victory over Germany, and he came to support Stockholm only when he was convinced that it would not lead to an Allied capitulation.

In a cable to Lloyd George at the beginning of July, Henderson insisted that 'we must be on our guard' against any 'appearance of coldness or neglect in our dealings with Provisional Government. Anything which injures their credit here can only operate to strengthen forces of disorder and to postpone the Restoration of Russia.'[88] He pointed out that there were two currents of opinion in Russia about the way to achieve peace:[89]

> One is for direct action on Western proletariate to provoke rising against capitalism and war together. The other is for Constitutional action by first converting labour and (?Socialist) parties and then trusting to pressure they will exercise on the Government.

The first view was the Bolshevik, the second the Menshevik and, Henderson concluded, the same distinction existed between the 'agitator and idealist in all countries'.[90] His firm support for the 'idealist' Provisional Government eventually brought him to favour the Stockholm project.

The event which sealed Henderson's change of mind about the conference was the ill-fated summer offensive, which was launched at the beginning of July to re-establish Russia's political standing among her Allies. After the Russian army had begun to disintegrate and the offensive had turned into a rout, he came to see that support for Stockholm was probably the only way to keep Russia in the war and to keep a moderate government in power.[91] He knew that Tsereteli and Skobelev were determined to see that the conference was convened, whether British Labour attended or not, and that the idea of Stockholm was extremely popular in Russia. In addition to accepting the inevitable, he also hoped that participation in an international socialist assembly would help clarify British war aims and thereby refute Bolshevik propaganda about the imperialistic nature of the war.

Given the available options, Henderson was prepared after six weeks in Russia, to accept participation in the Stockholm Conference. Before he left Petrograd on 16 July, he even suggested the 'temporary relinquishment' of government office for delegates, so that the most prominent Labour leaders could attend. In Stockholm the next day, he discussed the subject further with the Swedish socialist Hjalmar Branting, and urged a further delay in convening the conference. More time was needed, he argued, since the project involved no less than the reconstruction of the socialist international 'from the bottom' up.[92] His dedication to this task was a direct outcome of his visit to Russia.

Henderson's change of mind about Stockholm shocked at least one man who had known him in Russia. Robert Wilton of *The Times* wrote bitterly six months after Henderson's visit:[93]

> He came to Petrograd a convinced opponent of the Stockholm Conference idea.... He expressed his disapproval of the underhand manner in which the invitation to this Conference had been issued by the Soviets. He even spoke rather strongly about the Russian Revolutionaries in general. But instead of his 'converting' them, they 'converted' him.

Robert Williams, the socialist leader of the transport workers, came to the same conclusion, stripped of its pejorative tone. He wrote on 28 July 1917 that Henderson's 'experiences in Russia have been such as to bring about a kind of spontaneous conversion to internationalism'.[94] Both men were right. Arthur Henderson did experience a type of 'conversion' in Russia, the political significance of which became apparent soon after his mission was over.

The aftermath

Henderson returned to England in late July on the same boat, as it happened, with four Russian socialists who were sent by the Petrograd Soviet to convince their Western colleagues to attend the Stockholm Conference.[95] The fact that the secretary of the British Labour Party already agreed with them in principle made their mission infinitely easier. No one could challenge Henderson's prestige in the party executive committee, and if it came to a vote in conference, his view would decide the issue. In fact, after he reported on his trip to Russia in the presence of the Soviet's four emissaries, the Labour Party NEC voted five to two to convene a special party conference on 10 August at which it would recommend 'to sanction the Party being represented at the Stockholm Conference'.[96] Henderson then went to Paris with MacDonald for consultations with the French socialists, who had declared for Stockholm on 15 July. Just before the special conference on 9 August, the Labour Party NEC reaffirmed its earlier decision with the qualification that the invitation to attend 'be accepted on condition that the Conference be consultative and not mandatory'.[97]

The next day Henderson told the special Labour Party conference in London why he had changed his mind. He reminded them that 'before I went to Russia some ten or twelve weeks ago I was opposed to the holding of an international conference'. On his arrival in Petrograd, he said, he had lost no time in informing the Petrograd Soviet of this fact. Since he knew that they had no intention of renouncing the conference, there were three courses which Henderson saw as available to him. One was a complete refusal of their request to attend the conference; the second was unqualified acceptance, and the third was to work to convert the conference into a consultation. After he had seen conditions in Russia and how desperate the situation really was, he could not in conscience advocate the first course; he dismissed the second, and set his sights on the third.

Henderson concentrated his argument in his speech on the possibility of an outright rejection of the Soviet's request for the support of British Labour in its quest for peace. To have slammed the door in their faces, as it were, 'would have been about the most fatal position that I could have taken up,' he said, 'either in a government capacity or as the representative of the great British Labour Movement.'[98] Why?

> The reason is simple. In my opinion, our case has never been properly stated and is certainly not properly understood to this day in Russia, and to have point blank refused to consider the question would have done incalculable harm.

During his mission, Henderson also encountered[99]

> not only confused by prejudiced ideas against the great Labour Movement, because of the mistaken notion of our attitude in supporting the war. Our objects have been perverted, and these perversions I found were being utilised to the full by enemy agents.

Since he knew 'that a conference had become inevitable, owing to the determination of the Russians', to reject the proposal would have been to play right into the extremists' hands. They would then have had additional support if the Russian socialists alone met delegates from the neutral and central powers at Stockholm. Hence, 'after great thought', he concluded that 'British representatives should attend the Conference' as long as its resolutions were not binding on the participants.[100] Above all, in considering the issue, he asked the delegates in London to:[101]

remember poor struggling Russia whose great miracle we welcomed with such delight a few weeks ago, and of whom it was universally admitted that it had done the finest thing that had ever been done during the whole War. Let us remember poor Russia, and if we cannot give the newest Democracy, the infant of Democracies, all she asks, I beseech you not to give her an entire point blank refusal.

The resolution to go to Stockholm was passed by more than a three to one majority.

The political consequences of this decision were far-reaching. A few hours after the vote was taken, the Cabinet decided 'not to permit British representation at the Conference' and determined to expel Henderson from the government.[102] His resignation was tendered and accepted the following morning.[103]

Although the Labour Party did not leave the Coalition at this time, the Stockholm incident was an important precipitating factor in its internal development. When Arthur Henderson spoke to the special conference and advocated attendance at Stockholm, the step he asked the party to take was, in effect, to begin a new political life.

Only after Petrograd did his commitment to a socialist policy to help end the war outweigh his sense of obligation to Lloyd George and the Cabinet.[104] His experiences in Russia thus prepared the way for his decision to assert Labour's independence, by the adoption of a foreign policy of which he knew the government disapproved.

After his return from Russia, Henderson knew that a political collision was inevitable. He told the Cabinet on 1 August of the importance which the Russian Foreign Secretary, Tereshchenko, attributed to the conference and of his (Henderson's) support for it. The only question which remained open was whether he would personally attend, and he told his colleagues that he had not yet decided.[105] But his determination to see a British Labour delegation at Stockholm could not have been in doubt. When he wrote to Lloyd George at noon on 10 August, after his speech to the Labour Party Conference, but before the vote was taken, he explained: 'I came to the conclusion that I could take no other course than to stand by the advice [in favour of Stockholm] I had given the day after my return to Russia.'[106] Nothing that had happened since that date had changed his mind.

Henderson also knew that the British government's view about Stockholm had turned to indifference after the failure of the Russian offensive. There was no reason by August 1917 why Lloyd George should tolerate a socialist peace offensive. The Cabinet decided therefore, on 8 August, that since the influence of the Petrograd Soviet 'was steadily declining', they would allow the discussion of foreign affairs only through the regular diplomatic channels. Hence 'the attendance of British delegates in Stockholm was', in their opinion, 'less important than formerly'. Furthermore, they made the pointed and condescending suggestion that it would be:[107]

> more conducive to the maintenance of good relations between the British Government and the Labour Party, that the working men themselves should refuse to attend rather than that the Government should announce their decision and thereby appear to dictate to the Labour Party.

Like any other social or political inferior, the 'working men' could choose to differ, of course, but they would have to be prepared to take the consequences.

Henderson chose not to tell the Labour Party Conference of the strong objections to Stockholm or, despite the disingenuous wording, the explicit command of the Cabinet for its rejection. He was no longer prepared to carry out Lloyd George's orders, and he had no intention of contributing further to the intimidation of Labour which the Prime Minister had practised so successfully in the past. At the same time, he did not want to obscure the central issue by making the vote one of disapproval or support for the government. A very different matter was at stake for which the Cabinet had little sympathy, namely, the fate of the socialist revolution in Russia.

The Stockholm Conference never took place, and this failure, in Henderson's view, 'assisted in weakening the influence previously possessed by the sane elements in the Soviet and provided the Bolshevik extremists with their most powerful weapon'. Their 'mischievous propaganda' made 'headway', he believed, only after the plans for the conference were abandoned.[108] What is more important than the validity of this appraisal is the evidence it provides of Henderson's commitment to do all he could to support a moderate socialist regime in Russia.

In effect, by August 1917, Arthur Henderson had adopted a

new political perspective which precluded his return to the subservient role he had played earlier in the war. The development of his political views preconditioned the thrust for power and not the other way around.[109]

THE PLANS FOR THE RECONSTRUCTION
OF THE LABOUR PARTY

After his visit to Russia, Arthur Henderson acknowledged Labour's obligation as well as its right in wartime to act from its own particular standpoint and in the light of its own interests which, as in the case of Stockholm, were international in scope. Without the shackles of government responsibility, he put his new convictions into practice in the task of reorganizing the Labour Party. Ramsay MacDonald was led to the same view, not (like Henderson) because of the successes of European socialism, but because of its failures. Together they supported Sidney Webb's efforts to create in the last year of the war a coherent programme and structure for British Labour.

Even before the Stockholm incident, Webb was engaged in the formulation of just such an independent socialist policy for the Labour Party. In his contribution to the Conscription of Riches programme of the WEC, which has been examined in detail above [110] he provided the framework for the commitment to socialism embodied in the statement of party aims in the 1918 constitution.

In July 1917 Webb drew up a memorandum on war aims[111] and helped to prepare a draft party constitution.[112] Both served as the foundations of post-war policy. The latter document offered the executive two alternative statements of the objectives of their organization. The first read: 'To secure for the producers by hand or brain the full fruits of their industry by the Common Ownership of all Monopolies and essential Raw Materials.'[113] The authorship of this first proposal is reflected in its striking similarity to Webb's position on the conscription of riches.[114] The second statement of party aims is broader and incorporated some of the spirit of the guild socialist critique of Webbian ideas. It read:[115]

> To secure for the producers by hand or brain the full fruits of
> their industry, and the most equitable distribution thereof
> that may be possible, upon the basis of the Common Owner
> ship of the Means of Production and the best obtainable

system of popular administration and control of each industry or service; ...

Why two competing formulations of party objects were offered to the NEC is not clear. Probably Webb was aware of the reluctance of men like Purdy to accept the second, more sweeping socialist platform, and therefore offered as a compromise the first statement of party aims, which he had formulated for the WEC. After Henderson had returned from Russia and had left the government, no such tactical compromises were needed.

Of equal importance was the fact that some of the infectious optimism of the Russian Revolution had spread to the West, so that by the summer of 1917, socialists began to recover their confidence and to feel that radical changes were imminent. The reconstruction of the Labour Party was accomplished in this euphoric atmosphere, which was all the more powerful since it followed the heavy gloom of the previous three years.

Henderson himself argued that the Labour Party had to be reorganized to reflect what he called 'the new democratic consciousness and the new social consciousness which have come to birth in the long agony of the present struggle'. It was also 'a fact of enormous importance', he argued, that the advance in popular political thought 'synchronises' with the extension of the franchise.[116] Most importantly of all, he believed that with the added support of millions of new electors, the Labour Party could 'prove that political methods are effective' to achieve the sweeping social reforms which were bound to come. The party, indeed, had to show 'that the Democratic State of to-morrow can be established without an intervening period of violent upheaval and dislocation'.[117]

To make of the Labour Party a moderate socialist alternative to extra-parliamentary action, or even to revolution, was all the more essential, Henderson insisted, because thousands 'have become habituated to thoughts of violence' during the war. The legacy of his visit to Russia may be seen in this passage from a pamphlet he wrote in late 1917 to explain the new party programme:[118]

Never before have we had such vast numbers of the population skilled in the use of arms, disciplined, inured to danger, accustomed to act together under orders. When the war ends this country and every other will be flooded with hardy veterans of the great campaigns. Among them will be thousands of men who have exercised authority over their fellows in actual warfare, and who will be capable of assuming leadership again if insurrectionary movements come into existence. We may be warned by a perception of these facts that if barricades are indeed likely to be erected in our streets they will be manned by men who have learned how to fight and not by ill-disciplined mobs unversed in the use of modern weapons, likely to be easily overcome by trained troops. Revolution, if revolution is indeed to be forced upon democracy, will be veritable civil war. . . . This is the alternative that unmistakably confronts us if we turn aside from the path of ordered social change by constitutional methods.

Henderson issued this warning shortly after the October Revolution in Russia. Just as he supported the Coalition government in Petrograd as a left alternative to Bolshevism, so he advocated a few months later the reconstruction of the Labour Party with a socialist commitment as the bulwark of the British parliamentary system.

In this cause, he was prepared to widen the party significantly, 'to bring in a larger infusion of the non-Trade-Unionists', that is, the middle class, and especially the intellectuals in their ranks.[119] 'The Labour Party had been too short of brains', was the way he put it to C. P. Scott of the *Manchester Guardian*.[120]

Throughout the latter half of 1917, therefore, Henderson joined Webb and MacDonald in the effort to create a national party with a comprehensive programme on internal and international affairs. Without the backing of the party secretary, no plan for reorganization could ever have emerged from the executive. But with the shift in Henderson's views, both Webb and MacDonald knew that they had a powerful ally who would support their plans to insert a socialist plank in the party platform. With this invaluable backing, Webb proceeded to draw up virtually every major statement issued on behalf of the Labour Party in the last year of the war.

Webb had been given charge by the NEC on 20 August of drafting a memorandum on war issues.[121] In early September he wrote to Middleton to suggest the publication of this paper as a party pamphlet. He added:[122]

If desired, I would do a few explanatory notes on each part for instruction. It would be extremely educative to our members; and would make them more self-respecting in politics as a Party – they have a programme beyond mere 'Labour', like the other parties!

On 26 September a joint sub-committee of the NEC and the PCTUC was formed to secure, after the failure to convene the Stockholm Conference, 'a working agreement as to Peace and War Aims between the working-classes of the Allied nations'. On this question, and on all others related to foreign policy, Henderson, MacDonald and Webb were authorized to act for the NEC.[123] The final memorandum which Webb drew up on their behalf was discussed by the NEC on 24 October, adopted on 12 December, and affirmed two weeks later at a special conference as the official position of the now united Labour movement.[124]

At the NEC meeting of 26 September at which the same three men were delegated to work out a Labour foreign policy, Henderson also

> presented a Memorandum proposing the reorganisation of the Party with a view to a wider extension of membership, the strengthening and development of local parties in the constituencies, together with the promotion of a larger number of candidatures and the suggestion that a Party programme should be adopted.

The NEC then appointed a sub-committee to consider these proposals. Again Webb, MacDonald and Henderson were the key men in the group.[125] On 10 October, a draft of the new constitution was circulated to the NEC, which chose the more sweeping statement of party aims.

At this meeting as well, the same three were asked to prepare a report on reconstruction after the war.[126] As in the case of the War Aims manifesto, Webb drafted the document, published in 1918 as *Labour and the New Social Order*. On 1 November 1917, the reorganization sub-committee, now composed of Henderson, MacDonald, Webb, Purdy, Middleton, and Peters, the party agent, reported to the NEC. Among their suggestions was the establishment of permanent advisory committees to assist the party executive in its work.[127]

Thus by the beginning of the last year of the war, the Labour Party NEC had adopted the fundamental ideas and structure which supported it for the next generation. In February 1918, after a month's delay, the new constitution was ratified in London by a special party conference.[128] Nine months later, the Labour Party left the war with an ideological commitment which it could not have made and in a form which it could not have accepted a year earlier, let alone before the outbreak of the First World War.

NOTES

1 See above, p. 188. Mr David Marquand, who is engaged on a biography of MacDonald, advised me that the MacDonald Papers, which are in his possession, contain little of interest on this phase of his work. MacDonald's diaries and correspondence are not available for corroboration until Marquand's biography of MacDonald appears.

2 Algernon Simon Papers, MacDonald to Simon, 10 September 1914.

3 MacDonald, 'Socialism during war', *Socialist Review*, 12, 71, October–December 1914, p. 351.

4 Labour Party Library, Webb-MacDonald Papers, MacDonald to the Mayor of Leicester, 18 September 1914.

5 LPEC, 19 May 1915. W. C. Anderson and E. P. Wake probably joined MacDonald in opposition. The PLP voted against coalition, nine to eight, and the NEC voted in favour nine to three. Since MacDonald voted twice, the total was seventeen to eleven in the joint vote.

6 MacDonald, 'What ought the Labour Party to have done?', *Labour Leader*, 3 June 1915.

7 Simon Papers, MacDonald to Simon, 25 April 1916.

8 LPEC, 7 December 1916. The vote was eighteen to eleven.

9 'Mr. MacDonald's view', *The Times*, 11 December 1916.

10 MacDonald, 'From a Labour bench', Glasgow *Forward*, 16 December 1916.

11 MacDonald, *Patriots and Politics*, Manchester, 1917, p. 10. Text of a lecture delivered on 15 April 1917 to the Glasgow ILP Federation.

12 MacDonald, 'What Labour should do now', Glasgow *Forward*, 29 September 1917.

13 British Library of Political and Economic Science, Morel Papers, Box 8, MacDonald to Morel, 13, 16 March 1906.

14 Morel Papers, Box 8, MacDonald to Morel, 24 August 1914.

15 On the 'UDC' as it was known, cf. Marvin Swartz, *The Union of Democratic Control in British Politics during the First World War*, 1971; and MacDonald's pamphlet, *War and the Workers: A plea for democratic control*, 1915.

16 The book was first published in German in 1911 and appeared in a second edition in English in 1915, with additional remarks on socialism and the war. MacDonald may have been flattered by the complimentary references to him in the book. Cf. *Political Parties*, trans. E. and C. Paul, 1915, pp. 99, 113n, 153, 163.

17 MacDonald, 'Is democracy possible?' *Socialist Review*, 13, 77, April–May 1916, pp. 134–47.

18 *Ibid.*, p. 146.

19 *Ibid.*, p. 141. My italics.

20 *Ibid.*, p. 142.

21 *Ibid.*, p. 143. My italics.

22 *Ibid.*, p. 145.

23 MacDonald, 'Socialism after the war', *Labour Leader*, 17 August 1916. Cf. also his short book *Socialism after the War*, Manchester, 1917, which incorporated much of his occasional writing.

24 See above, p. 13.

25 MacDonald, 'Socialism and the State', *Labour Leader*, 5 July 1917.

26 MacDonald, 'The Leeds Conference', *Herald*, 9 June 1917.

27 MacDonald, 'The recess', Glasgow *Forward*, 9 June 1917.

28 MacDonald, 'A living Labour Party', Glasgow *Forward*, 13 October 1917; and, 'From a Labour bench', Glasgow *Forward*, 3 November 1917.

29 Lloyd George Papers, F/27/3/1, Henderson to Lloyd George, 7 December 1916 on his joining the new government. All references to these papers are referred to as 'LG'.

30 *Labour Party Annual Report 1916*, p. 120. Henderson was also appointed in 1915 one of the three presidents of the Parliamentary Recruiting Committee. Cf. Hansard, 6th ser., 70, 10 March 1915.

31 LG, F/24/3/6, Henderson to Lloyd George, 13 January 1917.

32 LG, F/27/3/4–5, exchange of letters between Henderson and Lloyd George, 13 January 1917.

33 *Labour Party Annual Report 1917*, p. 82.

34 *Ibid.*, p. 137.

35 *Ibid.*

36 *Ibid.*, p. 105.

37 *Ibid.*, pp. 106, 110.

38 The Report exonerated Henderson of any responsibility for the deportations. Cf. the copy in the Labour Party Library, Middleton Papers, Miscellaneous file.

39 CAB. 23/1, no. 47 (10), 29 January 1917.

40 CAB. 23/1, no. 25 (4), 2 January 1917.

41 Labour Party Library, Henderson Papers, HEN 11/2ii.

42 CAB. 23/2, no. 104 (5), 26 March 1917.

43 CAB. 23/2, no. 107 (9), 28 March 1917. Cf. also O'Grady's report on his eight weeks in Russia in *Furnishing Trades Association Monthly Report*, June 1917, 15–16.

44 LPEC, 9 May 1917. The vote was nine to four.

45 *Ibid.* and CAB. 23/2, no. 136 (15), 11 May 1917. Arno Mayer is wrong when he claims in his *Political Origins of the New Diplomacy, 1917–1918*, New Haven, Conn., 1959, p. 215, that 'at the time of his departure [for Russia] Henderson was still uncommitted on the Stockholm question'. Ultimately Purdy withdrew from the deputation because he objected to being associated with ILP – men like

MacDonald and Jowett, who were also invited to Russia as minority delegates. Roberts declined to go for the more credible reason that 'as a member of the Government his inclusion in the Executive deputation might lead to misunderstanding'. They were replaced by Hutchinson and Clynes who both later changed their minds about going. Finally Roberts reversed his decision after consultation with the Cabinet, and Carter joined him with MacDonald and Jowett for the ILP and Julius West for the Fabian Society. But when they got to Aberdeen, with government permission to go, Havelock Wilson's National Sailors' and Firemen's Union refused to service a ship carrying known pacifists en route to consultations with the Germans who were then waging their policy of unrestricted submarine warfare. The boat left without the Labour Party delegates who agreed to go together or not at all. Cf. LPEC, 1 June, 7 June, 20 June 1917.

46 CAB. 23/2, no. 136 (15), 11 May 1917.

47 CAB. 23/2, no. 141 (15), 21 May 1917.

48 CAB. 23/2, no. 144 (1), 23 May 1917.

49 *Ibid.*

50 LPEC, 1 June 1917.

51 'Mr. Henderson's arrival', *The Times*, 2 June 1917; 'Mr. Henderson in Petrograd', *The Times*, 4 June 1917. The Russian use of the Julian calendar, which was thirteen days behind the Gregorian calendar used in the West, meant that Henderson arrived in Russia on 19 May, their time. I have used the Western dating throughout.

52 LG, F/59/1/16–17, Buchanan to Charlie [*sic*], 30 May 1917; 15 June 1917, on his fears about Henderson's visit and their subsequent friendship.

53 LG, F/27/3/13, Henderson to Lloyd George, 14 June 1917.

54 Rex Wade, *The Russian Search for Peace*, Stanford, Calif., 1969, chs 2–3.

55 Wade, 'Irakli Tsereteli and Siberian Zimmerwaldism', *Journal of Modern History*, 39, 4, December 1967, 425–31.

56 Public Record Office, Foreign Office Papers [Hereafter referred to as 'FO'] 371/3010, Buchanan's cable on his interview, dated 27 May 1917.

57 *Ibid.*

58 Wade, *The Russian Search for Peace*, ch. 4.

59 Henderson Papers, HEN/1/30.i, Henderson to Dowson, 19 June 1917.

60 Henderson Papers, HEN/1/29.i, Henderson to R. W. Raine, 19 June 1917. Dr Ross McGibbin, who is engaged in writing a biography of Henderson, helped me to identify these letters.

61 'Mr. Henderson's mission', *The Times*, 6 June 1917.

62 *Ibid.*, and FO, 371/3010, cable from Henderson to Lloyd George, 8 June 1917.

63 *Ibid.*

64 Henderson Papers, HEN/1/31.i, Henderson to Roberts, 21 June 1917.

65 'American mission in Petrograd', *The Times*, 18 June 1917.
66 Cf. Robert Wilton, *Russia's Agony*, 1918, *passim* for a full statement of his anti-semitic and anti-Bolshevik attitudes.
67 V. I. Lenin, *Collected Works*, Moscow, 1934, XX, Bk i, pp. 287–90.
68 Marc Ferro, *The Great War 1914–1918*, trans. N. Stone, 1973, p. 194, Ferro, *The Russian Revolution of February 1917*, trans. J. L. Richards, 1972, p. 238, from *Pravda* on 8/21 June 1917. Cf. also Zinoviev's speech to the Petrograd Soviet on 16 June, in G. H. Gankin and H. H. Fisher, *The Bolsheviks and the World War*, Stanford, Calif., 1940, pp. 623–6.
69 'Imperial and foreign news items', *The Times*, 14 June 1917; and Wilton's letter to the editor of *The Times*, 31 December 1917, signed 'Petrograd correspondent'.
70 'Mr. Henderson in Moscow', *Daily Chronicle*, 3 July 1917.
71 FO, 371.2997, cable of Buchanan to Foreign Office, 5 July 1917.
72 FO, 371.2997, Henderson to Lloyd George, 1 July 1917.
73 *Ibid.*
74 *Ibid.*
75 FO, 438/10, Lockhart to Buchanan, 23 July 1917. A copy of Henderson's speech and the reactions of his audience is in A. J. Sack (ed.), *The Birth of the Russian Democracy*, New York, 1918, pp. 374–6.
76 FO, 371/2997, Henderson to Lloyd George, 1 July 1917.
77 FO, 438/10, Lockhart to Buchanan, 23 July 1917.
78 *Ibid.*
79 FO, 371/2997, Lockhart to Buchanan, 3 July 1917.
80 R. H. Bruce Lockhart, *Memoirs of a British Agent*, 1932, pp. 187, 188.
81 FO, 37/2997, Henderson to Lloyd George, 1 July 1917.
82 Cf. this appraisal by the editor of the *Daily News*, A. G. Gardiner. Henderson concluded, according to Gardiner, that 'If the current of the Revolution was to be kept within reasonable bounds, the Kerensky regime must have unequivocal backing against the Bolshevik attacks'. Gardiner, 'Mr. Henderson and the Labour movement', *Atlantic Monthly*, 122, 2, August 1918, p. 225.
83 'Socialist peace terms', *The Times*, 7 June 1917. Text of letter dated 4 June to Petrograd Council: 'We are more than ever convinced that a plenary meeting to which would be admitted those who are supporting the present policy of the Majority Socialists in the Central Powers would be harmful and dangerous and would leave the doubt that a just and permanent peace is possible before the imperialism of aggression has been destroyed.'
84 LPEC, 20 June 1917, in which his cable of 17 June is printed.
85 'New Allied note to Russia', *The Times*, 8 June 1917; 'The French reply to Russia', *The Times*, 9 June 1917.
86 'Duma speaks out', *The Times*, 18 June 1917.
87 As cited in Wade, *The Russian Search for Peace*, p. 59. His source was a passage in Tsereteli's memoirs, also cited in Ferro, *The Russian Revolution of February 1917*.
88 FO 371/2997, Henderson to Lloyd George, 1 July 1917.
89 *Ibid.*

90 *Ibid.*

91 Buchanan's opinion was similar. He cabled the Foreign Office on 5 July: 'Nothing would I think help Kerenski so much at the present moment as announcement that Allied Government had accepted Russian proposal for Conference in early September.' FO, 371/2997.

92 'Mr. Henderson's visit to Stockholm', *The Times*, 24 July 1917.

93 Wilton's letter to the editor of *The Times*, 31 December 1917, signed 'Petrograd Correspondent'.

94 Williams, 'The portent of Stockholm', *Herald*, 28 July 1917. For the same point, cf. Mrs Cedar Paul, 'The turning tide', *Workers' Dreadnought*, 18 August 1917; and, A. Harrison, 'The Stockholm curtain raiser', *English Review*, 25, September 1917, p. 265.

95 Rex Wade, 'Argonauts of Peace: the Soviet delegation to Western Europe in the summer of 1917', *Slavic Review*, 26, 3, September 1967, pp. 453–67. One of the delegates 'found Henderson impressed with the ideals of the Russian Revolution but depressed over what he considered the leadership's "impracticability", that is their lack of concern over strikes and disorders and other matters he considered serious and wished to discuss'.

96 LPEC, 25 July 1917. The Russians argued that the conference could not be postponed beyond 22 August due to the Swedish and Russian elections at the end of August and September, respectively. Henderson probably argued in the terms he used in a letter to the American labour leader, J. P. Frey, cited in H. M. Pelling, *America and the British Left*, 1956, p. 111: 'When in Russia I became aware that as far as the Russian democracy was concerned they were determined to have a conference if possible, and decided to advise my Executive to send delegates.'

97 LPEC, 9 August 1917. The vote was nine to five. The minority wanted to leave the decision up to the conference without instructions.

98 *Labour Party Annual Report 1918*, p. 47.

99 *Ibid.*, p. 48.

100 *Ibid.*, pp. 48–9.

101 *Ibid.*, p. 51.

102 CAB. 23/3, no. 211 (1, 5), 10 August 1917, 6:15 p.m. Curzon, Milner, Bonar Law, Carson, and Lloyd George attended.

103 CAB. 23/3, no. 212 (1), 11 August 1917, 11 a.m.

104 Cf. Mary Agnes Hamilton, *Arthur Henderson*, 1936, p. 164: 'By far the most important long-range result' of the trip to Russia was the development of his 'international outlook, before dim and rather conventional, now gradually became vivid and personal and never again left him'.

105 CAB. 23/3, 202, 1 August 1917.

106 LG, F/27/3/14, Henderson to Lloyd George, 10 August 1917, noon.

107 CAB. 23/3, 207 (5), 8 August 1917.

108 Henderson, 'Russia's peril', *Nation*, 17 November 1917. For the same point, see his article 'No sliding scale peace', *Herald*, 8 December 1917.

109 The importance of the Russian visit for Henderson's attitude raises

serious doubts about the argument of Samuel Beer in *Modern British Politics*, 1965, ch. V, about the reconstruction of the Labour Party. To discuss British political ideas in 1917 without mentioning the Russian Revolution or Henderson's thoughts about it is to invite distortion. Beer's mistake is that he failed to separate in his analysis the reasons for the ratification of the constitution by the trade unions from the reasons for the formulation of the party constitution in the first place. His argument, as on p. 149, that 'The adoption of socialism as an ideology was functional to [the Labour Party's] choice for political independence' may explain the first, but it does not explain the second part of the problem.

110 See above, pp. 214–15.

111 Passfield Papers, Beatrice Webb's unpublished diaries, vol. 34, 1 April 1918.

112 LPEC, 19–25 July 1917. The text is inserted between the meetings of those dates. It is unsigned. There is no conclusive proof that Webb drafted the document, but since he was called upon to write the most important party papers, it would be extraordinary if he did not also have a hand in formulating this document. Middleton recalled, in M. I. Cole (ed.), *The Webbs and Their Work*, p. 172, that 'Webb's inspiration and practical assistance were prominent in the devising of the new Constitution of 1918'. A. M. McBriar, *Fabian Socialism and English Politics 1884–1918*, p. 343, asserts that Webb drafted the constitution himself.

113 LPEC, July 1917, draft constitution.

114 See above, p. 214.

115 LPEC, July 1917, draft constitution. Webb himself interpreted the constitution as a more radical document in his article 'New constitution of the Labour Party', *Observer*, 21 October 1917, in which he said: 'This declaration of the Labour Party leaves it open to choose from time to time whatever forms of common ownership, from cooperative store to the nationalised railway, and whatever forms of popular administration and control of industry, from national guilds to ministries of employment and municipal management [which] may in particular cases commend themselves.' Again the parallel to the WEC Conscription of Riches programme is apparent.

116 A. Henderson, *The Aims of Labour*, 1918, pp. 10, 13.

117 *Ibid.*, pp. 61–2.

118 *Ibid.*, p. 59. Cf. also his articles: 'The need for democratic solidarity', *Herald*, 1 December 1917; 'The outlook for Labour', *Contemporary Review*, 113, February 1918, pp. 121–30.

119 Tom Jones, *Whitehall Diary*, ed., K. Middlemas, 1969, vol. 1, 36, 10 August 1917; 1, 45–6, 12 January 1918.

120 T. Wilson (ed.), *The Political Diaries of C. P. Scott 1911–1928*, 1970, p. 316, 11–12 December 1917.

121 LPEC, 20 August 1917.

122 WEC, Box 28, From Food to Food, Webb to Middleton, 9 September 1917.

123 LPEC, 26 September 1917.

124 LPEC, 24 October, 12 December 1917.
125 LPEC, 26 September 1917.
126 LPEC, 10 October 1917.
127 LPEC, 1 November 1917.
128 The decision was put off for a month after it was first raised at the Nottingham conference in January 1918. There was little doubt about the outcome of the balloting, despite the delay. Cf. *Labour Party Annual Report 1918, passim.*

9

The Impact of the First World War on British Socialist Thought

If ever there was a historical movement to which *Realpolitik* presents a baneful and ominous threat, it is that of socialism.

Georg Lukács[1]

This book began with the assertion that socialism is understood best as a dual phenomenon. That is to say, it must be studied both as an ongoing theoretical debate about social conflict under capitalism and as a programme of political action. An account of the impact of war must return to this distinction.

On the one hand, it is clear that the First World War had neither a creative nor a decisive effect on the development of socialist theory in Britain. As we have seen, the most important theoretical statements were made before the outbreak of hostilities. Furthermore, the pre-war ideas of the principal figures of this book dominated socialist writing in the following decade. The continuity of their work in the years 1912–22 is the best evidence against the claim that the war inaugurated a new chapter in socialist thought.

But on the other hand, when we turn to more practical matters, we obtain a very different sense of the place of the 1914–18 conflict in socialist history. For it was not the theory but rather the political activity and influence of British socialism which changed under the impact of the First World War.

SOCIALIST POLITICS

Socialists have held divergent views about the Labour Party throughout its seventy-year history. But despite constant arguments about policy, most have learned to live with it, and within it. Some have struck out on their own, but without much success. For better or for worse, the party had become by 1918 what it is today: the political home of the overwhelming majority of the British socialist movement. This wartime fusion of ideas about socialist politics can be seen most clearly in the work of the principal figures of this book.

Under the impact of the 'labour unrest', the Webbs decided in 1912 to work exclusively within the Labour Party. Tawney and Cole, in different ways, spoke for another school of thought. They articulated the views of those socialists who disagreed with the Webbs' political strategy and who remained unconvinced that the pre-war Labour Party was ever likely to become the vanguard of the socialist cause. Cole's hostility to the Webbs' viewpoint in general and to the Labour Party in particular reflected his belief in the primacy of industrial action. Tawney's doubts about the Webbs' position, on the other hand, grew out of his scepticism about the effectiveness of any reform programme without a prior shift in popular ideas. The doctrine of parliamentary socialism received a searching examination in his pre-war Commonplace Book and was found wanting in a number of respects.

After four years of war, these two men no longer kept their distance from the Labour Party. Indeed they were prepared to work for it in several ways. Tawney's unsuccessful candidacy at Rochdale was one example. Their constant consultation with the Parliamentary Labour Party and their advisory work for the party's executive committee were other aspects of their new political activity.

At this time, many socialists made a similar commitment to the Labour Party. Hence, when Tawney and Cole joined Sidney Webb in the party's International Advisory Committee in March 1918 to discuss the formation of a League of Nations and the party's attitude to it,[2] they were demonstrating the new tactical unity of British socialism which was a direct result of the First World War.

By the end of the war, then, the Webbs had won the old dispute about socialist politics. This resolution of the antagonism between socialists and the Labour Party was hardly predictable before the outbreak of the war. In 1914 it was equally difficult to foresee that, within four years, the Labour Party would turn to the thinkers in its ranks for essential help and would adopt certain of their ideas in 'Clause Four' of the new party constitution.

Intellectuals and the Labour Party

Before the coming of war, the title 'intellectual' was used frequently in certain Labour circles as a term of abuse.[3] Such disdain was much less prevalent in 1918, because the pressure of war had forced the party to seek out the assistance of socialist thinkers. The War Emergency Committee, especially in its studies of 'Labour after the War' and the 'Conscription of Riches' played an important part in this development. In this committee union officials and socialist writers worked together throughout the conflict to formulate policy on matters of direct concern to the working class. Before the war many of the people who were to serve on the WEC simply did not speak the same language. Four years later, largely because of the achievements of this organization, intellectuals were encouraged to operate on a permanent basis in the centre of party affairs and not, as they did before, on the periphery.

The creation of the nine Labour Party advisory committees[4] is one manifestation of the way in which the WEC's wartime functions were incorporated into the party's new structure. In the years after the armistice, Webb, Tawney, and Cole dominated the work of these groups.[5]

In effect a dual process of adaptation had taken place during the conflict. The result was the establishment in the last year of the war of an informal partnership between party leaders, especially Arthur Henderson, and a number of socialist thinkers, the most important of whom were the principal figures of this book.[6] During the war these people had escaped, so to speak, from the political isolation to which they had been consigned or had chosen in the pre-war Labour movement. They could do so because the post-war party recognized that they provided services which were vital to its political work.

The political fortunes of the party's socialist intellectuals were on the rise in the last two years of the war. But one qualification must be made here. Before 1914 most of the party's thinkers were members of the Fabian Society or the Independent Labour Party. Even in the last stages of the conflict, the latter group suffered for its 'pacifist' reputation. One indication of such political ostracism was the decision to change the composition of the NEC and to cut the strength of socialist societies relative to other party groups. The 'patriotic' trade-union leaders were behind this move, which did constitute a setback to the party's socialist wing.

There were, however, counter-forces at work. The establishment of new local party associations made possible the recruitment of numerous professional and blue-collar workers. Among these new members were socialists whose presence would be felt in the determination of post-war party policy. On balance then, it may be concluded that the Labour Party in 1918 had a new, more varied, and much stronger socialist constituency.

Clause Four

Many men were drawn to the Labour Party at the end of the First World War because it was free of the onus of responsibility for the war effort.[7] Many people also turned to Labour in 1918 and in the years that followed because its political programme had changed. The new objectives adopted during the course of the First World War were embodied in the statement of principles or 'Clause Four' of the 1918 party constitution.

That the Labour Party lacked an ideology was an often-repeated – and valid – judgment among socialists in the years before 1914. What they meant was that the party had operated without a coherent idea of its political function. The experience of war corroborated this charge and exposed the consequences of the party's absence of purpose. The conflict also provided ample evidence, as Ramsay MacDonald himself admitted, that in future times of stress, a working-class party which remained only a collection of interest groups was doomed to division and failure.

Consequently, by the last year of the war many people were even more strongly convinced of the need to provide the Labour movement with a new political organization. All accepted the fact that the party needed new tools for work on a nationwide basis. What was more controversial was the decision of the NEC to frame the new party programme in terms of long-range objectives which were distinct ideologically from those of the other parties. The real question to which the party leadership addressed itself was: what would distinguish Labour from its political competitors? The answer was deceptively simple. The Conservatives and Liberals readily admitted that they acted from a belief in the merits of capitalism. Labour would stand alone and independent, it was argued in 1918, precisely because it had a different political outlook. The party's programme, drafted by Sidney Webb, rested on an indictment of capitalism and offered a pledge to mitigate, if not to end, the inequality and deprivation it bred. The purpose of the 1918 statement of party aims was thus to make the choice among parties one of conviction rather than just a comparison of personalities.

One must look to the setting of Britain at war to appreciate fully the causes for the reconstruction of the Labour Party and its formal adoption in 1918 of socialist aims. 'Clause Four' makes sense only when seen in the light of the attempt of Sidney Webb and other socialists in the WEC to think out a consistent wartime policy for the Labour movement. Its adoption took place in the heady days after the Bolshevik Revolution, when the scent of radical change was in the air throughout Europe. It was perhaps inevitable that after four years of war and two revolutions in Russia, socialist ideas counted for much more in Labour politics than they had before – and so did the advice and support of the men who formulated them.

The adoption of Webbian tactics

Why did the ideas of Sidney and Beatrice Webb in particular become the basis for Labour party policy at the end of the First World War? The answer to this question must be sought not only in the experience of Labour in wartime but also in terms of the nature of Webbian socialism.

The Webbs' views were adopted out of necessity rather than out of choice or conviction. Neither Tawney, nor Cole, nor any of their contemporaries had been able to present a viable alternative to Webbian socialism during the First World War, that is, at the very time that the Labour movement most needed intellectual leadership.

It was precisely the ability to explain how institutions worked and developed over time which gave the Webbs their greatest advantage. The theories which Tawney and Cole advanced before the war avoided, perhaps deliberately, the central problems of comprehensive institutional change, a subject on which the Webbs were authorities. Other theorists never explained adequately how a socialist society would actually work or how it might be brought about. The failure of the Webbs' critics to construct and to defend an alternative theory of social change out of which a tactical approach could grow was decisive after 1914, when socialism had to produce precise political answers.

To borrow Arnold Toynbee's phrase, war presented challenges to the Labour movement which Webbian socialism was best prepared to meet. The Webbs' ideas had many limitations, but they were able to provide the framework for the only programme advanced by British Labour to deal with the problems of war and its aftermath. The significance of the WEC once more becomes apparent.

In this organization, Sidney Webb put into effect with far-reaching consequences the institutional approach to political problems which he held (and in fact personified) throughout his life. Webb lived largely through committees, and the work which had to be done during the war suited him perfectly. The social and economic mobilization of the entire population and the resultant increase in the power of the state made his organizational ability indispensable to the Labour movement during the conflict. In addition, his incurable optimism shielded him from the oppressive meditation on the horrors of war which at times immobilized his wife. He thus was able both temperamentally and intellectually to approach the war effort as a vehicle for progressive social change.

In the WEC, Webb successfully united the efforts of both those who believed, with him (and Tawney), that the conflict presented unique opportunities for the advancement of socialism and those who argued (like Cole) that the world crisis was a serious setback and distraction from more important tasks. All could contribute without difficulty to the WEC's search for remedies to the distress brought about by the war. British Labour thereby found an alternative to the unceasing strife and recrimination which crippled many European socialist parties.

Once more we can see how the Webbs' ideas were useful to the Labour movement during the war. Their views on social policy provided the essential common denominator between the party's pacifist and patriotic elements. There is much truth in Beatrice's claim that by December 1917 'Sidney has become the intellectual leader of the Labour Party'.[8] It was his work in the WEC which had earned him this new and important role.

The meeting of 5 August 1914 which brought the WEC into existence was chaired by Arthur Henderson, who was also instrumental, indirectly, in the fulfilment of its work. His sense of political priorities changed in 1917, largely as a result of his mission to Petrograd. His 'conversion' in Russia to an internationalist approach to ending the conflict and his subsequent expulsion from the Cabinet were key stages in the formal transformation of the Labour Party into an organization committed to socialist aims. His experience illustrates one aspect of the impact of the Russian Revolution on British socialist thought.

After the first socialist government in history had taken power and had held it for longer than the hundred days of the Paris Commune, few could deny that socialism was once more a major force in European politics. Lenin's seizure of power ensured the emergence of new, revolutionary parties within each combatant country. Men of all political persuasions were forced to take stock of the full revival of the militant left.

The events in Russia and their repercussions in the West both heartened and frightened the more conservative leaders of the British Labour movement, who by 1918, were ready to join moderate socialists to rebuild the Labour Party as a progressive constitutional alternative to revolution. It is in this context that one must place the party's acceptance of the new constitution.

On initial reflection, the Webbs' accomplishments during the war seem to have been quite substantial. Their ideas were appropriate for war, during which their influence reached its zenith. In the years that followed, though, they were much less effective, both as politicians and propagandists. How permanent, then, were their wartime political achievements? After all, the significance of the collectivist manifestos of 1918 rested heavily on the Labour Party's willingness and ability to make of socialism more than a set of electoral slogans. In other words, despite the socialist rhetoric, was there ever much chance that the reconstructed party would be able to escape from the 'normal' alternation of the political 'ins and outs'? Could the party dedicate itself single-mindedly, as the Webbs hoped, not to the pursuit of power for its own sake, but rather to the achievement of a socialist programme?

At the end of the First World War, optimistic answers to these questions were common and not entirely unfounded. But as the months passed after the armistice, many of the goals of social reconstruction which had seemed almost within reach, slowly receded into the distance. With them went the dream of inaugurating through parliamentary action the beginning of the end of the capitalist era.

Such sentiments had been based on a somewhat exaggerated opinion of the Labour Party's strength and on an insufficient appreciation of the difficult conditions under which it would have to operate in the generation after the war. The story of the failures of the post-war years – the Triple Alliance, the General Strike, and the Labour Government of 1929–31 – would require a book in itself. Such a discussion must take account of the reasons for the virtual eclipse of the party's aims as they were formulated in the 1918 constitution. Here the personal element, as in the case of MacDonald in 1931, must not be ignored. Attention must be focussed also on the erosion of the strength of the industrial wing of the Labour movement, as it is exhibited in the precipitous drop in trade union membership from its high point of over 8·3 million in 1920 to only 4·4 million in 1933.[9] But surely some responsibility must be placed as well on the shoulders of the party's socialists, who were unable to provide the leadership and vision essential to every socialist movement.

SOCIALIST THEORY

The pattern of socialist political activity in the inter-war years was set by 1918, but the overall strategy and the political theory which supported it remained incomplete and often contradictory. The deeper difficulties within British socialist thought were unresolved at the end of the First World War. No synthesis of the various elements in the theory of socialism emerged either before the first Labour government came to office in 1924 or in the years which have followed.

The heterogeneity of socialist ideas in this period is their most striking characteristic. The term 'Fabianism' is inappropriate as a blanket description of the positions examined in this study. A brief recapitulation of the ideas of Cole, Tawney and the Webbs will serve to illuminate some of the lines of conflict within British socialist thought.[10]

G. D. H. Cole based his social theory on the assumption that the only way to root out inequality and to end social strife was to alter class relationships. This goal, he thought, could be achieved only by eliminating the subservient position of the working man in each factory and on every shop floor. From his point of view, such radical changes in the way industry was run, in the industrial infrastructure itself, took precedence over all other socialist measures. The trade union movement, then, had to shed its defensive character and work towards the achievement of what he called 'self-government in industry'. This assertion of the primacy of industrial issues is similar in many ways to the philosophy of 'economism' which Lenin criticized so severely in *What Is To Be Done?*

In contrast, Tawney maintained that changes in moral – and not class – relationships were the key element in any socialist experiment. He operated mainly on the level of what one recent writer has called 'the individual pirouette of solitary repentance';[11] for he was convinced that the attitudes of ordinary people about social status and privilege had to change before reforms of any nature could take effect. Without such preliminary conversions in the way people approach all human association, the old pattern of domination and exploitation would recur, Tawney predicted, regardless of the future form of political or industrial control. Socialists, therefore, had to work constantly to undermine what he called 'the religion of inequality', in the celebrated phrase of one of his post-war books.[12] Hence he looked first to education, defined as organized moral and intellectual development, to generate the attitudes necessary for socialism. The line of thought which runs from Robert Owen and F. D. Maurice to the work of more contemporary social philosophers, such as Martin Buber and Paul Tillich, may be found as well in the writings of R. H. Tawney.[13]

Both Tawney and Cole argued that important adjustments in social life could come about without a prior change in the political superstructure. In other words, they did not believe that the long-term success of socialism depended primarily on electoral victories or civil service reform, even though they both came to place greater importance on the work of the Labour Party at the end of the First World War. After the armistice they continued to argue that political developments were the reflections of changes which took place outside of Parliament. Political and administrative advances were undeniably important, but they remained secondary factors in the process of social transformation which they envisaged, each in his different way.

This was not the view of the Webbs. They were convinced, like Lenin, that the state and the men who control it had to lead the way to socialism. There are many interesting similarities between the ideas of the Webbs and Lenin on the role of a professional, intellectual vanguard in the socialist strategy of 'all-sided political agitation'.[14] Of course, there are also major differences between them. Nothing could have been further from Lenin's doctrine than the Webbs' view that the rate of social change was determined by the speed of administrative progress. Unlike Lenin, they held that the violent seizure of the state was pointless, since the organs of collective control were not yet ready for the social tasks of the future; nor would these bodies be strengthened by the disruptive turmoil of revolution. Webbian strategy relied on the gradual development of what its formulators called 'the social tissue', that is, the network of local and national organizations which would ultimately manage most public affairs. But despite these important disagreements, both Lenin and the Webbs shared the belief that parties and the dedicated men who led them held in their hands the fate of the socialist movement.

The Webbs' political strategy, Cole's guild ideas, and Tawney's Christian social theory are not as unrelated as the above discussion inadvertently may suggest. Their views overlap, but never enough to obscure the real and vital differences among them.

Their disagreement over fundamental issues became apparent during the pre-war restatement of socialist ideas. Consider, for example, their positions on the question whether social conflict is an inevitable part of social affairs or rather a passing phase in the historical development of a more mature, and by definition, a more placid social order. Tawney's Christian belief led him to the view that conflict was inherent in all human association. In contrast, both Cole and the Webbs, however else they differed in their theoretical writing, at least agreed that capitalism and conflict were synonymous, as were socialism and social peace.[15] What they consistently failed to explain, though, was how the measures they advocated would convert a society which had always known social strife into a stable, well-integrated, and peaceful community of men.

The aftermath of war

The ideas of each of these thinkers were severely tested during the war. Of the three, only Cole was forced to modify elements of his theoretical work. The adjustments he made, however, were only temporarily effective. After a few more attempts to work out the difficulties of guild socialist theory, he abandoned the movement which he had helped to build in the previous years. In contrast, Tawney and the Webbs were older than Cole and approached the conflict with a greater degree of intellectual stability and maturity. They found that the war confirmed their deepest beliefs and offered opportunities for the realization of their somewhat different hopes. In the years after the armistice, they pressed forward along the separate lines which they had advanced before 1914.

The post-war continuity in the Webbs' thought is demonstrated clearly in the study they published in 1920 entitled *A Constitution for the Socialist Commonwealth of Great Britain*. This work is a restatement, at times verbatim, of the arguments which they had presented in their articles on 'What Is Socialism?' which appeared in the *New Statesman* before the war. There is, though, one interesting adjustment in their views which reflects their response to the contemporary criticisms of the tyranny of the over-centralized state. In 1920, the Webbs offered what appeared to be a new definition of the state and revised their notion of its optimal organization. But in the light of their earlier writings we can see that even these alterations were made within the framework of their pre-war ideas.

Before the First World War, they wrote of the capitalist state as a coercive body whose powers were based on 'the authoritarian conception of dominion (*Verwaltung, autorité régalienne*)'. The socialist state, in contrast, was to be an instrument which would both provide services and embody the interests which all citizens shared as consumers.[16]

In 1920, this distinction was dropped. The Webbs now divided the future socialist state into two parts, one of which would handle, through a Political Parliament, the problems of 'national defence, international relations and the administration of justice'.[17] There was to be a separate and co-equal power in the form of a Social Parliament, 'to which is entrusted the national administration of the industries and services by and through which the community lives'.[18] The Webbs distinguished the jurisdiction of these two 'coordinate national assemblies' in familiar terms: 'The sphere of the one is *Verwaltung, autorité régalienne*, police power; that of the other is *Wirtschaft, gestion*, housekeeping.'[19] The form is new, but the ideas and even the words are the same.

In the *Constitution*, the Webbs also repeated their earlier rejection of syndicalism and their negative judgment of the 'exclusiveness' of producers' associations.[20] They also reiterated their belief that socialist society would be free from most traditional forms of social conflict. In the future, they asserted:[21]

we must rid our minds of battle cries and turn our backs on battle formations. In a society in which all adults will be workers, so long as fulness of health and strength lasts, and [in] which all will have equal chances from birth to death, of enjoying a civilized existence, there will be no room, as the Socialists recognise, for class consciousness and the class struggle.

The Webbs retained these ideas in later years, that is, even after they turned to Soviet Russia after the failure of the Labour Government of 1929–31 and the onset of the world depression.

The cultivation of old ground immediately after the war is apparent also in the writing of G. D. H. Cole. The case for guild socialism which he argued in the four years which followed the armistice varied only slightly from the one he presented in his earlier work.[22] His pluralism is perhaps more salient in a book he published in 1920 entitled *Guild Socialism Re-stated*. Here he dissociated himself from the Webbs' definition of the state as an association of consumers. Cole thought consumers could be represented more effectively by other organizations.[23]

The continuity in Cole's thought was broken in 1922. In that year he withdrew from the guild socialist camp. Two developments had undermined Cole's faith in his early work. First came the disappointments of the Building Guild experiment, the only serious attempt to put guild ideas into practice. After a brief flurry of activity, it perished in the post-war contraction of trade.[24] Second, there was the parting of the ways with many of the pioneer guildsmen, who left Cole's movement to join the Communist Party.[25]

One such renegade was William Mellor, with whom Cole had worked so closely since 1913. In November 1921, Mellor published a scathing attack on Cole and his ideas. His comments, though vituperative, are not without interest. 'Anyone who has been closely associated with the inner workings of the National Guilds League (as I have),' Mellor began, 'must recognise that from the very start, ineffectiveness has been its lot.' Despite its short-comings, he admitted, 'Guild Socialism grew and waxed fat' from 1912 to 1917:[26]

It was the doctrine of the middle class man. Fabianism was dying and the Russian Revolution had not come. Here was a theory which seemed to have taken the best out of all the existing proposals and that seemed to hold out, if not to the workers, at any rate to the workers' advocates, hopes of cudos and ultimate power.

But then came the Bolshevik seizure of power which, Mellor argued, brought into sharp relief the fundamental weakness of guild socialism, which was 'that it had not the vaguest idea of how it proposed to get to the beautiful goal that its theorists had sketched'. The inevitable result, he maintained, was the collapse of the guild movement. In his account Mellor stressed[27]

> the part played by Mr. Cole in Guild Socialism; for if one can understand his psychology, one can understand the real failure of the movement to which he belongs. Like him it is neither revolutionary nor reformist. It is neither Utopian nor realist. It hovers in a state of uneasy equilibrium between the medievalists and the revolutionaries. . . . It likes to contemplate the idea of a break, sudden and definite, with capitalism, but it hates the thought of the suffering and trouble entailed in the process of that break. . . . It still thinks of peaceful change, and advocates proposals that involve war.

The testimony of an ex-member of a political group rarely provides the best evidence about its activities and problems. But in this case, the force of the criticism was soon recognized by the very man against whom it had been directed. In mid-1922, at the age of thirty, Cole decided that his work as a guild socialist was over. The bitterness with which he surveyed the ruin of his plans is unmistakable. In an article in the *New Statesman*, he concluded, perhaps with an element of personal projection, that 'At the end of forty years of continuous agitation, the British Socialist Movement has all the appearances of failure'. He was still of the opinion, though, that:[28]

> There will always be room in this country for propagandistic societies devoted to the spreading of a particular Socialist Gospel. But it is of the essence of such bodies to be ephemeral, and to succeed one another rapidly as fresh issues and aspects of Socialism come to the front, for the penalty of survival is atrophy.

But Cole's efforts, at least, would be directed to the centres of power. We can see in the following statement the final resolution of the tension between the militant and the moderate in his political thought:[29]

> Socialism as a large-scale organised movement, has now done its work in Great Britain, and in future the preaching of Socialism, and the bringing home of Socialist ideas to the larger bodies which alone have power to make them realities will be mainly in the hands of small mobile leagues and groups, easily formed and easily dissolved, succeeding one another as fresh interests and problems force their way to the front. Socialism has ceased to be a single coherent body of doctrine, capable of finding expression through a national organisation. It remains as a source of ideas and policies, from which it is the task of the Labour Party and of the Trade Unions – and, indeed, of others besides – to select or reject, modifying and transmuting what it uses into practical precepts of political and economic activity.

Cole's turn to the Webbian centre of socialist thought was complete.

In contrast, the structure of Tawney's beliefs was strong enough to withstand the test of war and its aftermath. He experienced little of the disillusionment from which Cole and others suffered at this time because of their misplaced hopes and false expectations. Nor did he flirt with Communism as the harbinger of a new age. Tawney needed no ideological re-orientation after the war because his fundamental position had remained unshaken.

His experience as a member of the Sankey Commission on the Coal Mines in 1919 deepened his pre-war critique of economic privilege, which he then expounded in various pamphlets and in an article for the *Hibbert Journal*,[30] later published in expanded form as *The Acquisitive Society*. In this book and in other post-war writings, we can see that Tawney moved closer to a guild socialist position. The guild idea was important, he argued, because it would help to bring[31]

> English socialism out of the back-waters and bypaths of government regulation, in which it was boring itself ten years ago, into the mainstream of the Socialist tradition, which has as its object not merely the alleviation of poverty, but an attack on the theory of functionless property.

His advocacy of the nationalization 'of the great foundation industries' could not have been in doubt.[32] But he maintained that 'collectivism by itself is too simple a solution' to the problem of the reorganization of industry. Essential work had to be done, and indeed was under way, in the Co-operative Movement, which 'has already [1921] substituted the motive of communal service for that of profit' and has shown the way to develop 'an effective partnership between consumer and producer'.[33] A third party in the assertion of the social control of economic life was constituted, he believed, by those engaged in 'the experiments in "industrial self-government" such as are now [1921] being made in the building industry'.[34] The failure of this experiment did not diminish Tawney's commitment to the notion of economic freedom behind it; for it had been merely one among many possible ways of expressing this freedom.

The stability of Tawney's outlook is its most striking characteristic. His post-war writings bear the same distinctive marks of the moral approach to socialism which he had outlined a decade earlier in his Commonplace Book. A passage from the introduction to *The Acquisitive Society* should suffice to prove this point. Tawney insisted that:[35]

An appeal to principles is the condition of any considerable reconstruction of society, because social institutions are the visible expression of the scale of moral values which rules the minds of individuals, and it is impossible to alter the institutions without altering that valuation. Parliament, industrial organisation, the whole complex machinery through which society expresses itself, is a mill which grinds only what is put into it. When nothing is put into it, it grinds air.

In 1922 he delivered at King's College, London, the first Scott Holland Memorial Lectures, which had been established to commemorate the work of the late Anglican theologian. Tawney was a particularly appropiate choice as the first lecturer in this series, which had as its general subject 'the religion of the Incarnation in its bearing on the social and economic life of man'.[36] The title Tawney chose for his inquiry was 'Religious Thought on Social and Economic Questions in the Sixteenth and Seventeenth Centuries'.[37] These lectures were published four years later as *Religion and the Rise of Capitalism*. This influential study grew out of Tawney's reflection on the simple question he had posed in his pre-war Commonplace Book, without the assistance of Max Weber: 'I wonder if Puritanism produced any special attitude towards economic matters.'[38] The same concerns which underlay his socialist theory may be found as well in his creative contribution to historical scholarship. And as in the cases of Cole and the Webbs, the decade surrounding the First World War forms a distinct phase in Tawney's life and thought.

Conclusion

On 24 April 1934, the eminent liberal historian Élie Halévy delivered an address at Chatham House, London, on the subject of 'Socialism and the Problem of Democratic Parliamentarianism'.[39] His remarks remain important for any student of socialist ideas. He observed that there is always an inner tension in socialist thought between the thrust towards liberty and the competing and often opposed impulse towards organization. In the case of the Webbs' ideas, there can be no doubt about which way the balance between these tendencies was tilted. The First World War helped to push their ideas even further to the organizational side of the argument, and to develop a view of socialism which received its most complete presentation in their *Soviet Communism: A New Civilization*, published in November 1935. Their admiration of government from above, even at the price of authoritarianism, is apparent throughout their writings. Their illiberalism attains its ultimate expression in this massive defence of Stalin's dictatorship which appeared after the trial of Zinoviev and Kamenev, when the great purges had begun.

It is one of the ironies of British socialism, then, that the only school of thought which had a chance of political success was precisely the one least likely to realize the idealism which is at the centre of the socialist position. Here lies the ultimate importance of the theoretical writings of R. H. Tawney and G. D. H. Cole. They kept alive the socialist alternatives to the desiccated élitism of Sidney and Beatrice Webb.

At the same time, however, the inability of Tawney and Cole to deal effectively with the theoretical and practical problems of organizing a political movement, let alone a modern industrial state at war, severely limited the ultimate impact of their critiques. Unlike the Webbs, their positions lacked appeal largely because they did not speak to the most pressing problems of the day. The

Webbs at least knew what matters needed immediate political attention.

In the first quarter of the twentieth century, then, British socialists were confronted with a difficult choice among three widely differing alternative political theories, none of which was fully adequate to the needs of the Labour movement. On the one side stood the bureaucratic approach of the Webbs, rigid and unattractive, but, as they proved during the First World War, admittedly the most effective socialist position. Opposed to it were the more humane and much more utopian ideas of Tawney and Cole. There were no other options until the formation of the Communist Party in 1920. Even after this event, most socialists were and many still are in search of a more complete socialist political philosophy. To inform the calculations of the planner and the tactics of the politician with a humanitarian vision has always been a formidable task. It is no less a challenge today than it was fifty years ago.

NOTES

1 G. Lukács, *Political Writings, 1919–39*, ed. R. Livingstone, 1972, p. 6.
2 Labour Party International Advisory Committee Minutes, 14 June 1918.
3 CPB, 29 April 1912, for George Lansbury's pejorative use of the term. The Labour press abounds with other examples.
4 See above, p. 262.
5 Labour Party Library, Middleton Papers, Lists of advisory committee personnel for 1920; letters of Cole to Middleton of 5 March and 18 July 1920 on his work as overall secretary of the committees. Cole resigned from this post in the summer of 1920, but he continued to take an active part in the work of at least six groups.
6 Beatrice Webb's unpublished diaries, vol. 35, 24 September and 7 October 1919 on Cole and Henderson, who also served as secretary and chairman of the National Industrial Conference of 1919. On Webb and Henderson, see the Webbs' General Correspondence, Henderson to Sidney Webb, 17 May 1919. Tawney's work on the Sankey Coal Commission kept him in constant contact with the Parliamentary group.
7 C. A. Cline, *Recruits to Labour*, Syracuse, New York, 1963, ch. 2.
8 M. I. Cole (ed.), *Beatrice Webb's Diaries 1912–24*, 1952, p. 99.
9 H. Pelling, *A History of British Trade Unionism*, 1962, pp. 262–3.
10 While ideological labels are unimportant, it still may be useful to characterize G. D. H. Cole, in his guild socialist phase as a 'class' theorist, Tawney as a 'status' theorist, and the Webbs as 'party' theorists, in the Weberian sense of these terms. For Weber's formulation, see H. H. Gerth and C. W. Mills (eds), *From Max Weber:*

Essays in Sociology, 1948, pp. 180–95, and for a highly suggestive discussion of these distinctions, see W. G. Runciman, 'Class, status, power?', in his *Sociology in Its Place and Other Essays*, Cambridge, 1970, pp. 102–40. I have followed Runciman in the presentation of the political theories examined here.

11 R. D. Laing, 'The obvious', in D. Cooper (ed.), *The Dialectics of Liberation*, Harmondsworth, 1968, p. 16.

12 Tawney, *Equality*, 1931, ch. 1.

13 Cf. J. F. C. Harrison, *Robert Owen and the Owenites in Britain and America*, 1969; C. Raven, *Christian Socialism*, 1920; M. Buber, *Paths in Utopia*, New York, 1950; P. Tillich, *My Search for Absolutes*, New York, 1967.

14 V. I. Lenin, *What Is To Be Done?*, trans. S. V. and P. Utechin, Oxford, 1963, ch. 3, sections c, d.

15 It may be useful to turn to sociological theory to illustrate this point. The distinguished German sociologist Ralf Dahrendorf has suggested that two separate 'images' or 'faces of society' have appeared in contemporary (1957) social theory. The first he names 'the *integration theory of society*' which 'conceives of social structure in terms of a functionally integrated system held in equilibrium by certain patterned and recurrent processes'. The second is called 'the *coercion theory of society*'. This position maintains that the social structure is 'a form of organisation held together by force and constraint and reaching continuously beyond itself in the sense of producing within itself the forces that maintain it in an unending process of change'. Dahrendorf adds that, 'Like their philosophical counterparts, these theories are mutually exclusive'. See his *Class and Class Conflict in Industrial Society*, 1964, pp. 158–65. The same distinction applies to the theoretical models which many socialists have constructed first to characterize the way society has operated in the past and secondly, the way it would operate in a post-capitalist environment. The Webbs and Cole, in their descriptions of capitalism, used what Dahrendorf terms a 'coercion theory', adjusted to accept the possibility of an end to social strife. When they envisaged socialism, they may be said to have turned to an 'integration theory'.

16 See above, p. 36.

17 Sidney and Beatrice Webb, *A Constitution for the Socialist Commonwealth of Great Britain*, 1920, p. 111.

18 *Ibid.*

19 *Ibid.*

20 *Ibid.*, pp. 19, 48.

21 *Ibid.*, p. 277.

22 See Cole's evidence before the Sankey Commission, 1919 Cd 359, xi, 373, 2, especially questions 13,124–13,295.

23 Cole, *Guild Socialism Re-stated*, 1920, p. 32n.

24 F. Matthews, 'The Building Guilds', in A. Briggs and J. Saville (eds), *Essays in Labour History 1886–1923*, 1971, pp. 332–50.

25 W. Kendall, *The Revolutionary Movement in Britian, 1900–21*, 1969, part 2, especially ch. 16.

K*

26 W. Mellor, 'A critique of guild socialism', *Labour Monthly*, 1, 5, November 1921, pp. 398–9.
27 *Ibid.*
28 Cole, 'The position of British socialism', *New Statesman*, 20 May 1922.
29 *Ibid.*
30 Tawney, 'The sickness of an acquisitive society', *Hibbert Journal*, 18, 3, April 1919, pp. 353–70, reprinted under the same title by the Fabian Society in 1920.
31 Tawney Papers, 'Speeches on Various Occasions', untitled speech, p. 1.
32 Tawney, *The Acquisitive Society*, 1921, p. 153.
33 *Ibid.*, pp. 152–3.
34 *Ibid.*, p. 153.
35 *Ibid.*, p. 3.
36 From the prefatory note by Bishop Charles Gore, in Tawney, *Religion and the Rise of Capitalism*, 1926, p. xxi.
37 These lectures most likely were published under the same title in *Journal of Political Economy*, 31, August, October, December 1923, pp. 461–93, 637–74, 802–25.
38 CPB, 16 September 1912.
39 É. Halévy, 'Socialism and the problem of democratic parliamentarianism', in R. K. Webb (ed.), *The Era of Tyrannies*, 1967, pp. 191–203.

Bibliography

Place of publication is London unless otherwise stated.

UNPUBLISHED MANUSCRIPTS

Collections deposited in libraries

Balliol College, Oxford
  A. L. Smith Papers
Beaverbrook Library
  Lloyd George Papers
Bodleian Library, Oxford
  Hammond Papers
British Library of Political and Economic Science, London School of Economics
  Beveridge Papers
  City of London Independent Labour Party Papers
  Lansbury Papers
  Morel Papers
  Passfield Papers
  Reports and Papers on the Relief of Distress
  Algernon Simon Papers (from the University of Wisconsin; on microfilm)
  Tawney Papers and Lectures
British Museum
  Shaw Papers
Corpus Christi College, Oxford
  R.C.K. Ensor Papers
Labour Party Library, Transport House
  Educational Advisory Committee Minutes and Memoranda
  Arthur Henderson Papers
  International Advisory Committee Minutes and Memoranda
  Labour Party Executive Minutes, 1910–24
  Middleton Papers

War Emergency: Workers' National Committee Papers: Boxes numbered in order of examination, 1 October 1968; the titles are Middleton's:

1 General
2 General and miscellaneous
3 Order 1915
4 Annual Report. Orders. Rent Law Appeal 1917
5 From Belgian Refugees to Coloured Labour
6 Food Prices to 1918
7 From Food Vigilance Committee to Housing
8 Industrial Compulsion to Labour After the War
9 Literature Orders to Local Government Board
10 Military Service Files
11 From Milk to Miscellaneous
12 From Municipal Activity to Munitions
13 Pensions (War) Allowances
14 From Postal to Prisoners of War
15 From Provision of Meals to Relief
16 From Relief to Rent
17 From Rent Appeal to Seamen
18 From Ships to Trades Union Congress
19 From War to War Office
20 From Acts to Agriculture
21 From Air Raids to Asylums
22 From Conference to Conference
23 From Conferences – Food to Consumers' Council
24 From Contracts to Contracts
25 Contracts
26 From Co-operative Representation to Enlistment
27 From Executive to Food
28 From Food to Food
29 From Food to Food Prices
30 From Labour After the War to Legal
31 From Maternity to Milk
32 From National Relief Fund to Old Age Pensions
33 Pensions (War) Allowances (2)
34 From Pensions to Postal
35 From Unemployment to War Charities
36 From War Savings to Women's War League

Lambeth Palace Library
  Life and Liberty Papers
Nuffield College, Oxford
  J. P. Bedford Papers
  Cole Collection on Guild Socialism
  Cole Papers
  Fabian Society Papers
Public Record Office, London
  Cabinet Papers, 1910–18
  Foreign Office Papers
  War Office Papers

Private collections

Clifford Allen Papers in the possession of Lady Allen of Hurtwood
Middleton Papers in the possession of Mrs Lucy Middleton
Reckitt Papers in the possession of Mr M. B. Reckitt
Tawney-Vyvyan Papers in the possession of Mr Michael Vyvyan

BIBLIOGRAPHY

Unpublished theses

CARPENTER, L. P., 'G. D. H. Cole: An Intellectual Biography', Harvard Ph.D., 1966.

GREGORY, R. G., 'The Miners and Politics in England and Wales', Oxford D.Phil., 1963.

HOBSBAWM, E. J., 'Fabianism and the Fabians, 1884–1914', Cambridge Ph.D., 1950.

MCGIBBIN, R. I., 'The Evolution of a National Party: Labour's Political Organisation, 1910–24', Oxford D.Phil., 1970.

MEWS, S. P., 'The Effects of the First World War on English Religious Life and Thought', Leeds M.A., 1967.

PUBLISHED SOURCES

Newspapers and contemporary periodicals

Amalgamated Engineers Monthly Journal and Report 1911–18
American Economic Review 1918
Athenaeum 1917
Atlantic Monthly 1918
Board of Trade Labour Gazette 1911–18
Challenge 1919
Christian Commonwealth 1911–18
Church Socialist 1914–18
Crusade 1911–12
Contemporary Review 1914–18
Daily Citizen 1913–15
Daily Herald (later *Herald*) 1911–18
Daily News and Chronicle 1914
Economic Journal 1906–14
Economic Review 1899–1914
English Review 1917–18
Fabian News 1912–18
Glasgow *Forward* 1911–18
Glasgow *Herald* 1906–8
Guildsman 1917–18
Hibbert Journal 1910–22

Highway 1910–18
Journal of Political Economy 1923
Labour Leader 1911–18
Labour Monthly 1921
Manchester Guardian 1911–18
Morning Post 1907–8
Nation 1912–18
New Age 1911–18
New Statesman 1913–22
Nineteenth Century (later *Nineteenth Century and After*) 1883, 1913
Observer 1918
Political Quarterly 1914
Proceedings of the Aristotelian Society 1914–16
Railway Review 1911–18
Rochdale Observer 1918
St. Martin's Review 1928–9
Socialist Review 1910–19
Sociological Review 1908–14
The Times 1911–18
The Times Educational Supplement 1917–18
Toynbee Record 1903–5
Venturer 1919
Women's Industrial News 1910–11

Selected writings of G. D. H. Cole, R. H. Tawney, and Sidney and Beatrice Webb: works cited in this study or of special relevance to it

G. D. H. Cole (Items written jointly with William Mellor are marked with an asterisk throughout)

*The Greater Unionism, Manchester, 1913.
Jean-Jacques Rousseau, The Social Contract and Discourses, 1913 (introd., transl. by G. D. H. Cole).
The World of Labour, 1913.
Labour in Wartime, 1915.
Trade Unionism in Wartime, 1915 (with H. H. Slesser).
The Munitions Act and the Restoration of Trade Union Customs, 1916.
Self-government in Industry, 1917.
Trade Unionism on the Railways, 1917 (with R. Page Arnot).
An Introduction to Trade Unionism, 1918.
Labour in the Commonwealth, 1918.
*The Meaning of Industrial Freedom, 1918.
The Payment of Wages, 1918.
Why Labour Left the Coalition, 1918.
Chaos and Order in Industry, 1920.
Guild Socialism Re-stated, 1920.
Social Theory, 1920.
Studies in World Economics, 1934.
William Morris as a Socialist, 1960.
'Oxford socialism from within', Socialist Review, 6, 34, December 1910.
'Fabian excursions', Daily Herald, 10 December 1913.
*'The need for Greater Unionism. Lessons of the fight at Chipping Norton', Daily Herald, 24 February 1914.
*'The class war and the state', Daily Herald, 3 March 1914.
'The free state of the future II', Labour Leader, 26 March 1914.
*'The bondage of iron', Daily Herald, 12 May 1914.
*'The wage system and the way out', Daily Herald, 26 May 1914.
*'The wage system and the way out II: guild socialism or social bureaucracy, Daily Herald, 28 May 1914.
*'Industrial unionism and the guild system', New Age, 25 June 1914.
*'The world for the workers: guild socialism and syndicalism', Daily Herald, 30 June 1914.
*'Co-operators and the war', Daily Herald, 13 August 1914.
*'Playing capital's game', Daily Herald, 20 August 1914.
*'Industrial unionism and the guild system', Amalgamated Engineers Monthly Journal and Report, 9, September 1914.
'Conflicting social obligations', Proceedings of the Aristotelian Society, 15, 1914–15.
*'Trade unions in war-time', Daily Herald, 2 January 1915.
*'Rumours of class war', Herald, 13 March 1915.
*'Compulsory arbitration', Daily Herald, 27 March 1915.
'The state and the engineers', Amalgamated Engineers Monthly Journal and Report, 4, April 1915.
'At the sign of the book', Highway, 7, 84, September 1915.
*'A second open letter to the Trades Union Congress', New Age, 2 September 1915.
'The meaning of the Trades Union Congress', Nation, 11 September 1915.

'The Munitions Act: a plea for reconsideration', *Nation*, 16 October 1915.

*'What of the state?' *Herald*, 13 November 1915.

*'The need for unity', *Herald*, 4 December 1915.

'Thrift for some people', *Herald*, 11 December 1915.

'Symposium: the nature of the state in view of its external arrangements', *Proceedings of the Aristotelian Society*, 16, 1915–16 (with C. Delisle Burns and B. Russell).

*'The price of dilution to labour', *Amalgamated Engineers Monthly Journal and Report*, January 1916.

'The Labour Party Conference', *Nation*, 29 January 1916.

*'Labour after the war: the problem', *Herald*, 4 March 1916.

*'Labour after the war: the problem – the class struggle', *Herald*, 21 March 1916.

*'Labour after the war: state control of industry', *Herald*, 8 July 1916.

'The busy rich class', *Herald*, 23 December 1916.

'The ILP and trade unionism', *Labour Leader*, 18 January 1917.

'The Whitley Report I', *Herald*, 7 July 1917 (with W. N. Ewer).

'The Whitley Report II its uses and abuses', *Herald*, 14 July 1917 (with W. N. Ewer).

'The Whitley Report III is it control?' *Herald*, 28 July 1917 (with W. N. Ewer).

'The Whitley Councils', *Guildsman*, June 1918.

'Recent developments in the British Labour movement', *American Economic Review*, 8, 3, September 1918.

'A call to industrial Labour', *Herald*, 23 November 1918.

'The position of British socialism', *New Statesman*, 20 May 1922.

R. H. Tawney (See also: J. M. Winter, 'A bibliography of the published writings of R. H. Tawney', *Economic History Review*, 2nd ser., 25, 1, February 1972).

The Agrarian Problem in the Sixteenth Century, 1912.

Education and Social Progress, Manchester, 1912.

Poverty as an Industrial Problem, 1913.

The Establishment of Minimum Rates in the Chain-making Industry under the Trade Boards Act of 1909, 1914.

The Establishment of Minimum Rates in the Tailoring Industry under the Trade Boards Act of 1909, 1915.

Continued Education under the New Act, 1918.

The Nationalization of the Coal Industry, 1919.

The Sickness of an Acquisitive Society, 1920.

The Acquisitive Society, 1921.

Religion and the Rise of Capitalism, 1926.

G. Unwin, *Studies in Economic History*, 1927 (ed., introd. by Tawney).

Equality, 1931.

Why Britain Fights, New York, 1941.

The Attack and other papers, 1953.

The Workers' Educational Association and Adult Education, 1953.

The Radical Tradition, 1964 (R. Hinden, ed.)

R. H. Tawney's Commonplace Book, Cambridge, 1972 (J. M. Winter and D. M. Joslin, eds).

'The *Daily News* Religious Census of London', *Toynbee Record*, 16, 6, March 1904.

'The university and the nation', *Westminster Gazette*, 15–17, 23–4 February and 2–3, 10 March 1906.

'Employment exchanges', *Westminster Gazette*, 7 November 1906.

'School and scholars', *Morning Post*, 16 August 1907.

'Unemployment and its remedies. The example of Germany I–IV', *Morning Post*, 27–9, 31 October 1908.

'The theory of pauperism', *Sociological Review*, 2, 4, October 1909.

'The economics of boy labour', *Economic Journal*, 19, December 1909.

'A report of a visit to Germany made by members of the Rochdale branch of the W.E.A.', *Highway*, 2, 18, March 1910.

'Municipal enterprise in Germany', *Economic Review*, 20, 3, October 1910.

' "Blind alley" occupations and the way out', *Women's Industrial News*, 52, October 1910.

'The halving of boy and girl labour', *Crusade*, 2, 6, June 1911.

'An experiment in democratic education', *Political Quarterly*, 1, 2, May 1914 (also published by the WEA as a separate pamphlet).

'The *personnel* of the new armies', *Nation*, 27 February 1915.

'Some reflections of a soldier', *Nation*, 21 October 1916.

'The attack', *Westminster Gazette*, 24, 25 October 1916.

'Democracy or defeat', *Welsh Outlook*, IV, 37, February 1917.

'A national college of All Souls', *Times Educational Supplement*, 22 February 1917.

'Educational programme', *Manchester Guardian*, 10 March 1917.

'The philosophy of power I', *Athenaeum*, April, May 1917.

'The sword of the spirit', *Athenaeum*, December 1917 (supplement).

'*Labour and Capital after the War*, (1918), (S. J. Chapman, ed.), Ch. 5.

'Prussianism in the schools', *Daily News*, 14 February 1918.

'John Ruskin his message for today', *Observer*, 9 February 1919.

'The sickness of an acquisitive society', *Hibbert Journal*, 18, 3, April 1919.

'The army and religion. A symposium', *Challenge*, 10 October 1919 (with F. R. Barry and H. F. Houlder).

'Religion and Business. A forgotten chapter of social history', *Hibbert Journal*, 21, October 1922.

'Religious thought on social and economic questions in the sixteenth and seventeenth centuries, I–III', *Journal of Political Economy*, 31, August–December 1923.

'Beatrice Webb, 1858–1943', *Proceedings of the British Academy*, 29, 1943.

'In memory of Sidney Webb', *Economica*, 14, 56, November 1947.

'Social democracy in Britain', in *The Christian Demand for Social Justice*, W. Scarlett (ed.), New York, 1949.

'J. L. Hammond, 1872–1949', *Proceedings of the British Academy*, 46, 1960.

'The conditions of economic liberty' in R. Hinden (ed.), *The Radical Tradition*, 1964.

Sidney and Beatrice Webb

The Co-operative Movement in Great Britain, 1891. (Beatrice)

Industrial Democracy, 1897; 2nd ed. 1902. (Sidney and Beatrice)

The Webbs' Australian Diary 1898. A. G. Austin, ed., Melbourne, 1965. (Sidney and Beatrice)

The Decline in the Birth-Rate, 1907. (Sidney)

How to Pay for the War, 1916. (Sidney, ed.)

Labour and the New Social Order, 1918. (Sidney)

The Principles of the Labour Party, 1918. (Sidney and Beatrice)

A Constitution for the Socialist Commonwealth of Great Britain, 1920. (Sidney and Beatrice)

The History of Trade Unionism, 1666–1920, 1920. (Sidney and Beatrice)

The Decay of Capitalist Civilisation, 1923. (Sidney and Beatrice)

Soviet Communism: A New Civilization, 1935; 3rd ed. 1944. (Sidney and Beatrice)

My Apprenticeship, 1938. (Beatrice)

Our Partnership, 1948. (Beatrice)

Beatrice Webb's Diaries 1912–24 M. I. Cole, ed., 1952. (Beatrice)

Beatrice Webb's Diaries 1924–32. M. I. Cole, ed., 1956. (Beatrice)

'The social crisis in Japan', *Crusade*, 3, 1, January 1912. (Sidney and Beatrice)

'China in revolution', *Crusade*, 3, 3, March 1912. (Sidney and Beatrice)

'The moral of the labour unrest', *Crusade*, 3, 7, July 1912. (Sidney)

'What syndicalism means', *Crusade*, 3, 8, August 1912 (supplement). (Sidney and Beatrice)

'The minimum wage and how to get it', *Fabian News*, 24, 2, January 1913. (Beatrice)

'Weapons of Socialism', *Christian Commonwealth*, 26 February 1913. (Beatrice)

'Some impressions of the Labour Party Conference', *Fabian News*, 24, 4, March 1913. (Beatrice)

'What is socialism?', *New Statesman*, April–September 1913. (Sidney and Beatrice)

    1 'Revolt', 12 April 1913.

    2 'Change of heart', 19 April 1913.

    3 'The application to society of the scientific method', 26 April 1913.

    4 'Participation in power and the consciousness of consent', 3 May 1913.

    5 'An inference from the law of rent', 10 May 1913.

    6 'The transformation of property', 17 May 1913.

7 'The expansion of local government', 24 May 1913.

8 'National housekeeping', 31 May 1913.

9 'Organisation from below as the safeguard of liberty', 7 June 1913.

10 'Co-partnership between producer and consumer', 14 June 1913.

11 'Voluntary groupings of producers and consumers', 21 June 1913.

12 'The approach to equality', 28 June 1913.

13 'Freedom for the woman', 5 July 1913.

14 'Protection for the child', 12 July 1913.

15 'The development of science, art, and religion untrammelled by plutocracy', 19 July 1913.

16 'The maintenance of nationality by the growth of internationalism', 26 July 1913.

17 'The guardianship of the non-adult races', 2 August 1913.

18 'The real safeguard against the nightmare of the servile state', 9 August 1913.

19 'Our protection against the disastrous illusion of the distributive state', 16 August 1913.

20 'In itself a demonstration of the impossibility of syndicalism and anarchism', 23 August 1913.

21 'The great alternative (1) the answer of pessimism', 30 August 1913.

22 'The great alternative (2) the optimist view', 6 September 1913.

'The awakening of woman', *New Statesman*, 1 November 1913 (special supplement). (Beatrice)

'Special supplement on co-operative production and profit-sharing', *New Statesman*, 14 February 1914. (Sidney and Beatrice)

'Voteless women and the social revolution', *New Statesman*, 14 February 1914. (Beatrice)

'Special supplement on women in industry', *New Statesman*, 21 February 1914. (Beatrice, ed.)

'Special supplement on the working of the Insurance Act', *New Statesman*, 14 March 1914. (Sidney)

'Motherhood and citizenship' in 'Special supplement on motherhood and the state', *New Statesman*, 16 May 1914. (Beatrice)

'Special supplement on the co-operative movement', *New Statesman*, 30 May 1914. (Sidney and Beatrice)

'Personal rights and the women's movement I–V', *New Statesman*, 4, 11, 18, 25 July, 1 August 1914. (Beatrice)

'Behind the fighting line', *Daily Chronicle*, 25 August 1914. (Sidney)

'Behind the firing lines', *Daily Chronicle*, 26 August 1914. (Sidney)

'Prevention – not alleviation', *Labour Leader*, 27 August 1914. (Beatrice)

'Special supplement on state and municipal enterprises', *New Statesman*, 8 May 1915. (Sidney and Beatrice)

'Special supplement on English teachers and their professional organisation', *New Statesman*, 2 October 1915. (Beatrice)

'The chains of Labour', *Labour Leader*, 9 November 1916.
'The new constitution of the Labour party', *Observer*, 21 October 1917. (Sidney)
'Reminiscences 1–6', *St. Martin's Review*, October–December 1928, January–March 1929. (Sidney: 1, 3–5; Beatrice: 2, 6)

Other secondary works

ARNOT, R. P., *History of the Labour Research Department*, 1926.
ARNOT, R. P., *The Impact of the Russian Revolution in Britain*, 1967.
ARNOT, R. P., *South Wales Miners*, 1967.
ASHLEY, M. P. and SAUNDERS, C. T., *Red Oxford*, Oxford, 1933.
ASHTON, T. S., 'Richard Henry Tawney 1880–1962', *Proceedings of the British Academy*, 48, 1962.
ASKWITH, G. R., *Industrial Problems and Disputes*, 1920.
BALL, O. H., *Sidney Ball*, Oxford, 1923.
BALL, SIDNEY, 'The Socialist ideal', *Economic Review*, 9, 4, October 1899.
BARKER, E., *Political Thought in England 1848 to 1914*, 1963.
BARKER, R., *Education and Politics 1900–1951*, Oxford, 1972.
BARNETT, H. O., *Canon Barnett: his Life, Work, and Friends*, 2 vols, 1918.
BARNETT, S. A., 'Our present discontents', *Nineteenth Century*, 83, 432, February 1913.
BARNETT, S. A., 'Practicable socialism', *Nineteenth Century*, 63, 74, April 1883.
BEER, M., *A History of British Socialism*, 1919, 1920.
BEER, SAMUEL H., *Modern British Politics*, 1965.
BELL, T., *Pioneering Days*, 1941.
BELLOC, HILAIRE and MACDONALD, J. R., *Socialism and the Servile State*, 1911.
BEVERIDGE, JANET, *Beveridge and His Plan*, 1954.
BEVERIDGE, JANET, *An Epic of Clare Market*, 1960.
BEVERIDGE, WILLIAM, *Unemployment: A Problem of Industry*, 1910.
BIDDISS, M., 'Racial ideas and the politics of prejudice', *Historical Journal*, 15, 3, September 1972.
BLEWETT, N., *The Peers, the Parties and the People: the General Elections of 1910*, 1972.
BOLT, C., *Victorian Attitudes to Race*, 1971.
BRAITHWAITE, W. J., *Lloyd George's Ambulance Wagon*, 1957.
BRIGGS, A. and SAVILLE, J. (eds), *Essays in Labour History*, 1960.
BRIGGS, A. and SAVILLE, J. (eds), *Essays in Labour History 1886–1923*, 1971.
BROWN, E. H. PHELPS, *The Growth of British Industrial Relations*, 1960.
BROWN, P. A., *The French Revolution in English History*, 1918.
BUBER, MARTIN, *Israel and the World*, New York, 1963.
BUBER, MARTIN, *Pointing the Way*, New York, 1957.
BUCHANAN, G., *My Mission to Russia and other diplomatic memoirs*, 2 vols, 1923.
BUTLER, D. and FREEMAN, J., *British Political Facts 1900–1960*, 1963.
CAMPBELL, G. L., *The Manchesters*, Manchester, 1916.

CARPENTER, N. H., 'The literature of guild socialism', *Quarterly Journal of Economics*, 34, August 1920.

CHAPMAN, GUY (ed.), *Vain Glory*, 2nd ed., 1968.

CHAPMAN, S. J. (ed.), *Labour and Capital after the War*, 1918.

CHESTERTON, C., 'The decline and fall of the Labour party', *New Age*, 11 May–17 August 1911.

CHURCHILL, RANDOLPH, *Winston S. Churchill: Young Statesman 1901–14*, 1967.

CLARKE, P. F., *Lancashire and the New Liberalism*, Cambridge, 1971.

CLINE, C. A., *Recruits to Labour*, Syracuse, New York, 1963.

'The coal trade dispute', *Board of Trade Labour Gazette*, 20, 4, April 1912.

COLE, MARGARET I., *Beatrice Webb*, 1945.

COLE, MARGARET I., *Growing Up Into Revolution*, 1949.

COLE, MARGARET I., *The Life of G. D. H. Cole*, 1971.

COLE, MARGARET I., *The Story of Fabian Socialism*, 1961.

COLE, MARGARET I., (ed.), *The Webbs and Their Work*, 1949.

COLLER, F. H., *A State Trading Venture*, 1925.

Colliery Strike Disturbances in South Wales. Correspondence and Report. Cd 5568, 64, 1911.

'Conference on the Whitley Report', *Fabian News*, 29, 2, January 1918.

COOPER, D. (ed.), *The Dialectics of Liberation*, Harmondsworth, 1968.

Co-operative Congress Annual Report, 1914–18.

COURT, W. H. B., *Scarcity and Choice in History*, 1970.

DAHRENDORF, R., *Class and Class Conflict in Industrial Society*, 1964.

DAHRENDORF, R., *Essays in the Theory of Society*, 1968.

DANGERFIELD, G., *The Strange Death of Liberal England*, 2nd ed., 1936.

DEANE, H. J., *The Political Ideas of Harold J. Laski*, New York, 1955.

DENMAN, R., *Political Sketches*, Carlisle, 1948.

DOUGLAS, R., 'The National Democratic party and the British Workers' League', *Historical Journal*, 15, 3, September 1972.

DURBIN, E. F. M. and BOWLBY, J. M., *Personal Aggressiveness and War*, 1939.

ELTON, G. R., *The Future of the Past*, Cambridge, 1968.

FAINSOD, M., *International Socialism and the World War*, Cambridge, Mass., 1935.

FERRO, M., *The Russian Revolution of February 1917*, trans. J. L. Richards, 1972.

FERRO, M., *The Great War 1914–1918*, trans. Nicole Stone, 1973.

FIGGIS, J. N., *Churches in the Modern State*, 1913.

FOLLETT, M. P., *The New State*, 1918.

FORD, P. and FORD, G., *A Breviate of Parliamentary Papers 1900–1916, 1917–1939*, Oxford, 1957, 1961.

GANKIN, G. H. and FISHER, H. H. (eds), *The Bolsheviks and the World War*, Stanford, Calif., 1940.

GARDINER, A. G., 'Mr Henderson and the Labour movement', *Atlantic Monthly*, 122, 2, August 1918.

GERTH, H. H. and MILLS C. W. (eds), *From Max Weber: Essays in Sociology*, 1948.

GILBERT, B., *The Evolution of National Insurance in Great Britain*, 1966.

GILBERT, M. (ed.), *Plough My Own Furrow*, 1965.

GLASIER, J. B., *James Keir Hardie: A Memorial*, Manchester, 1915.

GLASIER, J. B., *The Meaning of Socialism*, Manchester, 1919.

GLASS, S. T., *The Responsible Society*, 1966.

GLEASON, A., *What the Workers Want*, 1920.

GRAUBARD, S., *British Labour and the Russian Revolution*, 1956.

GRAY, A., *The Socialist Tradition: Moses to Lenin*, 1946.

GREENWOOD, A., *Juvenile Labour Exchanges and After-care*, 1910.

GREGORY, R., *The Miners and British Politics 1906–1914*, 1968.

HABAKKUK, H. J., *Population Growth and Economic Development since 1750*, Leicester, 1971.

HALÉVY, É., *The Era of Tyrannies*, ed., trans. R. K. Webb, 1967.

HALÉVY, É., *Histoire du socialisme européen*, Paris, 1948.

HALÉVY, É., *History of the English People in the Nineteenth Century. Epilogue. The Rule of Democracy*, trans. W. I. Watkin, 2 vols, 1952.

HAMILTON, M. A., *Arthur Henderson*, 1938.

HAMMOND, J. L., 'The war and the mind of Great Britain', *Atlantic Monthly*, 123, 4, March 1919.

Hansard's Parliamentary Debates, 1910–18.

HARRIS, J. F., *Unemployment and Politics: A Study in English Social Policy, 1880–1914*, Oxford, 1972.

HARRISON, A., 'The Stockholm curtain raiser', *English Review*, 25, September 1917.

HARRISON, J. F. C., *Robert Owen and the Owenites in Britain and America*, 1969.

HENDERSON, A., *The Aims of Labour*, 1918.

HENDERSON, A., 'The new Labour party constitution', *Fabian News*, 29, 2, January 1918.

HENDERSON, A., 'The outlook for Labour', *Contemporary Review*, 23, February 1918.

HENDERSON, A., 'Russia's peril', *Nation*, 17 November 1917.

HINTON, J., 'The Clyde Workers' Committee and the dilution struggle', in Briggs and Saville (eds), *Essays in Labour History 1886–1923*, 1971.

HOBSBAWM, E. J., *Labouring Men: Studies in the History of Labour*, 1964.

HOWE, M. (ed.), *Holmes-Laski Letters*, 2 vols, Cambridge, Mass., 1953.

HURWITZ, S. J., *State Intervention in Great Britain*, New York, 1949.

HYAMS, E., *The New Statesman*, 1963.

HYNES, E., *The Edwardian Turn of Mind*, 1968.

Independent Labour Party Annual Reports, 1911–18.

IREMONGER, F. A., *William Temple, Archbishop of Canterbury*, 1948.

JOHNSON, P. B., *Land Fit for Heroes*, 1968.

JOLL, J., *1914 The Unspoken Assumptions*, 1968.

JONES, R. L., 'The invasion of a university', *Highway*, 3, 35, August 1911.

JONES, THOMAS, *Whitehall Diary*, vol. 1, K. Middlemas ed., 1969.

KEELING, F., *The Labour Exchange in Relation to Boy and Girl Labour*, 1910.

KEELING, F., *Keeling Letters and Recollections*, E. Townshend, ed., 1918.

KEMSTER, F. and WESTROPP, H. C. (eds), *Manchester City Battalions of the Ninetieth and Ninety-First Infantry Brigades Book of Honour*, Manchester, 1916.

KENDALL, W., *The Revolutionary Movement in Britain 1900–21*, 1969.
KIERNAN, V., *The Lords of Human Kind*, 1969.
KING, P. and PAREKH, B. C. (eds), *Politics and Experience*, Cambridge, 1968.
KNOWLES, K. G. J. C., *Strikes: A Study in Industrial Conflict*, Oxford, 1952.
Labour Party Annual Reports, 1910–18.
LASKI, H. J., *Authority in the Modern State*, New Haven, Conn., 1919.
LASKI, H. J., *Studies in the Problem of Sovereignty*, New Haven, Conn., 1917.
LENIN, V. I., *Collected Works*, 12 vols, Moscow, 1934.
LENIN, V. I., *What Is To Be Done?* trans. S. V. and P. Utechin, Oxford, 1963.
LOCKHART, R. H. B., *Memoirs of a British Agent*, 1932.
LUKÁCS, G., *Political Writings, 1919–39*, ed. R. Livingstone, 1972.
LUXEMBURG, ROSA, *The Junius Pamphlet: The Crisis in the German Social Democracy*, 1967.
LYMAN, R., 'James Ramsay MacDonald and the leadership of the Labour party, 1918–22', *Journal of British Studies*, 2, 1962.
MCBRIAR, A. M., *Fabian Socialism and English Politics 1884–1918*, Cambridge, 1962.
MACDONALD, J. RAMSAY, 'Is democracy possible?' *Socialist Review*, 13, 77, April–June 1916.
MACDONALD, J. RAMSAY, *Patriots and Politics*, Manchester, 1917.
MACDONALD, J. RAMSAY, *Socialism after the War*, Manchester, 1917.
MACDONALD, J. RAMSAY, 'Socialism during war', *Socialist Review*, 12, 71, October–December 1914.
MACDONALD, J. RAMSAY, *The Socialist Movement*, 1911.
MACDONALD, J. RAMSAY, *War and the Workers: A Plea for Democratic Control*, 1915.
MCGIBBIN, R., 'James Ramsay MacDonald and the problem of the independence of the Labour Party', *Journal of Modern History*, 42, 2, June 1970.
MARTIN, B. K., *Father Figures*, 1966.
MARTIN, B. K., *Harold Laski 1893–1950*, 1953.
MARWICK, A., *Britain in the Century of Total War*, 1968.
MARWICK, A., *Clifford Allen: the Open Conspirator*, 1964.
MARWICK, A., *The Deluge*, 1965.
MATTHEWS, F., 'The Building Guilds', in Briggs and Saville (eds), *Essays in Labour History 1886–1923*, 1971.
MAYER, A., *Political Origins of the New Diplomacy, 1917–18*, New Haven, Conn., 1959.
MELLOR, W., 'A critique of guild socialism', *Labour Monthly*, 1, 5, November 1921.
MEYNELL, H., 'The Stockholm conference of 1917', *International Review of Social History*, 5, pts 1–2, 1960.
MICHELS, R., *Political Parties*, trans. E. and C. Paul, 1915.
MIDDLETON, J. S., *Farewell*, 1944.
MILIBAND, R., *Parliamentary Socialism*, 1961.
MOWAT, C. L., *The Charity Organization Society 1869–1913*, 1961.
MUGGERIDGE, K. and ADAMS, R., *Beatrice Webb*, 1967.
MURPHY, J. T., *Compromise or Independence?*, Sheffield, 1918.

MURPHY, J. T., *Preparing for Power*, 1934.
NABOKOFF, K. O., *The Ordeal of a Diplomat*, 2 vols, 1921.
NAMIER, L., *In the Margin of History*, 1939.
NGL Vigilance Committee on After-War Problems, *Observations on the Interim Report of the Reconstruction Committee on Joint Industrial Councils*, 1918.
ORAGE, A. R. (ed.), *National Guilds*, 1914.
ORTON, W. A., *Labour in Transition*, 1921.
PATEMAN, C., *Participation and Democratic Theory*, Cambridge, 1970.
PELLING, H., *America and the British Left*, 1956.
PELLING, H., *A Short History of the Labour Party*, 1961.
PELLING, H., *A History of British Trade Unionism*, 1962.
PELLING, H., *Popular Politics and Society in Late Victorian Britain*, 1968.
PENTY, A. J., *A Guildsman's Interpretation of History*, 1920.
PIMLOTT, J. A. R., *Toynbee Hall, 1884–1934*, 1935.
PRIBICEVIC, B., *The Shop Stewards' Movement and Workers' Control 1910–1922*, Oxford, 1959.
PRICE, T. W., *The Story of the Workers' Educational Association from 1903 to 1924*, 1924.
'Proposal to change the constitution', *Fabian News*, 26, 5, April 1915.
RAVEN, C., *Christian Socialism*, 1920.
RECKITT, M. B., *As It Happened*, 1941.
RECKITT, M. B. and BECHHOFER, C. E., *The Meaning of National Guilds*, 1918.
Reform Committee of South Wales Miners, *The Miners' Next Step*, Tonypandy, 1912.
REINDERS, R., 'Racialism on the Rhine', *International Review of Social History*, 13, 1, 1968.
REPINGTON, C.A'C., *The War in the Far East*, 1905.
'Research department', *Fabian News*, 29, 9, August 1918.
REYNOLDS, S. and WOOLLEY, B. and T., *Seems So! A Working-Class View of Politics*, 1911.
RIDER, D., *Ten Years' Adventures among Landlords and Tenants*, 1927.
ROBERTSON, J., 'The idea of a Labour party', *Contemporary Review*, 113, June 1918.
Royal Commission on the Poor Laws and the Relief of Distress. *Reports and Evidence*, 1910 Cd 5068.
ROSE, M., *The Relief of Poverty 1834–1914*, 1972.
RUNCIMAN, W. G., *Relative Deprivation and Social Justice*, 1966.
RUNCIMAN, W. G., *Social Science and Political Theory*, Cambridge, 1963.
RUNCIMAN, W. G., *Sociology in its Place and Other Essays*, Cambridge, 1970.
RUSSELL, BERTRAND, *The Autobiography of Bertrand Russell*, 3 vols, 1967–8.
RUSSELL, BERTRAND, *German Social Democracy*, 1896 and 1965.
RUSSELL, BERTRAND, *Political Ideals*, 1917.
RUSSELL, BERTRAND, *Portraits from Memory and Other Essays*, 1956.
RUSSELL, BERTRAND, *Principles of Social Reconstruction*, 1916.
RUSSELL, BERTRAND, *Roads to Freedom*, 1918.
SACK, A. J. (ed.), *The Birth of the Russian Democracy*, New York, 1918.
Sankey Coal Industry Commission. *Reports and Minutes of Evidence*, 1919 Cd 359, 11; 1919 Cd 360, 12.

SCARLETT, W. (ed.), *The Christian Demand for Social Justice*, New York, 1949.

SEARLE, G. R., *The Quest for National Efficiency*, Oxford, 1971.

SELVER, P. P., *Orage and the New Age Circle*, 1959.

SIMPSON, J. D. H., *Rugby since Arnold*, 1967.

SIRES, S. J., 'Labour unrest in England 1910–1914', *Journal of Economic History*, 15, 3, September 1955.

SLESSER, H. H., *Judgment Reserved*, 1941.

SMILLIE, R., 'The future of trade unionism', *Herald*, 19 December 1914.

SMILLIE, R., *My Life for Labour*, 1924.

STOCKS, M., *The Workers' Educational Association*, 1953.

SWARTZ, M., *The Union of Democratic Control in British Politics during the First World War*, 1971.

TALBOT, BISHOP E. W. *et al.*, *Christianity and Industrial Problems*, 2nd ed., 1928.

TAYLOR, A. J. P., *Politics in Wartime and Other Essays*, 1964.

TAYLOR, A. J. P., *The Troublemakers*, 1957.

TEMPLE, W., 'The Life and Liberty movement', *Contemporary Review*, 113, February 1918.

THOMPSON, L., *The Enthusiasts*, 1971.

TILLETT, B., *History of the London Transport Workers' Strike, 1911*, 1912.

TILLICH, P., *My Search for Absolutes*, New York, 1967.

TOYNBEE, A., *Acquaintances*, 1967.

Trades Union Congress Annual Reports, 1910–18.

TSUZUKI, C., *H. M. Hyndman and British Socialism*, Oxford, 1961.

ULAM, A., *Philosophical Foundations of English Socialism*, Cambridge, Mass., 1951.

WADE, REX, 'Argonauts of Peace: the Soviet delegation to Western Europe in the summer of 1917', *Slavic Review*, 26, 3, September 1967.

WADE, REX, 'Irakli Tsereteli and Siberian Zimmerwaldism', *Journal of Modern History*, 39, 4, December 1967.

WADE, REX, *The Russian Search for Peace*, Stanford, Calif., 1969.

WALLAS, GRAHAM, *The Great Society*, 1914.

WALLAS, GRAHAM, *Human Nature in Politics*, 1908.

WALLAS, GRAHAM, *Our Social Heritage*, 1921.

WEBER, MAX, *The Protestant Ethic and the Spirit of Capitalism*, trans. T. Parsons, 1930.

Whitley Committee on Joint Industrial Councils, *Reports*, 1917–18 Cd 18 and 1918 Cd 9002.

WIENER, M., *Between Two Worlds: The Political Thought of Graham Wallas*, Oxford, 1971.

WILLIAMS, J. R., TITMUSS, R. and FISHER, F. J., *R. H. Tawney: A Portrait by Several Hands*, 1960.

WILSON, T. (ed.), *The Political Diaries of C. P. Scott 1911–1928*, 1970.

WILTON, R., *Russia's Agony*, 1918.

ZYLSTRA, B., *From Pluralism to Collectivism. The Development of Harold Laski's Political Thought*, Assen, 1968.

Index

303